FROMM

EasyGuide

TO

LONDON

By
Jason Cochran

Easy Guides are ✦ Quick To Read ✦ Light To Carry
✦ For Expert Advice ✦ In All Price Ranges

FrommerMedia LLC

Published by

FROMMER MEDIA LLC

Copyright © 2016 by Frommer Media LLC, New York City, New York. All rights reserved. No part of this publication may be reproduced, stored in a retrieval system, or transmitted in any form or by any means, electronic, mechanical, photocopying, recording, scanning or otherwise, except as permitted under Sections 107 or 108 of the 1976 United States Copyright Act, without the prior written permission of the Publisher. Requests to the Publisher for permission should be addressed to the Permissions Department, Frommer Media LLC at partnerships@frommermedia.com. Frommer's is a registered trademark of Arthur Frommer. Used under license. All other trademarks are the property of their respective owners. Frommer Media LLC is not associated with any product or vendor mentioned in this book.

ISBN 978-1-62887-186-9 (paper), 978-1-62887-187-6 (e-book)

Editorial Director: Pauline Frommer
Editor: Shelley Bance
Production Editor: Donna Wright
Cartographer: Andrew Murphy
Indexer: Maro Riofrancos
Cover Designer: Howard Grossman

For information on our other products or services, see www.frommers.com. Frommer Media LLC also publishes its books in a variety of electronic formats.

Manufactured in the United States of America

5 4 3 2 1

HOW TO CONTACT US

In researching this book, we discovered many wonderful places—hotels, restaurants, shops, and more. We're sure you'll find others. Please tell us about them, so we can share the information with your fellow travelers in upcoming editions. If you were disappointed with a recommendation, we'd love to know that, too. Please write to: Support@FrommerMedia.com

FROMMER'S STAR RATINGS SYSTEM

Every hotel, restaurant and attraction listed in this guide has been ranked for quality and value. Here's what the stars mean:

★ Recommended
★★ Highly Recommended
★★★ A must! Don't miss!

AN IMPORTANT NOTE

The world is a dynamic place. Hotels change ownership, restaurants hike their prices, museums alter their opening hours, and buses and trains change their routings. And all of this can occur in the several months after our authors have visited, inspected, and written about these hotels, restaurants, museums and transportation services. Though we have made valiant efforts to keep all our information fresh and up-to-date, some few changes can inevitably occur in the periods before a revised edition of this guidebook is published. So please bear with us if a tiny number of the details in this book have changed. Please also note that we have no responsibility or liability for any inaccuracy or errors or omissions, or for inconvenience, loss, damage, or expenses suffered by anyone as a result of assertions in this guide.

A foreword TO THIS
EASY GUIDE TO LONDON
BY
ARTHUR FROMMER

Friends:

Stumbling off the plane after an overnight flight to London, I used to be startled by the appearance of the people staffing the customs and immigration counters at Heathrow Airport. They were in civilian clothes. They were in normal business suits, unlike the uniformed staff performing the same function in other airports around the world. "Good morning," they would quietly say, in the stately tones of a Shakespearean actor. "May I know the purpose of your visit?"—the latter uttered as if they were apologizing for this intrusion into my privacy. And whether it was my first visit or my fiftieth, I was made sharply aware that I had arrived at the center of a remarkable civilization.

Those customs officials are today—drat!—in uniforms. But the special courtesies and civilities of London remain as pleasant and powerful as ever. For a tourist who will show the same polite attitude to the British you meet, a stay in Britain's capital will be a refreshing change of pace from the harsher life we sometimes know at home.

It will also be an immersion into an intense world of learning and ideas. Though London is not the only city to possess scores of theaters, concert and lecture halls, bookstores, great museums, universities and schools of every sort, it nevertheless possesses more of these than any tourist could ever hope to visit. If you have even a smidgeon of interest in recent and ancient history, in parliamentary debates, in gatherings called to discuss public policies, you will find all these on every day and in every section of the city.

Theater is the major highlight of your stay—more playhouses and theater auditoriums than in any other city, more provocative plays presented at any one time than in any other city, more of an effort to introduce new—and sometimes outlandish—ideas through the mechanism of dramatic plays, more skilled productions of classical works, more outstanding actors than in any other place. Some people I know are so enamored of the London theaters that they attend three plays a day—a normal matinee, a 5pm matinee, and then an evening performance. Except for a very few super-hits, tickets are always available, and the avid theatergoer is constantly aglow at the ideas and talents they encounter here.

Be sure, as well, to attend a production of Shakespeare at the re-created Globe Theater near the Thames; and make the trip there even if you don't have a reservation. Tell the ticket attendant that you are willing to be a "groundling," standing in front of the stage (and sometimes leaning on it) as Londoners of the 1600s did.

There's more than theater to attract you. Unlike most other capital cities, the great national museums of London are almost always free of admission charges. From the British Museum to the British Library, from the National Gallery to the Victoria and Albert, you pay not a single cent—not even a "suggested contribution"—to while away the days amid many of the most fascinating collections on earth.

To write this *Easy Guide to London,* we at Frommer Media concluded that we needed to assign it to a very special talent—and in Jason Cochran, we found an author worthy of the task. Jason is a heavily published author in many fields, and currently the Editor-in-Chief of our own Frommers.com. He is a person of strong tastes who regards travel—as we also do—as a precious learning activity and the essential of a civilized life. He does not write down to his audience; if he regards a popular London attraction as a waste of time, he says so; and though his travel writings may sometimes provoke the reader, they delight a great many more. His books are invariably bestsellers among the many Frommer travel guides.

So here's his take on London, compressed by the Easy Guide formula into 288 pages, and therefore light enough to accompany you (in pocket or purse) as you enjoy the great city of London. "When a man is tired of London," said Samuel Johnson, "he is tired of life; for there is in London all that life can afford."

Enjoy your stay.

Cordially,

Arthur Frommer

CONTENTS

ABOUT THE AUTHOR

Jason Cochran was twice awarded Guide Book of the Year by the Society of American Travel Writers' Lowell Thomas Travel Journalism Competition and by the North American Travel Journalists Association for his writing on London and for Frommer's *EasyGuide to Disney World, Universal, and Orlando*. He also wrote the London, Orlando, and San Francisco guides for the Pauline Frommer series. He has written for publications including *Travel + Leisure, the New York Post, USA Today,* and *Scanorama* (Sweden) and been on staff at *Entertainment Weekly, Budget Travel,* and AOL Travel (Executive Editor). He devised questions for the first American prime-time season of *Who Wants to Be a Millionaire* (ABC) and produced and hosted *AfterShark*, the post-show for *Shark Tank* (ABC). He has appeared as a commentator on, among others, *CBS This Morning, The Early Show* (CBS), *BBC World, Good Morning America,* CNN and the CBC, and he is a video host on AOL. He attended Northwestern University's Medill School of Journalism and New York University's Graduate Music Theatre Writing Program. He is Editor-in-Chief of Frommers.com.

Sharing the inspiration and essence of London with other people has been one of the great pleasures and privileges of my life. It was an honor to create this edition with the friendship, expertise, and support of Hilary, Steve, and Jake Bowsher; Yhago Maia; Curtis Moore; Tracy Temple; Robin Oakley; Brian Fairbairn; Karl Eccleston; and many others.

ABOUT THE FROMMER'S TRAVEL GUIDES

For most of the past 50 years, Frommer's has been the leading series of travel guides in North America, accounting for as many as 24 percent of all guidebooks sold. I think I know why.

Although we hope our books are entertaining, we nevertheless deal with travel in a serious fashion. Our guidebooks have never looked on such journeys as a mere recreation, but as a far more important human function, a time of learning and introspection, an essential part of a civilized life. We stress the culture, lifestyle, history, and beliefs of the destinations we cover and urge our readers to seek out people and new ideas as the chief rewards of travel.

We have never shied from controversy. We have, from the beginning, encouraged our authors to be intensely judgmental, critical—both pro and con—in their comments, and wholly independent. Our only clients are our readers, and we have triggered the ire of countless prominent sorts, from a tourist newspaper we called "practically worthless" (it unsuccessfully sued us) to the many rip-offs we've condemned.

And because we believe that travel should be available to everyone regardless of their incomes, we have always been cost-conscious at every level of expenditure. Although we have broadened our recommendations beyond the budget category, we insist that every lodging we include be sensibly priced. We use every form of media to assist our readers and are particularly proud of our feisty daily website, the award-winning Frommers.com.

I have high hopes for the future of Frommer's. May these guidebooks, in all the years ahead, continue to reflect the joy of travel and the freedom that travel represents. May they always pursue a cost-conscious path, so that people of all incomes can enjoy the rewards of travel. And may they create, for both the traveler and the persons among whom we travel, a community of friends, where all human beings live in harmony and peace.

Arthur Frommer

THE BEST OF LONDON

Whether you realize it or not, London shaped your destiny. There's hardly a quarter of the globe that it hasn't changed. The United States was founded in reaction to London's edicts. Australia was first peopled with London's criminals. Modern Canada, South Africa, and New Zealand were cultivated from London. India's course was irrevocably changed by the aspirations of London businessmen, as were the lives of millions of Africans who were shipped around the world while Londoners lined their pockets with profits. That you bought this book, written in English somewhere other than in England, is evidence of London's reach across time and distance. And its dominion continues to this day: London is the world's most popular destination for foreign tourists.

London is inexhaustible. You could tour it for months and barely get to know it. Few cities support such a variety of people living in remarkable harmony. That diversity makes London like a cut diamond; approach it from a different angle each day, and it presents an entirely fresh shape and color. From famous stories to high style, London is many things in every moment.

LONDON'S best ATTRACTIONS

- **British Museum** (p. 90): Some of the most astounding treasures of the classical world are housed in one overwhelmingly glorious neoclassical building.
- **British Library** (p. 86): The finest and rarest books on the planet, plus the Magna Carta, are laid open for your eyes.
- **Churchill War Rooms** (p. 102): A time capsule of the tense days of World War II and the most advanced biographical museum in existence.
- **Museum of London** (p. 123): Beside a remnant of a Roman wall, the city's spectacular story is retold with the nonstop dazzle of precious finds.

- **National Gallery** (p. 95): Some 2,000 masterpieces, the cream of every genre, reside at what may be the best fine art collection in the world.
- **Natural History Museum** (p. 111): For kids, it's all about the dinosaurs, but this "cathedral of nature" has major chops as a research facility.
- **St Paul's Cathedral** (p. 124): Sir Christopher Wren's masterpiece is the icon of London and a shrine to historic events and people.
- **Tate Modern** (p. 120): Bankside's hymn to the "shock of the new," a former power station, makes for an unforgettable riverside afternoon.
- **Tower of London** (p. 128): Britain's gruesome underbelly and its glittering Crown Jewels coexist in one sprawling city castle of stone.
- **Victoria and Albert Museum** (p. 113): Always evolving and growing, this is probably the world's finest collection of decorative arts.
- **Westminster Abbey** (p. 105): Be awed by Britain's ancient spiritual heart, where nearly 1,000 years of monarchs have been crowned and many are buried.

LONDON'S essential EXPERIENCES

- **Climbing the Dome of St Paul's Cathedral:** Wren's baroque masterpiece stirs emotion in everyone who lays eyes on its lead-coated wooden dome. But it's the climb to the Golden Gallery for a 360° panorama that will stay with you forever. As for Wren, he was forced to add the balustrade for Queen Anne. "Ladies think nothing well without an edging," he complained. See p. 124.
- **Surveying the City from Southbank:** In 1957, the Thames was declared "biologically dead." Today, it flows with life. Alongside it, as restaurants, bars, and creative developments continue to pop up, a walk along the South Bank from Westminster Bridge to Tower Bridge has become one of the world's great promenades. The ever-changing perspective from Parliament to the Tower is ceaselessly inspiring.
- **Following in Royal Footsteps:** London is where some of the most famous characters in history played their scenes. Nearly every British monarch since 1066 was crowned in **Westminster Abbey** (p. 105). Henry VIII strutted around **Hampton Court Palace** (p. 141), Charles I lost his head at **The Banqueting House** (p. 108), and Queen Elizabeth resides at **Buckingham Palace** (p. 101). And the story goes on: The future King George VII is probably being diapered elsewhere in **Kensington Palace** (p. 110) even as you explore it.
- **Flying High on the London Eye:** Ride to the top of our generation's contribution to London's beloved landmarks for a far-reaching shot of the cityscape. Time your trip for early evening as the sun starts to sink and the lights come on across the metropolis. See p. 118.
- **Honoring the struggles of World War II:** More than 70 years later, the Blitz isn't far from many Londoners' minds. Dig into the power of their

resistance at the superlative time capsule of the **Churchill War Rooms** (p. 102), the immersive **Museum of London Docklands** (p. 134), the floating military museum **HMS** *Belfast,* and by seeing original bomb scars on the side of the **V&A** (p. 113).

o **Taking Afternoon Tea:** Look smart at **Brown's, The Goring, Fortnum & Mason,** or the **Langham** (p. 69), where the traditional tea ritual carries on as it did in Britain's colonial heyday.

o **Spending an Evening at a West End Theatre:** London is the theatrical capital of the world. The live stages of **Theatreland** around Covent Garden and Soho offer a combination of variety, accessibility, and economy—but the shows of the Fringe are where the future can be found. See p. 180.

LONDON'S best FOOD

o **Tucking into Honest British Ingredients:** After many lost years of too much boiled cabbage and bread, the English have fallen back in love with farm-fresh ingredients. The gastropub movement, epitomized by its still-potent pioneer, **The Eagle** (p. 74), is just the beginning. Delectable English traditional cooking can be found from the oldest establishments (**Rules,** p. 66) to the neighborhoody holes in the wall (**Andrew Edmunds,** p. 61; **10 Greek Street,** p. 60).

o **Sinking a Pint in a Traditional Pub:** From Tudor coaching inns to riverside taverns, London's pub culture spans the centuries. Raise a pint where Shakespeare did at **The George,** immerse yourself in an ale at Dr. Samuel Johnson's local **Ye Olde Cheshire Cheese** (p. 85), and drink in a Victorian jewel box of etched glass at **The Princess Louise** (p. 84). Then repeat. See "20 Pubs You'll Love" on p. 79.

o **Mining the Stalls at Borough Market:** The top weekend port of call for London foodies is the market under the railway by London Bridge station— not least for the free samples dished out by vendors keen to market their wares. It's gourmet heaven. See p. 72.

o **Enjoying the New English Comfort Food:** London's first Indian restaurant opened in 1810, and Asian food of every origin is now the capital's most popular cuisine. The dozens of curry houses on **Brick Lane** (p. 76) pitch for your business at the curb; or take in a traditional meal under the gold silk wallpaper at Covent Garden's **Punjab Restaurant** (p. 68), opened by an Indian wrestler back in 1947.

o **Chowing Down on Farmhouse Cheese:** England produces hundreds of artisan cheeses. Check out the West Country cheddars, red Leicester, and goat's cheeses at cheesemongers like **Neal's Yard Dairy** (p. 73) or eat a gloppy, gooey plate of raclette at **Kappacasein** (p. 73). But get your fill while you're here: You can't get it back through Customs.

o **Tasting Britain's Fading Traditions:** As young English diners insist on flashier fare, the older ways of cooking become rarer. Whether it's jellied eels in the protected interior of **M. Manze** (p. 73), the deep-fried goodness at the linoleum-lined "chippie" **Fryer's Delight** (p. 75), or the traditional "caff" of the **Regency Café** (p. 71), mid-century Britain is still steaming along—affordably.

LONDON'S best HOTELS

By 2016, London will have 136,000 hotel rooms—some better than others.

o **Meet the Locals at a Family-run B&B:** Mom-and-pop inns have taken a hit because of the dominance of corporate hotels. But you can still find some stellar homegrown hospitality where owners put you first, including the Valotis and Cabrals of the **Alhambra Hotel** in St Pancras (p. 24), the Beynons of Bloomsbury's **Jesmond Hotel** (p. 26), and the Callises of **22 York Street** in Marylebone (p. 40).

o **Lose Yourself in a Grande Dame:** The first all-service grand hotel in Europe, the **Langham,** was built in 1865 and it's still extending top-flight hospitality to guests with taste—and cash (p. 39). **Claridge's** (p. 39) and **Brown's** (p. 38) have attracted royalty and creative misadventures since the mid-1800s, while the world-famous **Savoy** still stands atop her field for luxury, legends, and Thames views (p. 29). Best of all, you can tour their ground floors without being a guest.

o **Pay Less Than $50:** You may not think it's possible, but with advance planning, you can get a new, impeccably maintained private room in the center of town for only £29 a night. Book ahead with the British chains **Premier Inn, Travelodge,** or **easyHotel,** or with the imported budget brands **Ibis** or **Tune,** and London is yours, cheap. See p. 47.

o **Sleep Where History Happened:** Rather than tear it down, Londoners would rather revitalize it. There's no more luscious restoration than that of the swoony spires of Gilbert Scott's neo-Gothic **St Pancras Renaissance Hotel** (p. 22). Have a chlorine-free swim where printing presses once printed the morning news at **One Aldwych** (p. 28), or take a room with a four-post bed where the great thinker William Hazlitt breathed his last at the dusky **Hazlitt's** in Soho (p. 27).

o **Enjoy Style for Less:** "Boutique" hotels are encroaching deeper into budget territory than ever before. At **Z Hotel Piccadilly** (p. 33) and **Hub By Premier Inn** (p. 32), surrender a little space but none of the chic at a berth near Trafalgar Square. In Southwark, buzzy Dutch boutique **CitizenM** (p. 42) has huge beds and a loopy personality, but a small price.

LONDON'S best FOR FAMILIES

o **Cruising London's Waterways:** In addition to the grand River Thames, London has a working canal system that once kept goods flowing to and from the city's docks. The best value trips are on the **Regent's Canal** (p. 152) and on the **Thames Clipper** passing under Tower Bridge. See p. 256.

- **Losing Your Way in the World's Most Famous Hedge Maze:** The green labyrinth at **Hampton Court** twists and turns for almost half a mile. When you manage to extricate yourselves, stroll through centuries of architectural styles at this stunning palace, home of many an English monarch. Don't forget to pick up a kids' activity trail. See p. 141.

- **Seeing Peter Pan in Kensington Gardens:** You'll feel like a character from a Victorian novel as you see Sir George Frampton's beloved 1902 statue of the boy who played the panpipe. There's no better way to admire and enjoy the "green lung"—the largest and most popular open space in a city that holds the record for the most green space for a city of its size. See p. 151.

- **Going Botanic in Royal Kew:** The **Royal Botanic Gardens,** Kew, house more than 50,000 plants from across the planet, including Arctic and tropical varieties. Youngsters will love the 200m (656-ft.) high Treetop Walkway, up in the Garden's deciduous canopy. See p. 142.

- **Asking How, Where, and Why:** Inside South Kensington's **Science Museum,** the Atmosphere and Launchpad galleries use interactive exhibits to keep inquisitive minds occupied. Or pilot a simulated ship at the kid-centric **National Maritime Museum.** See p. 112 and 137.

- **Learn the Panto Lingo:** From November to early January, join one of Britain's most delightful holiday experiences: Pantomime, which are slapstick musical romps through famous stories, usually starring D-list celebrities. Hiss at villains, shout instructions for heroes, and giggle at good-natured drag. Try the **Theatre Royal Stratford** (www.stratfordeast.com), the **New Wimbledon** (www.atgtickets.com), the **Hackney Empire** (p. 185), or **The Richmond Theatre** (www.richmondtheatre.net).

LONDON'S best FREE & DIRT CHEAP EXPERIENCES

- **Visiting the Great Museums:** London's state museums and galleries—including most of the big names—show off their permanent collections for free. Locals need the break—the average monthly rent here for a one-bedroom is £1,600 but the average salary is only £300 more. They include the **British Museum, National Gallery, National Portrait Gallery, Tate Britain, Tate Modern, Natural History Museum, Science Museum, V&A,** the two **Museums of London,** and the **British Library.** See chapter 5.

- **Taking in Fresh Air and a City View:** North of the River Thames, **Hampstead Heath** offers miles of woodland trails, historic pubs, and sumptuous mansions. To the south, the heights of **Greenwich Park** enjoy a panoramic sweep that takes in the royal borough's 18th-century maritime architecture and the steel-and-glass of Canary Wharf. See p. 151 and 150.

- **Dining on the Cheap:** Away from the main tourist drag and the Michelin-starred hotspots, London is surprisingly well equipped with affordable, tasty places to enjoy a full meal for under £10. Among the best are two of the West End's most venerable budget pit stops, **Café in the Crypt** at St Martin-in-the-Fields and the **Stockpot.** See p. 64 and 65.

o **Going to the Library:** The **British Library**'s free exhibitions include priceless manuscripts (p. 86) that will blow your mind. And check out **Jeremy Bentham,** stored like an on old book in a case at University College London! He is stuffed and on display. See p. 92.

o **Catching a Free Event in the Center of the City:** From the Lord Mayor's Show to the Notting Hill Carnival, almost every major public event in the capital costs nothing to attend. See "London Calendar of Events," p. 259.

THE best HISTORIC EXPERIENCES

o **Meeting the Heroes and Villains of History:** Get face-to-face with a rogue's gallery from the past at the **National Portrait Gallery,** where faces seem to watch you across time with a sparkle in their eye. The gang's all here, from a supercilious Henry VIII to a pugnacious Hogarth to a kind-eyed Princess Diana, already becoming a memory. See p. 97.

o **Taking a Tour of Royal London:** From palaces and parks to the royal art collections, history, geography, and culture have been shaped—or owned—by centuries of aristocratic rule. You can see the best of it in a day, including the Queen's favorite grocer, **Fortnum & Mason** (p. 162), plus any one of 800 other Royal Warrant holders (p. 167).

o **Peering into a Time Capsule:** Some museums preserve scenes that were frozen in time. No reconstructions or fakery here: You'll gaze upon authentic World War II military operations at the **Churchill War Rooms** (p. 102); admire the graves of great artists and the location of epic rituals at **Westminster Abbey** (p. 105); and roam the very rooms used in daily life by kings and queens at **Buckingham Palace** (p. 101), **Hampton Court Palace** (p. 141), **Kensington Palace** (p. 110), and **Windsor Castle** (p. 229).

o **Shopping in the Grandest Department Stores of Them All:** And, no, it isn't Harrods. **Liberty of London,** founded in 1875 and moved to its current half-timbered, mock-Tudor home in 1924, and **Selfridges** (p. 164), both designed and built by Americans, redefined sales methods and played crucial roles in world history. See p. 163.

o **Imagining Domestic Life Through the Ages:** At the **Geffrye Museum** (p. 133) period re-creations of interiors from the spartan 1630s to the flashy 1990s allow visitors to understand how home life has changed. But nothing immerses you in the past quite like the brain-bending role-playing of a night visit to **Dennis Severs' House** (p. 133).

SUGGESTED ITINERARIES & NEIGHBORHOODS

Few great modern cities are as multilayered, intricate, and yes, *messy* as London, Western Europe's most populous city (8.3 million in 2015), and that's because history was knitted into its very layout. London is mostly the haphazard product of blind evolution, which piled up over successive generations to produce a complicated metropolis. One could say that London simply happened.

As recently as the early 1800s, London—and by London, I mean what we now call The City, between St Paul's and the Tower—was a compact, teeming monster where many lives, birth to death, were carried out within the same few blocks. Within that frenzied cluster, districts developed out of logic or bias—the main streets ran south to the river and not east or west, for example, the smoke of industry was banished downwind, and kings lived near the Thames for easy transportation. All around The City were dozens of villages, many of which retain their names as modern neighborhoods and, if you're lucky, a whiff of their original personalities.

Quickly, London swelled to swallow its current territory. Yet because of ancient echoes, neighborhoods remain surprisingly small—many are just minutes across by foot, and all but the most crucial streets can change names several times. It's still possible to stroll along and sense sudden shifts in energy and character. In many ways, London is still a complex system of hamlets. It's one of the many delights that makes it so surprising. It also means it can take a lifetime to scratch its surface.

Addresses sometimes reflect this improvisation; a building numbered 75 may sit across the street from one numbered 32. Despite this, it's immensely difficult to get lost. The City maintains some 1,200 Legible London map **"Finger Posts"** throughout town. Wherever you are, a map is near.

If you want a map, forgo the oversimplified one your hotel might offer and don't tax your data plan. The most cherished paper map is the *London A-Z* (www.az.co.uk), first compiled by the indefatigable Phyllis Pearsall, who walked every mile of The City for the 1936 debut edition and commanded the resulting cartography empire until her death 60 years later. Its *London Mini A-Z Street Atlas* (£6) fits into a pocket. (Don't buy the app, which drains your smartphone's batteries quickly.) Just be sure to call it the "A to Zed" or you'll get a funny look; in England, the last letter in the alphabet is, quite sensibly, pronounced so it doesn't rhyme with eight other letters.

LONDON IN 1 DAY

First of all, what were you thinking? If you're in town on a layover, didn't you know that many airlines will allow you to stick around for a few days at no charge? Never mind. What's done is done. Eat a huge breakfast and make your way to Tower Hill.

1 The Tower of London ★★★

Start here (p. 128) because it usually opens an hour earlier (9am) than most attractions. Spend about 2 hours making stops at the **Crown Jewels** and the **White Tower,** and snap that requisite photo of the **Tower Bridge** (p. 127) from the quay. Grab a triangle sandwich (the quintessential London lunch).

Tube it west on the Circle or District lines to Westminster.

2 Westminster Abbey ★★★

Allot a rushed 2 hours to see the effigies of kings and queens (p. 105). Of the **Chapel of Henry VII,** Washington Irving wrote: "Stone seems, by the cunning labor of the chisel, to have been robbed of its weight and density, suspended aloft as if by magic, and the fretted roof achieved with the wonderful minuteness and airy security of a cobweb." Outside, take in the **Houses of Parliament** (p. 103) and **Big Ben's Elizabeth Tower** from across the street.

Walk up Whitehall, passing No. 10 Downing Street (the Walking Tour on p. 204 will guide you).

3 The National Gallery ★★★

At **Trafalgar Square,** a symbolic heart of The City, you can finally see some of the world's most famous paintings in person (p. 95). Park guards also turn a blind eye to tourists climbing alongside those famous bronze couchant lions, each of them 20 feet long. But don't mount them—they're cracking.

From the Strand, head to the back of Charing Cross station and cross the Thames.

4 London Eye ★★

There's time for a revolution on London's favorite contemporary icon and the new focal point of national celebrations (p. 118). In the colder months, you'll be there to watch the sun go down slowly as **Big Ben** gongs.

Finish just north of the Gallery, around Leicester Square.

5 West End Show ★★★

Curtains go up around 7:30pm (p. 180). Enjoy an ice cream during interval (intermission)—it's a custom here. Afterward, head to a **pub** and raise a pint to a city where you've barely scratched the surface (see p. 79 for ideas).

LONDON ON A 2ND DAY

You're going to have to move fast, but you'll be able to see some highlights. Take the Tube to Mansion House, Blackfriars, or St Paul's.

1 St Paul's Cathedral ★★★

As you appreciate the underside of her dome, also appreciate the grave fact that before the 1940s, her flanks were crowded with buildings. Bombings devastated the structures that once hemmed her in.

Cross the Thames on the Millennium Bridge (the Walking Tour on p. 212 will help).

2 Tate Modern ★★★

Here's a museum (p. 120) in a colossal structure that can be more memorable than what's on display inside it—although Rothko's paintings for the Four Seasons restaurant can't fail to put you in a restive mood. If it's summer, catch a matinee at **Shakespeare's Globe** (p. 119), just a few yards east; in summer, an afternoon pint at the wooden-galleried **George Inn** (p. 81), noted by Dickens and Shakespeare alike, will recharge you.

Take the Jubilee line from Southwark to Green Park.

3 Green Park ★★

Walk south through Green Park (p. 150) to behold the front of **Buckingham Palace** (p. 101); if you're here in March, you may be lucky enough to see fields of daffodils in bloom. Return to Piccadilly to browse the classy shops lining it, including **Fortnum & Mason** (p. 162).

Take the Tube's Piccadilly line (notice the century-old tilework) to Russell Square.

4 The British Museum ★★★

You'll spend the afternoon roaming it (p. 90), but you'll scarcely be able to wrap your brain around the age, rarity, and craftsmanship of what you see. Such aesthetic exertions may induce cravings for cream tea at its Great Court Restaurant.

Catch Bus 55 toward Oxford Circus. Sit on the top level for the views!

5 Oxford Circus ★★

Wind up the afternoon with a dive into the bustling fitting rooms of the shops on **Oxford Street, Regent Street,** and **Carnaby Street** (p. 160), where you'll find a huge selection of cool clothes at what Londoners call "High Street" prices—meaning they're sane. Walk southeast for a few minutes to Frith Street in Soho and have dinner at **Arbutus,** a

Michelin-starred neighborhood gem that charges prices far below its rank, and afterward, stroll past the lights of **Piccadilly Circus.** If you still have juice left, walk down Haymarket, turn left on Cockspur, and follow it down Strand to Aldwych.

6 Radio Rooftop Bar ★★

The haute, polished architecture of the ME London hotel is a flashy counterpoint to the antiquities you've been absorbing all day, and the breathtaking panorama of The City from the terrace of its glassy 10th-floor bar more than justifies the luxury price of its cocktails (www.radioat melondon.com; © **020/7395-3440;** Sun–Wed to 1am, Thurs–Sat to 2am; Tube: Temple). You're standing on the site of the old Gaiety Theatre, where 100 years ago the famous "Stage Door Johnnys" came shopping for wives among the chorus girls. History is in every footprint here.

LONDON ON A 3RD DAY

Follow the itinerary for 2 days in London, but add in one of The City's South Kensington museums, preferably the **Victoria and Albert** (p. 113), and follow that with a walk through **Hyde Park** (p. 151), possibly to see the **Diana, Princess of Wales Fountain,** and to tour the public areas of her son's and grandchildren's London home, **Kensington Palace** (p. 110), in adjoining **Kensington Gardens.** Take the Tube or a bus to Westminster, and dive into the time capsule of the **Churchill War Rooms** (p. 102). Follow that with a stroll along South Bank from Westminster to London Bridge, taking your pick among the pubs and restaurants you find along the path.

AN ITINERARY FOR FAMILIES

There's no bad neighborhood to stay in if you've got kids, because London is low-rise and manageable. But make sure they're ready to climb stairs if you're taking the Tube. On paper, some of London's museums sound as if they'd be too dry, but in reality, they bend over backward to cater to children—sometimes even at the expense of adult minds. Every major museum, no exceptions, has an on-site cafe for lunch.

Day 1: Double-Deckers & Thames Clippers

Forget expensive open-top tours: Start your day seeing Piccadilly Circus, Trafalgar Square, St Paul's Cathedral, the Tower of London, and much more for the price of bus fare on an antique, double-decker **Routemaster bus** with an old-style staircase on the end. Take route 15, every 15 minutes. After the Tower, head to the ferry dock outside and see The City from the river on a **Thames Clipper** (p. 256). Disembark at **Tate Modern** (p. 120), which comes fully loaded for young exploration with family trails, a learning zone on Level 5, and some very cool video tablets for interpreting the art. Take the Tube to Leicester Square for a **West End musical** (p. 180).

Day 2: Covent Garden & Coram's Fields

Make your way to Covent Garden's **London Transport Museum** (p. 94), where kids can pretend to drive a bus and explore other eye-level exhibits. Then bring your brood a 15-minute walk north to the **British Museum** (p. 90) and hook them up with crayons and pads, exploration backpacks, and the special object collections tour geared to young minds. If they're the daring types, the mummies never fail to impress. Just east you'll find a city park just for children: The 7-acre **Coram's Fields** (www.coramsfields.org) was set aside in 1739 for an orphanage at a time when 75% of London kids died before the age of 5. Its southern gate is where mothers once abandoned their babies in desperation. Today, no adult may enter without a child and this sad spot is now the scene of daily family joy; there's a petting zoo, two playgrounds for all ages, sand pits, and a paddling pool.

Day 3: The Brompton Road Museums

Today is devoted to exploration of the Brompton Road museums, a trio of world's-bests for kids: Take the Piccadilly line to South Kensington, where the **V&A** (p. 113) has hundreds of hands-on exhibits for kids (look for the hand symbol on the maps), such as trying on Victorian costumes or trying on armor gauntlets. Next door, the plain-speaking signs and robotic dinosaurs of the **Natural History Museum** (p. 111) impress kids as much as the airplanes and space capsules over their heads at the **Science Museum** (p. 112)—both institutions furnish even more kids' trails and activities for free. Go east on the Circle or District lines to Temple, and you're at the dancing water jets of the **Somerset House** courtyard (home of the Courtauld Gallery, p. 93). But if the weather doesn't suit that, the **London Eye**'s capsules are safe, climate-controlled, and move imperceptibly—the view will stimulate and inspire kids.

A DISCOVERY WEEKEND

The *Frommer's EasyGuides* are designed to give you a firm introduction to the sights, hotels, and restaurants that speak most to a visitor about what's going on in each destination. But authentic London doesn't begin and end with these pages, and if you dip into the way that London locals live, your visit will be immeasurably richer.

Day 1: Brixton & Bollywood

When Victoria was Queen, families flocked to live near the incandescent lights of Brixton's Electric Avenue, which in 1888 became one of

London's first shopping streets lit by electricity. Today, it's a boisterous immigrant community. By day, explore the glazed awnings of its markets, where to inhale the aroma of meat and exotic spices is to walk through a portal to Jamaica, India, or China, and to be reminded that London, like few others, is a truly worldly city. In the evening, experience London's huge South Asian population—Indians are nearly 2% of the population, and one of Britain's richest men, Lakshmi Mittal, is Indian-born—by attending a Bollywood film at the Boleyn Cinema (www.boleyncinemas.com; Tube: Upton Park), a historic 1938 Art Deco building and the second-largest Bollywood screen in the country that loves the genre.

Day 2: Go Football Mad or Cricket Crazy

London hosts 13 professional football (soccer) teams, more than any other city on Earth. From mid-August to mid-May, catch matches at some of the best Premier League teams: **Chelsea** (www.chealseafc.com), **Arsenal** (London's first club; www.arsenal.com), **Fulham** (www.fulhamfc.com), or **West Ham United** (www.whufc.com), which in 2016 takes up residence in the former Olympic Stadium at Stratford. Filling the gap from April to September, and less likely to pelt you in the skull with a beer bottle, is cricket. Attend "test matches" at Marylebone's **MCC Lord's Cricket Ground** (www.lords.org) or Oval's **Surrey County Cricket Club** (www.surreycricket.com). If you figure out how the game works, fill me in, won't you? It's a little like baseball—and a lot like watching grass grow.

Day 3: Ale, Yorkshire Pudding & Tough Questions

On Sunday afternoons, find a pub with an inviting garden for **Sunday Roast,** a spread of meats with the trimmings, Yorkshire pudding (a pastrylike shell), and gravy, washed down with copious amounts of beer. It's the more leisurely equivalent of brunch: After a long week of working for the Man, Londoners hang out until they're ready for Monday. On Sundays, some pubs also hold **pub quizzes,** another staple of British life. Form teams and answer trivia for lame prizes, but be warned: Foreigners always fold on the sports and politics questions.

Neighborhoods in Brief

London's neighborhoods were laid out during a period of wagon and foot traffic, when districts were defined in narrower terms than we define them today; indeed, for centuries people often lived complete lives without seeing the other side of town. Ironically, in our times, the Tube has done much to divide these districts from each other. Visitors are likely to hop a train between them and don't often realize how remarkably close together they really are.

Are these the only areas of interest? Not even close. Literally hundreds of fascinating village clusters abound, many with names as cherishable as Ponders End, Tooting, and The Wrythe. And considering that a third of Londoners now belong to an ethnic minority and more than 200 languages are spoken, the flavor of your experience shifts as you go. But visitors are likely to spend time here:

London is chopped into geographic parcels, and you'll see those post-codes on street signs. The heart of The City, in postcode terms, is near the Chancery Lane Tube stop. From there, areas are given a compass direction (N for north, SW for south-west, and so on) and a number (but ignore that, since a number greater than 1 doesn't mean the area is in the boonies). In the very heart of town, addresses get an extra C for "centre," as in WC1, which is where Covent Garden is located. Every address in this book includes its postcode, which corresponds to the neighborhood in which you'll find it. Don't worry—you won't need to memorize these because each listing also includes the nearest Tube stop to help you quickly place locations on a map. Here are some of the most common post-codes:

WC1 Bloomsbury
WC2 Covent Garden, Holborn, Strand
W1 Fitzrovia, Marylebone, Mayfair, Soho
W2 Bayswater
W6 Hammersmith
W8 Kensington
W11 Notting Hill
SW1 Belgravia, St James's, Westminster
SW3 Chelsea
SW5 Earl's Court
SW7 Knightsbridge, South Kensington
SE1 Southwark
SE10 Greenwich
EC1 Clerkenwell
EC2 Bank, Barbican, Liverpool Street
EC3 Tower Hill
EC4 Fleet Street, St Paul's
E1 Spitalfields, Whitechapel
E2 Bethnal Green
E14 Canary Wharf/Isle of Dogs
N1 Islington
NW1 Camden Town
NW3 Hampstead

BLOOMSBURY & FITZROVIA

Best for: *Museums, affordable inns, residential streets, universities, and homewares and electronics shops on Tottenham Court Road*
What you won't find: *Evening entertainment, nightclubs*

Bloomsbury's dark-brick, white-sashed residential buildings and leafy squares date mostly from the Georgian period, when the district became the first in a chaotic city to be planned—it was an early version of the modern suburban development. The refined air attracted the intelligentsia nearly from the start, and its two universities are both 19th-century institutions. The British Museum settled here, too. Bloomsbury became a place of remembrance on July 7, 2005; of the 52 who died that day, 26 perished underground on a bombed Piccadilly line train between King's Cross and Russell Square stations, and 13 were killed on a double-decker bus passing through Tavistock Square. Bloomsbury's cozier sister

Fitzrovia, similar in character but devoid of major attractions, lies on the western side of Tottenham Court Road. Famous residents include George Bernard Shaw and Virginia Woolf, who both lived (at different times) at 29 Fitzroy Square.

KING'S CROSS

Best for: *Budget hotels, trains heading north (and south to Paris), alternative/down-and-dirty nightlife, student housing, take-away counters*
What you won't find: *A large restaurant selection, shopping*

Recently, the area around King's Cross station was an unsavory tenderloin of porn stores and warehouses. Behind the station, millions of pounds just transformed once-derelict industrial infrastructure into Granary Square, a canalside center for arts hotspots, restaurants, colleges, and tech HQs. Legend (surely apocryphal) says the Celtic queen Boudica rests somewhere near Platform 8 of King's Cross. Fans of Harry Potter know that

From Arthur Frommer's *Europe on $5 a Day* (1957)

"All you've heard to the contrary, Londoners are among the warmest people of Europe, and London is a friendly and inviting city. It has charm and a politeness of attitude that belie its big-city status. You'll want to extend your stay . . . Can you live in London on $5 a day? There's nothing to it."

the young wizard boards the Hogwarts Express at the (fictitious) Platform 9¾; the movie versions have shot at Platforms 4 and 5 but used prettier St Pancras station, next door, as a stand-in facade. Change came, as it often has in English history, from France. The Channel Tunnel Rail Link is the starting point for Eurostar train trips to France and beyond.

MARYLEBONE & MAYFAIR

Best for: *Luxe shopping, hotels, restaurants, small museums, strolling, embassies*
What you won't find: *Historic sights, affordability*

The middle-class hubbub of Oxford Street west of Regent Street divides high-hat Marylebone from its snobbish southern neighbor, Mayfair. Both play host to upscale shopping and several fascinating, if overlooked, museums, but there the similarities end. World-famous Mayfair, typified by hyperluxe bauble shops and blue-blood heritage (the present Queen was born at 17 Bruton St. in a building that is no longer there), has a high opinion of itself as a starchy enclave of wealth, much of it from other countries, and it has less to offer the casual tourist. (The title of the musical *My Fair Lady* is witty wordplay on how its Cockney heroine, Eliza, would have pronounced "Mayfair lady.") Marylebone (*Mar-le-bun*), on the other hand, benefits from convenient Tube and bus connections and lively sidewalks crowded with evening celebrants, particularly around James Street. Also, thanks to a territorial local authority, its main shopping drag (Marylebone High St.) remains one of the last important streets in London that isn't awash with the ubiquitous corporate chain stores. Oxford Street is The City's premier shopping corridor; the western half between Oxford Circus and Marble

Arch is the classier end, with marquee department stores such as Selfridges and Marks & Spencer.

SOHO, COVENT GARDEN & CENTRAL WEST END

Best for: *Shopping, restaurants, theater, cinema, nightlife, opera, free art (National Gallery and National Portrait Gallery), star sightings*
What you won't find: *Elbow room, hotel values, silence*

London's undisputed center of nightlife, restaurants, and theater, the West End seethes with tourists and merry-makers. After work, Old Compton Street and Covent Garden overflow with people catching up with friends; by 7:30pm, the theaters and opera houses are pulsing; by midnight, the action has moved into the nightclubs of Leicester Square and lounges of Soho; and in the wee hours, you might find groups of partiers trawling Gerrard Street, in teeny Chinatown, hunting for snacks. Prim Trafalgar Square, dominated by the peerless National Gallery, has often been called London's focal point. On a sunny day, you'll find few places that exude such well-being.

WESTMINSTER, INCLUDING ST JAMES'S

Best for: *Historic and government sights, river strolls, St James's Park*
What you won't find: *Affordable hotels, a wide choice of restaurants*

This is near the central West End, but its energy is different. It's a district tourists mostly see by day. South of Trafalgar Square, you'll find regiments of robust government buildings but little in the way of hotels or food. Whitehall's severity doesn't spread far. Just a block east, its impenetrable character gives way to the proud riverside promenade of Victoria Embankment overlooking the London Eye, and just a block west, to the greenery of St James's Park, which is, in effect, the Queen's front yard, since Buckingham Palace is at the western boundary of this area. North of the park, the staid streets of St James's are even more exclusive than Mayfair's, if that's possible. Prince Charles lives there.

THE CITY

Best for: *Old streets, the Tower of London, St Paul's, financial concerns*

What you won't find: *Nightlife or weekend life, affordable hotels*

Technically, this is the only part of London that's London. Other bits, including the West End, are under the jurisdiction of different local governments, such as Westminster or Camden. The City, as it's called, is where most of London's history happened. It's where Romans cheered gladiators. It's where London Bridge—at least 12 of them—touched shore. It's where the Great Fire raged. And, more recently, it's where the Deutsche Luftwaffe focused many of its nocturnal bombing raids, which is why you'll find so little evidence of the aforementioned events. Outside of working hours, the main thing you'll see in The City is your own reflection in the facade of corporate fortresses; west of Liverpool Street station, even most of the pubs close on weekends. Although this is where you'll find such priceless relics as the Tower of London, St Paul's Cathedral, the Tower Bridge, the Bank of England, and the Monument, many remnants are underfoot, since much of the spider web of lanes and streets dates back to the Roman period, and often their names give a hint of their former lives (Walbrook is where the river Walbrook, now hidden underground, flowed down to the Thames; Honey Lane, Bread Street, Milk Street, and Poultry all once hosted food markets.) Buildings have come and gone, but the veins of The City have pumped in-situ for thousands of years.

THE SOUTH BANK, SOUTHWARK & BOROUGH

Best for: *Museums, memorable pubs, strolls, gourmet foods and wines*

What you won't find: *Shopping, parks*

During the recent rehabilitation of Southwark (*Suth*-urk) from a crumbling industrial district, its blighted power station became one of the world's greatest museums (the Tate Modern), a master playwright's theater was re-created (the Globe), and a sublime riverfront path replaced the coal lightermen's rotting piers. Now it's where London goes to fall in love with The City. It's a 1-mile riverside stroll between the London Eye and the Tate Modern, and every step is a pleasure. Once-dank railway viaducts are filled with cafes and reasonable restaurants, Western Europe's tallest skyscraper, The Shard, lords over from above, and the nation's dramatic showpiece (the National Theatre) anchors them. But it's gratifying to see that some things never change; Borough Market, which attracts gourmet foodies from around the world, is the descendant of a market that fed the denizens of that medieval skyscraper over the water, London Bridge.

VICTORIA & CHELSEA

Best for: *Boutiques, low-cost lodging, town homes, wealthy neighbors*

What you won't find: *Transit options, street life, museums*

Victoria doesn't technically apply to the neighborhood around the eponymous train station—Belgravia (to the west) and Pimlico (south and east) take those honors—but the shorthand stuck. Most of the area, which is residential or uninterestingly workaday, was developed starting in the 1820s in consistent patterns of white stucco-terraced homes. The area around the station, which is being redeveloped in a massive works project, contains two outlier West End theatres, but little else. Just north, you'll face the brick walls of Buckingham Palace Gardens. Chelsea, to its south, has a history of well-heeled bohemianism—Oscar Wilde, James McNeill Whistler, and the Beatles all lived here—although it's known more as one of The City's most exclusive (and some would say insular) communities. A stroll past boutiques and pocket-squared residents on the King's Road, turning ever-more corporate and indistinct, is not the adventure it once was.

KENSINGTON, KNIGHTSBRIDGE

Best for: *Museums, shopping, French pastries, hotels, celebrities*
What you won't find: *Historic sights*

Here, one expensive neighborhood genuflects to another, and barely anyone you meet was born in England. South Kensington and Brompton draw the most visitors to their grand museums; and Knightsbridge is where moneyed foreigners spend and show off—London now has the most billionaires in the world, nearly twice as many as New York or Moscow. Privilege has long had an address in Kensington—that's a reason those edifying institutions were located here to begin with, away from the grubby paws of the peasants—but it also is home to a core of French expats; you'll find the cafes catering to them on Bute Street. Kensington Palace, at the Gardens' western end, is where Prince William and Kate live when they're in town. When you travel west to Earl's Court, you experience a considerable drop in voltage. It's a frumpy zone deprived of a contingency to the park with undistinguished eats and sleeps; the rise of King's Cross and Shoreditch for younger travelers has reduced it to near-negligible stature.

SHOREDITCH & SPITALFIELDS

Best for: *Nightclubs, music, food of all types, galleries, clothing*
What you won't find: *Museums, parks*

If Mayfair is London's champagne, the East End hoods have been its hangover. For centuries it was an impoverished, squalid slum for poor immigrants and shifty souls. Jack the Ripper slashing and the Elephant Man suffering jibes—it happened here. That's in the history books now. Spitalfields (*Spit*-all-fields), named for its excellent covered market (p. 83) and increasingly threatened by an unstoppable cancer of soulless, open-plan office buildings from The City, blends into Shoreditch, big on restaurants, shopping, and name-dropping up-and-coming designers and party promoters as if you knew who they were. Dalston, young and bohemian, is north of that. East of Spitalfields, in ancient homes that have long housed waves of immgirants (French, then Jewish, now South Asian), you'll find the famed restaurants of Brick Lane (p. 76), the cafes and dance clubs of the converted Old Truman Brewery, and the art-savvy neighborhood of Whitechapel. Prostitutes are out, £4.50 coffee is in—which may not be an improvement.

GREENWICH

Best for: *Museums, antiques and food markets, river views, strolls, pubs*
What you won't find: *Hotels, bustle*

Greenwich, on the south bank across from the Canary Wharf developments, retains the tranquility of an untouched village. Such lovely insularity exists because the Tube (well, the DLR) didn't connect it to the greater city until 1999—all the more remarkable when you consider the town's illustrious pedigree as a royal getaway (it's got the oldest royal park in London), as a scientific capital, and as one of the world's most crucial command centers. If it all sounds like a living museum, it is: On top of being a UNESCO World Heritage Site (Maritime Greenwich), the village is literally the center of time and space, since it inhabits the exact location of Greenwich Mean Time, and of longitude 0° 0′ 0″. Set away from town there's the colossal O_2 dome, The City's iconic concert venue.

Other Popular London Neighborhoods

Mostly because of iffy transit connections (for example, service by a single Tube line that, should it go on the blink, would derail your vacation), this book doesn't focus on these neighborhoods as prime places to stay, but they're still vital parts of The City.

BAYSWATER & PADDINGTON

Best for: *Cheap inns, ethnic food, well-preserved Victorian thoroughfares*
What you won't find: *Attractions, non-chain stores, street life, adorable bears*

Its whitewashed, terraced houses were briefly the most fashionable in The City (Churchill and Dickens were residents), yet today, the sizable transient population deprives it of sustained energy, and its hotels tend to be for immigrant tradesmen. Crowning the muddle is Queensway, a popular shopping street containing White-leys, a 1911 department store edifice converted into a mall with fairly unexciting tenants. Although Paddington station is one of London's most beautiful train hubs (it was built by the legendary architect Isambard Kingdom Brunel in 1838), it's also the most inconvenient—although Heathrow and Windsor trains go from it.

DOCKLANDS

Best for: *Developments, ancient warehouses, super-cheap chain hotels*
What you won't find: *Street life, nightlife*

Most of far east London along the north side of the Thames is ignobly called by a single, sweeping name: Docklands. Yet Captain Cook set off on his explorations from here, and its hand-dug basins once teemed with ships bearing goods from around the planet. Docklands made colonial Britain successful—and thus America, Canada, Australia, and South Africa, too. After a fallow generation, East London's hand-dug pools are under constant redevelopment by corporations in stacks of fluorescent-lit office cubes, and the Olympics settled here in 2012. Away from the river, in salt-of-the-earth neighborhoods like Bethnal Green, Stratford, and West Ham, The City's Pakistani and Indian populations flourish, with marvelous but unglamorous food and shops.

ISLINGTON

Best for: *Antiques, gastropubs, theater, street markets, cafes, strolls*
What you won't find: *Museums, hotels*

Few neighborhoods retain such a healthy balance between feisty bohemianism and groomed prosperity, and almost none retain streetscapes as defiantly mid-century as Chapel Market. Islington's leafy byways are dotted with antiques dealers, hoary pubs with backroom theater spaces, beer gardens, and most pleasingly on a sunny day, pedestrian towpaths overlooking Regent's Canal. Why more tourists don't flood Islington is a mystery—and a blessing.

CAMDEN

Best for: *Alternative music, massive clothing markets, junk souvenirs, pubs*
What you won't find: *Elbow room, hotels, upscale restaurants*

Name a British tune that got under your skin, and chances are it received its first airing in the beer-soaked concert halls of Camden Town. London's analogue to San Francisco's Haight-Ashbury District, it was big in the countercultured '60s and '70s and is still grotty enough for Amy Winehouse to have expired in. The area's shoulder-to-shoulder markets, which hawk touristy hokum, cheap sunglasses, and £5 falafel in the former warehouses and stables serving Regent's Canal, can be pretty awful, and the sort of places where you feel compelled to carry your wallet in your front pocket. They're so thronged with young tourists, who seem drawn here more out of duty than for any true mission for commerce, that the inadequate Tube station only serves exit-only traffic on weekends.

NOTTING HILL

Best for: *Markets, village vibes, restaurants, pubs, touristy strolls, antiques*
What you won't find: *Well-priced shopping, museums, Hugh Grant*

Thanks partly to Hollywood, this westerly nook of London, known to locals for race riots, appears high on many visitors' checklists. Its Saturday Portobello Road market, the principal draw, is fiendishly crowded but short on truly wonderful wares. In fact, it's touristy.

WHERE TO STAY

From 19th-century grand hotels to boutique inns hatched by design firms, from eccentric quarters above pubs to family-run town house B&Bs, London's range of accommodations is as diverse as the city it serves. But because occupancy is at its highest rate in 20 years, lodging will be the single biggest expense of your trip, so make sure the place you choose spotlights the city at its best.

London's housing market is diseased—and the affliction is foreign cash. The city has always attracted the richest of the rich, but recently, they began parking their fortunes in its real estate en masse. Russian oligarchs, Middle Eastern magnates, and Chinese officials are snapping up prime real estate—in 2014, a 16,000-square-foot flat at One Hyde Park sold for an insane £140 million—squeezing out the middle class, shutting down family-run B&Bs, and turning a place to sleep into a major financial drain for everyone else. There are more than 11,000 five-star rooms in London, so it's rougher on budget, and even mid-level, travelers than it has ever been before.

Against that backdrop of extreme wealth, more than 500,000 migrants from the European Union flooded into the U.K. between 2010 and 2015, and 70% of them took low-skilled jobs such as hotel desk staff. Of the 15 initial members of the E.U., only Greece and Portugal pay their workers less than the U.K. Affording London is rough.

Fortunately, there is superlative value to be found in all the neighborhoods where you are most likely to be. First, don't get caught up in star ratings. In Britain, more stars does not necessarily mean more comfort. A hotel can earn an extra star simply because it will serve you food. In fact, the more stars a place has, the more likely it is to charge for using its amenities, so focus instead on the location and the price. This book filters out the inconvenient and shabby neighborhoods for you—Bayswater and Earl's Court, once tourist standbys, no longer make the grade—and focuses on central locations.

London's non-corporate hotels are good about sticking to their posted rates; in fact, every property is required by law to post the *maximum* rate in the lobby. They're also increasingly unabashed about quoting insanely high prices given any uptick in demand. Beware dates around the London Marathon (Apr), bank holidays, Wimbledon (June), New Year's, and summer. Most corporate hotels

London Hotel Price Categories	
Hotels are categorized by the lowest en suite double rate (suite prices are not included).	
Expensive	£181 and up
Moderate	£126 to £180
Inexpensive	Under £125

will grant a discount for nonrefundable bookings, and family-run places tend to cut deals if you stay longer.

Accommodations are subject to a Value Added Tax (VAT) of 20%. Happily, almost all small B&Bs include taxes in their rates, although you may be charged 3% to 5% to use a credit card. More expensive hotels (those around £150 or more) tend to leave taxes off their tariffs, which can result in a nasty surprise at checkout, so it never hurts to ask if the rate "excludes VAT."

KING'S CROSS & BLOOMSBURY

King's Cross hotels may have small rooms but they are served by six important Tube lines and they tend to be recently renovated. Meanwhile, Bloomsbury's chocolate-colored Georgian brick town houses lie within a 20-minute walk of Soho and Covent Garden, and they're near the Piccadilly Line to Heathrow. To be honest—and let's spill a dirty secret here—these places are better located than many of London's most expensive hotels.

Expensive

Great Northern Hotel ★★ Of all of London's major railway terminal hotels, from the outside the Great Northern is the plainest—and the smallest. Its crescent-shaped building went up quite early, in 1854, and as a consequence isn't as bombastic as its brethren, although it swaggers with the high ceilings and wide corridors of its epoch. The front door is so inauspicious and the reception so closet-like as to make you wonder if you're going in the delivery entrance, but since the original lobby has been converted into a sophisticated cocktail bar, I think the trade was just. Rooms aren't capacious, either, a quirk the renovation alleviated with smart modern design that includes—daringly for a hotel—cream-colored carpeting. The smallest rooms are now called "couchettes" because the sled-style queen beds, attached at head and foot to the walls, are said to have been inspired by railway sleepers. (Don't worry—they have much more space for your luggage, although the result is something less than ideal for families.) Etched glass and cute little curved banquettes complete the allusions to trains. Other high-standard perks pack the other spaces—a good British restaurant, Plum & Spilt Milk (named after a color scheme) is one. The combined effect of historical import and unparalleled transport connections (six Tube lines downstairs, trains and Eurostar to either side) justifies its upper-moderate pricing.

Kings Cross St Pancras Station, Pancras Rd., N1. www.gnhlondon.com. ✆ **020/3388-0800.** 91 units. Doubles from about £195. Tube: King's Cross St Pancras. **Amenities:** Restaurant; bar; snack bar; free Wi-Fi.

London-Wide Hotels

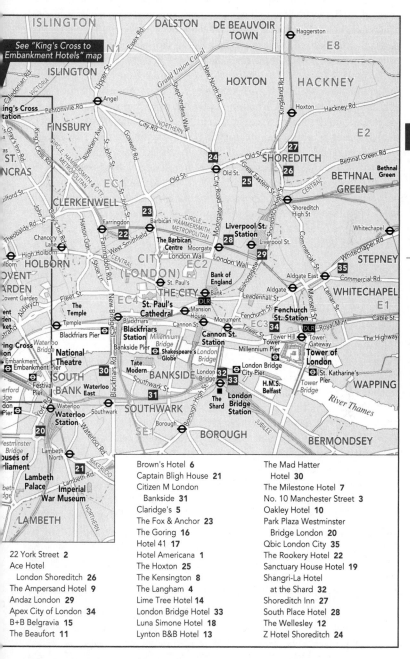

Brown's Hotel **6**

Captain Bligh House **21**

Citizen M London
  Bankside **31**

Claridge's **5**

The Fox & Anchor **23**

The Goring **16**

Hotel 41 **17**

Hotel Americana **1**

The Hoxton **25**

The Kensington **8**

The Langham **4**

Lime Tree Hotel **14**

London Bridge Hotel **33**

Luna Simone Hotel **18**

Lynton B&B Hotel **13**

The Mad Hatter
  Hotel **30**

The Milestone Hotel **7**

No. 10 Manchester Street **3**

Oakley Hotel **10**

Park Plaza Westminster
  Bridge London **20**

Qbic London City **35**

The Rookery Hotel **22**

Sanctuary House Hotel **19**

Shangri-La Hotel
  at the Shard **32**

Shoreditch Inn **27**

South Place Hotel **28**

The Wellesley **12**

Z Hotel Shoreditch **24**

22 York Street **2**

Ace Hotel
  London Shoreditch **26**

The Ampersand Hotel **9**

Andaz London **29**

Apex City of London **34**

B+B Belgravia **15**

The Beaufort **11**

St Pancras Renaissance Hotel ★★ This Gothic red brick palace, built in the 1870s as a castle-like terminal hotel for a railway line, is one of London's most distinctive buildings, and its 2011 restoration, overseen with exactitude, not only rescued a Victorian icon from neglect but also created a distinctive property. Premium rooms have an unforgettable view down the ribbed, cast-iron cavern of the train shed, where Eurostar arrives and departs for Paris. There, the most expensive Chambers rooms have 5.5m (18-ft.) ceilings and details such as (now-decorative) fireplaces, arched windows, and substantial wooden doors. Rooms in the newly built Barlow wing lack those long views but are spacious, modern, and suit corporate hotel tastes. Echoing public spaces is a gilt-and-tile parade of self-important Victorian excess, from the winged Grand Staircase to the lushly carved, The Gilbert Scott brasserie (named for the architect; local star Marcus Wareing oversees it) and the old wooden Booking Hall, now a bistro where old English punch cocktails are revived. The building was "too good for its purpose," lamented Scott, whose own son went mad and died in one of the rooms, and it's worth a wander even if you're not staying here—management knows it's a jewel, and it welcomes visitors.

Euston Rd., London, NW1. www.stpancrasrenaissance.co.uk. ℂ **020/7841-3540.** 245 units. Doubles £235–£450. Tube: King's Cross St Pancras. **Amenities:** Restaurant; 2 bars; indoor pool; gym; spa; free Wi-Fi in Chambers rooms, otherwise £15/day.

Moderate

The Megaro ★ This old office building has been tarted up with brassy colors with a cluttered mural, which the neighbors must hate, but inside, the theme is spacious and virtually Scandinavian, with open wood floors, unadorned paneling, smart slide-out make-up desks and workspaces, and fresh tea leaves for your cuppa. Rooms on the main road have killer views of St Pancras and the plaza in front of King's Cross (no. 504, a corner, is the best for that), but if traffic noise irritates you, go for one facing the other way (no. 508, with a small balcony, picturesquely peeks over the pipe chimneys of the nearby town houses). The tariff comes with a free newspaper you can download to your iPad. If you're traveling with a platonic companion, ask for a room in which your bathroom isn't encased in glass walls; some are, some aren't. Next door, its sister **The California** (www. thecalifornialondon.com; ℂ **020/7837-7629**) a converted town house, is tighter and lift-free, but 40% cheaper.

Belgrove Street, WC1. www.hotelmegaro.co.uk. ℂ **020/7843-2222.** 49 units. Average price £165 single, £185 double. Rates include breakfast. Tube: King's Cross St Pancras. **Amenities:** Restaurant; bar; free Wi-Fi.

Staunton Hotel ★ The Staunton is an admirable, welcoming, small B&B. Although it's situated in a pair of 230-year-old town houses on the corner of two loud streets (Store and Gower), windows have been double-glazed and adorned with treatments, which tamps down a bit on aural clutter.

King's Cross to Embankment Hotels

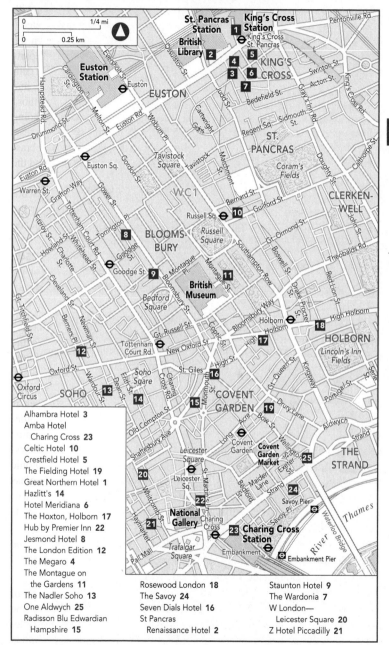

Alhambra Hotel **3**
Amba Hotel
  Charing Cross **23**
Celtic Hotel **10**
Crestfield Hotel **5**
The Fielding Hotel **19**
Great Northern Hotel **1**
Hazlitt's **14**
Hotel Meridiana **6**
The Hoxton, Holborn **17**
Hub by Premier Inn **22**
Jesmond Hotel **8**
The London Edition **12**
The Megaro **4**
The Montague on
  the Gardens **11**
The Nadler Soho **13**
One Aldwych **25**
Radisson Blu Edwardian
  Hampshire **15**

Rosewood London **18**
The Savoy **24**
Seven Dials Hotel **16**
St Pancras
  Renaissance Hotel **2**

Staunton Hotel **9**
The Wardonia **7**
W London—
  Leicester Square **20**
Z Hotel Piccadilly **21**

WHAT TO EXPECT AT town house hotels

Unfortunately, the once-famous English B&B is an endangered species, at least in central London. There's a drastic housing crunch. Neighborhoods that were recently dependable for cut-price lodging (Gloucester Place in Marylebone, Ebury Street in Victoria, Gower Street in Bloomsbury) are being sold to the ultra-rich, and B&Bs that don't convert to luxury apartments must jack up rates to uncompetitive levels or sell out to company-managed hotels that hire foreign-born desk staff who know London no better than you do.

The ones that survive usually occupy "listed" buildings. What does that mean? It means that it has historical or architectural importance—for example, it's an example of a fine Georgian town house or an original stately Victorian terrace home. To keep developers from knocking down a gem, "listed" buildings are protected. Changing anything down to the color of the paint requires permission. American tourists who are unused to London's listed buildings often post huffy online reviews about the very things that define town house hotels, penalizing London inns for being London inns. That hotel is not a dump! It's historic.

Rooms are small by American standards. Interior walls were added to subdivide the original rooms, but don't blame the current owners. Most subdivision was done in after World War II to fill a housing gap after many of the city's big hotels were destroyed, and now, even removing those slapped-up walls requires civic approval, which is nigh impossible. You are unlikely to have a

Well-appointed rooms also have safes, and air conditioning, which is uncommon in Georgian-era buildings like these, but no lift, which is why we imagine the owners charge more than the B&B average. The rooms are ever slightly larger-than-usual, as well having the formidable location within walking distance of the entire West End.

13-15 Gower St., WC1. www.stauntonhotel.com. ℗ **020/7580-2740.** 17 units. £156–£215 double, 15% less for 30-day advance purchase. Rates include full breakfast. Tube: Goodge Street. **Amenities:** Free Wi-Fi.

Inexpensive

Alhambra Hotel ★★★ A friendly, family-run find, the comforting Alhambra is an inn with heart, and a top value. Its proprietors, whose lineage has owned the land for decades and isn't at risk of being elbowed out, take pride in the business and they keep prices low. Picture simple but dignified rooms (LCD TVs but no phones, always spotless) squeezed into old spaces and freshened up with bright bedspreads; inviting royal blue carpeting; and built-in desks with chairs. Frank Valoti, the patriarch, does the cooking, and he dabbles in art, too; in the basement breakfast area, check out the pastel still life he drew to show Europeans what's included in his generous full English breakfast. Bruno Cabral, his attentive son-in-law, handles the hotel's modernization, such as the addition of free Wi-Fi (fiber-optics were just installed) and in-room safes, a rarity for this price point. If you share a bathroom, there are plenty to go around. Guests can use the lobby computer. The same family closet and in some rooms suitcases can be hard to open without using the bed. The largest rooms in such B&Bs usually face the front.

Bathrooms are even smaller. In the old days, guests shared bathrooms. Now, to suit changing tastes, landlords wedged booths containing the staples (toilet, shower, sink) into rooms that weren't designed to have them.

Don't expect an elevator, or "lift." It takes years of begging and a small fortune to convince the council to permit the installation of an elevator. Assume you'll have to use the stairs. They may be narrower than you're used to. Rooms on higher floors require climbing, but they also receive more light, less noise, and often cost less.

Ceilings get lower as you go higher. Until the 20th century, the floors of fashionable town houses served distinct functions. The cellar was for kitchens and coal storage. The ground floor was usually used for living rooms. The first and second floors were reserved for bedrooms, and the top floor was for servants and for the children's nursery, which accounts for the slightly lower ceilings there.

Not all windows are double glazed. You think you hear traffic now? Imagine when horses and carriages clattered up the cobbles at all hours. If you're a light sleeper, simply ask for a room at the back. Rooms on back stairway landings often don't adjoin other rooms, either, which takes care of more ambient noise.

runs an annex across the street that has the same high standards. In winter, it's easy to negotiate rates down by as much as 30%.

17-19 Argyle St., WC1. www.alhambrahotel.com. ✆ **020/7837-9575.** 52 units. £83–£108 single, £90–£124 double. Rates include full breakfast. Tube: King's Cross St Pancras. **Amenities:** Lobby computer; free Wi-Fi.

Celtic Hotel ★★ In 2007, the Duke of Bedford evicted the beloved St Margaret's budget hotel after a residence of a half-century. As its devotees howled, the premises were swiftly converted to an expensive boutique hotel. The St Margaret's operators, the eccentric but dedicated Marazzi family ("We were swindled!" one exclaimed to me), decamped nearby to the Celtic, transforming a bleak guesthouse (near the British Museum and the Tube to Heathrow) into their new, charismatic budget citadel. Few other budget hoteliers put as much heart into making sure guests are acclimated to London by answering questions, obliging special dietary requests, and filling bellies with a cooked breakfast that's so enormous (try the banana yogurt) that lunch might become optional. To keep attracting longtime regulars, the Celtic retains the top-value features that made Maggie's a quirky stalwart: rooms do not have TVs or phones, furniture is endearingly mismatched, and the lounge is a hub for socializing with fellow guests. Add £6 to £21 if you don't want to share a shower or toilet. You must book directly.

61-63 Guilford St., WC1. www.celtichotel.com. ✆ **020/7837-6737.** 30 units. Singles from £61, doubles from £82. Rates include cooked breakfast. Tube: Russell Square. **Amenities:** 2 lounges; free Wi-Fi.

Crestfield Hotel ★★   Every city needs a few unabashedly basic, secure choices that aren't grim. Rooms are tiny, freshly painted in grey-blue, and the breakfast area is trim and modernized, but there's no lift. Rooms also boast TVs (albeit teeny ones), but no phones. Bathrooms (most units have their own, with toilet) are essentially tiled cubicles with drains in the floor, but the £120 family room for four is a true steal. Room no. 9, a double, is located on a landing facing the back, so it's even quieter than most. If you're only staying on weekdays, ask for a special deal, because the hotel sees a lot of weekend trade. Private bathrooms cost £10 to £15 more. Seriously, what more do you require? Okay, the hotel has a dog: Jack the terrier.

2-4 Crestfield St., WC1. www.crestfieldhotel.com. ✆ **020/7837-0500.** 58 units. Singles from £45, doubles from £65. Rates include continental breakfast. Tube: King's Cross St Pancras. **Amenities:** Bar; free Wi-Fi.

Hotel Meridiana ★   This is what a value hotel should be: not lavish, but you happily get what you pay for. Walls can be thin, rooms truly teeny, many rooms share bathrooms, but everything is spotless, and breakfast (served in a room so small that sometimes you have to wait your turn) is a proper cooked one. Heating and hot water are reliable, too, which isn't always the case in buildings of this age, and some rooms have drawers, another relative curiosity. If you just want a place to sleep where you'll have no regrets about hygiene or price, this no-frills B&B is a decent choice. You're unlikely to get as much value for the price elsewhere.

43-44 Argyle Sq., WC1. www.hotelmeridiana.co.uk. ✆ **020/7713-0144.** 27 units. Singles from £45, doubles from £64. Rates include full breakfast. Tube: King's Cross St Pancras. **Amenities:** Free Wi-Fi.

Jesmond Hotel ★★★   I have a soft spot for this place. I stayed here often when I was out of college (in room no. 3, a cozy single on the rear landing—still there, still snug). Back then, the Beynon family, who took over the Jesmond in 1979, had a young son, Glyn. Today, Glyn is a grown family man and he's in charge—and he's doing a solid job of updating the family B&B in a historic Georgian town house (ask to read the history he wrote of it) far beyond the expectations of its tariff range. He installed new bathrooms with all-new piping, accounting for the larger-than-average showers, he soundproofed the front windows to keep out the roar of Gower Street's traffic, and he converted the house's 18th-century coal chute into a cellar breakfast room and day lounge. He also converted the former parlor, with its antique (nonworking) fireplace, into room no. 2, a spacious double. It's classic (not all units have bathrooms), and it's still one of London's last "they're charging *how* much?" values. Pay for 6 nights from November to March, and you can stay for 7. Don't confuse this place with the Jesmond Dene, a B&B on Argyle Square—it's very good, too, but not as central.

63 Gower St., WC1. www.jesmondhotel.org.uk. ✆ **020/7636-3199.** 15 units. £60–£70 single, £90–£120 double. Rates include full breakfast. Tube: Goodge Street. **Amenities:** Free Wi-Fi.

The Wardonia Hotel ★   The Wardonia is for those times when you need a place to be super cheap, no matter the sacrifice: Rooms are wee—like *sooooo* tiny, like the walls and the bed are in a death match for dominance—but you won't complain about cleanliness. The rooms' style is just as basic—very simple in blue and white fabrics and plain brown wainscoting, bathrooms with showers but not tubs—although the crazy low rates, which are a third of what other budget places charge and haven't gone up in half a decade, are something to astound. Everything's en suite, so it doesn't seem like the owners have cut corners to deliver low rates apart from not serving breakfast. The Wardonia is plainly a value champion. Prices dip about £10 lower in winter.

46-54 Argyle St., WC1. www.wardoniahotel.co.uk. ✆ **020/7837-3944.** 65 units. £40 single, £55 double/twin, £70 triple. Tube: King's Cross St Pancras. **Amenities:** Free Wi-Fi.

SOHO, COVENT GARDEN & WEST END

This is the middle of London. The part of town that offers everything you need outside your door. The area that also offers streets crawling with inebriated 20-year-olds singing drinking shanties in full voice after midnight. You may not care, because staying centrally can save on Tube fare more than it costs in shoe leather. Sunday through Thursday are the cheapest nights here.

Expensive

Hazlitt's ★★★   A stay is like a slumber in a time machine. Each room is its own individual historic universe, the centerpiece of which is a deep oak or carved four-poster bed. Around you is a bathroom with vintage fixtures and heavy silk curtains that, when pulled closed, make you feel as if you were the master of your own Georgian town house—plus, of course, modern expectations such as air conditioning, flatscreen TV, and safes. Breakfast including fresh-baked croissants arrives on a tray every morning, delivered by miraculously discreet staff. When you step out your front door, you can retreat to the library or step into the thick of Soho, completing the opulent fantasy. "Dandyism is a variety of genius," wrote William Hazlitt, a great writer of his age. I don't think that statement is true, but it sounds good. He died here when it was a rooming house, in a small bedroom at the back of the third floor, in 1830 at age 52.

6 Frith St., W1. www.hazlittshotel.com. ✆ **020/7434-1771.** 30 units. Rooms £215–£354. Tube: Tottenham Court Road. **Amenities:** Room service; free Wi-Fi.

The London Edition ★★   Style superstar Ian Schrager turned his attention to a worn-out, century-old hotel on the tatty Tottenham Court Road end of Oxford Street in Fitzrovia—convenient to much on foot—and opened the doors on an instant hotspot. On the surface, it would seem to be a calculated mix of classy and irreverent—look closely and you'll see those photographic homages to Rembrandt depict a girl wearing toilet paper rolls around her ears—but look deeper and you'll find a carefully run hotel where staff is more friendly than their current cool status should dictate. Rooms don't slouch—faux fur sculpturally strewn on your bed, speakers to which you can stream music from your phone—although the dark wood panel decor may remind you of a 1970s basement rumpus room. Laptops can be loaned from the front desk. It's also—this must be said—the place to stay if you love hot guys, since the porters and desk staff seem to have been hired as much for the cornflower blue of their eyes as for their service credentials. The adjoining lobby bar (get the Elderflower Power Sour cocktail) is a scene for one and all.

10 Berners St., W1. edition-hotels.marriott.com. ✆ **020/7781-0000.** 173 units. £285–£415 double. Tube: Tottenham Court Road. **Amenities:** Room service; 24-hr. fitness center; free bottled water; loaner laptops; free Wi-Fi.

The Montague on the Gardens ★ It's not easy these days finding typically British midpriced hotels that aren't mired in gloomy antique dinginess, but the conjoined town houses of the Montague deliver Englishness in demonstration as much as in word. Downstairs, a large staff pays close attention to guest needs, and rooms, always tasteful and richly comfortable, are a mishmash of styles as if in a moneyed home. They're also a mix of sizes, given the age of the buildings, but they're silent, plush, embellished with fine toiletries and "pillow mist" bedtime spray and otherwise appointed with more than you need. It's comfortable, dignified, and a homey upscale bolthole for Central London explorations—the British Museum is right across the road.

15 Montague St., WC1. edition-hotels.marriott.com. ✆ **020/7637-1001.** 100 units. Rooms £199–£356. Tube: Russell Square. **Amenities:** Restaurant; bar; air conditioning; free bottled water; free Wi-Fi.

One Aldwych ★★★ The pie-shaped, onetime headquarters of the *Morning Post*, built in 1907, contains a consistently high-quality boutique with two restaurants; a double-tall, sculpture-filled lobby lounge; and a theatrically lit, chlorine-free underground swimming pool where the printing presses used to be. Rooms are contemporary and designed with environmentalism in mind, have beds to sink into, and some even sneak a view of the Thames. The staff is truly five-star in that it tries to meet guests' needs without being asked, and its location feels impossibly considerate, too: steps from Covent Garden and Trafalgar, a walk down Strand to St Paul's, and a quick and gorgeous stroll over the Waterloo Bridge to the glories of Southbank. Deals on Lastminute.com save up to £100, and booking more than 90 days ahead can knock 20% off the rate.

1 Aldwych, WC2. www.onealdwych.com. ✆ **020/7300-1000.** 105 units. £264–£312 double. Tube: Covent Garden or Temple. **Amenities:** 2 restaurants; cocktail bar; indoor pool; gym; free Wi-Fi.

Radisson Blu Edwardian Hampshire ★ You can't do better for a location: on the south side of Leicester Square, facing the TKTS booth and all the movie premieres, and abutting the National Portrait Gallery. But what an odd hotel—'90s-era fixtures, floral touches that are English Country, pottery that's Pan-Asian, and an ornate red-brick facade (it was once a dental hospital). Never mind. The staff is attentive, the facilities, though aging, are clean and spacious enough for Central London, the price is remarkably low for where it is, and all you have to do is trip out the front door to wind up somewhere worth seeing. You may never take the Tube again. Ask for a room at the back, though, because the Square can brim with partiers.

31-36 Leicester Square, WC2. www.radissonblu-edwardian.com/hampshire. ℱ **020/ 7839-9399.** 127 units. Rooms £200–£288. Tube: Leicester Square. **Amenities:** Bar/ restaurant; fitness center; free Wi-Fi.

Rosewood London ★★★ The city's hottest new hotel, opened October 2013 after £85 million of investment, is entered through a stone courtyard arch of a gloriously elaborate edifice (constructed with pomp as the Pearl Assurance insurance citadel). It's the *ne plus ultra* of London's modern luxury properties. A foyer sheathed in brass! Songbirds by the lifts! Toilet paper as indulgently soft as puppies' ears! Rooms are so quiet you could hear your champagne bubbles pop. They're also lush: giant 46-inch flatscreen TVs are standard, as is Italian bedding you sink into like a swimming pool. Push a button to ring down your window blinds and sip homemade sloe gin from the minibar. If it weren't for the hard reality of the tariff, it'd be enough to sour you that the rest of the planet can't be executed with such theatricality. The neighborhood seems at first to be too dry, but the pleasures of the British Museum and Covent Garden are both 5 minutes away.

252 High Holborn, WC1. www.rosewoodhotels.com/london. ℱ **020/7781-8888.** 262 units. Rooms £320–£510. Tube: Holborn. **Amenities:** Restaurant; bar; lounge; fitness center; spa; free Wi-Fi.

The Savoy ★ Few cities can claim hotels as iconic as the Savoy, which merits a visit even if you, like most people, cannot afford to stay there. From the shimmering gleam of its Art Deco porte cochere to the palatial receiving rooms off the lobby, the Savoy has vibrated with high history, half Edwardian and half Jazz Age, since 1889. The American Bar has been a hushed laboratory for upscale cocktails for a century. A small museum about the Savoy's history, open to anyone, reminds you how much happened here: Churchill puffing, Chaplin mugging, Wilde and Bosie dallying, Gilbert and Sullivan pattering in its theater, Monet and Whistler painting the Thames from their windows. Your every need, from floral to gourmet, will be addressed with abject elegance and for a dear price, but would you be surprised to learn that the hotel, run by Fairmont and owned by the nephew of the King of Saudi Arabia, now tackily exploits its Hollywood past by hanging kitschy paintings of movie stars in its Thames Foyer and placing photos of them on nightstands? Good night, Burt Lancaster.

Strand, WC2. www.fairmont.com/savoy-london. ℱ **800/257-7544** (U.S.) or 020/7836-4343 (London). 268 units. Rooms from £390. Tube: Embankment or Temple. **Amenities:** 3 restaurants; 2 bars; indoor pool; gym; spa; business center; Wi-Fi £10/day.

W London—Leicester Square ★   London's only outpost of Starwood's self-consciously cool brand looks like a glass hippopotamus wallowing beside Leicester Square, and it's marked for effortful preening (crowd-control ropes appear at the entrance at night—whether they're needed or not—and guests can order a record player and vinyl LPs to their rooms—but who actually does that?), so it attracts a crowd that's, in a word, aspirational. Standard ("Wonderful") rooms are funky—a central bar contains both bathroom sink and desk, walls are hung with silvery curtains instead of art, the shower and WC are concealed behind mirrored doors (*lots* of mirrors in this place, including hundreds of disco balls), and your exterior view is partially obscured by a dotted glass curtain. The conceits are fun and the hotel's well situated for midnight Soho romps (though rooms are remarkably well insulated from the raucousness outside). You either dig W's shtick or roll your eyes to its beat.

10 Wardour St., WC2. www.wlondon.co.uk. ℂ **020/7758-1000.** 192 units. Rooms from £279. Tube: Leicester Square or Piccadilly Circus. **Amenities:** Restaurant; bar; air conditioning; Wi-Fi £16/day.

Moderate

Amba Hotel Charing Cross ★   The railway terminal hotel above Charing Cross Station was opened in 1865 and underwent many lives (and Blitz damage). Now it's a well-run, upper-moderate hotel that dips its toes into luxury trimmings (heated bathroom floors, illuminated wardrobes, walk-in showers, and so forth). The location is spectacular—steps from Trafalgar Square in one direction and morning strolls on the Thames in the other—and even though that would be enough to fill a lesser property, the staff doesn't slack off. Breakfast (crowded) is taken with a view toward St Martin-in-the-Fields, and at night, candles are placed throughout the hallways and up the sweeping grand staircase. You sense the privilege of a more genteel age without enduring the arrogance that sometimes accompanies such trappings.

The Strand, WC2. www.amba-hotel.com. ℂ **0871/376-9012.** 200 units. Rooms £169–£324. Tube: Charing Cross or Embankment. **Amenities:** Restaurant; bar; business center; free Wi-Fi.

The Fielding Hotel ★★   It's nearly impossible to beat the location, just steps from Covent Garden food and shopping, which is why you overlook the size of the rooms at this well-run, family-owned hotel. In this early-19th-century warren of tight staircases and fire doors, the appealingly cramped, attractively decorated, and sometimes slightly airless, tiny rooms snuggle you with a certain throwaway charisma. Room no. 10 is a double with a sitting area that catches lots of afternoon light, thanks to its corner position and copious windows. Everything's en suite (but mostly shower only). Trivia: Oscar Wilde was convicted of gross indecency in the Bow Street Magistrates' Court next door.

4 Broad Court, Bow St., WC2. www.thefieldinghotel.co.uk. ℂ **020/7836-8305.** 24 units. £90–£100 single, £140–£180 double. Tube: Covent Garden or Holborn. **Amenities:** Pass to nearby fitness center; free Wi-Fi.

The Hoxton ★★★   It's called Hoxton because that's where this boutique hipster hotel brand began (the original is listed on p. 46). This one is newer (2014) and busier—so book many months ahead to keep the price down—and delightfully, it's also just a few minutes' walk south of the British Museum in Holborn, in the middle of it all. There's a restaurant, a bar, and a too-cool-for-school beauty salon. It sounds heartbreakingly hip, but it's actually endearing—the lobby is always milling with life (maybe *too* much life, as it seems the whole neighborhood piles in for the free Wi-Fi) and the vibe is inclusive and welcoming. You get a smallish but beautifully antique-styled room with a double bed with a duck down duvet, fun throwback touches like wooden desk units, vintage-looking music players and mini-libraries of classic paperbacks, chubby duvets, and an hour's worth of free calls every day—even if you call all the way home, which you might do just to brag about how much you dig your hotel. Also helpful: Extend your checkout to 4pm for £5 an hour. Every room is a strong value—that's the point—but they all have the same amenities no matter the size, so why not go for the cheapest, the 129-square-foot "Shoebox"?

199-206 High Holborn, WC1. www.hoxtonhotels.com. ✆ **020/7661-3000.** 174 units. Rooms £149–£255. Rates include continental breakfast. Tube: Holborn. **Amenities:** 2 restaurants; bar; coffee house; salon; 1 hr. free calls daily; free water and milk; free Wi-Fi.

The Nadler Soho ★★★   The Nadler gets moderate lodging right by providing style without pretension or henpecking guests with extra fees. Quiet, high-design rooms are compact but nonetheless kitted out with twists such as wide beds, mini-kitchens with a third tap for filtered water, a microwave, big glassy bathrooms with rain showers, plenty of power points plus a loaner plug adapter, a half-hour of free national calls a day, and flatscreen TVs that double as music players. Deluxe rooms, at the top of the middle-rate scale, sleep up to four. There's no restaurant (breakfast can be delivered at prices that aren't marked up), but all of Soho is heaving right outside your door—reason alone to book here. At press time, a 73-room **Nadler Victoria** was under construction near the southern wall of Buckingham Palace; that location is more convenient but may yield higher rates.

10 Carlisle St., W1. www.thenadler.com. ✆ **020/3697-3697.** 78 units. Rooms £135–£255. Tube: Tottenham Court Road or Piccadilly Circus. **Amenities:** Free Wi-Fi.

Park Plaza Westminster Bridge London ★   It looks like a carburetor on a curb, but you won't believe the view some rooms have: straight down Westminster Bridge at the Houses of Parliament and Big Ben's tower, like a floor-to-ceiling fantasy. That view won't be accompanied by a charismatic experience but by a business-class formula; this modern, glassy mega-hotel is dominated by a central atrium that feels more like a convention center (the "Internal Facing" rooms get that booby prize; the "Iconic View" rooms get the goods), but that means lots of less-desirable rooms are more likely to be discounted in low season. Studio rooms have microwaves, fridges, and pullout beds, and there's a dark and soothing indoor pool. And the location, of course, is why you check in at all.

200 Westminster Bridge Rd., London SE1. www.parkplaza.com/westminster. ℗ **0844/415-6780.** 1,019 units. £177–339 double, 3-night minimum in some periods. Tube: Waterloo or Westminster. **Amenities:** 2 restaurants; bar; indoor pool; fitness center; spa; free Wi-Fi.

Sanctuary House Hotel ★ Once, many pubs ran nondescript inns as sidelines. The pub here is just a so-so Fuller's location (it owns hundreds of them), but the hotel upstairs is a creaking, well-tended reward unto itself for value and charm, and the staff is unusually responsive for such a small property. The look plays up its Victorian origins with faux-antique telephones and plenty of handsome wood trim, but the modernized bathrooms and soft beds betray the fact that it's the beneficiary of some recent renovations by intelligent hoteliers. Even more miraculously, it's so near Big Ben that you can hear the bell peal. (Across the street, the InterContinental charges twice as much.)

33 Tothill St., SW1. www.sanctuaryhousehotel.co.uk. ℗ **020/7799-4044.** 34 units. £140–255 double. Tube: St James's Park or Westminster. **Amenities:** Air conditioning; free Wi-Fi.

Inexpensive

Captain Bligh House ★★★ For a delicious taste of local London life without venturing far from the center of town, the Bligh, where Captain William Bligh lived after that sordid mutiny affair, is a transporting choice. Artists Gayna and Simon approach their wee guesthouse, built in the 1780s (before the invention of the lift), as a quiet home from home: Units have little kitchens for cooking up market ingredients, but you also get a starter pack of breakfast supplies. Although the Imperial War Museum (p. 118) is across the street, it's not a neighborhood crawling with tourists, so you'll kick back at the local pub and jump the many bus lines that go past. The value is over-the-top.

100 Lambeth Rd., SE1. www.captainblighhouse.co.uk. ℗ **020/7928-2735.** 5 units. £88–114 double. Tube: Lambeth North. **Amenities:** In-room kitchen; free Wi-Fi.

Hub by Premier Inn ★★★ This new budget hotel concept, which opened in late 2014, strips out everything you don't want without losing style and crispness. Sleek, cannily designed rooms (just 11.4 sq. m, or 123 sq. ft.) are tight as airlocks, packing in a platform bed for two with storage underneath, a bright and clean-lined shower/toilet module, well-located power outlets and USB charging ports, a fold-down desk, a lime green chair. It may be inexpensive, the staff won't do much, but the Hub is still cutting-edge: You can dim or extinguish the lights, watch TV (movies are free—the Wi-Fi is mercury-fast, too), or turn on the "do not disturb" light using an app, if you wish—which is handy when the room is pitch black. Because that's the thing, besides a good mobile phone signal, that you give up here: a view. You may have a window, but it may be small and frosted over. Still, the Hub is probably the best-located hotel of any we recommend in London. You can grab your breakfast from the inviting downstairs cafe (£8) and eat it every morning on the steps of the National Gallery in Trafalgar Square, which is a 90-second walk away. By night, the West End theaters and pubs are pulsing all around you. Deservedly, the best rates sell out months in advance (book online only), but when you get one cheap, you win the crash pad lottery.

110 St Martin's Lane, WC2. www.premierinn.com. ℮**0333/321 3104.** 163 units. £89–£161 double. Tube: Leicester Square. **Amenities:** Breakfast (paid); free movies; free Wi-Fi.

Seven Dials Hotel ★   There are nearly no budget hotels near Covent Garden. If you're this central, you can charge more. Here, though, everything is little: the stairway, the rooms—and correspondingly, the rates. Furniture and bathroom doors wrestle for supremacy, but still, there's usually enough storage space, a TV mounted on an armature, a basic writing desk, teeny clean bathrooms, and firm beds, albeit ones covered with dowdy bedspreads. Forget the lack of a lift and all the ways it's average. Its situation on Monmouth Street, steps from a rainbow of pubs, shops, and bars clustering around Covent Garden, is without comparison. Dump your bags and go play, because the price is right.

7 Monmouth St., WC2. www.sevendialshotel.com. ℮ **020/7681-0791.** 18 units. £90–£100 single, £85–£120 double. Rates include full breakfast. Tube: Covent Garden. **Amenities:** Free Wi-Fi.

The Z Hotel Piccadilly ★★★   Please say it "Zed," which rhymes with "bed." Now that you've got that down, here's the formula: extremely compact rooms, but lots of room under the duvets; glassy sleek style; a thrilling location on a quiet side street near the south end of Leicester Square; and a perfume-smelling lobby that's always abuzz with breakfast, coffee, or wine. Breakfast is particularly fun: top-shelf cheeses and honey served in the honeycomb. The formula works because the staff provides surprisingly strong service for the price, and there are design smarts where they count: Shower nozzles swivel the way you need them to, towels are plump and copious. They poured a lot of cash into the bedding and the 40-inch TVs, but did without closets and drawers. Rooms in the cellar (which you reach by passing through a small, strange basement parking lot) have no windows and as a consequence save you £15. Note that if you share a room with a platonic friend, bathrooms are enclosed by panels of fogged glass. All in all, it's a dream for the price and a most welcome addition to the budget hotel scene. The first Z Hotel is at the southeast edge of Soho (17 Moore St., W1; ℮ **020/3551-3701**, rooms start at £85 but are usually £145–£195; Tube: Leicester Square), and although we like it and it has a roof deck, it's noisier and the configuration is more unpredictable—try that one as a second choice.

2 Orange St., WC2. www.thezhotels.com. ℮ **020/3551-3720.** 112 units. Rooms £80–£130. Tube: Piccadilly Circus. **Amenities:** Cafe/bar; air conditioning; free evening wine and cheese; free Wi-Fi.

ALL IN THE timing

To save money on guesthouses and inns, remember five simple rules:

1. **Off-season is cheaper.** Many big hotels have two seasons: April through September and October through March (excluding holidays). Prices will be 10% to 25% cheaper in winter. Interestingly, very few family-owned B&Bs and inns bother with this system, pricing uniformly.

2. **To save, stay longer.** I haven't found a family-run hotel that wasn't willing to lower prices for anyone staying more than 5 or 6 nights.

3. **Mind the crowds.** Soho, a party zone, is cheaper on weekdays; The City, a business enclave, is cheaper on weekends.

4. **Go mom-and-pop.** Their rates usually include taxes, but big hotels' rates don't.

5. **Last-minute deals are rare, but do exist.** Routes for looking into deals are Hotwire.com, Priceline. com, and the same-day booking app Hotel Tonight.

KENSINGTON, VICTORIA & KNIGHTSBRIDGE

As affordable prospects develop in King's Cross and South Bank, it makes less sense to put up with the Tube ride required to stay here, so for budget tourists, South Ken and Victoria have slipped many notches in desirability, although people with higher budgets who don't require nightlife or cheap transportation are still attracted. The stores and restaurants of Knightsbridge are now so skewed to free-spending Persians that it's not a prime tourist hotel spot anymore, and the increasingly obsolete fleabag hotels in Earl's Court, just west, are now pretty much off the radar.

Expensive

The Beaufort ★ Quiet as a dropped pin, this upscale hotel down a dead-end residential street just west of Harrods distinguishes itself by offering more services than the standard: free afternoon tea with homemade scones, free cocktails by evening, and 24-hour staff that keeps tabs on guests' preferences, as its wealthy clientele prefers. Rooms, most of which are hidden somewhere in a tortured maze of corridors resulting from the combination of several town houses, are spacious for London, tastefully and conservatively decorated with delicate wallpaper and big cushy beds, and finely equipped. The museums of South Ken are a 5-minute walk away, as is Hyde Park.

33 Beaufort Gardens, SW3. www.thebeaufort.co.uk. ℰ **020/7584-5252.** 29 units. Singles from £200, doubles from £276. Tube: Knightsbridge. **Amenities:** Free cocktails; free afternoon tea; free Wi-Fi.

Hotel 41 ★★ A secret romantic nest only steps from Buckingham Palace, Hotel 41 is a hushed hideaway on the top floor of its moderate-priced cousin, the Rubens. You take a tiny private lift and trod a snug network of creaking corridors to reach its heart, a two-level, galleried conservatory bedecked like something to make Henry Higgins howl: mahogany shelves, inviting seating, sculptural busts and an oversized globe, and a yawning skylight to let the light in. There, staff makes the rounds, quietly addressing guests by name and filling glasses with champagne and plates with an endless flow of scones and hors d'oeuvres. People forget to go outside and see London. The rooms are equally individualized and top-flight: done nearly entirely in black and white and lacking nothing. There's no on-site restaurant or spa and some rooms have no view to speak of—the focus is on intimacy, service, and discretion. The duplex Master Suite, with a skylight over the bed, is popular with newlyweds and other nuzzling couples.

41 Buckingham Palace Rd, SW1. www.41hotel.com. ✆ **020/7300-0041.** 30 units. Rooms £312–£500. Tube: Victoria. **Amenities:** Bar; free snacks; access to nearby gym; free Wi-Fi.

The Goring ★   Only one five-star hotel has the Royal Warrant from the Queen for Hospitality Services. Only one has been run by the same family since 1910. Only one hosted Kate Middleton, the wife of a future king and mother of another, in her final night as a single girl before she walked down the aisle of Westminster Abbey. This is the Goring, classic but not self-importantly so, assiduously appropriate in style and rich in expensive fabrics, down to the Gainsborough silk on the walls, yet still goofy enough to put a stuffed sheep in every room and a statue of the founder in its huge back garden. The fleet of doormen wears bowler hats, and the signature canary-yellow china at its hotly pursued afternoon tea (4-month wait, from £43, p. 69) is made just for the hotel. The effect is something like an English country house, especially as you look out oversized windows at back gardens, kept lush as your personal enclave.

Beeston Place, SW1. www.thegoring.com. ✆ **020/7396-9000.** 69 units. Rooms £336–£840. Tube: Victoria. **Amenities:** Restaurant; bar; gym access; free Wi-Fi.

The Kensington ★   The family-owned Irish-boutique hotelier Doyle operates this upscale, classic town-house hotel 2 blocks south of the Natural History Museum. Everything that makes a Kensington town house iconic—two-story ceilings, floor-to-roof windows with flowing curtains, wainscoting and wood floors—has been assembled in rooms as comfortable as ones in our century. The rain showers are powerful enough to wash a Saint Bernard while four-poster beds, duck down duvets, and chandeliers add the right Regency tone. Breakfast is continental with an edge (goat cheese and spinach tarts!), but you can order cooked food at a charge.

109-113 Queen's Gate, SW7. www.doylecollection.com/Kensington. ✆ **020/7589-6300.** 150 units. £246–£284 double. Tube: South Kensington. **Amenities:** Restaurant; bar; gym access; free Wi-Fi.

The Milestone Hotel ★★★   The Milestone steeps itself in all things Anglophilic. First is the location on the southern edge of Kensington Gardens—upper-floor rooms have a view of Kensington Palace itself. The hotel is actually three townhouses that have been combined, so each room is distinct in size and shape, and the furnishings—antique paintings, rich rugs, enormous beds, fat couches—make you feel like you're staying in a rich relation's country mansion rather than a citified hotel. You're awash in thoughtful amenities, from a welcome cocktail in the glass conservatory to a small bag of prunes and another of handmade hard candy waiting bedside at night. Staff, from the top-hatted doormen to the butler that attends to higher-level rooms, is alert yet unfussy.

1 Kensington Court, W8. www.milestonehotel.com. © **020/7917-1000.** 63 units. Rooms from £350. Tube: High Street Kensington. **Amenities:** Restaurant; tea room; welcome beverage; bar; conservatory; fitness center; spa, indoor resistance swimming pool; room service; free bottled water; free Wi-Fi.

Moderate

The Ampersand Hotel ★★   This grand hotel from 1888 was given a makeover that's both sassy and reverently British, and now it's got its cool back for the first time since Victoria. Cleverly, the rooms, set over seven floors, are gently themed to poke the disciplines mastered at the museums nearby: astronomy for singles and doubles, music for superior rooms, ornithology for deluxe rooms, and so on. They don't skimp on goodies, from the quality of the towels to the free soft drinks in the minibar, and ceilings are high. The basement bar, the Mediterranean-themed Apero, is cheerfully snazzy, while the Modern English-style Drawing Rooms do double duty as tea room and champagne bar. All in all, the frisky interior is a stylish counterpoint to the 19th-century pomp of the exterior, and it's literally steps from the Tube.

10 Harrington Rd., SW7. www.theampersandhotel.com. © **020/7589-5895.** 111 units. Singles from £170, doubles £163–£286. Tube: South Kensington. **Amenities:** Restaurant; bar; gym; free Wi-Fi.

Lime Tree Hotel ★★   Matt and Charlotte Goodsall brightened a once-frumpy guesthouse into a place that feels as current as it is friendly. The conjoined brick town houses are historic, so no lift is permitted, but everything is updated with slate-and-white paint, fresh curtains, and touches such as bedside reading lights. If you have a first-floor room on the front, you'll have a small balcony over busy Ebury Street; in the back, you'll overlook the cute flower garden. Only three rooms have their own bathrooms; the rest share. A basement room added in 2014 is larger than the others but has no view. The Lime Tree is popular so the owners have no need to discount for longer stays.

135-137 Ebury St., London SW1. www.limetreehotel.co.uk. © **020/7730-8191.** 27 units. £110 single, £165–£195 double. Rates include full breakfast. Children 4 or under not permitted. Tube: Victoria or Sloane Square. **Amenities:** Free Wi-Fi.

Inexpensive

B+B Belgravia ★★   Although it follows the form of a typical town house hotel (rooms of various sizes, mostly small; stairs instead of lifts), it dares to have a strong sense of style and doesn't stint on hospitality. An ocean of white paint has been applied to every surface, and a futuristic glass-floored bridge was constructed at great expense to link the ground-floor sitting area (stop by the free espresso machine) with the light-drenched kitchen and dining area. The bathrooms, with cylinder sinks and pleasingly detailed tilework, bear little resemblance to the dated closets at other establishments. You won't spot a yard of chintz, although Ikea is well represented. Down the street at 82 Ebury, it rents a few more "Studio" rooms with compact, self-catering kitchens that can be slightly cheaper.

64-66 Ebury St., SW1. www.bb-belgravia.com. ✆ **020/7259-8570.** 26 units. Rooms £89–£140. Rates include full breakfast. Tube: Victoria. **Amenities:** Free Wi-Fi.

Luna Simone Hotel ★   Because this prototypical town house B&B began as two hotels that were conjoined in the 1990s, you'll sometimes see it called the Luna & Simone. Although it's a protected building with old metalwork on the banisters and oddly sized guest rooms, the owners have taken pains to keep up by way of fresh, inexpensive furniture and modernist prints. Its two large morning rooms, done up like a diner, have a weird undulating blue ceiling that makes scooping your cereal feel a bit like doing the backstroke (and eat quickly—the English breakfast ends early, at 9am). Everything is in excellent condition, which is a surprise when you consider that the owners have been at it since 1970. There's no lift, but also no sharing of bathrooms.

47-49 Belgrave Rd., SW1. www.lunasimonehotel.com. ✆ **020/7834-5897.** Singles from £75, doubles £100–£140. Rates include English breakfast. Tube: Victoria or Pimlico. **Amenities:** Free Wi-Fi.

Lynton B&B Hotel ★   Strictly old-school, the Lynton is the kind of affordable family-run crash pad with which London once charmed the world. Brothers Mark and Simon Connor took it over from their nan, who ran it since the mid-'60s (it's been a guesthouse since after the World War II, but a century ago was the home of a local horse doctor). The Gentrification Fairy has not yet pummeled the Lynton with her merciless wand—it's pleasingly dog-eared, like the house of a favorite aunt who keeps a spare room ready for visitors, and the Connors, some of the last London-bred B&B proprietors left on Ebury Street, dispense genial local wisdom like favorite uncles. Expect quarters that are entirely sufficient but not deluxe, which at these prices is a dream come true unto itself.

113 Ebury St., SW1. www.lyntonhotel.co.uk. ✆ **020/7730-4032.** 13 units. £65–£70 single, £80–£115 double. Rates include English breakfast. Tube: Victoria. **Amenities:** Free Wi-Fi.

Oakley Hotel ★   The rates channel a bygone era, which is why this long-running B&B endures. But there's a trade-off: a 20-minute walk to the Tube or a 10-minute bus ride from Victoria Station and rooms with no phones or TVs (only in the lounge). Although half the units share bathrooms, there are so many WCs that you won't have to wait even if everyone else has just consumed a pork vindaloo. Since the mid-'80s, owner Brian Millen has kept the 1850s house in fine condition and he's got some gorgeous furniture, much of it older than the house itself. The double with a four-poster bed was a favorite of the dissolute football superstar George Best, who regularly stayed here,

SHOULD I pack IT?

Mind the culture gap! Don't let these quirks take you by surprise:

- Although all hotels include towels and linens, you'll find for the most part that travelers are expected to bring their own washcloths.

- Many beds have duvets but not top sheets. It's just a European style; locals would probably explain that the duvet cover is the top sheet.

- You may find that your bed is made each day but your sheets aren't changed. This, too, is normal, and it saves on water, electricity, and detergent. If you want them changed, simply request it.

- In the budget category, nearly all rooms have TVs these days, but not cable, so expect only four or five broadcast (or "terrestrial") channels.

- Ask for a loaner hair dryer or curling iron because your non-British one probably can't handle the increased voltage. New non-British hair curlers fare better, although they may get hotter than they do back home.

- Not every small hotel stocks irons, sometimes for safety reasons.

- Family-run B&Bs can't afford a porter, but rare is the place that doesn't have at least one strong person to help with your baggage if asked.

- Many places don't have air-conditioning because during a normal summer London doesn't get that hot. If there's a heat wave, though, you'll be glad to have it.

presumably during his binges. About 90m (295 ft.) away, you'll find the tranquillity of the Thames, the cast-iron Albert Bridge, and soothing Battersea Park.

73 Oakley St., SW3. www.oakleyhotel.com. ℂ **020/7352-5599.** 12 units. £49 single, £49–£95 double. Rates include full cooked breakfast. Tube: Sloane Square or South Kensington. **Amenities:** Full shared kitchen; free Wi-Fi in lounge.

MARYLEBONE & MAYFAIR

For visitors who want a balance of central location and private residential vibe, Marylebone's the place. A 10-minute walk takes you to the "smart" end of Oxford Street and Mayfair to the south or the wide-open fields of Regent's Park to the north.

Expensive

Brown's Hotel ★ History is in every creak: The first-ever phone call was placed from its ground floor, and in 1907, Mark Twain scandalized the press by appearing in its lobby in his blue bathrobe. "Mark Twain exhibited himself as an eccentric today," tittered the *Times* on the front page, "and every staid Londoner who witnessed the exhibition fairly gasped." While staying here, FDR and Eleanor honeymooned, Agatha Christie plotted mysteries, Rudyard Kipling finished *The Jungle Book,* and Stephen King started *Misery.* Yet despite its heritage, the rambling Mayfair hotel (est. 1837) won't make commoners feel out-of-place. A contemporary update kicked out the dowdiness, yet the eagle-eyed staff doesn't let you down. If you're staying elsewhere, you still can satisfy yourself with the servile atmosphere and live piano at its afternoon tea, one of London's finest, for £40.

30 Albemarle St., W1. www.brownshotel.com. ⓒ **020/7493-6020.** 117 units. Rooms £395–£675. Tube: Green Park. **Amenities:** Restaurant; bar; tea room; spa; gym; fee local calls; free throttled Wi-Fi (£16/day unrestricted).

Claridge's ★★★ The red brick Claridge's is the quintessential luxury Mayfair hotel, decade after decade proudly proclaiming good taste in discretion as administered through glittering Deco accents. The building dates to 1894 (when Gilbert & Sullivan's producer rebuilt it), but modern amenities are installed among the gilded plasterwork and (non-working) fireplaces, the fitness center and spa are huge and up-to-date, and neither floorboards nor exacting staff grumbles upon your approach. From the bathrooms—heated floors, high-tech toilet/bidets—to cavernous wardrobes and plump beds as wide as some studio apartments, there's not much to complain about. Its main lift is the last in Central London to be operated by hand—there's a sofa inside should you tire during your five-level journey to the top floor—and its clubby cocktail bars and Fera restaurant are favored by modern-day fashion icons (your Von Furstenbergs, your Jaggers, your Eltons—wealthy Americans, in particularly, love it, and so did the Queen Mum) who value luxury and exclusivity without the snooty exclusivity that can make the Ritz such a drag. One room we stayed in recently even had an original Picasso. It isn't cheap, but it sets the flawless tone for five-star hotels around the world.

Brook Street, W1. www.claridges.co.uk. ⓒ **020/7629-8860.** 203 units. Rooms from £450. Tube: Bond Street. **Amenities:** Restaurant; 2 bars; spa; fitness center; business center; free Wi-Fi.

The Langham ★★ In 1863, while Americans were shooting each other in farmyards, London was assembling the first and most celebrated grande dame hotel in Europe. She survives, but it was touch and go during the 20th century. The polished lobby is perfumed, the lifts swathed in leather, each room a private cocoon of ordered wainscoting, enveloping beds, and bathrooms with toiletries in pink paper cartons kept in a box by the sink. Its Palm Court has been serving high tea (£40) since 1865, and its frivolous cocktail menu is deemed one of the world's cleverest. For its brag-worthy reputation, the Langham is favored by moneyed tourists from the Far East, and for service and discretion, along with that long history, there are few peers. The tariff is also something for the record books, but that's the price you pay to be in the company of Lady Di, Wallis Simpson, and Winston Churchill, who rightly favored it, and Arthur Conan Doyle, who sent Sherlock Holmes here in several stories. It's a few short blocks from Oxford Street's best shopping.

1c Portland Place, Regent St., W1. www.langhamhotels.com. ⓒ **020/7636-1000.** 380 units. Rooms £312–£444. Tube: Oxford Circus. **Amenities:** 2 restaurants; 2 bars; indoor pool; spa; business center; free Wi-Fi.

The Wellesley ★★★   A jewel box overlooking Hyde Park, the Wellesley, which despite its Art Deco panache opened only in 2012, caters to the ultra top end of the market, but the fact it's only 36 rooms, mostly suites, means coziness and indulgence are held paramount. The tiny Oval restaurant alone is one of the prettiest dining rooms in the city. It's also London's only hotel in a Tube station: The Hyde Park Corner ticket hall of the early Piccadilly Line was once behind its iconic 1906 facade of arched oxblood-red tiles, although everything has been exquisitely rebuilt for your comfort and, it must be said, your ego. Your 24-hour butler, just a button's push away, heeds your every command. You might find some amenities—Europe's largest hotel cigar humidor and a Rolls-Royce (license plate: WEII SLY) that will chauffeur you anywhere nearby—like some contemporary satire of Gatsby. I think it's rather delicious, although I did fight the urge to command the driver to take me to Superdrug.

11 Knightsbridge, SW1. www.thewellesley.co.uk. © **020/7235-3535.** 36 units. Doubles from £268. Tube: Oxford Circus. **Amenities:** Restaurant; bar; cigar lounge and humidor; jazz lounge; Rolls-Royce shuttle; free Wi-Fi.

Moderate

22 York Street ★★   You might wonder at first if you have knocked on the door of a private home of some bohemian doctor or lawyer. Inside, Michael and Liz Callis are going for a farmhouse feel, with warm wooden floorboards, plenty of antiques and oriental rugs, and large bathrooms, almost all of which have tub/shower combinations. Guests get their own keys and are let loose to treat the five-level premises as their own, which includes plenty of tea, coffee, and biscuits for munching. Adding to the home-away-from-home feel, breakfasts are served in the kitchen at a communal country table where you meet your fellow guests. The food includes some fantastic *pain au chocolate*. Although they're not explicitly banned, kids may not feel comfortable.

22 York St., W1. www.22yorkstreet.co.uk. © **020/7224-2990.** 10 units. Singles from £95, doubles from £150. Rates include continental breakfast. Tube: Baker Street. **Amenities:** Free Wi-Fi.

Hotel Americana ★   Beige-simple, without unnecessary flourish, but extremely well-maintained, the Americana is a strong value in a neighborhood besieged by rising rates. Robert, the chatty and opinionated longtime manager, is exactly the kind of authority on London (and on everything, really) that you wish to encounter behind a B&B desk. Room no. 124, a twin, is slightly larger than the others, but all have showers, tiny TVs, safes, and plenty of light. Although it's comprised of two conjoined town houses, there's a wee lift, and it's also very near Regent's Park and, unusually, steps away from a launderette. Rates can go even lower in winter or if you agree to stay for longer than 3 nights.

172 Gloucester Place, NW1. www.americanahotel.co.uk. © **020/7723-1452.** 29 units. £129–£156 double. Rates include breakfast buffet. Tube: Baker Street or Marylebone. **Amenities:** Free Wi-Fi.

No. 10 Manchester Street ★★   There's precious little to pick apart in this very good red brick hotel located on a quiet street behind the Wallace

FINDING HOTELS online

You may be used to booking through sites such as Expedia.com or Travelocity.com for the best prices, but when it comes to London, think again. Many London hotels, particularly the most affordable ones, are privately owned, and many of them are represented on the Web by third-party travel agents and booking engines that pad the price with a few extra bucks, which they'll skim off for themselves as commission. If you call the hotel directly for your bookings, you'll not only get the lowest price, but you'll also have the power of negotiation.

Another danger of making an online reservation: There are heaps of lousy budget hotels in London, particularly around Paddington and Earl's Court, that post misleading images on the Web, and it's easy to end up in a seedy one.

Mobissimo.com, **Momondo.com**, and **Kayak.com** are three "aggregator" sites that scan dozens of sites for deals and pull them all together. If you hit them, you don't need to hit Travelocity or the like, because it includes them in the search. Some major chains have teamed up to create **RoomKey.com**, which collects discounted rates from only their holdings.

Visit London, the city's official tourism office, has an area on its website (www.visitlondon.com) for discounted bookings, although it's maintained by LateRooms.com. At Heathrow, St Pancras, and Victoria, plus at 17-19 Cockspur Street near the southwest corner of Trafalgar Square, stop by the **British Hotel Reservation Centre** (www.bhrc.co.uk; ✆ 020/7592-3055), which also books for free online. **Lastminute.co.uk** is one of the most popular booking sites in the U.K., but its rates don't always represent savings, and the apps **Hotel Tonight** and **Hotels Now** sometimes bear cheap fruit. Other popular offshore hotel sites include **Booking.com, Eurocheapo.com, Hotels Combined.com, Laterooms.com**, and **Venere.com**. **Priceline.com** and **Hotwire.com** operate here. And **Tingo.com** refunds the difference if a hotel price drops after you book. As with all bid-for-travel sites, you could end up with a deal, but remember that as hotels add star levels, they also add extra charges.

Collection (p. 117) and near Oxford Street. Rooms are relatively large and the big beds and rain showers may tempt you away from exploring the city. For all its surface Edwardian style, it's modernized: On the ground floor, there's a dedicated cigar-smoking terrace and humidor room—some of its guests are businessmen from moneyed Muslim countries and they can't drink alcohol in the bar. Americans can finally get a legal taste of Cuban cigars there. This solid, perfectly sized hotel could charge a lot more than it does, and it delivers a distinctly London cultural experience.

10 Manchester St., W1. www.tenmanchesterstreethotel.com. ✆ **020/7317-5900.** 45 units. £175–£265 double. Tube: Baker Street. **Amenities:** Restaurant; bar; cigar lounge; free Wi-Fi.

THE SOUTH BANK, SOUTHWARK & BOROUGH

Since medieval times until about 15 years ago, "respectable" Londoners wanted nothing to do with this once-industrial area. They wish they'd bought property now. It's actually a terrific place to dwell in good weather, when the area comes alive with walkers, booksellers, pub-goers, and playgoers reveling in the nearby re-creation of Shakespeare's Globe. Furthermore, moderate hotels are proliferating.

Expensive

Shangri-La Hotel at the Shard ★★   Be warned that if you decide to book at the Shangri-La, you must be prepared to never leave it. Staying here, on the 36th to 52nd floors of this glass-sheathed skyscraper, means that your room will be encased with floor-to-ceiling windows overlooking the entire city. No structure in London will be higher than you. When you take a bath (in your marble-coated washroom with heated floors), you may feel as if you're flying over the Tower of London, and when you swim in your horizon pool in the sky above St Paul's, the vista is so surreal that you may wonder if it's all a dream. Such glassy heaven comes with interiors that are clean-lined, simple, and inflected by the Asian culture from which the Shangri-La brand hails (for example, in-room amenities might be stored in a bento-style box). The famous Borough Market is near its base. Rates are higher than other luxury hotels in town but so are the rooms, and that seems to justify it to nearly everyone's satisfaction.

31 St Thomas St., SE1. www.shangri-la.com/london/shangrila. ℂ **020/7234-8000.** 202 units. King rooms from £375. Tube: London Bridge. **Amenities:** Restaurant; bar; indoor pool; fitness center; free shoe shine; free newspaper; free in-room Nespresso coffee and tea; free Wi-Fi.

Moderate

CitizenM London Bankside ★★★   This affordable Dutch hotel chain is blossoming, deservedly so, and its welcome concept of smart-and-stylish quarters without interference from groveling staff or added fees makes it the best casual choice in Southwark. The glassy open-plan lobby, a playpen of designer coffee-table books and orange-and-white Penguin classic paperbacks, seems to hum day and night with people sipping coffee and telecommuting. Check-in is self-guided by kiosk, and rooms are compact—almost podlike—but arranged with genius. Platform beds are massive and piled with body pillows, curvy bathrooms slotted into the space with calculated aplomb, and you control everything from motorized blinds to the color of the room's mood lighting with a bedside tablet. There's even a hefty library of free movies (including porn of all persuasions—it's a Dutch company, and it's sassy). In 2015, CitizenM will become a major London player for affordable stays: New properties offering the identical concept in Holborn, Tower Hill, and Shoreditch have been announced.

20 Lavington St., SE1. www.citizenm.com/london-bankside. ℂ **020/3519-1680.** 192 units. £109–£189 double. Tube: Southwark or London Bridge. **Amenities:** Free movies; free Wi-Fi.

London Bridge Hotel ★★   A 1916 telephone exchange building near the base of the Shard has been gussied with current flourishes such as

HOW TO GET YOUR HOTEL FOR free

What if I told you that you could spend 6 nights in London, airfare and hotel included, for $1,149 in late summer? Or for around $1,049 over the American Thanksgiving holiday weekend? It's called an **air-hotel package,** and it can cost about the same as airfare alone—except it *also* comes with hotel, breakfast, and often a tour or two thrown in. How do they do it? Contracted rates and bulk buying.

The lowest prices are from eastern American cities such as New York and Boston, but for a few dozen dollars more, you can leave from just about any other American city. You can also often extend the return by as much as a month without having to buy more hotel nights (but you can do that, too). The catch is this: Many of the least expensive hotel options are pillow mills that have seen better days. For a little more peace of mind, upgrade to a slightly more expensive property.

The king of affordable air-hotel deals is **Go-Today.com** (www.go-today.com; ✆ 800/227-3235), which usually offers 4- and 6-night packages to London, sometimes paired with other European destinations, including local flights between the cities (as low as $1,300 for 6 nights—that's a touch over $200 a day). Other big brokers: **Virgin Vacations** (www.virgin-vacations.com; ✆ 888/937-8474), **Gate 1 Travel** (www.gate1travel.com; ✆ 800/682-3333), and **British Airways Holidays** (www.baholidays.com; ✆ 877/428-2228), which may be priced higher than others. Beware of airline-run sales, because those hotel rates may not be the cheapest.

walnut floors and red suede furniture, making for a casually distinguished, mid-level hotel. Deluxe rooms come with a few blessings you don't find in many other London hotels, including walk-in closets and DVD players. Not a chain, its independence results in an attentive management, which is why it attracts repeat guests. On weekends, rates can plummet to around £100, so check its website for offers. This is not the same property as the Mercure with the same name.

8-18 London Bridge St., SE1. www.londonbridgehotel.com. ✆ **020/7855-2200.** 138 units. £109–£324 double. Tube: London Bridge. **Amenities:** Restaurant; bar; gym; free Wi-Fi.

The Mad Hatter Hotel ★★ Decent pub hotels, which are hotels above pubs, are a dying breed in London. Here, sizable, good-value rooms feel like they were lifted from a business hotel. Think decent-size bathrooms with tub/showers, rose-colored bedspreads matching painted accent walls, a lift, and ice machines—rare as diamonds in the U.K. You'll pay around £150 for advance bookings and rates rarely crack £200, which is a big deal for someplace so central: 5 minutes from the Tate Modern and just over Blackfriars Bridge from the City. Some rooms can be conjoined for families.

3-7 Stamford St., SE1 www.madhatterhotel.co.uk. ✆ **020/7401-9222.** 30 units. £86–£181 double. Rates include full breakfast. Tube: Southwark or Blackfriars. **Amenities:** Pub; free Wi-Fi.

THE CITY & SHOREDITCH

Not long ago, the City went to sleep at 7pm and only an office worker would think of staying there. Now, with Shoreditch and Spitalfields revitalized, there's a good reason for creative types to stay there. Some of London's prime party zones are within steps of hotels where rates bottom out on weekends. The Liverpool Street station area lacks character, but it's near things that have it, and it's also a nucleus of the Night Bus system. Just be wary of going *too* far east: There are corporate choices in the Canary Wharf district and temptingly cheap rooms by the ExCeL convention center in the Docklands region, but from there it will take you 45 minutes to reach Piccadilly Circus by the Tube and DLR.

Expensive

Andaz London ★★   The Great Eastern, once one of London's great train station terminal hotels that's practically atop the Liverpool Street station, was renovated well past its Victorian origins and is now one of the City's more pleasant hotel surprises, with rooms both decently sized and luxurious. The Andaz, owned by Hyatt, makes a point of offering service that mixes ultra-casual (there's no check-in desk; staff greets you with an iPad) with an attentiveness appropriate to the price point. It also piles on the freebies: You pay nothing extra for a minibar stocked with water and juices, snacks, in-room gourmet coffee, local calls, and Wi-Fi. Breakfast is taken in a glorious showpiece restaurant capped with glass cupolas, and ask to see the astonishing Grecian Masonic temple; this once-secret space with £4 million inlaid marble floors is now an events venue Freemasons can't afford. The Andaz is extremely well connected by bus and rail, and a few blocks north and east, you'll find the art and nightlife of Spitalfields and Shoreditch and the "real" London of Bethnal Green.

40 Liverpool St., EC2. www.london.liverpoolstreet.andaz.com. ℭ **020/7961-1234.** 267 units. £205–£285 double. Tube: Liverpool Street. **Amenities:** 3 restaurants; pub; wine bar; champagne bar; gym; local calls; free in-room beverages and snacks; free Wi-Fi.

The Rookery Hotel ★★★   In the 1990s, three derelict houses and shops were converted into a hotel, and using the same formula as their Hazlitt's in Soho—Georgian and 17th-century oak and four-poster beds, antique desks, era wood paneling and top-line attention and discretion—the owners fashioned this tucked-away realm of open fireplaces and polite staff that give a sense of what it must have been like to live with money in the 19th century. It's elegant, but not like a stuffy dowager aunt's parlor—more like an eccentric professor's study. Each huge room is a unique, rambling surprise of Persian rugs, gilt-framed mirrors, and oil paintings, but not neglectful of modern necessities. The result is one of London's most unique and repeatable hotel experiences that's romantic beyond measure. There's no restaurant, but you can get food brought to your room, as your breakfast will be. Note that some rooms' tubs have European-style hand-held shower nozzles. The location is quiet and off the main road.

Peter's Lane, Cowcross St., London EC1. www.rookeryhotel.com. © **020/7336-0931.** 33 units. £222–£312 double. Tube: Farringdon or Barbican. **Amenities:** Free Wi-Fi.

South Place Hotel ★★★ Plugged-in, stylish, and sexy: That's the crowd this hotel goes for, and you'll feel that way, too. The first hotel to be built from the ground up in the Square Mile for a century, every inch was run through the design filter, and much of the art was commissioned by celebrated contemporary artists. Rooms, charcoal-grey with wool carpets, are large and hushed and fully up-to-date with luxury expectations, so you'll find plenty of outlets, AV connections, blackout blinds closed from a bedside panel, and a big bed you can flop around in. By evening, the two restaurants, Angler and a 3 South Place Bar & Grill, have lured both named chefs and some of the liveliest professionals from The City before they head just east to the party grounds at Spitalfields. Despite the hot scene, it never ignores the relaxation of its guests. On weekends, rates can dip to £170.

3 South Place, EC2. www.southplacehotel.com. © **020/3503-0000.** 80 units. Doubles from £213. Tube: Moorgate or Liverpool Street. **Amenities:** 2 restaurants; 3 bars; guests' lounge; gym; spa; business center; free Wi-Fi.

Moderate

Ace Hotel London Shoreditch ★★ In 2014, a blah mid-level business hotel was remade into the epicenter of Shoreditch Cool. A stay here isn't about service but about style, since the Ace's agreeable pretentions have become a "lifestyle brand" for the fashionably impressionable. Pretty people tap away on laptops all day at the lobby workbenches, pretty people dine at its restaurant (Hoi Polloi), which publishes its menu on newsprint just 'cause, and well-dressed revelers thump away in its basement club until all hours. Accommodations are cushy where it counts (huge beds and bathrooms, room-width built-in window sofas) and styled with self-knowing false irreverence when it won't affect your comfort (instead of drawers, you use plastic crates, as if you were still in kindergarten, your bedspread is denim, and there's a guitar—an Ace signature). It's inauthentic, but fun, and the rates aren't crazy. If you've grown up enough to have some cash but not enough to demand much of hotel staff, the Ace wins.

100 Shoreditch High St., E1. www.acehotel.com/london. © **020/7613-9800.** 97 units. £135–£279 double. Tube: Shoreditch High Street or Liverpool Street. **Amenities:** Restaurant; rooftop bar; basement club; gym; free Wi-Fi.

Apex City of London ★★★ An excellent contemporary boutique brand from Scotland that appeals to high standards for space and style, Apex is a friendly and peaceful urban retreat that actually looks like its pictures. You'll find it literally steps from the Tower of London, and a few rooms glimpse the Tower Bridge—along with the balcony, worth the upgrade of £15 to £30. During the weekend, when The City is deader than Old Marley, it can be a steal. It's handsomely designed in hardwood and walnut, Nespresso pods instead of awful instant coffee, and bathrooms larger than many B&Bs' guest rooms, including walk-in power showers. The only downside is The City is personality-free off-hours. The **Apex London Wall,** just as good, is on the side streets north of Bank station, and the **Apex Temple Court,** off Fleet Street, is also tops, but for the views and its affordable proximity to the river, it's a solid choice.

No. 1 Seething Lane, London EC3. www.apexhotels.co.uk. ℂ **020/7977-9500.** 179 units. £140–£340 double. Tube: Tower Hill. **Amenities:** Restaurant; bar; gym; free local calls; free Wi-Fi.

The Fox & Anchor ★ We all claim to want an old-fashioned English inn, but do you really want the chintz, the lace curtains, and the blank walls? In the thick of Smithfield's nightlife (so bring earplugs if you require them), this fun little find took a tiny old-fashioned pub hotel and upgraded it so it only *looks* old—brass saddle-bowl sinks, mullioned windows, wood floors, and in the case of the Smithfield room, a freestanding tub in the room (that fills fast), yet they're also current with sound systems and flatscreen TVs. This is a case of making a leap forward by looking back. Downstairs, of course, there's a Victorian-era pub of mahogany, brass, and etched glass. It was also upgraded from the authentic original.

115 Charterhouse St., London EC1. www.foxandanchor.com. ℂ **020/7550-1000.** 6 units. Doubles from £120. Rates include full breakfast. Tube: Barbican or Farringdon. **Amenities:** Restaurant; bar; free Wi-Fi.

Inexpensive

The Hoxton ★★ The advent of "the Hox" a decade ago changed the way London thought of budget lodging: Chintz and linoleum went out, to be replaced by good-looking staff that knows the local hotspots, lobbies that attract writers and artists day and night, and compact but all-you-need rooms that pack in more style and cleverness than the low price would allow. You sleep on a crib-like platform bed under exposed brick walls and among set pieces like Union Jack pillows and steamer trunks for chests of drawers. You bathe under a rain shower in a futuristic cylinder. Your continental breakfast is delivered each morning via a bag you hang on the door, which can make you feel like a monkey at the world's hippest zoo, and there's free water and milk for your little fridge and an hour of free telephone calls a day, even if you call internationally. Downstairs there's a grill, a bar, and coffee and free Wi-Fi flowing at all hours, make it as much a gathering place for the neighborhood as it is a way station for travelers. Book as far ahead as possible to keep the price under £200—you could get more space and service elsewhere for any than that.

1 Austin St., E2. www.hoxtonhotels.com. ℂ **020/7550-1000.** 208 units. Rooms £99–£269. Tube: Aldgate or Tower Hill. **Amenities:** Restaurant; 1 hr. free local calls; free Wi-Fi.

Qbic London City ★★ From a growing affordable design hotel chain in Holland, Qbic is a wacky antidote to the formula budget hotels. Everything you need—bed, outlets, bathroom with a rain shower, TV—is a part of a pre-fabricated bed/bathroom structure that dominates the center of the room. It's not a capsule hotel, just one that came up with a multipurpose hospitality unit with plenty of room to walk around and stash your suitcase. Your lamp is made out of coiled garden hose, your clothing rack a strange ladder/planter of some sort—it's just fun. There are free coffee and tea machines on every floor and a preposterously funky lobby where organic continental breakfast is served. You'll be within walking distance to Spitalfieds/Shoreditch (15 min.) and the Tower of London (15 min.) and you'll be amused to learn that the United States' Liberty Bell was made on the very same block at the Whitechapel Bell Foundry, which you can see from courtyard-facing rooms. As a bonus, the managers are hip to local culture and give solid advice.

42 Adler St. E1. london.qbichotels.com. ℭ **020/3021-3300.** 171 units. Windowless ("Smart") rooms from £69, windowed doubles ("Cosy" and "Fun") from £79. Tube: Aldgate East. **Amenities:** Lounge; free coffee; free Wi-Fi.

Shoreditch Inn ★ Budget hotels are few and far between in this part of London, which now marks hipness above accessibility, but here you find a modern value-priced hotel that won't frighten you. Encumbered by none of the lifestyle-obsessed frills that its preening neighbors obsess over, it's simply clean and recently refit with the little touches that distinguish it as a standout of its price class: double-glazed windows, quality toiletries, roomy quarters, and enough selection at breakfast, even if said breakfast is taken in the basement. That it's in the middle of the Shoreditch action and front rooms that overlook a church from 1740 have me wondering when the dream will end and the owners will put the price out of reach. They could ask for more.

1 Austin St., E2. www.shoreditchinn.com. ℭ **020/3327-3910.** 14 units. £79–£139 double. Rates include continental breakfast. Tube: Bethnal Green. **Amenities:** Free Wi-Fi.

Z Hotel Shoreditch ★★★ New as of 2015, this fourth London location for the ingenious Z Hotel formula gives budget lodgings dignity by imbuing them with design panache. Rooms are laid out by a simple but winning concept: no closet, but spacious platform beds, ample washroom cubes encased in fogged glass, individual thermostats, 48-inch TVs with free movies, and free evening wine meet-and-greets in the lobby. The Z team pitches their hotel as a place for a short break, but its prices are usually low enough for many people to see it as their price savior. Its "inside" rooms lack windows, a quirk that saves you £15 a night. Right outside the door, you'll find the myriad restaurants and bars of the ever-burgeoning Shoreditch neighborhood.

136-144 City Rd., EC1. www.thezhotels.com. ℭ **020/3551-3700.** 111 units. Rooms £99–£199. Tube: Old Street. **Amenities:** Lounge; free evening wine and cheese; free movies; free Wi-Fi.

THE BUDGET HOTEL CHAINS, CITYWIDE

The biggest tourism headline in the past decade is the boom in hotel chains that lure bookings with predictable standards, decently sized rooms, and unbeatable lead-in rates for people who pay months ahead of time. Be warned—these brands' reservation search engines will return results that are deep in distant suburbs, so you must consult a map before taking the bait of a low price. Also, so many people habitually turn to them that prices frequently rise far past the point of value, particularly close to the dates of stay. In addition to these names, look into **Motel One** (24-26 Minories, EC3, www.motel-one.com, ✆ **020/7481-6420**, doubles from £98), a stylish and ultra-cheap but cramped German newcomer in the somewhat inconvenient neighborhood of Tower Hill.

easyHotel ★　This is how you do London super-cheaply while avoiding hostels. Reservations typically cost £25 for double rooms if you book 6 months ahead, and £35 to £90 if you procrastinate. Its revelation is, to others, a curse: prefabricated room units that differ only in how little floor space you're given (the smallest are 6 sq. m/65 sq. ft.). Beds are double-size with white duvets, with rarely an inch of space between mattress and wall. No phone, no hair dryer, no frills at all. You may find a long ledge on which to pop a travel alarm clock, but bathrooms aren't more than plastic cubicles combining a shower, toilet, and sink in one water-splashed closet. The cheapest rooms don't even have windows. Want to watch TV? You'll pay £5 for 24 hours. Want housekeeping? £10. Wi-Fi is pay-as-you-use. This is no-nonsense sleep.

www.easyhotel.com. No phone reservations. 5 locations in Central London. Rooms £25–£90. **Amenities:** Wi-Fi £10/day.

Ibis Hotels ★★　This 600-strong French chain by the Accor hotel giant is distinguished by its trademark 3-foot-square windows, its just-off-the-margins locations, and its simple but cheerful decor. You'll get a double bed, bathroom with shower, climate control, a 24-hour kitchen, TV, phone, free Wi-Fi, at least one outlet, and a built-in desk. The breakfast charge varies per property (£8 is typical), but food is usually served from 4am, making this a smart choice if you need to catch an early flight or train. The fresh-baked breakfast baguettes are delicious—hey, it's French. There's also **Ibis Styles,** the "all-inclusive" brand that is slightly more upscale and includes breakfast and Wi-Fi, and **Ibis Budget,** a bare-bones, shower-only crash pad once known as Etap or Formule 1; rooms there have style but are very simple, sleep up to three people, and have free Wi-Fi and TV, but practically nothing else.

www.ibishotel.com. No English-reservations hotline. 6 locations around the city (see website and map in this guide). Rooms £101–£218, varying by season and location. **Amenities:** Free Wi-Fi.

Premier Inn ★★★　This is many British travelers' favorite hotel brand. Opening a new location in the U.K. on average once a week, it's the largest hotel chain in the country, and rooms (maximum of two adults) offer a king-size bed, bathtub and shower with all-purpose shower gel, tea- and coffee-making facilities, TV, phone, iron, air conditioning (sometimes), at least three outlets, and a desk. Increasingly, it requires you to check in at a kiosk, eliminating interaction, but that tells you about the tourist churn that this company is going for. Many locations include a mass-appeal bar/cafe, Thyme. Unlike Travelodge, there are in-room phones and hair dryers. Its prices start at £19 nearly a year ahead, but final prices can be poor value, rivaling a much nicer hotel's. Like airline tickets, prices rise as availability dwindles. Clip £10 off prices by booking ahead with a nonrefundable reservation.

www.premierinn.com. ℭ **0845/099-0095.** More than 12 locations around the city. Rooms £80–£126, depending on season and location. **Amenities:** Bar/cafe; 30 mins. free Wi-Fi daily, then £3/24 hr.

Travelodge ★   Rates start at a head-slapping £19 for a non-flexible reservation if you book 11 months ahead. That more than makes up for the thinnest amenities of the economy brands, which has some two dozen properties in Greater London. It's nicer than the American Travelodge brand, which isn't related to it. Expect king-size beds, bathtub and shower, TV (but no phone, hair dryer, or toiletries), paid in-room movies, a wardrobe, at least one power point, and a desk. Breakfast, if your property offers it, is about £8 more. "Family rooms" have a pullout couch for two kids but cost the same as a double. Prices go down to £25 if you're first to book but they skyrocket in peak periods.

www.travelodge.co.uk. ℭ **08719/848484.** More than 12 locations around the city. Rooms £65–£116, depending on season and location. **Amenities:** Bar/café (often); Wi-Fi £3 a day.

Tune Hotels ★★   This modern-design Malaysian import provides everything you need but nothing else: en-suite power shower, round-the-clock reception, air conditioning, but not even a closet—you get hangers. If you want more, you pay a few pounds at a time: towel rental, TV, Wi-Fi, safe, hair dryer, and even windows come at a price. The a la carte model keeps costs down but isn't a path to luxury, yet the facilities are clean and designed with minimalist zip. Don't write off a windowless room's power to mediate jet lag. Prices are as low as £35 months in advance and go to £125 or so last-minute.

www.tunehotels.com. No phone. 5 locations in the city. Rooms £35–£125. **Amenities:** Wi-Fi £4 per device per day.

RENT A ROOM

Airbnb is old news in England. English hosted accommodations were long one of the world's great travel bargains. Londoners have always been eager to make a few pounds by welcoming you into their homes, and as they vie for your business, they make for some great places to find cheap deals. One potential hidden advantage of this sort of stay comes if you've got a car—for example, if you're stopping in London during a drive round the island. Staying with a family in Zone 3 or 4 may enable you to park your car cheaply. What's included? At the minimum, a bed and breakfast. Everything else depends, since homestays are as unique as the hosts themselves. Your hosts may offer to show you the town or they may leave you in peace. They may have searingly fast Wi-Fi or they may think electric kettles are the cutting edge of technology. Armed with your wish list, these brokers should be able to pair you with suitable options:

- **At Home in London** (www.athomeinlondon.co.uk; ✆ **020/8748-2701**). Operating since 1986. Properties in West London, near the Tube: mid-£80s (central London) to £30 a night (Zones 2 & 3).
- **The Bed and Breakfast Club** (www.thebedandbreakfastclub.co.uk; ✆ **01243/370-692**). Operating since 1988. Provides luxury of the kind you might see spotlighted in a decorators' magazine: from £80 to £125 with a cooked breakfast.
- **London Bed and Breakfast Agency** (www.londonbb.com; ✆ **020/7586-2768**). Finds trustworthy hosts for single female travelers: between £70 and £120.
- **London Homestead Services** (www.lhslondon.co.uk; ✆ **020/7286-5115**). Operating since 1985. Rooms in traditional homes found in commuter neighborhoods a good half-hour train ride from town: £18 to £40 for both doubles and singles.
- **Happy Homes** (www.happy-homes.com; ✆ **020/7352-5121**). Operating since 1992. Specializes in rooms in southwest London, about a 25-minute commute to the West End: £25 to £40, plus a one-time fee of £35 to £65 per room.
- **Annscott Accommodation Service** (www.holidayhosts.free-online.co.uk; ✆ **020/8540-7942**). Operating since the early 1990s. Rooms about 30 minutes by train from the city: £17 to £54 single, £34 to £90 double.

RENT A FLAT

If you don't want to rent a room in a home, rent a whole flat. When you arrive, you'll often find a folder that schools you in the best local shops and restaurants, and you may encounter neighbors keeping an eye on the place and on your welfare (at one property I know of, the owner herself pops round and pretends to be a helpful neighbor), which is an advantage if you want to learn more city secrets. Many properties have minimum stays of 5 to 7 nights. Renters such as **Airbnb.com**, **FlipKey.com**, **Housetrip.com**, and **VRBO.com** can charge as much as nice hotels. Those become a value when you've got a group.

For higher-quality results, we recommend booking through a London rental specialist—one who has vetted the unit and has a relationship with its owner. Our favorite, for its interesting span of 60-odd homes from mid-range to fantasy, is **Coach House Rentals** (chslondon.com/london; ✆ **020/8133-8332**), run for 15 years by the passionate Harley Nott. It shines brightest in West London and Westminster. Large, well-appointed units go from around £115 to £300 a night—as much as hotels, but for spaces that sleep up to 10 people. Discounts kick in after 6 nights.

The highly recommended **New York Habitat** (www.nyhabitat.com; ✆ **212/255-8018** in U.S.) represents hundreds of flats and has a licensed, U.S.-based office. Units for two range £80 to £250, but they come larger.

Loving London Apartments (www.lovinglondonapartments.com; ℭ **800/961-8138** from the U.S.), a clearinghouse for flats, vets every property. What began in 2003 for Spanish vacation villas spread to London in 2005. You can find late-breaking "hot deals" on its site; using those, £100 a night is an advance-booking standard.

Set up in 1995, **Outlet 4 Holidays** (www.outlet4holidays.com; ℭ **07974/729-099**) has flats better located for tourists than perhaps any other firm's. Locations are around Soho's cafe-and-club scene, smack in the West End. £130 a night is the norm, but there are extra fees for checking in outside of business hours. Should trouble arise, its office is in Soho, so you won't have far to go for assistance.

A high-end renter, **One Fine Stay** (www.onefinestay.com; ℭ **7826/529-286** (U.K.), **845/200-3489**) shoots its flats as if it's photographing a fashion spread, which tells you something about its target market. Central London digs are over £200 a night, with impeccable design and service to match.

A variety of properties exist for the sole purpose of renting flats to visitors. Flats are renovated with complete current fittings, including Wi-Fi, air conditioning, full kitchens and washer/dryers, and yet there's a staff on property to respond to your needs. One of the most gorgeous is **AKA West End** (5 Bentinck St., Marylebone, W1; www.stayaka.com; ℭ **020/7467-5930**; from £380 double; Tube: Bond Street), in the former London offices of Russia's notorious KGB; the surviving circular lift is a treasure. At the peak of the range, in Knightsbridge, is the 21-unit **Beaufort House** (45 Beaufort Gardens, SW3; www.beauforthouse.co.uk; ℭ **020/7584-2600;** from £324 nightly, £2,058 weekly for a fully equipped and serviced 1-bedroom apartment with health club access; Tube: Knightsbridge), converted from a few conjoined town houses 2 minutes' walk west of Harrods.

Citadines (www.citadines.com; ℭ **011-33-141-/05-79-05**) runs corporate-style hotel rooms fitted like little apartments, and it has five locations citywide. In order of centrality: Trafalgar Square, Holborn, South Kensington, Barbican (cheapest, from £87), and St Mark's-Islington.

HOME EXCHANGES

You'd be surprised how many Londoners are dying to visit your own stomping grounds, and if you make contact with the right people, you can swap homes (sometimes simultaneously). It sounds strange, but nothing tends to get stolen because swappers often become good friends. Not just that, but neighbors will often pop by to check up on you, so you have a built-in source of insider advice.

So which club should you choose? Here are the biggies, in alphabetical order:

Digsville.com (ℭ **877/795-1019**): This free, popular, and well-designed site allows users to see photos of their prospective swap and even read feedback from others who have traded with its owner.

HomeExchange.com (© **800/877-8723**): This service has some 65,000 listings. This is important because the more members, the more potential swaps. Results can be broken down by interest. It costs $10 a month to list.

Homelink.org (© **800/638-3841**): Popular with British and Australian travelers (with reps in 27 countries), this service costs $95 per year.

Intervac (www.intervacus.com; © **800/756-4663**): Intervac has been around for 6 decades and its claim to fame is that some 80% of its listings are international (30,000 families are represented), which means (as it puts it), "you compete with fewer Americans for overseas properties." Access to all listings is $99 a year, but you can take a limited 2-week trial for free.

Additional exchange sites include **SabbaticalHomes.com** catering to academics; and **HomeAroundtheWorld.com** (© **020/7564-3739**) for gays and lesbians (£45 for a year). Or you could roll the dice with a website like **CouchSurfing.com**, on which folks (generally younger) offer spare space to visitors. That's free, but there is no vetting system, so consider the risks before taking an offer.

CHEAP DORM ROOMS

Staying in a college room in holiday periods is an ideal budget saver for visitors of any age. Reservations are accepted starting in spring. At all of them, expect a wood-frame bed with linen, a desk, a dresser, an in-room sink, the possibility of an equipped kitchen (although it might be shared), an en suite bathroom (usually), laundry facilities, breakfast (often at a reasonable charge), Wi-Fi, and phones in the room or in the hall.

London School of Economics (www.lsevacations.co.uk; © **020/7955-7676**): Check these out first. Its eight dorms are in terrific condition, with the dignity that you'd expect of a school that trains the world's power players in business. Rooms rent cheaply (£45–£73) for July, August, and the first chunk of September. A few rooms may be available at Christmas or Easter, too.

Some single "private accommodation" rooms at **City University London** (www.city.ac.uk/accommodation; © **020/7040-7040**) are available from early July to early September. Prices are around £210 a week.

University College London (www.ucl.ac.uk/residences; © **020/7631-8310**): Its dorms are less prestigious than LSE's, but they aren't depressing. From late June to mid-September, 10 residences are available for public use at £36 to £53, but only five properties have private bathrooms.

King's College (www.kingsvenues.com; © **020/7848-1700**): As of 2016, four halls are available for short rental from late June through mid-September. The candidates have kitchens but not utensils and cost £45 to £65.

International Students House (229 Great Portland St., W1; www.ish.org.uk; © **020/7631-8300**; Tube: Great Portland Street): Part dorm, part subdued hostel, in two buildings. Rates are mid-£20s in a gender-separated dorm, £50 single, £33 twin, £104 quad. Bathrooms are shared, and some are co-ed but partitioned. Other academic rooms are more private. Breakfast is included.

WHERE TO EAT

In 1957, Arthur Frommer visited London for his seminal *Europe on $5 a Day*. His report was gloomy: "With great despair, this book recommends that you . . . save your money for the better meals available in France and Italy. Cooking is a lost art in Great Britain; your meat pie with cabbage will turn out just as tasteless for 40¢ in a chain restaurant as it will for $2 in a posh hotel." The report today is different: Wow!

As it turns out, good English cooking wasn't a lost art at all. True, there are still plenty of places you'll find a crap meal, but cabbage is no longer the national affliction, as it was in the days of rationing. Now that London swarms with people from across the world, you'll find nearly every style of cuisine—food the British of 40 years ago were reticent to try. Countless restaurants now serve ingredients fresh from the farm. Fish and chips, for a time relegated to the suburbs, made a comeback, and Indian restaurants, or "curry shops," now serve the country's unofficial comfort food. Thai food and burgers are more common than them all. Even most of the major museums (listed starting on p. 86) run cafes that, surprisingly, more than pull their weight.

Don't like meat? London's greenie culture thrives, and virtually every menu will have plenty of dishes for vegetarians to eat. The situation for vegans isn't quite as obvious, but most kitchens understand vegan dietary requirements. The news is just as good for people with **food allergies:** A majority of potentially irritating ingredients is marked when you buy pre-made food at the major shops.

Beware of relying on Yelp, Google, or Apple Maps to find places. Online inventory is often vastly incomplete, opening hours are often way off, and the results favor chains, so you'll miss a lot of good things. You can sometimes find some meal deals on **OpenTable.co.uk** and **SquareMeal.co.uk**. The free app **Uncover** hooks you up with last-minute availability at the trendiest and busiest restaurants.

No place in this book is emptily trendy. Each was chosen to say something about London of the moment and you'll taste what it's like to eat like a Londoner today.

London-Wide Restaurants

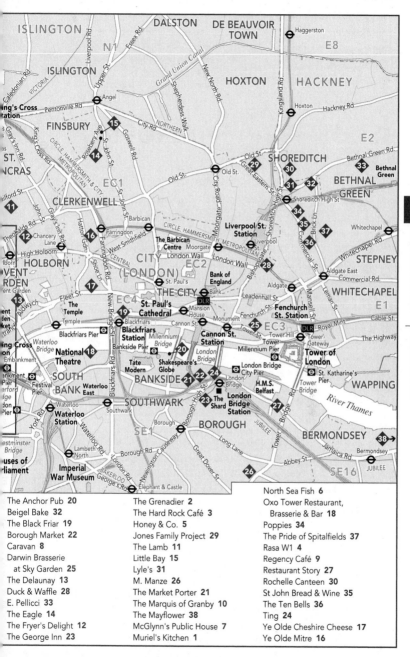

4 WHERE TO EAT | Introduction

The Anchor Pub **20**	The Grenadier **2**	North Sea Fish **6**
Beigel Bake **32**	The Hard Rock Café **3**	Oxo Tower Restaurant,
The Black Friar **19**	Honey & Co. **5**	Brasserie & Bar **18**
Borough Market **22**	Jones Family Project **29**	Poppies **34**
Caravan **8**	The Lamb **11**	The Pride of Spitalfields **37**
Darwin Brasserie	Little Bay **15**	Rasa W1 **4**
at Sky Garden **25**	Lyle's **31**	Regency Café **9**
The Delaunay **13**	M. Manze **26**	Restaurant Story **27**
Duck & Waffle **28**	The Market Porter **21**	Rochelle Canteen **30**
E. Pellicci **33**	The Marquis of Granby **10**	St John Bread & Wine **35**
The Eagle **14**	The Mayflower **38**	The Ten Bells **36**
The Fryer's Delight **12**	McGlynn's Public House **7**	Ting **24**
The George Inn **23**	Muriel's Kitchen **1**	Ye Olde Cheshire Cheese **17**
		Ye Olde Mitre **16**

Price categories are based on a typical main course.

- **Expensive**   £17 and up
- **Moderate**   £10 to £17
- **Inexpensive**   under £10

Doggy bags are frowned upon and most restaurants expect you to give up your table after 90 minutes to 2 hours. Always check the bill to see if service is included. If it is, you don't have to tip. If not, 10% to 15% is customary.

BLOOMSBURY, FITZROVIA & KING'S CROSS

Expensive

Dabbous ★★★ INTERNATIONAL   A white-hot table, Dabbous (the S is silent) shines through arty, crisp dishes using local and seasonal ingredients. The setting is kind of ugly, all concrete and exposed ducts, and the words on the menu give no hint of the inventiveness to follow, so the fun is putting yourself in Chef Ollie Dabbous' hands and seeing what inventions he's come up with: Coddled egg with smoked butter, then returned audaciously to the shell? Burrata cheese with wild strawberries and fennel pollen? Rather than over-salt or heavily spice, he'll lightly char something or create a suspended emulsion of another thing. Downstairs in Oskar's Bar, cocktails are made with homemade infusions and there's a shortened menu of barbecued meat. More, please.

39 Whitfield St., W1. www.dabbous.co.uk. © **020/7323-1544.** Set 4-course lunch menu £28; 4-course dinner menu £48. Mon–Fri noon–2:30pm and 5:30–11:30pm; Sat noon–2:30pm and 6:30–11:30pm. Reservations required. Tube: Goodge Street.

Moderate

Bill's ★★ INTERNATIONAL   A 5-minute walk from the British Museum and handy for many uses—big breakfasts, lunches, dinner, tea with scones and clotted cream, feeding kids, or downing cheap cocktails—this casual and affordable small group of restaurants started as a green grocer and is rigorous about quality ingredients. In few other London establishments will you find mac and cheese, burgers, pecan pie, and Caesar's salad together on the same menu. It's a lifesaver when you're indecisive or in need of drama-free grub served briskly, which is why you'll be glad to hear there are also locations near Piccadilly Circus (36-44 Brewer St., W1), off the Long Acre shopping street (St Martin's Courtyard, WC2; Tube: Covent Garden), and off Strand (21 Wellington St., WC2; Tube: Temple). The afternoon tea is £10 and not half bad, plus there's free Wi-Fi.

42 Kingsway, WC2. www.bills-website.co.uk. © **020/2742-2981.** Main courses £9–£13. Mon–Sat 8am–11pm; Sun 9am–10:30pm. Tube: Holborn.

West End Restaurants

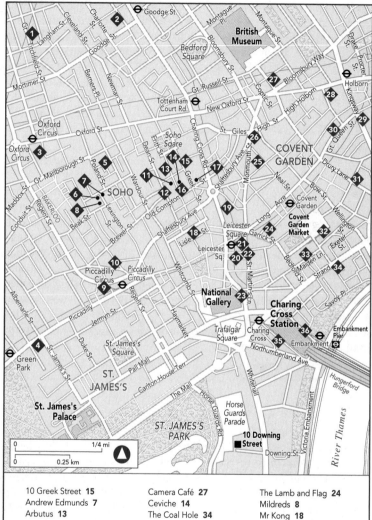

4

WHERE TO EAT | Bloomsbury, Fitzrovia & King's Cross

Caravan ★★ INTERNATIONAL   The redevelopment of the 67-acre industrial wasteland north of King's Cross station will take a decade, but construction is cooking along now, and even from square one, Caravan, in the old Granary building, made the changes cool. So basic and industrial-feeling (long blonde tables, canvaslike sheets for window shades, plain metal racks for bar shelves) that it feels like it could be converted to a ceramics shop overnight, Caravan (which is always busy but really cooks on nice days when its front patio is open) roasts its own coffee, bakes its own goods—the jalapeno cornbread is moist and kicky—and pushes its tapas-size dishes into fun flavor realms like salt beef terrine and chipotle ricotta in edible zucchini flower or coconut lime chicken salad. After dinner, kick back in its front yard in an amphitheater overlooking the Regent's Canal.

1 Granary Sq., off Goods Way, N1. www.caravankingscross.co.uk. ✆ **020/7101-7661.** Small plates £5–£7; pizzas £7–£9. Mon–Fri 8am–10:30pm; Sat 10am–4pm and 5–10:30pm; Sun 10am–4pm. No reservations during day on Sat–Sun, but otherwise recommended. Tube: King's Cross St Pancras.

Honey & Co. ★★ MIDDLE EASTERN   It's packed for good reasons: First, the food brilliantly adapts Middle Eastern dishes to sensitive London palates. Spectacular lamb schwarma is tender as brisket and spiked with pomegranate and mint, and is served in a little pot with hot and soft pita. Chicken dumplings come in a broth that smells like love. The "strawberry spliff" dessert proves that berries, filo, mint, and olive oil go well together. The other reason this place is packed is it's knee-knockingly tiny: 20 table seats and 4 in the window, so make a reservation or miss out on this assured, sometimes revelatory meal.

25A Warren St., W1. www.honeyandco.co.uk. ✆ **020/7388-6175.** Main courses £8–£15. Mon–Fri 8am–10:30pm; Sat 9:30am–10:30pm. Tube: Warren Street or Great Portland Street.

North Sea Fish ★★ SEAFOOD   Don't expect a linoleum-lined chippie, but a classy fish market-cum-restaurant, hidden on a lost-in-time side street. Every hotel manager within a walkable radius recommends it. Portions are huge, and there's always a selection of fresh fish (sole, salmon, halibut, and so on). If you need a healthier option, you can also get your fish grilled, and keep in mind that sitting down to eat will cost nearly double what using the takeaway desk does. Try the terrific homemade tartar sauce, or, for fans of little fishies, sample grilled sardines with salad.

7-8 Leigh St., WC1. www.northseafishrestaurant.co.uk. ✆ **020/7387-5892.** Main courses £10–£20. Mon–Sat noon–2:30pm and 5:30–10:30pm; Sun 1–6pm. Tube: King's Cross St Pancras or Russell Square.

Inexpensive

The Attendant ★ CAFE   They can only serve light meals here, but the scene is still worth a detour: a gourmet coffee cafe in an underground men's toilet. The facilities had been abandoned for 50 years and the conversion was so artful you might not realize it at first: Eight elaborate Victorian porcelain urinals are now eight individual coffee-drinking bays, and an overhead water reservoir became a lovely planter. Beans are roasted at Caravan (p. 58) and brewed in a La Rarzacco machine. If you're hungry, try the three-bean chili or peanut-butter caramel brownies (the "Elvis").

27A Foley St. at Great Titchfield St., W1. www.the-attendant.com. © **020/7637-3794.** Sandwiches and baked goods £3–£5. Mon–Fri 8am–6pm; Sat 10am–7pm. Tube: Oxford Circus or Goodge Street.

Camera Café ★ INTERNATIONAL   Most of the joints around the British Museum are imposters hawking British stereotypes to tourists, but this local's secret is squirreled away in the back of Aperture Photographic, a small shop specializing in Hasselblad lenses; the walls are decorated with shots taken by local artists. Food is simple (soups and sandwiches) but the management is thoughtful—there are lots of coffee-table books on art and Britain to borrow, plus a vintage Scrabble set, and you're encouraged to use its free Wi-Fi and outlets for further planning.

44 Museum St., WC1. www.cameracafe.co.uk. © **07887/930826.** Main courses £4–£7. Mon–Fri 11am–7pm; Sat noon–7pm. Tube: Tottenham Court Road or Holborn.

SOHO & LEICESTER SQUARE

Visitors spend much of their time around here, the dining and entertainment hub of London. So a miasma of dining also-rans, from junky steam-table buffets to overpriced bistros, sponge off tourists. Soho's southern fringe hosts a meager Chinatown in the neon-tinted 2-block section between Leicester Square and Shaftesbury Avenue. The district survives mostly as a tourist attraction, and I don't think many of its restaurants are distinguished enough to single out. Many of them use MSG, too, despite public health currents.

Expensive

Arbutus ★★★ CONTEMPORARY EUROPEAN   A pair of celebrated city chefs, Anthony Demetre and Will Smith, opened an exquisite restaurant with the intention of serving magnificent modern food at reasonable prices, and they have triumphed, winning a Michelin star for their efforts (and you can buy Demetre's cookbook on bistro food). The menu changes according to what ingredients are in season and top-quality, but might include saddle of rabbit, English pea soup, Lincolnshire smoked eel, Dorset crab, or braised pig's head. Some of these may sound dauntingly adventurous, but deliciousness rewards adventure. Service is also impeccable, and as another budget bonus, wines are available in carafes equal to a third of a bottle. Between 5 and 6:30pm, you'll find great deals such as £10 for the plat du jour plus a carafe of wine.

63-64 Frith St., W1. www.arbutusrestaurant.co.uk. © **020/7734-4545.** Main courses £19–£25; 3-course pre-theater set menu 5–6:30pm. Mon–Thurs noon–2:30pm and 5–11pm; Fri–Sat noon–2:30pm and 5–11:30pm; Sun noon–3pm and 5:30–10:30pm. Reservations recommended. Tube: Tottenham Court Road.

LONDON food chains I RECOMMEND:

London, like so many other cities, is experiencing an economic shift that is squeezing out mom-and-pop establishments in favor of better-heeled chains, so you'll often see these mid-priced, kid-friendly names cropping up on storefronts wherever you go. They're reliable, delicious, and English-owned too, so rely on them as well:

o **Busaba Eathai:** Peppy noodles and Asian dishes at communal tables.

o **Carluccio's:** New York–style Italian. Tile walls, pasta, fish, meats, coffees.

o **Giraffe:** Every kind of comfort food, extremely family-friendly.

o **Leon:** Free-trade, organic alternative to fast food includes "hot boxes" of Moroccan meatballs, halloumi wraps, and "superfood" salads.

o **Ping Pong:** Chinese dim sum in a vibrant, hip environment, plus cocktails.

o **Pizza Express:** Artisan-style pie. No one pays full price; see www.pizza-express.com/latest-offers for consistent discounts such as 25% off.

o **Simply Food:** Marks & Spencer's (p. 79) standalone shops for sandwiches, truly delicious ready-made dishes, and well-selected inexpensive wines.

o **Wagamama:** Hearty noodle bowls eaten at shared long tables.

o **Wahaca:** Substantial Mexican done well with British-grown ingredients.

The Ivy ★ TRADITIONAL BRITISH   A West End tent-pole for a century, it's where British brand names (Look! Hugh Grant! Ooh! Simon Cowell!) take their luncheon beneath its iconic wood paneling and harlequin mullioned windows. "The Ivy is like a safari park in which the rare and exotic creatures are nurtured," wrote the *Guardian.* A 2015 renovation auctioned off old artwork, cutlery, and linens and shook up the look with new Britart from the likes of Damien Hirst and new fare (barbecued squid salad, Togarashi popcorn rock shrimp with kewpie mayonnaise) set alongside Ivy classics like its famous hamburger and Shepherd's Pue. Despite the modernization, they didn't mess with the restaurant's enduring sophistication.

1-5 West St., WC1. www.the-ivy.co.uk. ℂ **020/7836-4751.** Main courses £15–£20; set menu until 6:15pm on non-matinee days: 2 courses £22, 3 courses £26. Mon–Sun noon–11:30pm (Sun 10:30pm). Tube: Leicester Square or Covent Garden.

Moderate

10 Greek Street ★★★ CONTEMPORARY EUROPEAN   Sometimes, restaurants get it so right—from friendly and knowledgeable staff to unfussy surroundings (chalkboard, mirrors) to pure, clean, well-made food—that you wonder why they can't all be this way. The menu, all choices a top value for the money, changes but the impeccable standards don't: frequent standouts include whole lemon sole with samphire (an edible coastal plant) and artichokes, zucchini flower stuffed with mushroom, elderflower sorbet, a continuous trickle of fresh-baked breads, and a wine list chosen with as much care as the fresh fish cuts. If there's a downside, it's that it will only take reservations for lunch, which means you risk missing out on dinner if you don't come early. Or just sit at the bar, where the people-watching is prime.

10 Greek St., W1. www.10greekstreet.com. ⓒ **0209/7734-4677.** Main courses £12–£19. Mon–Sat noon–11:30pm. Tube: Tottenham Court Road.

Andrew Edmunds ★★★ BRITISH The relaxed, town house-style storefront, a study in natural woods and candle-lit purity, has been going for 30 years and the fact it hasn't caved to Soho trendiness, and that its stupendous wine list is priced fairly, is central to its endurance. Chairs don't match, staff isn't in uniform, and the menu is hand-scribbled daily with a haste that belies the effort the chef puts into sourcing farmhouse meats and preparing seasonal ingredients—expect choices along the lines of skate wing with cauliflower and capers, free-range Aylesbury duck breast, and artichoke spaghetti with wild garlic and almond pesto, plus the occasional nose-to-tail adventure. Superb dessert cheeses are selected from area farms. It's very London, and the slick crowd can't commandeer it because bookings are only accepted a week out.

46 Lexington St., W1. www.blanchettesoho.co.uk. ⓒ **020/7437-5708.** Main courses £13–£17. Mon–Fri noon–3:30pm and 5:30-10:45pm; Sat 12:30–3:30pm and 5:30–10:45pm; Sun 1–4pm and 6–10:30pm. Reservations essential. Tube: Piccadilly Circus or Oxford Circus.

Aurora ★★ MODERN EUROPEAN When you're at a loss for where to find honest cooking among the food factories of Soho—or you've been turned away by the crowd at Andrew Edmunds (see above) across the street—try the intimate, French-style fare in this adorable, if cheek-by-jowl, setting of dim lights, low voices, scarlet walls, and tiny framed artworks that seem to hide a dozen stories. Selections, which shift monthly, are interesting without being gimmicky, and they might include duck confit, a scrumptious broccoli soup, or warm lamb salad, but it seems to excel most at fish, which gives it a slightly Mediterranean bent. It's possible to get in and out for £20, rare for this neighborhood—yet sacrifice nothing in terms of portions or culinary prowess. In good weather, ask to sit in the delightful back garden. This is the sort of place locals beg me not to publish in my guidebook—so let's keep this our little secret, shall we?

49 Lexington St., W1. www.aurorasoho.co.uk. ⓒ **020/7494-0514.** Main courses £12–£18. Mon–Sat noon–3pm and 5:30pm–midnight (last orders at 10pm); Sun noon–10pm (last orders at 9pm). Reservations suggested. Tube: Piccadilly Circus or Oxford Circus.

Blanchette ★ FRENCH Divinely assembled tasting plates, which change with seasons, focus on ingredients: grilled flavor-rich beef *onglet* (hanger steak) with snails or mushrooms, grilled asparagus with aged Comté cheese, hot bread delivered in a brown paper bag and soft dairy butter spread with a wooden paddle. The food may be crafted, but there's no formality in the welcome. The look is much like a casually urbanized French farmhouse of rough wood, exposed brick, and a long bar under caged light bulbs ideal for tasting charcuterie and sipping wine. And Blanchette wants you to love wine like the French: There are only two beers on the menu.

9 D'Arblay St., W1. www.blanchettesoho.co.uk. ℂ **020/7439-8100.** Small plates £3–£8. Mon–Sat noon–11pm; Sun noon–5pm. Tube: Oxford Circus.

Brasserie Zédel ★★★ FRENCH   When you descend its grand staircase, you feel like Toulouse-Lautrec in search of tonight's muse: The gilt-and-marble cellar dining room, awash in fin-de-siècle statements like platter mirrors and vested waiters, is a perfect piece of Paris off Piccadilly. This is not a crusty holdover but a modern pitch-perfect pastiche created from what was once part of the defunct Regent Palace Hotel, which in 1915 was the largest hotel in Europe: Its choices are as authentic as Pernod, pastis, oysters, quiche Lorraine, and sublimely seasoned steak tartare. The adjoining Bar Américain, a 1930s Art Deco treasure by an architect survivor of the *Lusitania,* does indulgently uptight cocktails and champagne, while its cabaret, The Crazy Coqs (shows at 7pm and 10:15pm, £15–35), has quickly risen as an elegant music venue for grown-up tastes. This taste of the Continental high life is not nearly as expensive as it looks, and its Gallic poise only adds to the deliciousness.

20 Sherwood St., W1. www.brasseriezedel.com. ℂ **020/7734-4888.** Main courses £13–£15; 2 courses £10; 3 courses £13. Mon–Sun 11:30am–midnight (Sun 11pm). Tube: Piccadilly Circus.

Ceviche ★★★ PERUVIAN   This is my firm favorite in Soho. Owner Martin Morales quit his job at Disney's European music division to pursue his true passion: food. Now he is a TV personality, a cookbook author, and runs this hopping, cheerful Peruvian hangout that pours the best *pisco* (brandy) sour in town. Flavors are indescribably punchy, citrusy, and unrepeatable anywhere else you've eaten. Favorite small plates include scallops with *pisco* and pomegranate, the *don ceviche* made with *limo chili* tiger's milk, and the succulent *corazón mío* of beef skewers marinated in *panca chili anticuchera.* Once your tongue tastes its first citrusy zip, you'll feel compelled to come back. They now give diners a spoon to lap up leftover tiger's milk—probably because I kept asking. In 2015, a second, spacious location opened just north of the Old Street Tube stop (2 Baldwin St., EC1), while the owner's similar **Andina** is in Shoreditch (1 Redchurch St., E2; www.andinalondon.com; ℂ **020/7920-6499;** Tube: Shoreditch High Street or Liverpool Street).

17 Frith St., W1. www.cevicheuk.com. ℂ **020/7292-2040.** Small plates £7–£12. Mon–Sun noon–11:30pm (Sun 10:15pm). Reservations suggested. Tube: Piccadilly Circus or Tottenham Court Road.

Ducksoup ★★ INTERNATIONAL   The sort of invisible hidey-hole you have to be told about, Ducksoup is barely marked. Indeed, when you first open its old door, the first thing you see is a stack of LPs and a record player, the sole sound system, that might be playing Grace Jones' "Nightclubbing" or Toots & the Maytals' "Funky Kingston." The day's menu hangs above the turntable on an office clip. The metal grill on the windows and life-beaten walls make it look like a greasy cafe that would sling a fry-up at you, but instead, there's a funky wine list and solid, whole-food selections such as steak tartare, grilled artichoke with lemon and capers, rabbit pappardelle, and chargrilled bream. The room feels like a London that went out with Thatcher, but dishes sit solidly within London's 21st-century passion for quality food.

41 Dean St., W1. www.ducksoupsoho.co.uk. © **020/7287-4599.** Main courses £8–£18. Mon–Sun noon–10:30pm (Sun 5pm). Tube: Tottenham Court Road.

Koya ★★ JAPANESE   A queue for a quick and cheap bowl of noodle soup? Well, ordinary soup wouldn't merit it. But this stuff is no mere soup. The dining room, which turns out customers quickly, is plain, bearing nothing more special than wood stick chairs, cheap chopsticks in cups, menu boards, and rows of metal coat hooks. Even the menu of *udon* (wheat flour noodles) and more *udon* would appear to have no tricks. But then the finished product arrives in several parts, ferried by impish waitresses, for you to mix your-self, and the fog lifts. Noodles are made fresh each day using traditional methods. The walnut miso enchants. The pork *udon* is made of spring onion, salty roast pork crumble, a mystically *umami* (savory taste) broth base, and 6 ounces of pure Colombian cocaine. I'm not actually sure about that last ingredient, but it would explain a lot. You will drink the dregs from the bowl.

49 Frith St., W1. www.koya.co.uk. © **020/7434-4463.** Main courses £7–£14. Daily noon–3pm; Mon–Sun 5:30–10:30pm (Sun 10pm). Tube: Tottenham Court Road.

Mildreds ★ VEGETARIAN   Usually packed, it's where vegetarians with palates go. The menu is ever-changing but always assembled with more care than the usual beans and tofu: Sri Lankan sweet potato and cashew nut curry, tortelloni with pumpkin and ricotta, and mixed mushroom and leek pie are three samples from its internationally derived menu. Big bowls and plates, appetizing presentation, and a vibe like a contemporary home have secured Mildreds a following even among carnivores—it even got a cookbook pub-lished. Save room for the peanut butter chocolate brownie—you won't believe it's gluten-free.

45 Lexington St., W1. www.mildreds.co.uk. © **020/7494-1634.** Main courses £9–£12. Mon–Sat noon–11pm. No reservations. Tube: Tottenham Court Road.

Inexpensive

Bar Italia ★★ COFFEE/ITALIAN   Italians settled Soho in the 1940s, and before they decamped for the suburbs, they installed a set of mod, gleaming coffee bars and cafes. This straggler from 1949 is a haunt of slumming celeb-rities and artists, yet modest enough for the rest of us. While this institution is busy all day—making simple sandwiches, delivering pastries—it swells with revelers after midnight. Even Rome doesn't have bars that steam, press, and shuffle coffee across such defiantly worn '50s linoleum with such gusto.

"Like everything in this city that Londoners really enjoy, it reminds us of being abroad," quipped the *Guardian*. Whatever; it practically leaks hipness.

22 Frith St., W1. www.baritaliasoho.co.uk. © **020/7437-4520.** Coffee £3–£4; pizza £10–£11; panini £7. Mon–Sun 6:30am–4:30am (Sun 2am). Tube: Leicester Square.

Café in the Crypt ★ INTERNATIONAL   The tastiest graveyard in town! Under the sanctuary of the historic St Martin-in-the-Fields church at Trafalgar Square, atop the gravestones of 18th-century Londoners, one of the West End's sharpest bargains is served. The menu at this dependable cafeteria changes daily, but the large portions always include a few hot meat main dishes, a vegetarian choice, soups, salads topped with meats, and red velvet or lemon drizzle cake, all homemade. This church keeps the wine and draft beer flowing, the soup-and-sandwich-or-pudding deal is £7 and afternoon tea is but £7. April to September, it also serves alfresco on the plaza at street level. Bottom line: It's fun, delicious, central, and a budget savior.

Trafalgar Sq., WC2. www.stmartin-in-the-fields.org. © **020/7766-1158.** Main courses £6–£9. Mon–Tues 8am–8pm; Wed 8am–10:30pm with jazz for ticket holders after 6:30pm; Thurs–Sat 8am–9pm; Sun 11am–6:30pm. Tube: Charing Cross.

Gordon's Wine Bar ★ INTERNATIONAL   The atmosphere is matchless at London's most vaunted and vaulted casual wine bar. It was established in 1890 (when Rudyard Kipling lived upstairs) and, thank goodness, hasn't been refurbished since—look in the front display window and you'll see some untouched champagne bottles that have intentionally grown furry with dust. These tight, craggy cellars beneath Villiers Street are wallpapered with important newspaper front pages from the 20th century—Thatcher's resignation, the death of King George VI—while ceiling fans threaten to come loose from their screws. Everything is suffused in a mustardy ochre from more than 42,000 past evenings of indoor tobacco smoke (no longer legal). Tables are candlelit, music is not played—not that you could hear it over the din of conversation. Dozens of wines and sherries by the glass are around £5, you can select from a marble display of English and French cheeses or a steam table of hot food, and in good weather, the event expands outside along Embankment Gardens with casual alfresco meals such as stuffed peppers and marinated pork loin. (The stone arch was built around 1625 as a palace gate on the Thames, but its mansion is long gone and the river moved 46m/150 ft. south.) Come down well before offices let out to secure seating; it won't accept bookings.

47 Villiers St., WC2. www.gordonswinebar.com. © **020/7930-1408.** Main courses £7–£10. Mon–Sat 11am–11pm; Sun noon–10pm. Tube: Charing Cross or Embankment.

Mr Kong ★★ ASIAN   One of Chinatown's late-night rabbles worth pausing for, Mr. Kong works from a lengthy Cantonese menu, and has worked it well since 1984. It's not much to look at (there's a lot more space downstairs), and its steely waiters treat patrons as little more than business transactions, but it's one of the few establishments in honky-tonk Chinatown to supplement Western-style Chinese dishes with daring ones (starring eel, soft-shell crab with chilies, and the like). In addition to laying claim to a following of

KEEPING THE BILL low

If you're watching your money, bear in mind these cultural differences:

Avoid soda: It costs more than £2, and often for a puny glassful, no refills.

Avoid over-tipping: Credit card slips may have a line for a tip—even if it was built in. Only tip (10%–20%) if the menu says "service not included" or similar.

Avoid rice dishes: It's customary to pay £2 to £3 for a side dish of plain rice, even if you think it should come with what you ordered.

Avoid eating in: Establishments are obliged by law to charge 20% in tax if you decide to eat your purchases there.

Avoid water: Well, avoid it bottled. If you just order "water," waiters may bring expensive bottled water, so if you want it for free, specify "tap water."

Avoid starters: Even where mains are £7, starters can be £4 to £6.

Avoid cocktails: Mixed drinks can cost a dizzying £8 to £11, and they're all the same middling strength because of measure standardization. If you do drink, stick to beer (£3–£4 a pint) or wine (around £5 a glass).

Asian-born devotees, who order razor clams, crispy duck, and scallops by the bowlful, it's kid- and vegan-friendly and serves until the wee hours. The menu's daunting, so consider the £11 set that decides for you.

21 Lisle St., WC2. www.mrkongrestaurant.com. ✆ **020/7437-7341.** Main courses £8–£12. Mon–Sun noon–2:45am (Sun 1:45am). Tube: Leicester Square.

The Stockpot ★ INTERNATIONAL   High on function and low on glitz, it has been indispensable to scrimping visitors and families for years. No dish, be it spaghetti Bolognese, pork steak, or coq au vin, will set you back more than £7, though everything's good and all portions overflow their plates, and even dessert is £3—and that's the essence of its appeal. Staff waits around with dishrags at the ready on their shoulders, and the wall is hung with old drawings of gentlemen, just to class things up. On one memorable visit, a brief power outage interrupted dinner. "Just like the food," my neighbor inveighed, "it has a certain Eastern Bloc flavor." For those who can barely afford to visit London, the Stockpot is salvation. Forget the ravens at the Tower. When the Stockpot goes, London is over.

18 Old Compton St., W1. ✆ **020/7287-1066.** Main courses £6–£7; 2-course set menu £8. Mon–Tues 11:30am–11:30pm; Wed–Sat 11:30am–midnight; Sun noon–11:30pm. Tube: Leicester Square or Tottenham Court Road.

COVENT GARDEN

The area was once more interesting in general, but CAPCO, which governs the leases, has adopted a policy of squeezing out oddballs in favor of imported brands such as Shake Shack, Le Pain Quotidien, Apple, and Balthazar. The food within the market is tourist-priced, but if you simply must eat there, head to the lower level where you'll find £6 *tartines* (open sandwiches) at Chez Antoinette and good cheese at the Crusting Pipe wine bar.

Expensive

The Delaunay ★★ INTERNATIONAL   In 2012 Jeremy King and Chris Corbin, who did the acclaimed Wolseley (see below), opened another pitch-perfect evocation of a Continental cafe from a lost age. This one, just south of Covent Garden, is fitted with Art Deco brass fittings and lots of dark wood, and its menu, which includes all three meals, is decidedly Teutonic, what with its schnitzels, seared mackerel, beef Stroganoff, and wieners. Next door, its much more affordable casual cafe, the Counter, is retro Viennese, and it's tempting to while away an afternoon sipping espresso, eating Sacher torte (£5) and fresh-made croissants (£2), and reading one of the provided newspapers at one of the benches with the crane-necked jeweler's lamps. There, it serves a £13 tea after 3pm and sandwiches (salt beef, croque monsieur, and so forth).

55 Aldwych, WC2. www.thedelaunay.com. ✆ **020/7499-8558.** Main courses £15–£27; counter cakes from £2; sandwiches £5–£7. Restaurant: Mon–Fri 7am–midnight; Sat 8am–midnight; Sun 9am–11pm. Counter: Mon 7am–7:30pm; Tues–Fri 7am–10:30pm; Sat–Sun 10:30am–10:30pm (Sun 5:30pm). Tube: Temple.

J. Sheekey ★★ SEAFOOD   Smartly turned out waiters prep you with so many strange fish-eating utensils that your place setting starts to look like a workstation at Santa's workshop. Such presentational flourishes are appropriate to theaterland, where this has been a bistro-style classic for years, and although prices aren't generous, portions and quality are. The least expensive main dish, fish pie, is fortunately its trademark, but there are plenty of other choices, from shrimp-and-scallop burgers to a delectable lemon sole, plus a changing slate of game and meats for the fish-averse. For all the folderol, children are welcomed. The adjoining horseshoe-shaped Oyster Bar (same hours without a mid-afternoon break) has a limited menu that includes a velvety rich crab bisque with cognac (£9).

28-32 St. Martin's Court, WC2. www.j-sheekey.co.uk. ✆ **020/7240-2565.** Main courses £16–£42; weekend set-lunch menu: 3 courses £27. Mon–Fri noon–3pm and 5:30pm–midnight; Sat–Sun noon–3:30pm and 5:30pm–midnight (Sun 11pm). Reservations recommended. Tube: Leicester Square.

Rules ★★ TRADITIONAL BRITISH   For a high-end kitchen that takes British cuisine seriously, go with an icon. In fact, Rules is London's oldest restaurant, having been cooking since 1798, and its patrons have included Graham Greene, Charles Dickens, Evelyn Waugh, and Edward VII, who regularly dined here with his paramour Lillie Langtry. (The management is less than discreet about it; the nook they used is named for him.) Being a major stop on the tourist trail has gone slightly to its head, and its view of a dining experience is steeped in its own hype; beer comes in a "silver tankard," for example, and the landmarked dining rooms are an overdressed mélange of yellowing etchings, antlers, and rich red fabrics. But what's on the table is indisputably high-class London: English-reared meat like roast loin of roe deer, whole roast squab or grouse (it serves 18,000 game birds annually), and cocktails like that famous one made of tonic, juniper, and quinine. Its nearest

Covent Garden | WHERE TO EAT

rival, Simpsons-in-the-Strand at the Savoy hotel (p. 29) has been going since 1828, but that has become overly touristy. This is the heartier choice.

35 Maiden Lane, WC1. www.rules.co.uk. ⓒ **020/7836-5314.** Main courses £18–£29. Mon–Sun noon–11:45pm (Sun 10:45pm). Tube: Covent Garden.

Sarastro ★ MEDITERRANEAN What if Mozart went insane on hollandaise sauce? He'd open this flamboyant paean to the opulence of opera. In a design that must give the fire marshal sleepless nights, Sarastro's every cranny has been gilded, sheathed in shimmering fabric, or filled with erotic statuary (you can't miss the self-pleasuring Diablo). Along the walls, 10 intimate opera boxes, reached up precarious stairs, survey the silliness, which is often embellished by musicians. The menu—like it matters amid such eye candy—is Turkish, though not as fun as the setting, with lots of meats (beef bourguignon, "Guinea fowl supreme") and no shyness about the sauces. Many nights, opera singers serenade diners. It's not dead cheap (two-course menus start at £16, three courses at £19), but it's an event. And not only tourists come—locals celebrate here, too, albeit slightly apologetically.

126 Drury Lane, WC2. www.sarastro-restaurant.com. ⓒ **020/7836-0101.** Main courses £15–£23. Daily 12:30–midnight. Tube: Covent Garden.

Moderate

Browns ★ TRADITIONAL BRITISH In London, there's a Browns for fashion, and a Brown's Hotel, but Browns the spacious brasserie is the Browns you can afford. Installed in the former Westminster County Courts, this high-quality, Brighton-based English chain serves updated English food and imported beer. The globe lanterns, enormous mirrors, and staff buttoned into crisp white oxford shirts impart the sense of a Gilded Age chophouse. Expect lots of indulgently hearty dishes such as fish pie in cream and white wine sauce; steak, mushroom and Guinness pie; a house salad with beets, quinoa, pumpkin seeds, artichoke hearts and more; or a nice fat wild boar and chorizo burger. British tradition—starchy but welcoming to tourists—is the main product here.

82-84 St. Martins Lane, WC2. www.browns-restaurants.com. ⓒ **020/7497-5050.** Main courses £9–£15; Sunday roast £11–£15. Mon–Fri 8am–10:30pm (Fri 11pm); Sat–Sun 10am–11pm (Sun 10:30pm). Tube: Leicester Square.

Great Queen Street ★★★ TRADITIONAL BRITISH Here, the people behind the seminal Eagle (p. 74) present the essence of gastropub cuisine in the more convenient environs of Covent Garden. There's a pub feel—scuffed wood floors, burgundy walls, sconces capped with fringed mini-shades—but here, waiters come to you. And how: On one visit, I had no fewer than five servers attend to me, and one of them voluntarily gave me a free Negroni cocktail out of sheer conviviality. The slow-cooked dishes are clean and reassuringly ingredient-proud. Samples (they change) include Old Spot (a breed of pig) pork chops with sticky shallots, griddled quail with celery salt; and lamb's shoulder cooked for 7 hours and accompanied by *gratin* *dauphinoise* (potatoes in crème fraîche)—that one feeds four, which hints at the social atmosphere encouraged here. The Cellar Bar, open until midnight, serves the cold dishes from the same menu.

32 Green Queen St., WC2. www.greatqueenstreetrestaurant.co.uk. © **020/7242-0622.** Main courses £12–£25. Mon–Sat noon–2:30pm and 6–10:30pm; Sun 1–4pm. Tube: Covent Garden or Holborn.

Wild Food Café ★★ VEGETARIAN   Upstairs in the Granola Triangle of Neal's Yard, beside the excellent homeopathic dispensary Neal's Yard Remedies, this popular and packed place serves vegetarian fare that's truly flavorful at prices Covent Garden left behind: olive and shiitake burgers, grilled-cheese sandwiches using unpasteurized sheep cheese from nearby Neal's Yard Dairy, pine nut quinoa with horseradish tahini, and raw chocolate as a component in some very impressive desserts. There's always a bunch-up of punters at the door. Don't be daunted; wait to get the next available seat whether it's at the bar or at a table. It's some of the best vegan food you'll find in the city, but even usual meat eaters depart stimulated and satisfied.

14 Neal's Yard, WC2. www.wildfoodcafe.com. © **020/7419-2014.** Main courses £8–£13. Sun–Mon noon–5pm; Tues–Sat noon–10pm. Tube: Covent Garden.

Inexpensive

Dinner Jackets ★ TAKE-AWAY   The Covent Garden standby is often overlooked because it's just a mobile kiosk (and the endless line at the nearby Shake Shack is so distracting), but this energy-packing standby makes carb-rich baked potatoes ("jacket potatoes") with fillings including chicken curry, veggie chili, tuna mayo, and the like. No need belaboring this one; you come for carbs, speed, and value, and you get it all. Park on the stone steps as the street performers entertain you. Along the same lines (cheap and carby): **Battersea Pie Station** a few steps away in the lower level of the Market Building, in the middle of the piazza.

Outside London Transport Museum, Covent Garden, W1. © **020/7240-2677.** Potatoes from £3. Daily 11am–6pm. Tube: Covent Garden.

Punjab Restaurant ★★★ INDIAN   Ignore that it looks like every other hack kitchen sponging off the Covent Garden tourist trade—this place predates the recent curry trend, which is why it survived the crest of the popularity wave. Punjab has been cooking since 1947, when it was opened by Gurbachan Singh Maan, a wrestler, and his fourth generation now runs it with striking professionalism. It proclaims itself the oldest North Indian restaurant in the U.K., and staff have worked here, beneath the gold silk wallpaper, for decades. Cooking is light on the oil and *ghee* (clarified butter). Meats and tandoori (the oven was installed in 1962) are well marinated, and so they arrive tender. Ask for something not on the menu: *anari gosht,* or pomegranate-flavored lamb. ("That's only for the regulars," the waiter tells me. "No problem.") The flavors dovetail gorgeously with every bite, winding up with a slight spicy twang. The menu is cheeky, too: "If you have any erotic activities planned for after you leave us, perhaps you should resist this sensational

STEEPED IN TRADITION: afternoon tea

Afternoon tea is an overpriced tourist's pursuit, to be sure, but that doesn't mean it's not delightful to pass a mid-afternoon by pretending to be fancy. Arrive hungry and you'll be served a never-ending banquet of scones, clotted cream, pastry, light sandwiches, and a bottomless brewed torrent. Dress up, if you please, and be discreet about photos. Hundreds of places throw teas, but these are among the most legendary or the best located. Most places will add champagne for £5 to £20 more.

Brown's Hotel: This Mayfair institution, open since 1837, offers exacting execution and a handsome paneled room but is not overly snooty, and there are three 90-minute seatings a day. "Tea-Tox" is its lower-fat, lower-carb version. (www.roccofortehotels.com; ✆ **020/7518-4155;** noon–6:30pm; £45)

Forntum & Mason: The venerable department store on Piccadilly has sold tea for 3 centuries, so naturally you choose from 150 types, many of which are supplied to the hotels on this list. (www.fortunumandmason.com; ✆ **020/7734-8040;** £40)

The Goring: Near Buckingham Palace, it's served on its own bespoke canary-yellow china in your choice of the blood-red lounge, the airy conservatory, or the garden. Book at least 3 months ahead, but sit as long as you want once you're there. (www.thegoring.com; ✆ **020/7396-9000;** 3–4pm; from £43)

Great Court Restaurant, The British Museum: Enjoy more sensibly priced scones under the courtyard's central glass canopy. It's a gorgeous setting you're sure to visit anyway. (www.britishmuseum.org; ✆ **020/7323-8990;** 3–5:30pm; £20)

Houses of Parliament: Take tea overlooking the Thames in its modern Terrace Pavilion rooms behind the House of Commons. (www.parliament.uk/visiting; ✆ **020/7219-4114;** times change, but generally 2pm and 3:45pm; £28 plus price of tour)

The Langham: The first London hotel to initiate the custom (in 1865) is still one of the best, with dazzlingly intricate pastries (chef Cherish Finden calls them "my collection"), but it's also one of the most commercial, having branded itself with a Wedgewood partnership. This Oxford Circus tradition is particularly popular with Asian tourists. (palm-court.co.uk; ✆ **020/7636-1000;** 5 seatings noon–5:30pm; £47)

The Milestone: The antiqued, library-like Park Lounge overlooking Kensington Gardens is your stop if you're near Kensington Palace. It doles out 11,000 doggy boxes a year for guests who can't finish—a courtesy that's uncommon in England. (www.milestonehotel.com; ✆ **020/7917-1000;** 3 seatings 1–5pm; from £38)

The Ritz: The only way most of us can afford the gilding, mirrors, and boisterous floral arrangements of the Ritz, on Piccadilly, is to submit to the formal attentions of the servile waiters in its Palm Court (1906), who handle 400 people daily. No jeans or sneakers, with jacket and tie required for men. Book 6 to 8 weeks ahead. (www.theritzlondon.com; ✆ **020/7300-2345;** 5 seatings 11:30am–7:30pm; £50 adults, £30 children)

garlic *naan.*" On a recent visit, two diners at a neighboring table ribbed each other about who had been coming here longer; the winner got hooked in 1987. Reserve ahead on weekends.

80 Neal St., WC2. www.punjab.co.uk. ✆ **020/7836-9787.** Main courses £7–£11. Mon–Sun noon–11:30pm (Sun 10:30pm). Tube: Covent Garden.

MAYFAIR, MARYLEBONE, KENSINGTON & KNIGHTSBRIDGE

Expensive

Hawksmoor ★★★ STEAK   Americans like to think they've mastered the almighty steak, but even they would have to dine here every day for a month to find a cut of meat that wasn't cooked beyond fault. Other than that, the menu is simple (sides, seafood), but the cocktails are inspired, starting with the signature Full Fat Old-Fashioned, featuring bourbon infused with butter in a *sous-vide* machine. Like most steakhouses, it'll lighten your wallet, but it also delivers romance with a clubby atmosphere signaled by a barely marked front door in its regal stone edifice off Regent Street. Until 6:30pm and after 10pm, get a starter and a rib-eye for £23, or £7 less than steak alone at peak dinnertime.

5a Air St., W1. thehawksmoor.com. ✆ **020/7406-3980.** Main courses £18–£36. Mon–Fri noon–3pm and 5–10:30pm (Fri 11pm); Sat–Sun noon–11pm (Sun 10:30pm). Tube: Piccadilly Circus.

The Wolseley ★★★ CONTEMPORARY EUROPEAN   "No Flash or Intrusive Photography please," chastises diners in a footnote on the menu. That's because this opulent bistro in the Grand European style, posing with every polished surface to appear like something Renoir would want to paint, is home base for celebrities and power lunchers. Built as a luxury car dealership for a doomed manufacturer, then used as a bank, a decade ago it became the caviar-scooping, oyster-shucking, tea-pouring hotspot that fools nearly everyone who sips its pea-and-lettuce soup that it's always been this way. Waiters are unattainably attractive and look down their noses as they gingerly place salad Niçoise and Swiss souffle, enacting the calculated Continental crispness we crave.

160 Piccadilly, W1. www.thewolseley.com. ✆ **020/7499-6996.** Main courses £15–£20; sandwiches £11. Mon–Fri 7am–midnight; Sat–Sun 8am–midnight (Sun 11pm). Tube: Green Park.

Moderate

The Hard Rock Café ★ AMERICAN   You'll find one in every town from Key West to Kuwait. Its burgers (though excellent and a ½-lb.) hit an outrageous £16, it's cramped, much of the so-called memorabilia consists of instruments that celebs played once and tossed, and waiting up to 90 minutes for a table chews up time that could be used for more authentic touring. But this Hard Rock was the world's first, having opened in 1971, so there is a grudging authenticity.

150 Old Park Lane, W1. www.hardrock.com. ✆ **020/7514-1700.** Main courses £11–£16. Mon–Sun 9:30am–11:30pm (Sun 11pm). Reservations recommended. Tube: Hyde Park Corner.

Rasa W1 ★ INDIAN   Oxford Street is for corporate stores and predictable chain food, but you can do better. This kicky Indian alternative, which shines a light on the fun flavors of southwest India, lies off a quiet side street just southeast of the Bond Street station. It may be casual like a standard Indian joint (pinkish walls, tablecloths too nice for its price point), but even everyday items are pumped up—what's just "coconut rice" on the menu is in fact blended with cashews, a leading crop of Kerala. The crab *thoran,* crab meat stir-fried with coconut, mustard seeds, and ginger, is touted as an owner's grandmother's recipe. And imagine this: mangoes and green bananas cooked in yogurt with green chilis, ginger, and fresh curry leaves. That's the sweet-and-sour *moru kachiathu,* and it's a menu highlight.

6 Dering St., W1. www.rasarestaurants.com. ☎ **020/7629-1346.** Main courses £11–£16. Mon–Sat noon–3pm and 6–11pm. Tube: Bond Street.

Inexpensive

Muriel's Kitchen ★★ AMERICAN/INTERNATIONAL   The window is a fantasia of icing-blobbed, fruit-topped, sugar-dusted pastry temptation, but the real reason to step inside this rustic-style, casual restaurant is locally grown, organic comfort foods such as beef lasagna; five-spice marinated pulled pork; chili con carne; and creamy chicken and apricot curry. The high, wooden tables feel like something from an American farmhouse even as they look out on the neighborhood's French residents and the families on their way to the big Kensington museums around the corner. Being one of the few noncorporate choices in South Ken has brought success; new locations just opened at 36-38 Old Compton St. in Soho and on the north side of Leicester Square.

1-3 Pelham St., SW7. www.murielskitchen.co.uk. ☎ **020/7589-3511.** Main courses £8–£10. Mon–Sat 8am–11pm; Sun 9am–10pm. Tube: South Kensington.

Regency Café ★★★ TRADITIONAL BRITISH   The mid-century "caff" diner, once a staple of London life, is rapidly being swept into Formica heaven by trendy bistros. Among the few holdouts still feeding Westminster's cops, security guards, and bureaucrats, is the 1940s Regency, a discount-Deco elegy to another age in yellowed white tiles and bolted-down plastic chairs. This isn't a gastronomic treasure (the fryer is in heavy use, white bread heaped high, sausage a food group); it's an anthropological one. Big-value food including homemade meat pie is prepared with lightning speed and your order is jarringly bellowed so that you can come fetch it. For another marvelous "caff," see E. Pellicci, later in this chapter.

17-19 Regency St., SW1. ☎ **020/7821-6596.** Main courses £3–£8. Mon–Fri 7am–2:30pm and 4–7:30pm; Sat 7am–noon. Tube: Pimlico or Westminster.

THE SOUTH BANK, SOUTHWARK & BOROUGH

For a casual street food meal, head behind the South Bank Centre for the South Bank Market, a collection of changing food stalls cooking up curries, duck confit burgers, sausages, grilled *halloumi* (cheese), and other cheap and ready-to-eats. It runs Fri–Sun starting around noon and wraps up by about 8pm.

Expensive

Oxo Tower Restaurant, Brasserie & Bar ★★ INTERNATIONAL

The Oxo commands a gratitude-inducing panorama of St Paul's and the City from Southbank, and its adjoining cocktail terrace is an ever-popular meeting spot. Chef Jeremy Bloor isn't one for faddish techniques, although he does keep a waffle machine for dishes such as sweet potato waffles with goat's cheese, beets, rosemary, and truffle honey dressing. Satisfyingly nuanced dinners are built around luxe proteins such as John Dory, Mallard, and South Devon beef, with a few sumptuous garnishes (lobster mash, oxtail spring roll) just to keep the fireworks going. The Brasserie section, which has live music in the evening, does less ostentatious food such as seared tuna and spring chicken for about £4 less per main course. If you don't have reservations, try to arrive early during the seating period.

22 Barge House St., SE1. www.harveynichols.com/restaurants. ✆ **020/7803-3888.** Main courses £22–£35; 3-course lunch £37. Mon–Fri noon–2:30pm and 6–11pm; Sat noon–2:30pm and 5:30–11pm; Sun noon–3pm and 6:30–10pm. Reservations recommended. Tube: Blackfriars or Waterloo.

Restaurant Story ★★★ MODERN BRITISH

The moment you sit, your server lights a white taper and you slide your menu from the leafs of *Sketches by Boz* by Dickens, who started his life penniless nearby. By the time a fusillade of about six *amuse-bouche* "snacks" hits you (paper-thin cod skin studded with emulsified cod roe, a sweet black eel mousse "Storeo"), your candle has quickly melted, you're told that the wax was actually edible beef fat, and you're handed a leather pouch of fresh-baked bread to sop up the rich drippings. And there are 10 more frivolously surprising, small-plate courses to go. The dramatic and whimsical delights are by hot young talent Tom Sellers, and his prix-fixe menu, which never stops amusing and dazzling with flavor duets, speaks of London cooking both old and new: scallop carpaccio with cucumber balls rolled in dill ash; Jensen's gin (Sellers loves gin) and apple consommé topped with garlic blossoms; and "Three Bears" porridge—one sweet, one salty, one just right. It's food you'll be talking about. Reserve ahead.

201 Tooley St., SE1. www.restaurantstory.co.uk. ✆ **020/7183-2117.** 6 courses £60; 10 courses £80. Tues–Sat noon–2:30pm and 6:30–9:30pm. Reservations essential. Tube: London Bridge or Bermondsey.

Inexpensive

Borough Market ★★★ INTERNATIONAL/TAKE-AWAY

A chronicle of overstimulation, it combines Victorian commercial hubbub with glorious, farm-fresh flavors, rendered as finger food for visitors. About a dozen green-market vendors sell their countryside meats, cheeses, and vegetables all week long, but the market blooms beneath its metal-and-glass canopy Thursdays through Saturdays, when more than 100 additional vendors unpack and the awe-inspiring, touristy scene hits overcrowded swing. The least crowded time is Thursdays between 11am and noon; Saturdays are plain nuts. Thursdays and Fridays from 12:30 to 2pm, there's a demonstration kitchen using market produce. It's best to pay with cash.

If there's any country that has farming down, it's England, and this market is its showplace. Follow the crowd across Bedale Street, past the artisan cacao at **Rabot 1745;** to the **Green Market,** along the fence by the cathedral; to **Kappacasein** dairy from Bermondsey (www.kappacasein.com), which places great wheels of Ogleshield cheese under burners and sloughs bubbling swaths of it onto plates of boiled new potatoes (it's called *raclette,* £6, and the only thing to rival it for decadence is the same booth's goopy grilled cheese, £5, which you'll taste all day after eating). **Roast Hog** (www.roasthog.com) slices pig off a turning spit; **Greedy Goat** scoops lactose-free goat mile ice cream. Under the breathtaking Victorian glass canopy of **Three Crown Square, Le Marché du Quartier** (www.marketquarter.com) does duck confit sandwiches (£5); you can't export either melt-in-your-mouth **Bath soft cheese** (www.parkfarm.co.uk) or aromatic unpasteurized **Gorwydd Caerphilly** cheese (www.trethowansdairy.co.uk). **Shellseekers,** the fishmonger in the center, is known for hand-dived Devon scallop, served in its own shell and topped with a bacon and sprout stir-fry (£6). **Roast** (www.roast-restaurant.com), which runs an expensive restaurant upstairs, has a stall for rich meats such as roast pork belly with crackling and Bramley applesauce and beef with horseradish cream (both £7). At **Maria's Market Café,** the moon-faced, second-generation proprietor slaves over a stove making fresh bubble (kind of a mushy version of home fries) for vendors and visitors alike (it's £4 on a roll). The **Brindisa** booth (www.brindisa.com) facing Stoney Street, feeds a steady line of punters its grilled chorizo sandwich with oil-drizzled pequillo peppers from Spain (£4). Outside on Stoney and Park streets, opposite the well-stocked **Market Porter** pub (p. 82), more finds: **Monmouth Coffee** (www.monmmouthcoffee.com), which sends emissaries to check its single-farm beans in the field and is one of London's most revered roasters; **Gelateria 3bis,** which has (among others) an ultra-creamy *fior di latte* flavor made from rich English milk plus a warm chocolate fountain for pre-filling cones; the casual sit-down restaurant **Elliot's,** specializing in preparations of market produce; and **Neal's Yard Dairy** (www.nealsyarddairy.co.uk), stacked high and tended by clerks in caps and aprons, which is the gold standard for English cheese. It's all food you can only enjoy in London.

8 Southwark St., SE1. www.boroughmarket.org.uk. ✆ **020/7407-1002.** Mon–Wed 10am–3pm; Thurs 11am–5pm; Fri noon–6pm; Sat 8am–5pm. Tube: London Bridge.

M. Manze ★★ TRADITIONAL BRITISH   If you're truly fearless or your palate is truly twisted, brave the classic East End dishes of jellied or stewed eels. But if not, there's still a reason to visit: a jewel box of a shop with green

Those who have been fortunate enough to travel broadly can attest to how sadly unusual it is to find places where people of wildly different colors, religions, and nationalities can live together without killing each other. London, though, like New York City, Toronto, or Sydney, is certifiably multi-ethnic—some 300 languages and 45 distinct ethnic communities—and the patchwork supplies the rare chance to sample cultures beyond the borders of our own. You'll find neighborhoods of all stripes everywhere, but here's the Tube or rail stop for some of the major concentrations so you can begin your own culinary world travels:

Bangladesh: Bethnal Green, Whitechapel
Caribbean: Brixton, Willesden Junction
Egypt: Shepherd's Bush

Ghana, Nigeria, Congo, West Africa: Seven Sisters, Hackney Central, or Hackney Downs (National Rail)
India, especially northern: Southall (National Rail)
Ireland: Kilburn
Kenya: Barking
Kurdistan: Manor House
Lebanon: Shepherd's Bush
Nigeria: Peckham Rye (National Rail)
Persia: Edgware Road
Poland: Hammersmith, Ealing Broadway
Somalia: Streatham (National Rail)
Sri Lanka and South India: Tooting (National Rail)
Syria: Shepherd's Bush
Turkey: Dalston Kingsland and Stoke Newington (National Rail)
Vietnam: Hackney Central or Hackney Downs (National Rail), Old Street

glazed Victorian tile and wooden benches, which is in such rare condition it's protected by the government. Manze, which has been serving since 1891, also does meat or vegetarian pastry pies—which to be fair, most customers prefer—as it has done since the days when this street was home to dock-workers and laborers. The parsley-made "liquor" sauce doesn't really taste like much, but the gravy and mash taste like nostalgia itself.

87 Tower Bridge Rd., SE1. manze.co.uk. © **020/7407-2985.** Main courses £3–£6. Mon 11am–2pm; Tues–Thurs 10:30am–2pm; Fri–Sat 10am–2:30pm (Sat 2:45pm).

THE CITY

Things tend to shut down around here after the bankers go home from work.

Moderate

The Eagle ★★★ TRADITIONAL BRITISH By now, the gastropub trend is so widespread the term is meaningless, but foodies note: It began here in 1991 (or so most agree) and shows no sign of fading (definitely). Behind the bar of a bare-to-the-wood former saloon, casual chefs prepare a changing selection of about a dozen flavorful and thoughtful dishes a day, from the likes of pork loin salad to pan-roasted sole to the house specialty, the insidiously spicy Bife Ana steak sandwich dripping with marinated garlic and onion. Tables are shared, furniture reassuringly shabby and mismatched, and foodie crowds reliably in force—come early to ensure your share. Order

THE HEIGHTS OF cuisine

London's skyscrapers are shooting up like bamboo, and with them, dining aeries to be remembered. The city's taste buds are too sophisticated to tolerate a top-floor restaurant with bottom-feeder grub—these places compete with terrific cuisine that's a pleasure to eat. Only the prices could be considered unpleasant. Reservations are suggested for all of them.

Duck & Waffle. The scene: All day and night—yes, it's 24 hours, and doubles as a skilled *cocktailerie*—it cycles through sharing plate menus that lean toward richness, including foie gras crème brûlée, braised cuttlefish, barbecue crispy pig ears, and the namesake dish with mustard maple syrup. The view: It's a little inland from the Thames, so the nearest views are of the Gherkin and the City. (40th Floor, 110 Bishopsgate, EC2; www.duckandwaffle.com. ℂ **020/3640-7310.** Sharing plates £9–13. Tube: Liverpool Street)

Darwin Brasserie. The scene: The multi-story atrium atop the "Walkie-Talkie" is like an upscale mini-mall of evening pursuits, including thump-thump-thump beats at Sky Pod bar and a seafood place, Fenchurch Seafood Bar & Grill. Our choice, Darwin, has an honest menu (Cornish lamb, Scottish rib-eye, fish and chips) on an elevated floor where some of the horizon may be obscured by the drooping eyelid roofline, but it's still spectacular, and you're free to soak in the panorama from elsewhere in the massive atrium after dinner. The airport-style security queue downstairs can be a drag but it thins out after sunset. The view: the Tower of London, the Thames, the Shard, and beyond. (Sky Garden, 36th Floor, 20 Fenchurch St., EC3; skygarden.london/Darwin. ℂ **0333/ 772-0020.** Dinner main courses £17–£26. Breakfast: Mon–Fri 7–10am; Sat 8–10am. Lunch: Mon–Sun 11:30am–4pm, Sun 11:30am–3:30pm. Dinner: Mon–Sat 5:30–10:30pm, Sun 5:30–8:30pm. Tube: Monument or Bank.)

Ting. The scene: Much more romantic than Duck or Darwin, the principal dining room of the Shangri-La hotel (p. 42) does exquisite but unadventurous classics like monkfish, slow-roasted piglet belly, Cotswold free-range chicken, and steak. The view: sweeping eastern panorama from Southwark, including London Bridge Station, the Tower of London, and Tower Bridge. Pair it with cocktails on the 52nd floor at **Gong**, the hotel's tight little bar. (35th floor, The Shard, 32 London Bridge St., SE1. www.ting-shangri-la.com. ℂ **020/7234-8108.** Dinner main courses £23–38. Daily 6:30–10:30am, noon–2:30pm, and 6–11:30pm. Tube: London Bridge.)

at the bar and get a beer while you're up there, because here, the food's the thing, and they'll bring your meal to you in their own sweet time. The point is to sit back and enjoy.

159 Farringdon Rd., EC1. ℂ **020/7837-1353.** Main courses £8–£15. Mon–Fri noon–3pm and 6:30–10:30pm; Sat noon–3:30pm and 6:30–10:30pm; Sun 12:30–4pm. Tube: Farringdon.

Inexpensive

The Fryer's Delight ★★ TRADITIONAL BRITISH/TAKE-AWAY   In this age, no one would dare name their joint something as hydrogenated as The Fryer's Delight. Fortunately, this joint is not of this age. It's a true

Brick Lane: 24-Hour Playground

Brick Lane, named for its medieval status as a source for bricks, was once a Jewish area but has become so strongly identified with immigrants from the Indian subcontinent that its name has transcended geography to become a sort of shorthand term for England's South Asian population. In the span of just a few blocks, most of which have signage in both English and Bengali, lines of Indian restaurants jockey for business. No discerning Londoner would claim that any serve the city's best Indian cuisine, and most of them are in fact run by Bangladeshi or Pakistani entrepreneurs catering to the average Englishman's milder notion of northern curries. But it's nonetheless a terrific place to stroll along, leverage competition, and sit down for a bargain meal. (Bring your own wine, though, since most are run by Muslims who don't sell alcohol.) By day, the connecting Dray Walk is a short block of sophisticated boutiques and laid-back cafes. On weekends, it hosts a handful of markets for vintage clothes, books, and art (www.bricklanemarket.com).

old-world chippy, where the fry fat is from beef drippings, chips come in paper wrappings, the wooden booths and checkered floor date to the lean postwar years, and the men behind the counter almost callously gruff. Prices are anachronistic, too: Nothing's more expensive than £6. Seamy? Order yours with mushy peas. It's a 10-minute walk east of the British Museum; look for the logo of a codfish tipping his bowler hat (seriously). If you like fish and chips more upscale, try **Bonnie Gull** in Fitzrovia (21 Foley St., W1; www.bonniegullseafoodshack.com; ℂ **020/7436-0921;** £15 at dinner) or **Golden Union** in Soho (38 Poland St., W1; www.goldenunion.co.uk; ℂ **020/7434-1933;** £12).

19 Theobald's Rd., WC1. ℂ **020/7405-4114.** Main courses £5–£6. Mon–Sat noon–10:30pm. Tube: Holborn or Chancery Lane.

Little Bay ★★ INTERNATIONAL   Rarely has paying so little afforded such extravagance: The menu changes, but on one visit, I received an astounding 22 mussels in my mussels marinara (shallots, garlic, and white wine) for my piddly £3—and yes, they were fresh and well sauced. Main courses are just as generous. Possibilities may include honey-glazed pork belly, confit leg of duck, or sweet smoked spare ribs—yes, for only £7, and there are frequent price cuts, too, such as three-course menus for £14. The decor is beyond loopy, like a penny arcade version of the Vatican—a Romanesque fun house of plaster murals, gnarled chandeliers, and a massive mask of Zeus. Sunday is roast day: £8 including potatoes and Yorkshire pudding, and on Thursdays and Saturdays after 8pm, just to slam home the iconoclasticism, there's an opera singer—one does Elvis songs. Little Bay is a budget find.

171 Farringdon Rd., WC1. www.littlebayfarringdon.co.uk. ℂ **020/7278-1234.** Main courses £7. Mon–Sun noon–midnight (Sun 11pm). Tube: Farringdon.

EAST END & DOCKLANDS

Much of the city's most exciting cooking for a fun night out has migrated to Shoreditch and Spitalfields, leaving Mayfair to cater to the expense-account gourmets and Soho to feed the beery hordes.

Expensive

Lyle's ★★ BRITISH   The kind of place where chefs like to eat, where the dishes appear simple and fluid and yet require authority to accomplish, Lyle's has a short, changing New British-meets-Nordic menu, but it runs deep with inventiveness and delicacy: lemon sole with buttermilk and sea aster (a salt marsh plant), raw beef with mussels that's actually chopped beef with shellfish emulsion, soured cream with chocolate as a dessert. Dishes are neatly creative, but flavors remain clean, even if the blank loft space in which they're served is a bit factory-like. If things are busy, you can always sit at the bar.

Tea Building, 56 Shoreditch High St., E1. Lyleslondon.com. ✆ **020/3011-5911.** Main courses £13–£29; 3-course set meal £39; small plates £4–£8. Mon–Fri 8am–11pm; Sat 6–11pm. Reservations recommended. Tube: Shoreditch High Street or Liverpool Street.

Moderate

Jones Family Project ★★ BRITISH   If you love beef, the way JFP's Josper grill can almost mystically seal in the flavors of its Yorkshire Longhorn could blow your mind, but then again, the burger topped with oxtail-stock mayo might also do it. It's not just about beef, though; fish, duck, and pork (that's cut like beef) are also knowingly prepared in generous portions—most proteins come from The Ginger Pig, a network of principled farmers. Sides such as truffled mac and cheese and tomato salad underscore the traditional cuisine goals, but the friendly, groovily '70s downstairs dining space makes for a clubby, convivial hideaway good for conversation and stretching out when you're in Shoreditch. It's an especially good stop on Sunday afternoons for its weekly roast, and the upstairs bar is open until midnight Monday to Saturday.

78 Great Eastern St., EC2. www.jonesfamilyproject.co.uk. ✆ **020/7739-1740.** Main courses £14–£27. Mon–Sat noon–3pm and 6–10:30pm; Sun 11am–6pm. Reservations Fri–Sun. Tube: Old Street.

Poppies ★★ SEAFOOD   Big crispy portions flopping on big oval plates eaten with a big knife and fork to big 1950s sock-hop music: The franchise-ready Poppies does for British fish and chips what peppy jukebox diners have done for midcentury American food. Amusingly, it wraps its chips in custom-printed newspaper since it's now illegal to use the chemical-laden real thing. For all its plastic theatricality, it hews to authenticity: The chief dish, cooked to order, is sustainably caught and sourced from third-generation fishmonger T. Bush at Billingsgate Market, and even the uniforms worn by the "Poppetes" waitresses—a red sailor frock with a jaunty, bellhoppy cap—come from Collectif in Camden's Stables Market. For those whose palates swerve differently, there's also chicken, the chance to try jellied eels, and Minghella ice cream hailing from the Isle of Wight. There's a second location near the markets of Camden Town (30 Hawley Crescent, NW1; © **020/7267-0440**).

6-8 Hanbury St., E1. www.poppiesfishandchips.co.uk. © **020/7247-0892.** Main courses £10–£12. Mon–Thurs 11am–11pm; Fri–Sun 11am–11:30pm (Sun 10:30pm). Tube: Shoreditch High Street or Liverpool Street.

Rochelle Canteen ★★ BRITISH A sublime secret is hidden away, discovered only if you ring a doorbell beside a green door in a brick wall. You'll pass through the grassy yard of an 1880s school, and in the old bike shed, join a daytime garden party. The changing menu is rigorously British, without flourish, high-quality, and fresh: green pea soup, roast sirloin, cuttlefish ink stew, leek and wigmore tart, fish and chips, loose-leaf tea. Your companions will be high-functioning artists, designers, and professionals, many of whom now lease space in the former school, plus the occasional kid, if they behave as well as a Victorian child. In fine weather, it's easier to find a seat because dining spills outdoors, the better to enjoy jugs of rhubarb and ginger fizz.

Rochelle School, Arnold Circus, E2. www.rochelleschool.org. © **020/7729-5677.** Main courses £13–£15. Mon–Fri 9am–2:30pm. Reservations suggested. Tube: Shoreditch High Street.

St. John Bread & Wine ★★ TRADITIONAL BRITISH Hand-in-hand with the gastropub trend is "nose-to-tail" eating. That's when your chef doesn't waste a single part of the animal, resulting in tastes that were commonplace to his agrarian English forefathers (heart, cockscomb, marrow, whole pigeon) but are new to most North American tongues. Most places charge, um, an arm and leg for it, but you can sample it at this lower-priced offshoot of the influential St. John restaurant, which in the 1990s brought back British cooking in a big way. Walls are simple white, chairs are plain wood, and the kitchen staff is serious about food, no matter its form. Experience dishes like cold lamb with chicory and anchovy, smoked sprat (sardines) with horseradish, and laver bread (made with seaweed) with oats and bacon. A meal here can be an adventure (ever eaten dandelion?).

94-96 Commercial St., E1. www.stjohnbreadandwine.com. © **020/7251-0848.** Main courses £7–£9 before 6pm, around £15 after 6pm. Mon–Sun 9am–11pm (Sun 9pm). Reservations recommended. Tube: Aldgate East or Shoreditch High Street.

Inexpensive

Beigel Bake ★★ BAKERY The city's most famous bakery, Jewish or otherwise, never closes but there's often a line. The queue moves quickly here even if time doesn't—signs still post an area code that hasn't been active since 2000. The patronage is a microcosm of London, ranging from bikers to hipsters to arrogant yuppies to the homeless. Its beigels (*bi*-gulls) are not as puffy or as salty as the New York "bagel" variety, and they even come filled for under £2—the same price, astonishingly, as a half-dozen plain ones. Its pastries are gorgeous, too: The chocolate fudge brownie, less than £1, could be nursed for hours. Watching the clerks slice juicy chunks of pink salt beef in

SAVE BREAD WITH sandwiches

You'll go all day without crossing paths with a bobby or a Cockney, but you can't walk a block without passing a sandwich shop The cheapest ones are what I call the **triangle sandwiches,** which are ready-made, sliced diagonally, and sealed into triangular containers. They are made fresh every day by the million, cost less than £5, and can rescue both time and money during your busy touring schedule.

A few ubiquitous chains in the triangle sandwich trade:

- **Eat** (www.eat.co.uk): Its quality is ahead of Pret, with a good selection of organics, wraps, and whole grains.

- **Pret A Manger** (www.pret.com): Right behind Eat in clever flavors, with gourmet fixings in snazzy combinations.

- **Gregg's** (www.greggs.co.uk): Its sandwiches are average in every way, but it also does pies and hot meat rolls.

- **Marks & Spencer** (www.marksandspencer.com): Lots of cheap stuff, well done, and around dinnertime, markdowns up to 50%.

the window, then slather it onto a beigel with nostril-clearing mustard from a crusty jar, is an attraction unto itself. Londoners complain it's gotten touristy, but what tourist trap serves 60p coffee?

159 Brick Lane, E1. ✆ **020/7729-0616.** Daily 24 hr. Tube: Shoreditch High Street.

E. Pellicci ★★★ TRADITIONAL BRITISH London's tradition of mid-century diners, or "caffs," is quickly being gentrified into nostalgia, but this fry-up on deeply authentic and unflashy Bethnal Green Road has been run by the affable Nevio family since 1900. Some of them were born upstairs, and the matriarch of the family commanded the kitchen since 1961. The Deco interior, a greasy spoon fantasia of sunburst icons, chrome, and primrose, was carved by a regular in 1946 and is now protected by law. You'll be boisterously welcomed with open arms—Mama, cooking her Italian specialties like cannelloni, may wave to you from the kitchen—and you'll spend a happy meal sharing a table with locals ("Where are you from?" "Looks like rain tomorrow."), sipping the best cuppa 70p tea you ever had, and as proof of your acceptance by the regulars, after you're done you may be sent out with a parting gift of homemade cake. There's no more iconic "caff" in town, certainly none happier.

332 Bethnal Green Rd., E2. ✆ **020/7739-4873.** Main courses £2–£8. Mon–Sat 7am–4pm. Tube: Shoreditch High Street or Bethnal Green.

20 PUBS YOU'LL LOVE

Pubs are the beating heart of British life, and they have been for centuries. Your neighborhood hangout is called your "local," but you might be shocked to learn that many of the oldest premises have been so well-loved (or so well-bombed) that their original features are gone, and most of them are company-owned and depressingly standardized and modern-looking, which may disappoint those looking for an evocative atmosphere. The following pubs, all centrally located, should do you right. All of them serve food of some kind (burgers, meat pies, and the like) for at least part of the day; you usually order at the bar, where you receive a numbered tag for your table so that servers can find you. Pubs commonly charge £4 to £5 for a pint of the favored serving size of about 20 American ounces, and the ABV percentage tends to be strong. Ale or stout is often not chilled—it's cool, because it's probably stored in the cellar—and it may be hand-pumped. Mixed drinks are also served, but don't expect a generous pour because measures are rigidly standardized across the country. They'll have bottled beer and cider, too. When the bell is rung, it's last call, and the landlord *will* turf you out precisely at closing time.

The Anchor Pub ★★   Few pubs meld abundant history with an enviable location as perfectly. This Thameside patio in sight of St Paul's dome is perhaps the most agreeable (and popular) spot in London at which to sit a spell with a fresh-pulled pint. There's been a tavern here at least since the 1500s, when Londoners ferried to Southwark by the hundreds to experience bear baiting, gardens, brothels, and Shakespeare (the playwright surely would have known the place). Diarist and royal confidant Samuel Pepys is said to have watched London burn to the ground from the safety of this shore in 1666. The industrial Anchor brewery that subsumed it for 200 years was cleared away in the 1980s, and the spacious (but always crowded) riverside terrace was added. Beer snobs kvetch that it has become a tourist draw, but that's all right with me; it's historic, and pubs have always been hangouts for the common man.

34 Park St., SE1. www.taylor-walker.co.uk. © **020/7407-1577.** Mon–Sat 11am–11pm (Sat midnight); Sun noon–10:30pm. Tube: London Bridge.

The Argyll Arms ★★   Having a beer in here can feel like drinking in a bejeweled, red velvet box. That's thanks to the acid-etched glass screens that subdivide the busy bar into dignified drinking areas. Originally installed in 1895 to prevent brawls between the working and middle classes at a time when even subway rides were segregated, the screens somehow survived the 20th century. Drinks are £1 more than they should be, but it's one of the prettiest pubs in London, and its location southeast of Oxford Circus makes it an easy stop.

18 Argyll St., W1. www.nicholsonspubs.co.uk. © **020/7734-6117.** Mon–Sat 10am–11:30pm (Sat midnight); Sun 10am–11pm. Tube: Oxford Circus.

The Black Friar ★★★   Deservedly protected by landmark status, this 1904 Art Nouveau masterpiece, a short walk from St Paul's, is as jolly as the fat friars that bedeck it in bronze, wood, and glass. Once it was snuggled down a few dark alleys, but neighboring demolitions liberated it and now it's blessed with a noisy outdoor patio and walls of windows are now bathed in afternoon sunshine from over the Thames. The back Saloon was intended for the upper classes, hence its exceptionally overbaked interior in marble and bronze, and the undulating front bar, where pop music plays and pub crawls frequently pass through to sign the guest book, is extraordinarily well-stocked with a range of cask ales and cider. Pricey food (£13 burgers, many meat pies) is shuttled from the upstairs kitchen via a hand-cranked dumb waiter.

174 Queen Victoria St., EC4. www.nicholsonspubs.co.uk. ℂ **020/7236-5474.** Mon–Sat 10am–11pm; Sun noon–10:30pm. Tube: Blackfriars.

The Coal Hole ★ A onetime haunt of actor Edmund Kean, who drank himself to an early curtain, was rebuilt in 1904 in the Arts and Crafts style and is still a hangout for performers at the adjoining Savoy Theatre. Use the entrance in back, by the stage door, to access the clubbier lower level. The antique street lamp on the Strand is a vestige of an experimental gaslight piping system that burned off sewage gases before the farty stink could overcome citizens. Bottoms up!

91 Strand, WC2. www.nicholsonspubs.co.uk/thecoalholestrandlondon. ℂ **020/7379-9883.** Mon–Thurs 10am–11:30pm (Thurs midnight); Fri–Sun 10am–12:30am (Sun 10:30pm). Tube: Charing Cross or Embankment.

The George Inn ★★★ Unquestionably one of the most important ancient pubs still standing, the George traces its lineage to at least 1542, when a map of Southwark first depicted it; the Tabard Inn, from where Chaucer's pilgrims left in *Canterbury Tales,* was then a few doors south (it's gone now). The oldest part of the current structure, a galleried wood-and-brick longhouse, dates to 1677, after a horrific fire swept the district. It later functioned as an 18th-century transit hub, and its courtyard was encircled on three sides with a tavern, a hotel, stables, wagon repair bays, and warehouses. Shakespeare knew it, and Dickens memorialized it in *Little Dorrit,* but the rise of a railway nearly saw it destroyed, and only one side of the former complex survives. The National Trust now protects it, and in 2012, Pete Brown traced some of its *dramatis personae* in the book *Shakespeare's Local.* Sip ale in the low-ceilinged timber-and-plaster chambers, or sit in the cobbled courtyard, in the Shard's shadow, and soak up the fading echoes of history.

77 Borough High St., SE1. www.nationaltrust.org.uk/george-inn. ℂ **020/7407-2056.** Mon–Sat 11am–11pm; Sun noon–10:30pm. Tube: London Bridge.

The Grenadier ★★★ They say this was the Duke of Wellington's local bar and the unofficial clubhouse for his regiment, hence the battlefield artifacts on display, and they also say someone was beaten to death here for cheating at cards, hence the routine ghost sightings. This tiny plank-floored, currency-festooned pub/restaurant, pretty as a picture in a cobbled mews, comes off like a boozer in some upcountry village, with only 15 places at its island bar, part of which is still faced with its original pewter top. Once a haunt for servants of the surrounding townhouses, clientele these days skews toward an international mix of students and businessmen. The pub is also unjustly known for its Bloody Marys (overrated). Find this secret spot by heading down Grosvenor Crescent from Hyde Park Corner station, hanging a hard right upon arriving at Belgrave Square onto Wilton Crescent, and taking your first right on Wilton Row.

18 Wilton Row, SW1. www.taylor-walker.co.uk. ℂ **020/7235-3074.** Daily noon–11pm. Tube: Hyde Park Corner.

The Lamb ★   Quiet, not too touristy, this east Bloomsbury choice (where Ted Hughes took Sylvia Plath on their early dates) is representative of a neighborhood local that still has some prime Victoriana from the old days. Check out the rare sunburst etched-glass snob screens obscuring the bar, built so you don't have to look the help in the eye. Or put 50p in the polyphon in the corner—that's a musical metal disc that works like a music box and was the gramophone of a century ago. The carpet is a tired tartan, the walls lined with sepia photograph cards of long-forgotten stage actresses, the cask beers out-of-the-ordinary enough to intrigue.

94 Lambs Conduit St., WC1. www.youngs.co.uk. ℂ **020/7405-0713.** Mon–Wed noon–11pm; Thurs–Sun noon–midnight (Sun 10:30pm); food served until 9pm. Tube: Russell Square.

The Lamb and Flag ★★   Too tiny and thronged after work to supply much respite, it is nonetheless the epitome of a city pub, tucked as it is down an atmospheric brick alley and blessed with an original fireplace. It has been known throughout its 380 years as both the Coopers Arms and the Bucket of Blood (the latter because it hosted illegal prizefights in the early 1800s), and its building is said to be Tudor in origin. No one can prove it, since it was heavily rebuilt in the 1890s. You'll find it on a lane just east of the intersection of Floral and Garrick streets. But you probably won't find a place to sit unless you start drinking after lunch, which the regular drinkers on its memorial wall surely did.

33 Rose St., WC2. www.lambandflagcoventgarden.co.uk. ℂ **020/7497-9504.** Mon–Sat 11am–11:30pm; Sun noon–10:30pm. Tube: Covent Garden or Leicester Square.

The Market Porter ★   Most tourists notice it because it faces the gastronomic mayhem of Borough Market, but in fact it's a lovely old timber-beamed boozer to drink in any time of the week. In fact, more times than most pubs, because its location earned a special license to open at 6am when vendors are working. Sundays and off-hours are pleasant for sitting by a double-sided fire drinking one of its nine traditional ales (choices change) or eating upstairs—ingredients all come from the market. It can also act: It appeared as the Third Hand Book Emporium in the third Harry Potter film.

9 Stoney St., SE1. www.markettaverns.co.uk. ℂ **020/7407-2495.** Mon–Fri 6–8:30am and 11am–11pm; Sat–Sun noon–11pm (Sun 10:30pm). Tube: London Bridge.

The Marquis of Granby ★   Amusingly, some pubs near the Houses of Parliament are equipped with a "division bell," which rings—rather like a fire alarm, which panics neophytes—to warn socializing MPs they have only 8 minutes to scurry back to vote. The Marquis, a single-room pub with bare floorboards and high wood walls, prides itself on real hand-pumped ale. Other pubs have division bells, too—St. Stephens Tavern on Bridge Street across from Big Ben and the Red Lion on Whitehall—but those are cloyingly touristy, while this is a pub supported by government types (it's not even open on weekends).

41 Romney St., SW1. www.nicholsonspubs.co.uk. ℂ **020/7227-0941.** Mon–Fri 10am–11:30pm. Tube: Westminster or Pimlico.

The Mayflower ★   The story goes that the sea captain Christopher Jones lived around here and in 1620, some dissenters recruited him, boarded his ship *The Mayflower* alongside this pub (then it was The Shippe; this building is from the 1700s), and set sail to Southampton, then Plymouth, and thence to the New World. It's hard to imagine, and otherwise, it's a fairly traditional pub (oak beams, wood paneling) with real ales and a fire. The tiny backyard on the Thames is a worthy place to raise a pint and mull your personal slice of the river on a summer day. Would the Pilgrims have called that a sin? Surely, but you're more fun than they were.

117 Rotherhithe St., SW16. www.themayflowerrotherhithe.com. ✆ **020/7237-4088.** Mon–Sat 11am–11pm; Sun noon–10:30pm. Tube: Rotherhithe.

McGlynn's Public House ★   McGlynn's isn't hundreds of years old, or even important, but it fulfills the image of a "local" where neighborhood folks hang out and the landlord welcomes new faces. Its coal-blackened brick corner building, painted in old-fashioned green and red trim, is hard to find (it's southwest of Argyle Square in King's Cross), which accounts for some of its appeal. It's the sort of place with a few "pokie" gambling machines jangling in the corner, and a rugby or football game on the TV every afternoon.

1-5 Whidborne St, WC1. www.mcglynnsfreehouse.com. ✆ **020/7916-9816.** Mon–Sat 11am–11pm; Sun noon–10:30pm. Tube: Russell Square or King's Cross St Pancras.

Meantime The Old Brewery ★★★   London's biggest craft beer success story began in 1999 in a Greenwich flat, but in 2010 it took up residence in Sir Christopher Wren's palatial Old Royal Naval College (a UNESCO World Heritage site where the Paris scenes in 2012's *Les Misérables* were shot), occupying the very brewery building that once furnished Napoleonic War veterans with their three daily pints. From here, practically on top of the Prime Meridian (and near Greenwich's sights), Meantime now supplies seemingly all of London's best restuarants with its meticulous creations, plus guest drinks of distinction. The large outdoor patio is a dream on a sunny day. Inside, there's a cafe by day and an upscale restaurant by night. In 2015, Meantime sold to beer giant SAB Miller, which will expand its product line for distant markets, but the original owners still operate this brewery with stubborn exactitude, and this is where they continue to pour unpasteurized, potent, small-batch brews.

The Pepys Building, Old Royal Naval College, SE10. www.oldbrewerygreenwich.com. ✆ **020/3327-1280.** Mon–Sat 11am–11pm; Sun noon–10:30pm. Tube: Cutty Sark DLR.

The Pride of Spitalfields ★★   Lovingly shabby, with a tired floral carpet and weary red upholstered banquettes, the backstreet boozer east of Brick Lane is the embodiment of a homey pub pulling pleasing pints. The upright piano is rarely played (recorded classic punk is preferred), the sewage system is finicky, the beer bottles are dusty, but the goings-on are lively and neighborly. Unlike in some neighborhood joints, they understand tourists, so if you're friendly, you'll have fun. In the afternoon, you can get cheap salt beef for a few pounds. James Hardiman, a suspect in the Jack the Ripper murders, was a "cats meats vendor" who drank here when it was called the Romford Arms, but today, a feline rules it: Don't accidentally sit on the entitled rescue house cat, Lenny, who has his own Twitter account (@LennyThePubCat) and the run of the place. He's the only pretentious one here.

3 Heneage St., E1. ✆ **020/7247-8933.** Mon–Sat 11am–11pm; Sun noon–10:30pm. Tube: Aldgate East.

The Princess Louise ★★★   This Victorian fantasia is worth a visit even if you don't drink, and it's just south of the British Museum, so you can do it conveniently. Your feeling that it's lost in time begins with the proud signage, a traditional marquee of gold lettering on black. The 1891 interior, built by the best craftsmen of its period and miraculously maintained in mint condition, astounds: Morris & Son etched glass, mirrors, mahogany privacy screens, cast-iron bar, Corinthian columns, Simpson & Son mosaic tile floor—even the men's room marble urinals are legally protected from alteration. There's no music, no TVs, and all of the libations are by the resolutely old-fashioned Samuel Smith, which has been brewing since 1758 in Yorkshire and still draws its water from its original well.

208 High Holborn, WC1. www.princesslouisepub.co.uk. ✆ **020/7405-8816.** Mon–Fri 11am–11pm; Sat–Sun noon–11pm (Sun 6:45pm). Tube: Holborn.

The Salisbury ★   The Covent Garden/Leicester Square location is unbeatable, and the ornate exterior and interior are unmistakably Victorian—ostentatious, just-how-drunk-was-the-designer Victorian, to be precise. Thrill to the Grecian urns in the brilliant-cut glass, the pressed-copper tables, and the nymphs entwined in the bronze lamps. Long a haunt of the city's theatrical community, it's now a suitable pit stop for any West End exploration. If you want food, try the "pie and a pint" including mashed potatoes, seasonal veggies, gravy, and beer, for £10—although it does burgers and fish and chips, too. Theater fans should check out the cellar, which is papered with posters, many of them rare, from '80s and '90s shows.

90 St Martin's Lane, WC2. www.taylor-walker.co.uk. ✆ **020/7836-5863.** Mon–Thurs 11am–11pm (Thurs 11:30pm); Fri 11am–midnight; Sat–Sun noon–midnight (Sun 10:30pm). Tube: Leicester Square.

The Ship & Shovell ★★   One of the most endearing configurations for any pub you'll ever see, it's cleft in two by an alley trod by commuters on their way to Charing Cross. On the north, there's a traditional Victorian-style space, and on the south, a cozier room with a languidly sloping floor and private snugs. A cellar links the halves. The bewigged tubby chap on the swinging sign is Admiral Cloudesley Shovell who, in 1707, wrecked his ship and drowned 800 sailors, which certainly gives the interior's nautical theme an ignoble context. It's special for another reason, too, being one of the few pubs in town to pour Dorset ales from Hall and Woodhouse brewers, a family brewer dating to 1777.

1-2 Craven Passage, WC2. www.shipandshovell.co.uk. ✆ **020/8391-1311.** Mon–Sat 11am–11pm; Sun noon–10:30pm. Tube: Charing Cross or Embankment.

4

20 Pubs You'll Love

WHERE TO EAT

The Ten Bells ★   It's said that Annie Chapman, one of Jack the Ripper's victims, downed her last beer at this Spitalfields boozer while another, Mary Kelly, picked up her clients outside, and for an icky period in the '70s, the pub capitalized on infamy by being renamed for their slayer. All that unsavoriness is past, and the hipsters are here. The pub's Victorian tilework has been restored, and a new mural was added to celebrate the modern artistic vitality of the neighborhood. Today the clientele is young and friendly, the furniture casually mismatched, and the pub is a cheerful specimen of a well-aled "local" that parties more intensely as the evening advances. Nicholas Hawksmoor's Christ Church, which towers next door, silently observes the latest mortals at play.

84 Commercial St., E1. www.tenbells.com. ℂ **020/7366-1721.** Mon–Wed and Sun noon–midnight; Thurs–Sat noon–1am. Tube: Liverpool Street.

Ye Olde Cheshire Cheese ★★★   Just the sort of rambling, low-ceilinged tavern you imagine London is full of (and was, once), it was built behind Fleet Street in the wake of the Great Fire in 1666, and because of steady log fires and regularly strewn sawdust, it still smells like history hasn't finished passing it by. In later generations, it played regular host to Dr. Samuel Johnson (who lived behind on Gough Square), Charles Dickens (who referred to it in *A Tale of Two Cities*), Yeats, Wilde, and Thackeray. You can get pretty well thackered yourself today: There are six drinking rooms, but the cozy front bar—of pallid light, candles in the fireplace, and antique paintings of dead fish—is the most magical. Observe the stuffed carcass of Polly the Parrot, enshrined above the bar since 1926 and "whose adept use of profanity would have put any golfer to shame," according to her obituary in the *New York American.* Don't confuse this place with the Victorian-era Cheshire Cheese pub at Temple.

Wine Office Court, off 145 Fleet St. ℂ **020/7353-6170.** Mon–Sat 11am–11pm. Tube: Blackfriars, Temple, or Chancery Lane. Bus: 4, 15, 26, 76.

Ye Olde Mitre ★★★   Suspended in a hidden courtyard and seemingly between centuries, this enchanter—no televisions, no music—was once part of a great palace mentioned by Shakespeare in *Richards II and III.* The medieval St Etheldreda's Chapel, the palace's surviving place of worship, stands outside. This extremely tiny pub (established in 1546 but built in its present form in 1772) has two entrances that feed either side of the bar. The one on the left grants you access to "the Closet," a fine example of a semiprivate sitting area called a "snug." The entrance on the right brings you face-to-face with a case containing a blackened stump said to be part of a cherry-tree maypole that Elizabeth I danced around. (Yeah, right, drink another one.) Suck down one of the house specialties: pickled eggs, for less than 80p. To locate this hidden idyll, seek a little alley among the jewelry stores on eastern Hatton Garden between 8 and 9 Hatton Garden. Leaving will be even more difficult.

1 Ely Court, off Ely Place, EC1. www.yeoldemitreholborn.co.uk. ℂ **020/7405-4751.** Mon–Fri 11am–11pm. Tube: Farringdon or Chancery Lane.

EXPLORING LONDON

England has been a top dog for 500 years, and London is where it keeps its bark. Many of the world's finest treasures came here during the Empire and never left. Most cities store their best goodies in one or two top museums. In London, riches hide everywhere. The major attractions could by themselves occupy months of contemplation. But the sheer abundance of history and wealth—layer upon layer of it—means that London boasts dozens of exciting smaller sights, too. You could spend a lifetime seeing it all, so you'd better get started.

Sightseeing discounts, such as 2-for-1s, are sometimes offered at **LastMinute.com** under Experiences. The heavily promoted **London Pass** (www.londonpass.com) gets you into a bevy of attractions for a fixed price (such as £52 a day or £71 for 2 days), but is unlikely to pay off in the small amount of time you're given to use it. Only the version that lasts 6 days (£116 adult, £80 child) would potentially pay off, but still only marginally and only if you don't take much time for meals.

Historic Royal Palaces operates The Banqueting House (p. 108), Hampton Court (p. 141), Kensington Palace (p. 110), Kew Palace (p. 144), and the Tower of London (p. 128). An annual membership pass will possibly save you money if you plan to see several of them; do the math (www.hrp.org.uk; ✆ **0844/482-7788;** £47 one adult, £71 two adults, £59 for one adult plus up to six children, £90 two adults plus up to six children).

BLOOMSBURY, FITZROVIA & KING'S CROSS

The British Library ★★★ MUSEUM   One of the planet's most precious collections of books, maps, and manuscripts, the **Treasures of the British Library** at the Sir John Ritblat Gallery, is displayed in a cool, climate-controlled suite of black cases and rich purple carpeting. It ought to be mobbed, but isn't. The library holds approximately 150 million items and adds 3 million each year, so when it puts the cream (about 200 items) on display, you will be positively astounded. The trove changes, but it has included:

Children's prices generally apply to those 15 and under. To qualify for a **senior discount,** you must usually be 60 or older. **Students** require ID for discounts. Some places offer **Family Tickets** with discounts for up to three kids with adults. Museums may post prices that include a voluntary **"gift aid"** donation, but you may ask to have it removed. In addition to closing on public holidays and on December 25 and 26 (Boxing Day), some heritage properties only open in the summer.

- Two of the four known copies of the **Magna Carta,** 800 years old in 2015
- The Beatles' first lyric doodles: "A Hard Day's Night" on Julian Lennon's first birthday card (with a choo-choo on it) and "Yesterday"
- The **Diamond Sutra,** the oldest known printed book, which was found in a Chinese cave in 1907 and was probably made by woodblock nearly 600 years before Europeans developed similar technology
- The *Codex Sinaiticus,* one of the two oldest Christian Bibles (the Pope has the other) and illuminated manuscripts from Buddhism, Jainism, and Islam
- Jane Austen's diary and writing desk
- Alexander Fleming's handwritten discovery of penicillin from 1928
- Michelangelo's letter to his dad telling him he had finished the Sistine Chapel and pages from **Leonardo da Vinci's notebook,** in mirror writing
- Works in the hand of Mozart, Handel, Beethoven, Dickens, Trollope, Charlotte Brontë, and more.
- An 11th-century copy of *Beowulf* on vellum, in Old English; it's the only surviving manuscript, written when Ethelred the Unready was king.

The King's Library, some 85,000 tomes assembled by King George III, floats in a glassed-in central tower and forms the core of the collection, like Thomas Jefferson's library does for Washington's Library of Congress—which means the King who lost America and a principal engineer of the loss provided the seed for their respective nations' libraries. The hall contains the **Philatelic Exhibition,** 500 vertical drawers containing thousands of rare stamps.

You can't handle books unless you're a scholar, but the Library encourages anyone to hang out in its public spaces. In addition to the Treasures, the Library presents about 150 annual talks featuring celebrities and historians and some strong temporary exhibitions (about £12; check www.bl.uk/whats-on), including recent ones on Gothic horror, comic books, and one on the Magna Carta that marked the first time Thomas Jefferson's handwritten copy of the Declaration of Independence was displayed in London, the city at which it was originally targeted. That's curator clout. Twice a day, you can book an £8 tour of the superlative facilities.

96 Euston Rd., NW1. www.bl.uk. ✆ **01937/546-060.** Free admission. Mon and Fri 9:30am–6pm; Tues–Thurs 9:30am–8pm; Sat 9:30am–5pm; Sun 11am–5pm. Tube: King's Cross St Pancras.

5

EXPLORING LONDON | Bloomsbury, Fitzrovia & King's Cross

London-Wide Attractions

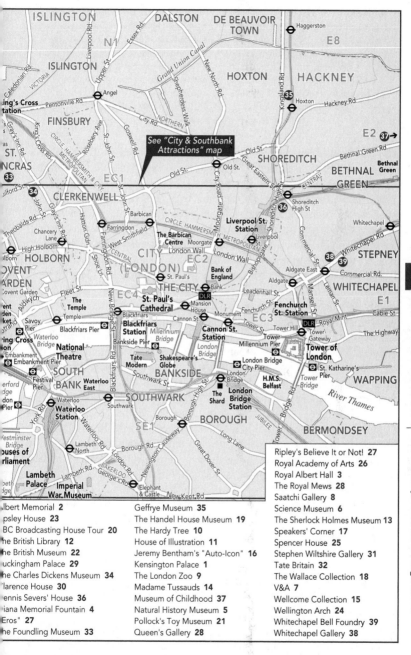

Ripley's Believe It or Not! **27**
Royal Academy of Arts **26**
Royal Albert Hall **3**
The Royal Mews **28**
Saatchi Gallery **8**
Science Museum **6**
The Sherlock Holmes Museum **13**
Speakers' Corner **17**
Spencer House **25**
Stephen Wiltshire Gallery **31**
Tate Britain **32**
The Wallace Collection **18**
V&A **7**
Wellcome Collection **15**
Wellington Arch **24**
Whitechapel Bell Foundry **39**
Whitechapel Gallery **38**

Albert Memorial **2**
Apsley House **23**
BBC Broadcasting House Tour **20**
The British Library **12**
The British Museum **22**
Buckingham Palace **29**
The Charles Dickens Museum **34**
Clarence House **30**
Dennis Severs' House **36**
Diana Memorial Fountain **4**
"Eros" **27**
The Foundling Museum **33**

Geffrye Museum **35**
The Handel House Museum **19**
The Hardy Tree **10**
House of Illustration **11**
Jeremy Bentham's "Auto-Icon" **16**
Kensington Palace **1**
The London Zoo **9**
Madame Tussauds **14**
Museum of Childhood **37**
Natural History Museum **5**
Pollock's Toy Museum **21**
Queen's Gallery **28**

Many of London's biggest museums are free to enter, but there's a catch: To make up the cash they miss out on, they find lots of other revenue streams. Many institutions charge £1 for a map and £10 or more for the most interesting temporary exhibitions. Many will also loan out their star works to other institutions around the world (so a marquee work named in this guide may be temporarily on vacation). Fortunately, this funding model also gives museums an incentive to operate superlative shops, publish wonderful keepsake guidebooks, and run gorgeous cafes that even attract people off the street.

The British Museum ★★★ MUSEUM Founded in 1753 and first opened in 1759 in a converted mansion, the British Museum is as much a monument to great craftsmanship as it is to the piracy carried out by 18th- and 19th-century Englishmen, who, on their trips abroad, plundered whatever goodies they could find and then told the bereft that the thievery was for their own good. Yet the exquisite taste of these English patriarchs is unquestionable, and now the British Museum may be the museum to beat all the rest. In fact, it's the top attraction in the country—6.8 million people visited in 2014. Put on your walking shoes because it's a gigantic tourism machine.

Dominating the glass-roofed **Great Court** like a drum in a box, the cream-and-gold, round **Reading Room,** completed in 1857, was once part of the British Library. Patrons had to apply for tickets, and they included Lenin and Karl Marx, who developed their political theories here; other habitués included Bram Stoker, Sir Arthur Conan Doyle, and Virginia Woolf, who wrote upon entering "one stood under the vast dome, as if one were a thought in the huge bald forehead which is so splendidly encircled by a band of famous names." The Reading Room is closed to the public.

If you don't know what to look for, the Museum will be a stupefying series of rooms of urns notable mostly for the zombified tourists staggering through them. Your forced enthusiasm may betray a dutiful, intellectual numbness, so do what you can to understand what you're seeing. Check the schedule of daily events by the pillar to the right as you enter the Great Court. Those will include some 15 daily free Eye-Openers, focused on particular rooms, and Hands On, which allow you to touch some things. Consider renting a hand-held audio/video tablet (£5, both adult and kids' versions) that spotlights 200 of the best objects. From 10:30am to 3pm on weekends, it lends free kids' backpacks including discovery maps. The website also has **free themed tour plans**—useful because staff rarely knows about anything except crowd control and maps range from £2 to £6 depending on the level of guiding information you want. Holdings are grouped in numbered rooms by geography, with an emphasis on the Greek and Roman Empires, Europe, and Britain. But don't miss:

o The museum's most famous, and most controversial, possessions are the so-called **Elgin Marbles,** gingerly referred to as **The Sculptures of** the **Parthenon** (rooms 18 and 19) to disguise imperialist provenance. These slab sculptures (called friezes and Metopes), plus some life-size weathered statuary, once lined the pediment of the famous Parthenon atop Athens' Acropolis but were defaced (literally—the faces were hacked off) by invading vandals (not literally—they were Persian) in the 500s. They suffered further indignities in a 1687 gunpowder explosion before being sawed off and carted away by Lord Elgin. They're laid out in the gallery in the approximate position in which they appeared on the Parthenon, only facing inward so you can admire them. Greece begs ceaselessly for their return, but the British have argued that they're better cared for in London. The smog-burnt portions left behind in Athens make a muddy issue of conservation and politics even murkier.

o Fragments of **sculptures from The Mausoleum at Halikarnassos,** one of the lost Seven Wonders of the Ancient World, loom in room 21. They're colossal in the original sense—one horse's head measures 2.1m (7 ft.) long.

o The pivotal **Rosetta Stone** (196 B.C.), in room 4, is what helped linguists crack hieroglyphics, and its importance to anthropology can't be exaggerated. Napoleon's soldiers found it in Egypt in 1799, but the British nabbed it in 1801. Consider it his first Waterloo. It now adorns everything from handbags to socks in the gift shops; free museums have to profit *somehow.*

o The grisly array of **Egyptian Mummies** in rooms 62, 63, and 64 petrify living children and on your visit, they'll probably be thronged as usual. In addition to the wizened, raisinlike corpses, there are painted coffins; the hair and lung of the scribe Sutimose, dating to 1100 B.C.; and scarabs galore. In room 64, check out the body from 3400 B.C., found in a fetal position without a coffin, which was preserved by dry sand. Beside it is another one, 400 years younger, that rotted to soil because it was laid to rest in a basket.

o Kids also stare moon-eyed at crumpled, leather-faced **Lindow Man** in room 50; he was discovered, throat slit, in a Cheshire bog nearly 2,000 years after his brutal demise. Preserved down to his hair and fingernails, he looks like he could spring to life and pound the glass of his case. Nearby (room 49) is the **Mildenhall Treasure,** a hoard of new-looking silver Roman tableware unearthed by Gordon Butcher, a Suffolk farmer, as he plowed fields in 1942; the saga of how Butcher was cheated of his fortune was chronicled by writer Roald Dahl. (Yes, pillage is something of a hidden theme in this place.) The **Lewis Chessmen** (room 40), made from walrus ivory, are whimsical favorites.

Room 70, on the upper floor, holds many remarkable holdings: the bronze **head of Roman Emperor Augustus,** found in the Sudan and unsettlingly lifelike (it still has its eyeballs of glass and stone); **The Portland Vase,** a black, cameo-glass jug that's very difficult to make even today; beside that, the historically important **The Warren Cup,** a First Century silver chalice

JEREMY BENTHAM'S "auto icon"

England's own Ben Franklin, Jeremy Bentham (1748–1832) was a philosopher, a progressive, and a subversive. Prison reformer, supporter of suffrage and the decriminalization of homosexuality, educator, and pen pal of U.S. president James Madison, Bentham worked to enable equal access to courts and schools, and he coined the words *international, maximize*—he codified *codification* itself.

He was so ahead of his time, he refused to stay in the past: His will stipulated eternal access to his corpse—the gift that keeps on giving, really. Starting years before his death, he purportedly carried around a pair of glass eyes that were intended for his future "Auto Icon" (auto = self, icon = image), which would represent him forever. After he expired, his body was dissected for students. In 1850, a colleague dressed his remains and Bentham's severed head was placed between his own feet. There his remains remain, in a lobby at University College London. His skeleton is under his original clothing and gloves. Unfortunately, his noggin was clumsily preserved and kids kept swiping it (in 1975, some hooligans held it for a £10 ransom), so today, it's stashed in the vaults, staring blankly with those long-pocketed blue eyeballs. You can see the real head on an electronic display. "Some visitors find it disturbing to look at," confesses the caption after you're already recoiling at the sight of the leathery thing. His new lifelike, doughy face sagely observes the current scholarly crop at UCL from beneath a straw hat. You'll find this freak show on the east side of Gower Street between University Street and Grafton Way, opposite the red-brick Cruciform Building. Go in the gates, veer right, and enter the door marked South Cloisters. Then hang a right and head for the stone lions (Tube: Euston Square).

graphically depicting homosexual sex in relief; and a 3rd-century Roman **crocodile-skin suit of armor.**

There's the **Great Court Restaurant** above the Reading Room that serves a full afternoon tea from 3pm for just £20—a bargain (© **020/7323-8990**).

Great Russell St., WC1. www.thebritishmuseum.org. © **020/7323-8299.** Free admission. Sat–Thurs 10am–5:30pm; Fri 10am–8:30pm. Closed New Year's Day, Good Friday, and Dec 24–26. Tube: Tottenham Court Road or Holborn or Russell Square.

Other Area Attractions

Pollock's Toy Museum ★ MUSEUM   Eddy Fawdry (and his wee dog Haggis) preside over this strange secret world of vintage toys, which he inherited from his grandparents and they from the Hoxton-based Pollock family, which made famous toy theaters. In room after creaky room, history stares back at you with doll's eyes: puppets, Gollywogs, the 1921 forerunner to G.I. Joe (Swiss Action Man), doll's houses, mechanical cast-iron banks, 1950s rocket toys, a board game based on the Falkland Islands invasion that was banned for being in poor taste. Stories are everywhere and the kitsch factor is through the roof, which brings us to the quirky, spirited building, which has been left leaning and unrestored since its erection in the 1780s (but received a new roof after the Luftwaffe blew off the original one). The ground-floor

In 1866, as laborers dug their way through his churchyard to create the new St Pancras Station, the Vicar of St Pancras noticed with horror that they were tossing aside thighbones and skulls. His cemetery contained the remains of Mary Wollstonecraft, J.C. Bach, Sir John Soane, and Ben Franklin's son, the last colonial governor of New Jersey, so the Vicar assigned Thomas, a young architecture student, with the unenviable task of overseeing the relocation of some 8,000 bodies. As he worked, Thomas carefully arranged their discarded headstones around a tree. The tree survives, and today its trunk grows around the markers. Now it is called the Hardy Tree—you see, young Thomas, who created this eerie living monument, was about to become the famous novelist Thomas Hardy. (St Pancras Old Church, Pancras Rd., NW1; www.posp.co.uk; ℭ 020/7424-0724; Tube: King's Cross St Pancras.)

shop stocks unusual, hard-to-find toys that don't cost much, including handmade items and cardboard theaters—the original inspiration for this one-of-a-kind time warp.

1 Scala St., W1. www.pollockstoymuseum.com. ℭ **020/7636-3452.** Admission £6 adults, £5 seniors and students, £3 children 3–16. Mon–Sat 10am–5pm; last admission 4:30pm. Tube: Goodge Street.

Wellcome Collection ★★ MUSEUM   Once upon a time, there was a very strange Midwestern pharmacist named Henry Wellcome. Henry got very rich and developed a taste for hoarding medical oddities, such as Napoleon's toothbrush, hair from George III, oil paintings of childbirth, and Japanese sex toys. When he died, he bequeathed a flashy museum for them, and which now makes for a highly amusing hour's visit. Besides the permanent collection, there's always one or two offbeat temporary ones pertaining to the human body and its uses—two recent ones were on sex research and corpse forensics. It's always one of the most compelling museums in town, and its sizable shop is one of the more intellectual.

183 Euston Rd., NW1. www.wellcomecollection.org. ℭ **020/7611-2222.** Free admission. Tues–Sat 10am–6pm (Thurs 8pm); Sun 11am–6pm. Tube: Euston Square or Warren Street.

SOHO, COVENT GARDEN & WEST END

The Courtauld Institute of Art Gallery ★★★ MUSEUM   Art historians consider the Courtauld one of the most prestigious collections on Earth, yet the tourist masses don't visit it, which makes for a very pleasant viewing experience. The small two-level selection is supreme, with several masterpieces you will instantly recognize. Among the winners are Manet's scandalous *Le Déjeuner sur l'herbe,* depicting a naked woman picnicking with two clothed men, and the artist's *A Bar at the Folies-Bergère,* showing a melancholy barmaid standing in front of her disproportionate reflection. There are multiple Cézannes, Toulouse-Lautrecs, and Tahitian Gauguins. Degas' *Two Dancers on a Stage* is iconic, as is Van Gogh's *Self-Portrait with Bandaged Ear.* Especially rare is a completed Seurat, *Young Woman Powdering Herself,* which depicts his mistress in the act of dressing and initially included his own face in the frame on the wall—he painted over it with a vase of flowers to avoid ridicule. **Somerset House,** its home, was once a naval center and later was where Londoners came to settle taxes and research family history. The central courtyard, beneath which lie the foundations of a Tudor palace, has a grove of 55 ground-level fountains that delight small children, and it's the scene of both popular summer concerts and a winter ice rink, plus a cafe by the popular charcuterie-bakery Fernandez & Wells. Check out the changing free exhibitions at the **East Wing Galleries** and see if anything interesting is showing at the **Embankment Galleries,** which charges £10 adults, £8 seniors/students, depending on what's on display. The terrace overlooking the Thames (from across the street) can be enjoyed for free.

Somerset House, Strand, WC2. www.courtauld.ac.uk. ℘ **020/7848-2526.** Admission £6 adults, £5 seniors, students, and children 18 and under; posted prices are higher and include a "voluntary donation." Daily 10am–6pm (9pm 1 Thurs/month). Tube: Temple.

The Foundling Museum ★★ MUSEUM Small but devastating, it tracks the history of the Foundling Hospital, which took in thousands of orphans between 1739 and 1953. This was a period in which kids were treated like rubbish: For example, in 1802 a law was passed limiting the time children could work in mills—to 12 hours a day. By that measure, it's clear that the benefactors were actually helping kids by locking them in this borderline prison. Don't miss the heartbreaking cases of tokens that mothers left at the doorstep with their babies. These tiny objects, into which a lifetime of hopes was imbued, never made it to their children lest they compromise anonymity. Also take the time to listen to the oral histories by some of the last kids to be raised by the Hospital; at the time of recording, they were elderly but still obviously quite shaken. Upstairs is a modest but respectable collection of 18th-century English works (Hogarth, Reynolds, Gainsborough), which believe it or not was one of the first permanent art exhibitions in the world. The composer Handel loved the Hospital. He wrote his *Messiah* as a benefit for the facility in 1754; a score is on display. The exercise grounds are now called Coram's Fields. Fittingly, it is the domain of the child; adults are not permitted to enter without one.

40 Brunswick Sq., WC1. www.foundlingmuseum.org.uk. ℘ **020/7841-3600.** Admission £8 adults, free for children 15 and under, £6 seniors and students. Tues–Sat 10am–5pm; Sun 11am–5pm. Tube: Russell Square.

London Transport Museum ★★ MUSEUM Try to imagine London without its wheeled icons: the red double-decker bus, the black taxi, and the Tube, which are the best of their kind in the world and a draw for visitors. In

Covent Garden's soaring cast iron-and-glass 1871 flower-selling hall where Eliza Doolittle would have bought her flowers, their development and evolution are traced with excellent technology (lots of ambient sounds and video displays, although some are getting grubby or outdated) and detail (there are even fake horse apples beneath the antique carriages). Besides a fleet of intact landmark vehicles you can board, such as Number 23, a steam locomotive that powered the Underground in its most unpleasant days ("a form of mild torture," wrote *The Times* then), there's also plenty of the system's famous Edwardian and Art Deco posters, many of which are so stunning they're art unto themselves—because of them, the gift shop, which doesn't require a ticket, is exemplary. Designers will appreciate the background on Johnston, the distinctive and oft-imitated typeface created by Frank Pick in 1916 for the Underground that could now be considered London's unofficial font. Along the way, you'll learn a great deal about shifts in London life, and you'll feel a twinge of embarrassment about the state of your own town's public transportation. It's a must for fans of London history and a good place to entertain children—but if you're childless, you'll need patience.

Covent Garden, WC2. www.ltmuseum.co.uk. © **020/7565-7299.** Admission £16 adults, £14 seniors and students, free for children 17 and under. Sat–Thurs 10am–6pm; Fri 11am–6pm; last admission 45 min. before closing. Tube: Covent Garden.

National Gallery ★★★ MUSEUM   When the bells of St Martin-in-the-Fields peal each morning at 10am, the doors promptly open on one of the world's greatest artistic fireworks shows—each famous picture follows an equally famous picture. Few museums can compete with the strongest, widest collection of paintings in the world—one of every important style is on display, and it's almost always the best in that genre. There are 2,300 Western European works, which is plenty to divert you for as long as you can manage, and 6 million visitors are drawn here every year, although most of them just wander around without getting properly close to the brushwork. Be different.

Galleries imperceptibly surge through time in a clockwise arrangement. The best course is to start in the Sainsbury Wing (through room 9 or from Pall Mall East), which will order viewings more or less chronologically. The map (£1) is a poor value since it omits many major works. To find a specific painting, track down a staffer wearing a lime green shirt. They're rare—the museum is focused on security, not on explication—but there's usually one in the Trafalgar Square lobby. Or just use the free Wi-Fi to look up the room number on the Gallery's website (you can recharge your phone in the downstairs Espresso Bar). Among the many noteworthy holdings:

Sainsbury Wing

o Piero della Francesca, one of the most sought-after Renaissance painters, is represented by ***The Baptism of Christ*** (1450s, room 66). With its then-advanced use of light and foreshortening, its faces verge on bemusement, and the dove, representing the Holy Spirit, seems to fly straight at viewers.

o Sandro Botticelli fell under the spell of the hardline reformer Savonarola. He burned many of his finest paintings in the Bonfire of the Vanities and changed to an inferior style, so his best works are rare; **Venus and Mars** (1485, room 58), depicting the lovers reclining, is one of them.

The Main Building

o Michelangelo's **The Entombment** (ca. 1500, room 8) is unfinished but powerful. The feminine figure in the red gown is now thought to be St John, but it's hard to know for sure, since the artist favored strong masculine traits.

o Kids love Holbein's **The Ambassadors** (1533, room 4), full of symbolic riddles that refer to the guy on the left, and famous for a stretched image of a skull that can only be viewed in proper perspective from the side. Get close; the fine brushwork extends even to the feathers on the shoes.

o Kids also love Quinten Massys' grotesque, porcine **An Old Woman** (*"The Ugly Duchess"*; 1513, room 5), thought to be a satire on ladies who try to look younger than they are, but possibly a woman suffering from a disease.

o Among other works, Rembrandt shows two self-portraits. One at age 34 (room 24, by the painting of a dragon eating a man's face off) is pridefully detailed to declare ego and prosperity; by age 63 (room 23), he's in simple clothes and broadly dolloping paint with a palette knife. The pair makes for a universal story of preening youth giving way to confident old age.

o George Stubbs' stark, life-size portrait of rearing stallion **Whistlejacket** (room 34) stops everyone in their tracks; it was painted in 1762 for its proud owner.

o The Gallery is rich in Peter Paul Rubens, with some 25 works attributed to him. His **Samson and Delilah** (1609–10, room 29) is known for Samson's muscular back and Delilah's crimson robe.

There's much more: George Seurat's almost-pointillist **Bathers at Asnieres** (1884, room 44), Van Gogh's **Sunflowers** (room 45, another in 46), Jan van Eyck's **The Arnolfini Portrait** (Sainsbury Wing, room 56), a mysterious but fabulously skillful depiction of light that dates to 1434, years ahead of its time. **Brueghels. Cézannes. Uccellos.** There's so much art here that you may want to go twice during your visit, and the Gallery is centrally located, so you can.

Posted signs are awfully straight-laced. Comprehensive audio tours covering 1,200 of the 2,000-odd works are £4 and come in themed varieties (impressionists technique), a $2 app catalogs more than 1,500 paintings, and a free version supplies 183 highlights. The website has some touring trail suggestions, but your visit would be best illuminated by some expert input. Check the info desk for events, such as the "Ten Minute Talks" about a single work; 45-minute, 1pm "Lunchtime Talks" about a specific work or artist; storytelling for kids; or the few hour-long tours (check the schedule online). Permanent displays are supplemented by temporary exhibitions, one free and one paid (£8–£18). The Gallery schedules most family activities for Sundays. The two restaurants are top-quality but overpriced, and besides, the view from the restaurant at the National Portrait Gallery (see below) is better. But don't miss the superlative gift shops, which will print you a color-matched custom copy of any of the 1,200 works or even mail a framed version home.

Trafalgar Square, WC2. www.nationalgallery.org.uk. ☎ **020/7747-2885.** Free admission. Daily 10am–6pm (Fri 9pm). Tube: Charing Cross or Leicester Square.

The National Portrait Gallery ★★★ MUSEUM   On paper, the concept of a portrait gallery sounds like Field Trip Hell. But actually, you'll be surprised how the best works capture the sparkle of life behind history's most charismatic shapers. Here, the names from your high school textbook flower into flesh-and-blood people, and the accompanying biographies are so sublimely evocative (Samuel Johnson is described as "massive, ungainly, plagued with nervous tics") that subjects come alive.

The ancient kings and queens have the most heft, partly because it's hard to wrap your brain around the fact that in many cases, the actual people posed in the same room as these very canvases. One of the most instantly recognizable paintings is the **Ditchley portrait of Elizabeth I** (room 2), in which the queen's jeweled gown spreads like wings and Her Majesty firmly glares at the viewer under stormy skies. Right away, it becomes clear that many artists are slyly commenting on the disposition of their sitters. The troublesome **Henry VIII** is shown in several likenesses. One is a delicate 1537 paper cartoon by Hans Holbein the Younger (for a mural at Whitehall—a rare survivor from that palace), in which the king suspiciously peers with flinty grey eyes—hinting at a shiftiness that His Majesty probably couldn't recognize in his own likeness, but that all who knew him feared (room 1). One painting of **King Edward VI,** painted when he was 9, is executed in a distorted perspective (called anamorphosis) that requires it to be viewed from a hole on the right side of its case (room 1). You'll also find **George Washington** (he was born an Englishman, after all), and one of the only authoritative images of **Captain James Cook** (room 14), who was so pivotal in colonial expansion. In room 12, look for the newly acquired **Chevalier D'Eon,** a male diplomat and fencing champion who lived as a woman in the late 1700s; in room 10 for the adorable little nose of William Hogarth in his terra-cotta bust; and in room 18, for the sketch of **Jane Austen** by her sister Cassandra—friends said it stank, but here it is. The **Brontë Sisters** appear together in an 1834 portrait found folded atop a cupboard in 1914; their alcoholic brother Patrick Branwell Brontë painted himself out but his ghostly image is eerily re-appearing (room 24).

Fortunately, the portraits don't stop when cameras were invented. **Margaret Thatcher** imperiously glaring over the grey gunwale of a dais at a Conservative Party Congress (room 32); Paul Emsley's warm oil-on-canvas of **Catherine, HRH The Duchess of Cambridge** (2012, room 39); a video of **David Beckham** sleeping in 2004 (room 38a). The bust of artist **Marc Quinn** is formed by 8 pints of his frozen blood (room 38). In contrast, a 1950

It's Free!

All of the following attractions charge no admission fees for their permanent collections. Not a shabby lineup!

The Bank of England Museum; The British Library; The British Museum; The Hunterian Museum; Museum of Childhood; Museum of London; Museum of London Docklands; The National Gallery; The National Maritime Museum; The National Portrait Gallery; The Natural History Museum; The Old Naval College, Greenwich; The Queen's House, Greenwich; The Royal Observatory (partly); Saatchi Gallery; The Science Museum; Sir John Soane's Museum; The Tate Britain; The Tate Modern; The V&A; The Wallace Collection; The Wellcome Collection.

sitting-room portrait of **Queen Elizabeth II** with her parents, **King George VI** and the **Queen Mum,** mines Rockwell-esque, just-us-folks imagery (Mum's about to pour tea, Dad's smoking) to make the Royal Family seem as normal and as middle-class as the Cleavers (room 31). Modern portraits tend to change often because there's simply not enough room to show everything. Just about everything can be printed as a poster in the gift shop.

Take the escalator to the top and work your way down over about 2 hours. The oldest works (Tudors, Jacobeans, Elizabethans) come first, and you'll progress forward in time—adding photography when canvas fatigue sets in. Frankly, it helps to know a little history so these pictures ring some bells, so consider visiting near the end of your trip, when many of these names will be fresh in your mind from your tours. The £3 audio guide starts out dull, but by the end, it uses archival recordings, which is cool, and there's a $2 smartphone app (there's free Wi-Fi) of the highlights. Bring kids; the desk lends free discovery trails for them.

Late Shift evenings (Thurs, Fri 6–9pm), programmed with DJs, talks, live music, and drawing sessions, are great fun. Also consider the pre-theater menu (£19 for two courses, £23 for three) served from 5:30 to 6:30pm in the rooftop Portrait Restaurant, which has a breathtaking view taking in Nelson's Column and Big Ben's tower, and it's better than the National Gallery's (© **020/7312-2490**).

St Martin's Place, WC2. www.npg.org.uk. © **020/7312-2463.** Free admission. Daily 10am–6pm (Fri 9pm); last admission 45 min. before closing. Tube: Leicester Square.

Sir John Soane's Museum ★★ MUSEUM   A doorman will politely ask you to check your bags. With good reason: These two town houses on the north side of Lincoln's Inn Fields are so overloaded with furniture, paintings, architectural decoration, and sculpture, that navigation is a challenge. The Georgian architect, noted for his egotistic neoclassicism (the Bank of England) as much as for his aesthetic materialism, bequeathed his home and its contents as a museum for "amateurs and students," and so it has been, looking much like this since 1837. It's as if the well-connected eccentric had just popped out to purloin another Greek pilaster, leaving you to roam his groaning wood floors, sussing out the *objets d'art* from the certifiable treasures. His oddball abode, which his will decreed must be left precisely as it was on the day he died, is a melee of art history in which precious paintings and sculpture jostle for space like baubles in a junk shop. Ask to join a tour of the **Picture Room,** built in an 1823 expansion, so you can watch its hidden recesses be opened, revealing layer upon buried layer of works (such as William Hogarth's 8-painting *The Rake's Progress,* a documentary of dissolution), filed inside false walls. Look sharp for Canalettos (which often fetch £9 million at auction) and a J. M. W. Turner (ditto). Curation appears convoluted and haphazard: The guides swear that although sunshine appears to pour onto the masterpieces through skylights, there are UV filters—yet architectural fragments from Whitehall Palace are plainly betrayed to the elements in the courtyard ("It was never covered because that's the way he wanted it," a guide says). You have to wonder how Soane could legally acquire antiquities such as the sarcophagus of Seti I, carved from translucent limestone, and you won't know because nearly nothing is marked. (Just how the Hogarth hoarder wanted it.) Download one of three free MP3 tours to make sense of the untidiness. Or take a 1-hour tour (£10): Tuesday and Friday at 11:30am, Wednesday and Thursday at 3:30pm. Mostly, a visit reminds you of the unseemly way in which privileged Englishmen used to stuff their homes with classical art as a way of stocking up on a sense of righteousness—but that doesn't mean it's not wondrous.

12 Lincoln's Inn Fields, WC2. www.soane.org. © **020/7405-2107.** Free admission. Tues–Sat 10am–5pm; candlelit nights 1st Tues of month 6–9pm. Tube: Holborn.

Other Area Attractions

The Benjamin Franklin House ★ LANDMARK   The only residence of the portly politico left standing is a sort of architectural preserve. Astonishingly, Franklin lived here in this boarding house by the Thames without his wife for nearly 16 years—he was here for the Boston Tea Party, the enactment of the Stamp Act, and his invention of the armonica—and it was only the Revolution (and scandal) that forced him to abandon his adopted home and move back to the Colonies. For much of his life Franklin was a fervent loyalist who, even as late as 1775, felt that the differences between Britain and the Colonies could be settled in "half an hour." Tours are conducted by a young actress playing the landlady's daughter, Polly Hewson, who became such a dear friend that she moved to Philadelphia and was with him when he died. In empty rooms, Polly tells wistful tales as recordings chime in with voices from her memory. (Mondays are for architectural tours without the actress.) Rewards are mixed. Exhibits are sparse (one exception is the ghoulish deposit of human bones in the backyard, likely left over from dissections by Franklin's doctor neighbor), and there are few kids' activities. But on the other hand, it's rare for a famous home of this age to have survived into our lifetime.

It's also humbling to see how this giant man made do with such small quarters. The worn wooden staircase, on which he got his exercise when French trollops weren't available, is so well preserved it feels ghostly.

36 Craven St., WC2. www.benjaminfranklinhouse.org. © **020/7925-1405.** Admission and tours (required) £7 adults, £5 seniors and students, free for children 15 and under; 5 timed tours daily. Mon and Wed–Sun noon–4:15pm. Tube: Embankment or Charing Cross.

The Charles Dickens Museum ★ MUSEUM Although Dickens moved around a lot, his last remaining London home, which he rented for £80 a year when he was 30, is now his testament. A museum since 1925, and restored to a period look in 2012 (when the attic and kitchen were opened for the first time), these four floors don't exude many vibes from the old guy; after all, he departed in 1839 after staying less than 2 years. It could be anyone's humble home. Still, his celebrity got a kick-start while he lived here: *Oliver Twist* and *Nicholas Nickleby,* arguably his biggest hits, were written while he was in residence, a short stroll from the Foundling Hospital for orphans. As you inspect his desk, his razor, bars from a prison where his spendthrift dad was locked up, an unpleasant realization sets in: Charles Dickens was a compelling character, but also a jerk. Tough on his kids and unfaithfully cruel to his wife, his greatest talent seems to have been for ego.

48 Doughty St., WC1. www.dickensmuseum.com. © **020/7405-2127.** Admission £8 adults, £6 seniors and students, £4 children 6–16. Daily 10am–5pm. Tube: Chancery Lane or Russell Square.

Cleopatra's Needle ★ LANDMARK Cleopatra's Needles—which Cleopatra had nothing to do with—were erected in Heliopolis, Egypt, around 1450 B.C., and inscriptions were added 200 years later. The Romans moved the granite spires to Alexandria, where they were toppled and buried in the sand, preserving them until the early 1800s. And after much peril during delivery, London's 224-ton needle was erected here on the river in 1878. New York City got one in 1881, and a third went to Paris. Two sphinxes were installed to guard it (some say backward, since they face the sculpture, not away from it). Just 140 years here wrecked what 20 Saharan centuries didn't: Pollution has rendered the hieroglyphs illegible. In 1917, German bombs scarred the western sphinx. The cast iron benches in the area were installed in preparation of its arrival in the 1870s. Look closely; you'll find sphinxes and camels hidden in the armrests.

Victoria Embankment. Tube: Embankment or Temple.

"Eros" ★★ LANDMARK When he finished his legendary fountain in the middle of Piccadilly Circus in 1893, sculptor Alfred Gilbert thought the playful maritime-themed sculptures on its base would be celebrated. Audiences have minds of their own. They responded to the archer god on top. But they even got that bit of admiration wrong—they thought he represented Eros, god of erotic love, when Gilbert had actually intended Anteros, god of requited love. Today, even Piccadilly Circus isn't a roundabout anymore—it's an interchange—but the ceaseless tourist crowd photographing Gilbert's misunderstood masterpiece at least puts the circus back into Piccadilly. Gilbert's fabulous fountain is now dry and full of McDonald's wrappers, but his misidentified god, ironically the one who punishes mortals for failing to return love, blesses the city as an icon.

Piccadilly Circus. Tube: Piccadilly Circus.

Hunterian Museum ★ MUSEUM   This ghoulish exhibition at the Royal College of Surgeons, now 2 centuries old, chronicles the life's work of John Hunter (1728–93), who elevated surgery from something your barber dabbled in to something a saw-wielding, germ-spreading "scientist" would, ahem, undertake. It's a macabre scene, crowded with thousands of specimens, including extinct animals, all tastefully presented in a modern, gleaming, two-level hall. Most of your time will be spent squeamishly perusing some 3,000 black-lidded jars of human and animal pathology and anatomy (many originally obtained by grave-robbers, a common practice then), plus a bone-grinding collection of crude surgical instruments that could rattle even the steeliest physician. Check out the cross-section of a chicken's head that Hunter grafted with a human tooth. Such Frankenstein projects were his stock in trade. In 1783, when a 7 ft.-7 in. man named Charles Byrne heard Hunter wanted to display his corpse after he died, he tried to escape that fate by being buried at sea in a lead-lined coffin; Hunter bribed fishermen to fetch it, and here the poor man's skeleton remains. Upstairs, as part of a history of surgery, you'll find an ill-conceived amputation buzz saw. In its first use, it became slick with blood, slipped, and lopped off a nurse's hand; both patient and nurse were killed by subsequent infection. Ask the good-humored staff questions, or else catch the weekly free guided tour, Wednesdays at 1pm (book ahead if possible).

35-43 Lincoln's Inn Fields, WC2. www.rcseng.ac.uk/museums. © **020/7869-6560.** Free admission. Tues–Sat 10am–5pm. Tube: Holborn.

WESTMINSTER & ST JAMES'S

For information on the Changing the Guard ceremony, please see p. 149.

Buckingham Palace ★★ HISTORIC SITE   If you were to fall asleep tonight and wake up inside one of the **State Rooms,** you'd never guess where you were. Is it opulent? No question. But if gilding, teardrop chandeliers, 18th-century portraits, and ceremonial halls could ever be considered standard-issue, Buckingham Palace is your basic palace. Queen Elizabeth's mild taste—call it "respectable decadence" of yellows and creams and pleasant floral arrangements, thank you very much—is partly the reason. Remember, too, that much of this palace was built or remodeled in the 1800s—not so long ago in the scheme of things—and that the Queen considers Windsor to be her real home. That's right: Buckingham Palace is a mere *pied-à-terre.*

All tickets are timed and include an audio tour that rushes you around too quickly. The route threads through the public and ceremonial rooms (nowhere the Royal Family spends personal time, and besides, the Palace is open only 2 months a year, when they're in Scotland) at the back of the Palace. (If you want to see highlights of the formal gardens, that's another £9.) Highlights include the 50m-long (164-ft.) **Picture Gallery** filled mostly with works amassed by George IV, an obsessive collector; the 14m-tall (46-ft.) **Ballroom,** where the Queen confers knighthoods; the parquet-floored **Music Room,** unaltered since John Nash decorated it in 1831, where the Queen's three eldest children were baptized in water brought from the River Jordan; and a stroll through the thick **Garden** in the back yard. It's definitely worth seeing—how often can you toodle around the spare rooms in a Queen's house, inspecting artwork given as gifts by some of history's most prominent names? But it's no Versailles. If you're in London any time other than August or September and spot her standard of red, gold, and blue flying above, you'll at least know the Queen is home. (If it's the Union Jack, she's gone.) So near, yet so far.

Buckingham Palace Rd., SW1. www.royalcollection.org.uk. ✆ **020/7766-7300.** Admission £21 adults, £19 seniors and students, £12 children 5–16. Apr and late July to late Aug daily 9:30am–7:30pm; Sept daily 9:30am–6:30pm; last admission 2¼ hr. before closing. Tube: Victoria or Green Park.

Churchill War Rooms ★★★ MUSEUM/HISTORIC SITE   One of London's most fascinating museums is the secret command center used by Winston Churchill and his staff during the most harrowing moments of Word War II, when it looked like England might become German. We regard the period with nostalgia, but a staggering 30,000 civilians were killed by some 18,000 tons of bombs in London alone and more than 65,000 innocent people were killed in Britain as a whole. Here, in the cellar of the Treasury building, practically next door to 10 Downing Street, the core of the British government hunkered down where one errant bomb could have incinerated the lot of them.

When the War ended, the bunker was abandoned, but everything was left just as it was in August 1945, and when it was time to make it a museum, everything was intact—from pushpins tracing convoy movements on yellowed world maps to rationed sugar cubes hidden in the back of a clerk's desk drawer. Although the hideout functioned like a small town for 526 people, with sleeping quarters, kitchens, radio rooms, and other facilities that would enable leaders to live undetected for months on end, it feels a lot more like your old elementary school, with its painted brick, linoleum walls, and round clocks.

Midway through, you disappear into the **Churchill Museum,** surely the most cutting-edge biographical museum open at this moment. Exhaustively displaying every conceivable facet of his life (his bowtie, his bowler hat, and even the original front door to 10 Downing St.), it covers the exalted statesman's life from entitled birth through his antics as a journalist in South Africa (where he escaped a kidnapping and became a national hero), to, of course, his stints as prime minister. You even learn his favorite cigar (Romeo y Julieta) and brandy (Hine). The entire museum is atwitter with multimedia displays, movies, and archival sounds, but the centerpiece will blow you away: a 15m-long (50-ft.) Lifeline Interactive table, illuminated by projections, that looks like a long file cabinet and covers every month of Churchill's life. Touch a date, and the file "opens" with 4,600 pages of rare documents, photos, or, for critical dates in history, animated Easter eggs that temporarily consume the entire table (select the original Armistice Day or the *Titanic* sinking to see what I mean). You could play for hours, dipping into his life day by day.

Clive Steps, King Charles St., SW1. www.iwm.org.uk. © **020/7930-6961.** Admission £16 adults, £13 seniors and students, £9 children 5–15; posted prices are higher and include a "voluntary donation." Daily 9:30am–6pm; last admission 5pm. Tube: Westminster.

Houses of Parliament ★★ LANDMARK   In olden days, England's rich overlords got together at the king's house, Westminster Palace, to figure out how to manage their peasants. Over time, the king was forced out of the proceedings and most of the Palace burned down. What remains is constructed to express the might of Empire riches and the lofty aesthetics of Gothic-revival architecture. Luckily, the nation allows you to tour a dozen stately halls and even to wander through its vaunted House of Lords and House of Commons when they're not in session. There are now two ways to see it: Choose a 100-minute guided group tour, which presents the usual issues of audibility and pace, or take it easy with the new 2-hour audio guide (and eavesdrop on groups whenever you want).

The historical highlight, oddly, is viewed almost in passing as a foyer where you buy rubber duckies with clock towers on their heads and commemorative magnets: massive Westminster Hall, one of the world's most precious spaces and a UNESCO World Heritage Site, was built in 1097 by William Rufus, son of William the Conqueror. Richard II commissioned its cherished oak hammer-beam ceiling before he was deposed in the 1390s. Charles I, William Wallace, Sir Thomas More, and Guy Fawkes were all condemned in it, monarchs lie in state in it—and your role in it is to pick up your audio tour. The rest of the Palace is roughly divided into three areas: those for the House of Lords (whose members inherit seats, done in rose with an unbelievable gilt sitting area where Queen Victoria would preside on designated occasions); the House of Commons (by far the most powerful, elected by the people, but plainer, with seats of blue-green under a hanging forest of microphones); and some flabbergasting lobbies, sitting rooms, and the "Robing Room" (golds, browns, burgundies), which the Sovereign flits through when she shows up once a year to kick off sessions. You walk right onto the floor of both Houses. Many delicious details are elucidated, from the knock-marks on the Commons door made by the Crown's emissary, the Black Rod, to the line in the carpet members may not cross when in the throes of vigorous debates. You can even see actress Glenda Jackson's staff mailbox; she's now an MP. Booking ahead is advisable, but you can try your luck for openings at the ticket office next to the Jewel Tower, across the street.

The Palace recently kicked off a popular new afternoon tea service (p. 69) overlooking the river. Frustratingly, the Elizabeth Tower (1859) beside the Houses—it contains the 13$\frac{1}{2}$-ton bell known as Big Ben plus four smaller bells—is only open to U.K. residents. If the green Ayrton Light atop it burns, Parliament is sitting after dark.

Bridge St. and Parliament Sq., SW1. www.parliament.uk/visiting. © **020/7219-4114.** Admission £25 adults, £20 seniors and students, £10 children 5–15, free for children 4 and under. Tours: Sat and most weekdays during Parliamentary recesses; times vary; always check ahead. Reservations recommended. Tube: Westminster.

Spencer House ★★ MUSEUM A home so lush that its current owner is Rothschilds banking company, which hosts diplomatic and corporate events here that make the world go round, is the only surviving London mansion with an intact 18th-century interior, and you can see tours of the ground floor and a portion of the first floor. The home was begun in 1756 as a love nest by Diana Spencer's ancestors (and, by extension, the future king's), and the lavish gilt and carved decor repeatedly invoke the symbols of fidelity and virility. Great War damage spooked the Spencer clan, who moved out in the 1920s, and since then, they've gradually transferred the most precious elements to their estate at Althorp, 193km (120 miles) north of the city, and replaced them with equally fantastic facsimiles—the fireplace library, for instance, took 4,000 hours to carve. The original Painted Room suite was once at the V&A. Groups are limited to 20, so arrive early to secure a spot.

27 St James's Place, SW1. www.spencerhouse.co.uk. © **020/7499-8620.** Admission £12 adults; £10 students, seniors, and children 15 and under. Sun 10am–4:45pm; closed Jan and Aug. Tube: Green Park.

Tate Britain ★ MUSEUM Tourists often wonder about the difference between the Tate Modern and this, its sister upstream on the Thames. Well, the Modern is for contemporary art of any origin, and the Britain, besides its calmer and more civilized affect, is mostly for British-made art made after 1500. Not to diminish the quality of the grade-A work on display here, but you won't spot many recognizable masterpieces. Britain has a historic knack for collecting masterpieces, not so much for creating them, so a lot of the work is rich with relevance but highly imitative of classical or Renaissance styles. The main collection has corporate sponsorship by BP, not as skilled with handling oil as the artists represented on the walls. Although the oldest portion of the collection, full of documentary or moralist works by William Hogarth, William Blake, and Joshua Reynolds, skillfully illustrates British life from centuries ago, it's hard to shake the feeling that, artistically speaking, Britain was playing catch-up with the rest of Europe. That changes when the galleries progress chronologically into the modern era, and works by visionaries such as Francis Bacon and James Abbott McNeill Whistler (granted, not English, but an American in England) reveal ebullient colors latent in the national mind.

Descriptions are academic ("this picture bridges the historical and the sublime") and paintings are hung salon-style, many at such altitude that

The Tate-to-Tate Boat

The most fun way to get between the Tates is not the Tube (a circuitous route) but the **Tate Boat** (www.tate.org.uk/visit/tate-boat; © **020/7887-8888**; £7 adults, half off kids 15 and under, Oyster rate 10% off, Oyster with Travelcard one-third off), a 220-seat catamaran that zips along the Thames every 40 minutes from 10am to 4:30pm (Mon–Fri) or 6:30pm (Sat–Sun) between the Tate Britain and the Tate Modern. Along the way, it supplies camera-ready views of the London Eye and the Houses of Parliament. Tate's entertainment! Buy at the piers or at a Tate.

lighting glare makes them inscrutable. The 1-hour tours go at 11am, noon, 2pm, and 3pm.

Shifting objectives consistently rotate beloved paintings into storage, a frustrating habit with Tate, but some masterpieces can be relied upon. J. M. W. Turner's trenchant *The Field of Waterloo* (room 1810) was painted in 1818, 3 years after the battle; its shadowy piles of corpses, and of bereaved family members searching them, made viewers question his patriotism. The oil-on-canvas *Carnation, Lily, Lily, Rose* (1840) is by another American who settled in London, John Singer Sargent, and it depicts children holding paper lanterns so luminous that when it was first exhibited in 1887, its worth was instantly recognized and it was purchased for the nation. John Everett Millais' depiction of a drowning *Ophelia* (1840) is also considered a treasure for its phenomenally tricky depiction of water; the artist painted the plants in the summer so he'd get them right and waited until winter to paint his model, a hat-shop girl, in a tub of water. Naturally, she caught a severe cold (he paid for her doctor's bill after her father threatened to sue). Check out the sculptures, too, including forms by **Henry Moore,** who gets two rooms, and Barbara Hepworth. But the crowning attraction here is the **Turner Galleries,** with their expansive collection of J. M. W. Turners. Turner (1775–1851), the son of a Covent Garden barber, was a master of landscapes lit by misty, perpetual sunrise, and the dozens of paintings testify to both his undying popularity and his doggedly British tendency to convey information purely by implication. Turner's work is lovely, if sleepy. Just don't sully his name in these halls; even his old sketchbook is dotingly preserved. A free app supplies expert audio descriptions of major works, but download it at home before going because it's over 100MB. Maps are £1.

Millbank, SW1. www.tate.org.uk/britain. © **020/7887-8888.** Free admission. Daily 10am–6pm; closes 10pm 1 Fri/month. Tube: Pimlico.

Westminster Abbey ★★★ HISTORIC SITE   If you have to pick just one church to see in London—nay, one church in the entire *world*—this is the one. The echoes of history are mind-blowing: The current building dates from the 1200s, but it was part of a monastery dating to at least 960. Every English monarch since 1066 has been crowned here (with three minor exceptions: Edward V, Edward VIII, and possibly Mary I). There are 17 monarchs interred here (their deaths date from 1066–1760), as are dozens of great writers and artists. Even if England's tumultuous history and the thought of bodies lying underfoot don't stir your imagination, the interior—in places, as intricate as lace—will earn your appreciation. A visit should take about 3 hours and should begin early, since entry lines are excruciating.

Unlike St Paul's Cathedral, which has an airy, stately beauty, the much smaller Westminster is more like time's attic, packed with artifacts, memorials, tombs, and virtuosic shrines. It's easy to feel overloaded after just a few minutes; by the time you've pocketed the (paltry) change from your admission ticket, you're already treading on the final resting place of poor William Bradford (died 1728 at age 32). It only gets busier from there. Take your time and don't get swept along in the current of visitors. Let them pass. There are stories to be told in every square meter of this place.

Inside the sanctuary, tourists are corralled clockwise from the North Transept. The royal tombs are clustered in the first half of the route, in the region of the High Altar, where coronations and funerals are conducted. The most famous rulers of all time are truly *here*—not in story, but in body, a few inches away behind marble slabs. Some are stashed in cozy side chapels (which once held medieval shrines before Cromwellians bashed them to pieces during the Reformation; some vandalism is still visible), but the oldest are on the sanctuary side of the ambulatory (aisle). The executed **Mary Queen of Scots** was belatedly given a crypt of equal stature to her rival, **Elizabeth I,** by Mary's son **James I,** who gave himself only a marker for his own tomb beneath **Henry VII**'s elaborate resting place. James I's infant daughter Sophia, who died aged 3 days, was given a creepy bassinet sarcophagus in the Lady Chapel.

If you have questions, approach anyone in a red robe; they're "vergers," or officers who attend to the church. They lead 90-minute tours (usually at 10am, but up to 5 times daily, for £3) and if you stump them, you may win an invitation to the atmospheric Library, a creaking loft that smells of medieval vellum and dust, where an archivist can answer you.

The South Transept is **Poet's Corner,** where Britain's great writers are honored. You'll see many plaques, but most (Shakespeare, Austen, Carroll, Wilde, the Brontës) are merely memorials. The biggest names who truly lie underfoot are Robert Browning, Geoffrey Chaucer (he was placed here first, starting the trend), Charles Dickens, Thomas Hardy (buried without his heart), John Gay, Rudyard Kipling, Dr. Samuel Johnson, Laurence Olivier, Edmund Spenser, and Alfred Lord Tennyson. Ben Jonson is commemorated here, but is actually buried in the Nave near Isaac Newton and Charles Darwin.

Now for a few Abbey secrets:

o That oak seat between the Sanctuary and the Confessors' Chapel, near the tomb of Henry V, is the **Coronation Chair.** Unbelievably, every English monarch since 1308 has been crowned on this excruciating-looking throne. The slot under the seat is for the 152kg (336-lb.) Stone of Scone, said to be used as a pillow by the Bible's Jacob, and a central part of Irish, Scottish, and English coronations since at least 700 B.C. After spending 7 centuries in the Abbey (except for when Scottish nationalists stole it for 4 months in late 1950), the Stone was returned to Scotland in 1996, where it's on view at Edinburgh Castle. It will return for every future coronation.

o **Oliver Cromwell,** who overthrew the monarchy and ran England as a republic, was buried with honors behind the High Altar in 1658. Three years later, after the monarchy was restored, his corpse was dug up, dragged to Tyburn (by the Marble Arch), hanged, decapitated, the body tossed into a common grave, and its head put on display outside the Abbey. (Didn't they realize he was already dead?) Today his much-abused cranium is at Sidney Sussex College in Cambridge. Cromwell's daughter, who died young, was mercifully allowed to remain buried in the Abbey.

o The **Quire** is where the choir sings; it comprises about 12 men and 30 or so boys who are educated at the adjoining Westminster Choir School, the last of its type in the world. The wooden stalls, in the Gothic style, are Victorian, but are so delicate they're dusted using vacuum cleaners.

The door to the **Chapter House** was made between 924 and 1030 and is Britain's oldest-known door. The Abbey's oft-overlooked **Museum,** in a vaulted undercroft, contains some astounding treasures, including **Edward III's death mask** (thought to be the oldest of its kind in Europe; it's made of walnut and doesn't ignore his facial droop, which resulted from a stroke), **ancient jewelry** "found in graves" (we know what that means—pried from skeletons), the **fake Crown Jewels** used for coronation rehearsals, 14th-century leather shoes and Roman tiles unearthed on the grounds, and the fateful **Essex Ring,** which Elizabeth I gave to her brilliant confidant Robert Devereux, telling him to send it if he needed her. He tried to, but his enemies intercepted it, and he was beheaded at the Tower of London in 1601. Oops.

Time seems suspended in the **Cloister,** or courtyard. But better gardens are hidden away. At the Museum, head for the corridor to the left and you'll find the fragrant and fountained **Little Cloister Garden,** blackened by 19th-century coal dust, and beyond that to the right, the wide **College Garden,** a tempting courtyard with daffodil beds, green lawns, and five plane trees dating to 1850. The garden is thought to be Britain's longest-established one, having been cultivated for nearly a millennium. Westminster School, started by the abbey's monks in the 1300s, stands nearby. (Incidentally, there haven't been monks in this complex for 550 years, yet Londoners persist in calling it an "Abbey.")

Get a real sense of the majesty of the space at a service. Evening prayer with choirs from around the world are at 5pm weekdays and sung Eucharist Sundays at 11am, plus a Sunday organ recital at 5:45pm and evening service with simple hymns at 6:30pm (but check ahead, since services are sometimes shuffled to smaller, but equally historic, chapels). Holy Communion is daily at 8am, Matins are at 10am, and Evensong is Saturdays at 3pm. Next door, pop into **St Margaret's Chapel** (free), which the monks built in 1523 so they'd be left alone in peace. The Germans didn't comply: Some southern windows were destroyed by a bomb and were replaced by plain glass, and in addition to damage to the north wall, Pew 3 remains charred.

Broad Sanctuary, SW1. www.westminster-abbey.org. ℭ **020/7222-5152.** Admission £20 adults, £17 seniors and students, £9 children 6–16, free for children 5 and under. Generally Mon–Tues and Thurs–Fri 9:30am–3:30pm; Wed 9:30am–6pm; Sat 9:30am–1:30pm; last admission 1 hr. before closing. Closed Sun for worship. Check ahead for closures. Tube: Westminster.

Other Area Attractions

The Banqueting House ★ HISTORIC SITE   The glorious palace of Whitehall was home to some of England's flashiest characters, including Henry VIII. In a wrenching loss for art and architecture—to say nothing of bowling heritage, since Henry had an alley installed—it burned down in 1698. But if you had to pick just one room to survive, it would have been the one that did, designed with Italianate Renaissance assurance by Inigo Jones and completed in 1622, which means Henry never set foot in it, but another fateful king set his *last* foot in it: In 1649, Charles I walked onto the scaffold from a window that stood in the present-day staircase, and met his doom under an axe wielded by Cromwell's republicans, many of whom (shades of modern fundamentalism here) thought that by executing the king of Divine Right, they were heralding the return of Christ himself. The reason to come here is to gape at the nine grandiose ceiling murals by Peter Paul Rubens in which the king is portrayed as a god. They give you a bold clue as to why the rabble would want to see His Highness brought low. Thoughtfully, mirrored tables help you inspect the ceiling without craning your head to behold why Charles lost his.

Whitehall at Horseguards Ave., SW1. www.hrp.org.uk. ℭ **084/4482-7777.** Admission £6 adults, £5 seniors and students (including audio tour), free for children 15 and under. Posted rates are higher and include a "voluntary donation." Daily 10am–5pm; last admission 45 min. before closing. Tube: Charing Cross or Westminster.

Clarence House ★ HISTORIC SITE   The Queen dictates who lives at which palace, and she herself lived at this four-story mansion, a part of St James's Palace, before she took the throne. Her mother dwelled here for nearly half a century until her 2002 death at age 101, and now it's chez Charles and Camilla. Charles, having a keener sense of public relations than any royal before him, decided to open the house, where royals have lived since 1827, during the summer when the family is away. You won't get to poke around the Prince's medicine cabinet since you can only see the ground floor. Clarence is more like a grand town house than a mansion fit for a king, and that reflects the Windsors' homey, cluttered style, heavy on paintings of horses and light on gilding and glitter.

Stableyard Rd., SW1. www.royalcollection.org.uk. ℭ **020/7766-7303.** Admission £10 adults, seniors, and students, £6 children 5–16. Aug Mon–Fri 10am–4:30pm; Sat–Sun 10am–5:30pm; last admission 1 hr. before closing. Tube: Green Park.

Jewel Tower ★ HISTORIC SITE   Built around 1365, it's one of only two remnants left from the 1834 fire that ravaged the Royal Palace of Westminster. This stone three-level tower, once a moatside storehouse for Edward III's treasures, has walls so thick it was later considered an ideal setting for taking accurate measurements. So you'll see some explanation of weights-and-measures standards and some relics dug up from the moat (a 1,200-year-old sword, a bulbous bottle from The Sun, a 17th-century tavern where Samuel Pepys drank). It's quiet and easily overlooked.

Abingdon St., SW1. www.english-heritage.org.uk. ℂ **020/7222-2219.** Admission £4 adults, £4 seniors and students, £3 children 5–15. Apr–Sept daily 10am–6pm; Oct–Nov 2 daily 10am–5pm; Nov–Mar Sat–Sun 10am–4pm. Tube: Westminster.

KENSINGTON & KNIGHTSBRIDGE

Apsley House ★★ MUSEUM   This is how you'd be rewarded if you became a national war hero: You'd get Hyde Park as a backyard. In 1815, Arthur Wellesley defeated Napoleon and became the Duke of Wellington and later, prime minister. The mansion, still in the family (they maintain private rooms), was filled with splendid thank-you gifts showered upon him by grateful nations, including a thousand-piece silver set from the Portuguese court, but he never seemed to get his nemesis off his mind. Under the grand staircase stands a colossal nude statue of Napoleon that the little emperor despised; the Duke cherished it as a token of victory. Apsley's supreme art stash, which was largely looted by the French from the Spanish royal family and never went home, includes a few Jan Bruegel the Elders, Diego Velazques' virtuosic *The Waterseller of Seville* (you can understand why it was the artist's favorite work, since just looking at it makes you thirsty); and Correggio's *The Agony in the Garden,* in a case fitted with a keyhole so the Duke could open it and polish it with a silk hanky. The Duke and his best friend lived here together after their wives died, and the whiff of faded masculine glory pervades the place like cigar smoke. In other circumstances, the Duke and Napoleon, who both liked fancy finery and fancier egos, would have been buddies. If you're also visiting Wellington Arch (see below), a joint ticket will save a couple of pounds.

149 Piccadilly. www.english-heritage.org.uk. ℂ **0870/333-1181.** Admission £8 adults, £7 seniors and students (including an audio tour), £5 children 18 and under. Apr–Oct Wed–Sun 11am–5pm; Nov–Mar Sat–Sun 10am–4pm. Check ahead for closures. Tube: Hyde Park Corner.

Diana Memorial Fountain ★ LANDMARK   In July 2004, the Queen came to Hyde Park, probably grudgingly, to open an unusual gated fountain designed to conjure the memory of the mother of her grandchildren and a longtime thorn in her side, Princess Diana. As designed by American architect Kathryn Gustafson, this graceful, O-shaped fountain undulates down a gentle slope, sending two flumes of water gurgling into a collecting pool. At three points, bridges carry you to the center. Rather than putting you in a state of remembrance, it may put you into a state of wanting to ride it on an inner tube. Reach it from the Alexandra Gate at Kensington Gore, Knightsbridge, up Exhibition Road, and don't confuse it for the Diana, Princess of Wales Playground in Kensington Gardens or the 17th-century Diana Fountain.

Between West Carriage Dr., Rotten Row, and The Serpentine, Hyde Park. www.royal parks.org.uk. ℰ **030/0061-2350.** Free admission. Nov–Feb daily 10am–4pm; Mar and Oct daily 10am–6pm; Apr–Aug daily 10am–8pm; Sept daily 10am–7pm. Check website for maintenance closures. Tube: South Kensington.

Kensington Palace ★ HISTORIC SITE   Most people know it as the place where Lady Diana raised Princes William and Harry with Prince Charles from 1984 to 1996, but now it's where Prince William, Kate, George, and Charlotte live when they're in town. (Sorry. You won't run into them in the bathroom.) It has been a royal domicile since 1689, when William and Mary took control of an existing home (then in the country, far from town, which inflamed William's asthma) and made it theirs. Handsome and haughty, with none of the symmetry that defined later English tastes, the redbrick palace is not as ostentatious as you might expect. At least from the outside. A 2013 "transformation" ruined the experience within. Historic Royal Palaces, grasping for currency, installed junky art installations (voices whispering from gramophones, graffiti-like quotations scrawled across carpets and walls) based on scandals that happened here. The venerable palace was stripped of most of its context and now it's a spook house for art snobs. The newly reopened King's Apartments, pegged to King George III and Queen Caroline, was explained to visitors not with a thoughtful historical dossier but with a scratch-and-sniff guide to odors that might have filled the palace once—kids may appreciate the costumed characters wandering about, but anyone who can reach the pedals knows it's all style over substance. Queen Victoria has her own section, but she's given the trashy treatment, too, and rather than teaching visitors what enabled a girl of 18 to rise to master the most powerful empire in the world, she is shown, misogynistically, in terms of gender roles: as a good girl, a loving wife, and a grieving widow. It's also misleading: One room draped in black leads you to believe Prince Albert died here, but no, he died at Windsor.

Thankfully, the walk-through still includes the magnificent King's Staircase, lined with delicate canvas panels whose perimeters are rigged with tissue paper slivers that will tear as a warning of shifting or swelling. The staircase is considered so precious that it was only opened to the public in 2004, 105 years after the rest of the palace first accepted sightseers. Also, in the Gallery there's a working Anemoscope, which has told the outside wind direction since 1694, and a map of the world as known in that year. You'll also get a chance to see gowns worn by HM the Queen, Diana, and Princess

Margaret, who also lived here. Overall, through, if you're short on time, this pandering Palace is no longer a must-see.

Kensington Gardens, W8. www.hrp.org.uk. ⓒ 084/4482-7777. Admission £15 adults, £12 seniors and students (including audio tour), free for children 15 and under; posted prices are higher and include "voluntary donation." Mar–Oct daily 10am–6pm; Nov–Feb daily 10am–5pm; last admission 1 hr. before closing. Tube: High Street Kensington or Queensway.

Natural History Museum ★★ MUSEUM   The commodious NHM, which attracts 5.3 million visitors a year (mostly families, and by far the most of the three big South Ken museums), is a true blockbuster and it's good for several hours' wander, but you'll have plenty of company. In all ways, it's a zoo. You get a hall of dinosaur bones, a taxidermist's menagerie, and case after case of stuffed goners. Mostly, you'll encounter the wildest creatures of all: lurching, wailing, scampering children in all their varieties. On weekends and school holidays, the outdoor queue can be an hour long, so go at opening and enter through Exhibition Road for lighter crowds. The trove is rich: At the top of the stairs, the **Treasures** gallery holds such historically meaningful stuff as a dodo skeleton and Britain's only moon rock. The pretend kitchen full of hiding places for insects and **Creepy Crawlies** (the **Green Zone**) are longtime visitor favorites, as is the **Red Zone** (the Earth Galleries), anchored by a toned-down, ride-along mock-up of a Japanese supermarket jolted by the 1995 Kobe earthquake. Even the dinosaurs (in the Blue Zone) are supplemented by scary robotic estimations of how they sounded and moved. The **Darwin Centre's** Cocoon looks like a seven-story egg laid in the back atrium; hidden inside are some 20 million bottled specimens (including those that came back on the *Beagle*) on 27km/17 miles of shelves, which you will not see. Most of the discussion here, and throughout the museum, is aimed at a child's mind, with signs answering such unasked questions such as why we study nature, but now and then you'll see an expert through a window into the stacks of Centre who can use a microphone to respond to more intelligent concerns.

Even if you don't give a hooey about remedial ecology, the cathedral-like 1880 Victorian building is unforgettable. Columns crawl with carved monkeys whimsically clinging to the terra-cotta and plants creeping across ceiling panels. Daily Nature Live talks are given at 2:30pm on a huge range of topics; they're put online, too. The Museum's brainiacs even cultivate a garden and pond (the Orange Zone; open Apr–Oct) that attracts a range of English creatures and flowers. Kids under 7 can borrow free Explorer backpacks with pith helmets, binoculars, and activities themed to Monsters, Birds, Oceans, or Mammals (they tend to run out early on weekends); and those 7 to 14 should look for the free Investigate hands-on lab in the basement (afternoons are less crowded). All that and the requisite ceiling whale.

Cromwell Rd., SW7. www.nhm.ac.uk. ⓒ 020/7942-5000. Free admission. Daily 10am–5:50pm. Tube: South Kensington.

Royal Albert Hall ★★ LANDMARK   In addition to being a great concert venue, the Royal Albert is also one of London's great landmarks, and you don't need a seat to enjoy it. Conceived by Queen Victoria's husband Albert and opened in 1871, a decade after his death from typhoid (Vicky was so distraught that she didn't speak at the opening ceremonies). You can take a 1-hour tour. The hall contains such oddities as Britain's longest single-weave carpet (in the corridors), the Queen's Box (still leased to the monarchy), and a spectacular glass dome (41m/135 ft. high and supported only at its rim). *Be warned:* You don't go backstage (that's for groups only). Some 320 performances a year are presented, many with less than 24 hours' set-up time, and a flow of sightseers would be in the way.

Kensington Gore, SW7. www.royalalberthall.com. ✆ **020/7589-8212.** Free admission to lobby, tours £12 adults, £10 seniors and students, £5 children 18 and under. Tours available most days; times vary, generally 9:30am–4:30pm. Tube: South Kensington.

Science Museum ★★ MUSEUM   It's really two museums, one old-fashioned and one progressive, that have been grafted together and embellished with a few tacky gimmicks and blatant corporate propaganda, but it's a firm family favorite. So many interesting exhibitions are on display here that you'll probably run out of time. The old-school section, which began collecting in 1857 and is split over six levels, is an embarrassment of riches from the artifact archives of science and technology: 1969's *Apollo 10* command module; "Puffing Billy," the world's oldest surviving steam engine; and the first Daguerreotype camera from 1839. In 2015, the rare clocks and watches of London's prestigious Clockmakers' Museum, most dating from 1600 to 1850, moved here from their overlooked space in Guildhall (p. 126). The upper floors are full of model ships and 1950s computers (second floor, where a £16.5 million hall about the Information Age has been installed), veterinary medicine (fifth floor), and in the hangarlike third floor, aviation. Highlights there: a complete De Havilland Comet, which was the first jetliner (1952), a slice of a jumbo jet, and a modified Vickers Vimy bomber, the first plane to cross the Atlantic without stopping. It was flown by Arthur Whitten Brown, who promptly became the first person to report jet lag. He called it something less catchy: the "difficulty of adjustment to the sudden change in time."

The high-concept wing buried in the back of the ground floor is easy to miss, but seek it out. A cobalt-blue cavern for interactive games and displays, it bears little relation to the mothballed museum you just crossed through. The Antenna exhibition (ground floor) is exceptionally cutting-edge, and updated regularly with the latest breakthroughs; past topics have included biodegradable cell phones implanted with seeds and building bricks grown from bacteria. The interactive exhibits of Launchpad (third floor; heat-seeking cameras, dry ice, and the like) enchant kids. But not everything in the museum is enchanting. The gift shop (mostly mall-style toys) and guidebook disappoint. And when you've got the actual Model T, why charge an extra £11 for a gimmicky IMAX 3D cinema or £6 on motion simulator rides? Fortunately, the merits override the patronization.

Exhibition Rd., SW7. www.sciencemuseum.org.uk. ✆ **087/0870-4868.** Free admission. Daily 10am–6pm. Tube: South Kensington.

V&A ★★★ MUSEUM   If it was pretty, well-made, or valuable, the British Empire wanted to possess it. As a decorative arts repository, the Victoria & Albert, occupying a haughty High Victorian edifice (it was endowed by the proceeds from the first world's fair, the Great Exhibition of 1851), is about the eye candy of objects—not so much for paintings—and if you're paying attention, it tells the story of mankind through the development of style and technique.

As for how to tour it, the ground floor, a jumbled grid of rooms, has lots of good stuff, but lots more bric-a-brac (Korean pots, 1,000-year-old rock crystal jugs from Egypt) that you'll probably walk past with polite but hasty appreciation. The second, third, and fourth levels have less space and therefore are more manageable.

Rooms are arranged by country of origin or by medium (ironwork, tapestries, and the like) but you'll want to see the **20th Century** (rooms 74, 76; level 3), which surprises by including objects you may have once kept in your home (a Dyson vacuum cleaner, mobile phones); the U.K.'s only permanent **Architecture** gallery (rooms 127–128a, level 4), for a nautilus-like preconstruction model of the Sydney Opera House; and endless slices of **medieval stained glass** (rooms 83–84, level 3). Wherever you go, if you see a drawer beneath a display case, open it, because many treasures are stored out of the light. More not to miss:

o The seven **Raphael Cartoons** (room 48a), 500 years old in 2015, are probably the most priceless items. These giant paper paintings—yes, paper—were created by the hand of Raphael as templates for the weavers of his 10 tapestries for the Sistine Chapel. Before Queen Victoria moved them here, they hung for around 175 years in the purpose-built Cartoon Gallery at Hampton Court Palace. The colors are fugitive, meaning they're fading: Christ's red robe, painted with plant-based madder lake, has turned white—his reflection in the water, painted with a different pigment, is still red. Yet the Queen recently decided people could take flash photos of it.

o None of the sculptures in the sky-lit **Cast Court** (rooms 46 and 46a) are original. They're casts of the greatest hits in Renaissance art, and they crowd the room like a yard sale. They were put here in 1873 for the poor, who could never hope to see the real articles for themselves. Find Ghiberti's doors to the baptistery at Florence's San Giovanni, whose design kicked off the artistic frenzy of the Renaissance. Michelangelo's *David,* floppy puppy feet and all; he was fitted with a fig leaf for royal visits. Depressingly, many of these replicas are now in better shape than the originals.

o Tipu Sultan of India hated imperialists. So, in the 1790s he commissioned an automaton of a tiger devouring one. A crank on **Tippoo's Tiger** (room 41) activates a clockwork that makes an Englishman's hand flail and an organ makes his gaping mouth moan. In the end, Tipu was killed by Europeans and the English got his Tiger after all. It has been a crowd favorite since 1808, when it was part of the East India Company's trophy museum.

o **The Great Bed of Ware** (room 57), a 10-by-11-foot four-poster of carved oak that dates to about 1590, was once a tourist attraction at a country inn, renowned enough for Shakespeare to mention it in *Twelfth Night:* "big enough for the bed of Ware." As you admire it, consider that in those days, bed canopies were installed to protect sleepers from insects that might tumble out of their thatched roofs and into their mouths. Canopied beds, a mark of luxury today, were a sign of a humbler home. Nearby is James II's silver-embroidered wedding suit (1673, room 56).

o The **Ardabil carpet** (room 42), the world's oldest dated carpet (copies lay on the floors of 10 Downing Street and Hitler's Berlin office alike), is from 1539. To preserve its dyes, it's lit 10 minutes at a time on every half-hour.

o The **Hereford Screen** (1862, Ironworks balcony) is a liturgical riot by Gilbert Scott, the architect of the "Eros" (p. 100) and the St Pancras Renaissance (p. 22). It took 38 conservators 13 months to restore the 8-ton choir screen to its full golden, brassy, painted, Gothic glory.

o The **Gilbert Collection** (rooms 70–73; closed until mid-2015) of impossibly fine jewel boxes, cameos, silver, and mosaics amassed by a rich enthusiast is so impressive it once had its own museum at Somerset House.

Questions about what you're seeing will be referred to the Info Desk, which in turn may be referred to a search on a computer screen, possibly your own. Such is the sad reality of today's heavily touristed museum. That's why planning pays off: Download a map and you'll save £1, and download its free app to see what hot-ticket exhibitions are coming. (The big one in 2015 was on Alexander McQueen for £16.) Free 1-hour introductory tours are given at 10:30am, 12:30pm, 1:30pm, and 3:30pm, with one for the Medieval and Renaissance galleries at 11:30am and another for the British galleries at 2:30pm. Kids can borrow delightful "Back-Packs" at a dedicated Families Desk in the Learning Centre, which contain activity sets that engage them in some of the museum's most eye-catching holdings. More goodies for kids are listed at www.vam.ac.uk/families and exhibited at the Museum of Childhood (p. 134). Even the cafe is gorgeous; have a coffee in the Gamble Room (1865–78), a visual feast in ceramic tile and enameled iron. Also visit the V&A's western exterior. Scarred during the Blitz, the stonework was left unrepaired as a memorial.

Cromwell Rd., SW7. www.vam.ac.uk. © **020/7942-2000.** Free admission. Daily 10am–5:45pm (Fri 10pm). Tube: South Kensington.

Other Area Attractions

Albert Memorial ★ LANDMARK Albert, Queen Victoria's German-born husband (and, um, first cousin), was a passionate supporter of the arts who piloted Britain from one dazzling creative triumph to another. But when he died suddenly of typhoid (some say Crohn's disease) in 1861 at age 42, the devastated Queen abruptly withdrew from the gaiety and remained in mourning until her death in 1901, shaping the Victorian mentality. She arranged for this astounding spire—part bombast, part elegy—to be erected in 1872 opposite the concert hall he spearheaded. Some of its nearly 200 figures represent the continents and the sciences, and some, higher up, represent angels and virtues. It's Victorian high-mindedness in stone. At the center, as if on an altar, is Albert himself, gleaming in gold. Guided explanations happen at 2 and 3pm on the first Sunday of each month, March to December (© **020/7936-2568;** no reservations required; £8).

Kensington Gardens. www.royalparks.org.uk. Tube: South Kensington.

Wellington Arch ★ LANDMARK When it was finished in 1830, it was intended as a triumphal entry to Buckingham Palace. Now it's the tourist equivalent of a shrug. Minor anecdotes of its relocation and the switch from Wellington's original statue on top to a smaller statue (*Peace descending upon War,* the largest bronze sculpture in Europe) are all this handsome landmark can muster in its little museum, which also discusses the period when the Arch served as a police station. If you buy a joint ticket with the Apsley House, across Piccadilly (see above), you'll save a couple of pounds; you can take an elevator up with the admission price.

Hyde Park Corner, Apsley Way, W1. www.english-heritage.org.uk. © **020/7930-2726.** Admission £4 adults, £4 seniors and students, £3 children 5–15. Apr–Sept daily 10am–6pm; Oct daily 10am–5pm; Nov–Mar daily 10am–4pm. Tube: Hyde Park Corner.

MARYLEBONE & MAYFAIR

BBC Broadcasting House Tour ★★ MUSEUM In 2014, the Beeb began admitting tourists to its lavish, newly renovated nerve center for news and radio. Expect a soft, low-impact 90-minute visit with lots of filler, such as how radio sound effects are recorded and listening to a recording of newsreader Bruce Belfrage supposedly delivering the news through a famous 1940 bombing raid (they don't tell you it's actually a 1950 re-enactment of the incident). You may not recognize many of the references to the programs that emanate from here, but the scope of the eight-story-high active newsroom (some 6,000 people work in the building, many in 12-hour shifts) and the histories of the older studios such as Radio Theatre are transfixing. A highlight is the old Broadcasting House, from which Winston Churchill made his "we shall fight on the beaches" speech and de Gaulle broadcast his resistance movement. The exterior sculpture of Prospero and Ariel was by the hand of Eric Gill, who is now famous for creating the Gill Sans font. You can also apply for tickets to tapings on the BBC website. There's a small kiosk for BBC-themed trinkets, and *Dr. Who* fans, rejoice: You can take pictures beside a Tardis at the tour's starting point. At night, look up at the illuminated column on the roof—it shoots a beam into the sky at 10pm, during the nightly news, to commemorate slain journalists.

Portland Place, W1. www.bbc.co.uk/tours. ☏ **0370/901-1227.** Admission £15 adult, £13 seniors, £11 students, £10 children 9–15. Children 8 and under not admitted; no same-day bookings. Daily 10am–6pm. Tube: Oxford Circus.

The Handel House Museum ★ MUSEUM/HISTORIC SITE   Here's a pleasant *Messiah* complex. This Mayfair building, the German-born composer's home from 1723 (he was its first tenant) to his death in 1759, has lived many lives—before the museum's 2001 opening, conservators chipped 28 layers of paint off the interior walls to uncover the original grey color. You'll see a video on Handel's life, and then move on, often attended by old dears serving as volunteers, to see the few humble rooms. They're furnished with period furniture that wasn't his, but not many artifacts. You're best off coming during one of the many concerts, held every week or so in a plain recital room (usually £9). Handel fans should also investigate the composer's collection at the Foundling Museum (p. 94), where he was a crucial patron.

25 Brook St., W1. www.handelhouse.org. ☏ **020/7495-1685.** Admission £7 adults, £6 seniors and students, £2 children 5–16 (free Sat–Sun). Tues–Sat 10am–6pm (Thurs 8pm), Sun noon–6pm. Tube: Bond Street.

Royal Academy of Arts ★ MUSEUM   Britain's first art school was founded in 1768 and relocated here to Burlington House, a Palladian-style mansion that now has a splendid courtyard in which to enjoy a coffee away from Piccadilly's fumes and an exclusive new restaurant, the Keeper's House. The art in a few of its 18th-century areas, the six John Madejski Fine Rooms, can only be seen on free tours. (Charles Darwin's *Origin of the Species* papers were delivered for the first time in the Reynolds Room on July 1, 1858.) The meat, really, is on the third floor. First, that's where to find Michelangelo's only marble sculpture in Britain, an unfinished circular relief of Mary with the babies Jesus and John. Because the main reason to come is whatever crowd-pleasing paid exhibition is on, you're always at risk of not having much fun. The biggest event, and always worth it, is the annual **Summer Exhibition,** which since the late 1700s has displayed the best works, submitted anonymously; careers are made by it. Don't miss the wooden red "Phone Box No. 1" tucked behind the front gate—it was the 1924 prototype for what we now recognize as an international icon.

Burlington House, Piccadilly, W1. www.royalacademy.org.uk. ☏ **020/7300-8000.** Free admission. Mon–Sun 10am–6pm (Fri 10pm); last admission 30 min. before closing. John Madejski Fine Rooms by free tour only: Tues–Fri 1pm; Wed–Fri also at 3pm; Sat 11:30am. Tube: Piccadilly Circus or Green Park.

Speakers' Corner ★ LANDMARK   Near the northeast corner of Hyde Park, where Edgware Road meets Bayswater Road, Londoners of yore congregated for public executions. By the early 1800s, the gathered crowds were jeering at hangings instead of cheering them, and the locale's reputation for public outcry became entrenched. An Act of Parliament in 1872 finally legitimized it as a place of free speech, and its tradition of well-intentioned protest has evolved into a quirky weekend attraction. Laborers and suffragettes fomented social change here, but these days, you're more likely to encounter a rogues' gallery of kooks and idealists. Anyone can show up, always on Sunday mornings after 7am, with a soapbox (or, these days, a stepladder), plus an axe to grind, and orate about anything from Muslim relations to the superiority of 1970s disco—but if they don't have the wit to appease the crowd, they stand a good chance of being jibed, or at the very least vigorously challenged. In true British style, most speakers refrain from profanity. Even the heckling is usually polite. ("Communists, violent racists, vegetarians," reported Arthur Frommer in 1957. "They undergo the finest heckling in the world, a vicious repartee . . .") While audience participation at this scholarly circus can be heated, it's usually based on facts rather than emotion—bellowing American talk radio hosts are not models for victory. The blather continues until late afternoon.

Tube: Marble Arch, exits 4, 5, 8, or 9.

The Wallace Collection ★★★ MUSEUM   A little bit V&A (decorative arts and furniture), a little bit National Gallery (paintings and portraits), but with a boutique French flair, the Wallace celebrates fine living in an extravagant 19th-century city mansion, the former Hertford House. Rooms drip with chandeliers, clocks, suits of armor, and furniture, usually of royal provenance, and there's not a clunker among the paintings. While other museums were stocking up on Renaissance works, the Wallaces, visionaries of sorts, were buying 17th-century and 18th-century artists for cheap, and now its collection shines. You might recognize Jean-Honoré Fragonard's *The Swing* (Oval Drawing Room), showing a maiden kicking her slipper to her suitor below. Peter Paul Rubens' *The Rainbow Landscape* is also here (East Drawing Room), as is the world's most complete room of furniture belonging to Marie-Antoinette (Study; look for her initials hidden around a keyhole on one cabinet). Thomas Gainsborough's *Mrs. Mary Robinson (Perdita)* (West Room) depicts the sloe-eyed actress in mid-affair with the Prince of Wales; she holds a token of his love, a miniature portrait, in her right hand. If she exudes a suspicious mood, it's for good reason—the Prince dumped her before the paint was dry. You must not miss the recently restored Great Gallery, a stupendous tour de force of world-class old master paintings. Red folders contain descriptions of pictures, and gold ones are for furniture—the information even tells who owned them before they got here. Be in the Ground Floor State Rooms at the top of the hour, when a chorus of golden musical clocks announce midday direct from the 1700s. Kids should grab a free trail map, which leads them to the most attention-holding works, but adults should get the audio guide which highlights 80 of the best items for £4. The Wallace Restaurant, in the covered courtyard, has an exemplary atmosphere but stupidly high prices, although its French-styled afternoon tea is under £20 or just £7 if you only want tea and scones.

Hertford House, Manchester Sq., W1. www.wallacecollection.org. © **020/7563-9500.** Free admission. Daily 10am–5pm. Tube: Bond Street.

THE SOUTH BANK, SOUTHWARK & BOROUGH

Imperial War Museum London ★★ MUSEUM   One of London's unexpectedly gripping museums has a deceptive name. It's not just for military buffs, and it's no gun-fondling armory. Instead of merely showcasing heavy implements of death which it does, the latest tenant of the commodious former mental hospital known as Bedlam takes great care to share the sensations, feelings, and motivations of soldiers and civilians caught in past conflicts. It is, in fact, a museum about *people* at war. In addition to easy-to-grasp background on major wars, the museum intelligently balances tanks and planes with intimate storytelling that unravels propaganda and connects you to the human experience. In 2014, the IWM was expensively renovated into a remarkably modern facility—while some exhibit areas were perhaps oversimplified, the First World War Galleries (reserve ahead in peak season) are the most advanced, best-stocked, most comprehensible, and most moving you'll ever see.

Lambeth Rd., SE1. www.iwm.org.uk. © **020/7416-5000.** Free admission. Daily 10am–6pm. Tube: Lambeth North or Elephant & Castle.

London Eye ★★★ OBSERVATIONAL WHEEL   The Eye was erected in 1999 as the Millennium Wheel, and like many temporary vantage points, it became such a sensation—and a money-spinner—that it was made permanent. It rises above everything in this part of the city—at 135m/443 ft. high, it's 1½ times taller than the Statue of Liberty. The 30-minute ride above the Thames affords an unmatched and unobstructed perspective on the prime tourist territory; there's no narration but six tablets elucidate what's before you. On a clear day, you can see to Windsor, but even on an average day, the entire West End bows down before you. That's why you should either go as soon as you arrive in the city, to orient yourself, or on your last day in town (my choice), when you can appreciate what you've seen. The whirl is adulterated by a lame "4D Experience" movie (a camera flies over London while a fan and bubbles blow in your face—it's Orlandofied twaddle) but it's included in the price and you can skip that if you want. Each of the 32 enclosed capsules, which accommodate up to 28 people, is climate-controlled and rotates so gradually that it's easy to forget you're moving—which means this ride will upset only the desperately height-averse. By the time you summit, you'll have true 360-degree views unobstructed by the support frame. The ticket queue often looks positively wicked, but it moves quickly, chewing through 15,000 riders a day, 800 per revolution. The Shard (p. 121) is much higher (and costs much more), which is why you have a much better chance of appreciating what you're seeing aboard the Eye. *Tip:* Booking on the Web saves waiting in the first queue and you'll save 10% off the price listed below. There's a host of options—basically, you pay up to £30 more to go anytime you want rather than stick to a reservation, but a standard ticket buys you the same view.

Riverside Building, County Hall, SE1. www.londoneye.com. © **0871/781-3000.** Admission £22 adults, £19 seniors (save 10% online at least 4 days ahead), £16 children 4–15, free for children 3 and under. Jan–Mar and Sept–Dec 10am–8:30pm; Apr–June 10am–9pm; July–August 10am–9:30pm. Tube: Waterloo or Westminster.

The Old Operating Theatre Museum & Herb Garret ★★

MUSEUM   In the mid-1800s, before general anesthesia, St Thomas' Hospital used the attic of a neighboring church for a space in which surgeries, mostly amputations and other quick-hit procedures, could be conducted where students could watch but other patients couldn't hear the agonized screams. When the hospital moved in 1862, it was abandoned, sealed away, and forgotten. It was considered lost until 1956, when an enterprising historian thought to look in the attic, and he found the secret surgical stadium behind a wall. Creep up the tight wooden spiral staircase once used by the bell ringer and you'll find the theater, now the centerpiece of a ghoulish, but carefully educational, museum delving into medical methods of the early 1800s, from herbal remedies to leeches. On a recent visit, a 7-year-old boy in a visiting school group nearly passed out during a mock bloodletting show-and-tell; the staff, accustomed to fainters, casually produced a pillow and a glass of water without halting the demonstration, proving that in the old days, medicine was less about science and more about soldiering on.

9a St Thomas St., SE1. www.thegarret.org.uk. © **020/7188-2679.** Admission £7 adults, £5 seniors and students, £4 children 15 and under. Daily 10:30am–5pm. Closed Dec 15–Jan 5. Tube: London Bridge.

Shakespeare's Globe ★ MUSEUM/LANDMARK

A painstaking re-creation of an outdoor Elizabethan theater, it tends to bewitch fans of history and theater, but it can put all others to sleep. Arrive early since the timed 40-minute tours fill up. Get a bad time, and you'll be stuck waiting for far too long in the UnderGlobe, the well-crafted but exhaustible exhibition about Elizabethan theater. Also avoid matinee days, since tours don't run during performances. The open-air theater was made using only Elizabethan technology such as saws, oak framing, pegs, and plaster panels mixed with goat's hair (the original recipe called for cow's hair, but the breed they needed is now extinct). The first Globe burned down, aged just 14, when a cannon fired during a performance caused its thatched roof to catch fire. It took a special act of Parliament, plus plenty of hidden sprinkler systems, to permit the construction of this, the first thatched roof in London since the Great Fire. The original theater was the same size (and stood 180m/591 ft. to the southeast), but it crammed 3,000 luckless souls. Today, just 1,600 are admitted for performances. If you'd like to see the location of the **Rose Theatre,** a true Shakespeare original, go around the corner to 56 Park St., where its foundations, discovered in 1989 and now squatted over by a modern office building, are

The South Bank, Southwark & Borough

open for visitors on Saturdays from 10am to 5pm. There's a video on how it was discovered and it also hosts regular performances (www.rosetheatre.org. uk; ℂ **020/7261-9565;** Sat 10am–5pm, free admission).

21 New Globe Walk, SE1. www.shakespearesglobe.com. ℂ **020/7401-9919.** Admission £14 adults, £12 seniors, £11 students, £8 children 5–15. Exhibition: early Oct to early Apr daily 9am–5:30pm; late April to early Oct daily 9am–5pm. Theater tours: daily 9:30am–5pm; check ahead for schedule changes. Tube: London Bridge.

Tate Modern ★★★ MUSEUM   In 2000, Bankside's most reviled eyesore, a goliath power station—steely and cavernous, a cathedral to soulless industry—was ingeniously converted into the national contemporary art collection and is now as integral to London as the Quire of Westminster Abbey or the Dome of St Paul's, with 5.3 million annual visitors, making it Britain's number-two attraction. The mammoth Turbine Hall, cleared of machinery to form a meadowlike expanse of concrete, hosts works created by major-league artists in its Hyundai Commission (once called the Unilever Series). People of every background frolic there as if it were a park. This building is a star.

Maps are £1. The galleries flow from floors two to six on the river side of the building. Holdings focus on art made since 1900 and are divided into four loose areas of thought: On Level 2, there's Poetry and Dream (about surrealism) and Making Traces ("works gathered in this wing capture making as

Museums: After Hours

Many attractions offer extended opening times for evening viewing. Often, extra inducements are tossed in, such as wine and sketch classes at the National Portrait Gallery and DJs at the V&A. These are the major "Lates" events that can really free up your daytime touring to include more sights:

Attraction	Late Opening
British Museum (p. 90)	Friday to 8:30pm
British Library (p. 86)	Tuesday–Thursday to 8pm
The Golden Hinde (p. 122)	Friday 7–11pm (first of month)
Handel House Museum (p. 116)	Thursday to 8pm
Hayward Gallery (p. 130)	Thursday–Friday to 8pm
London Canal Museum (p. 152)	Thursday to 7:30pm (first of month)
London Zoo (p. 148)	Friday to 10pm (selected nights)
National Gallery (p. 95)	Friday to 9pm
National Portrait Gallery (p. 97)	Thursday–Friday to 9pm
Natural History Museum (p. 111)	Friday to 10:30pm (last of month)
Royal Academy (p. 116)	Friday to 10pm
Science Museum (p. 112)	Wednesday to 10pm (last of month)
Sir John Soane's Museum (p. 98)	Tuesday to 9pm (first of month)
Tate Britain (p. 104)	Friday to 10pm (once bi-monthly)
Tate Modern (p. 120)	Friday–Saturday to 10pm
Victoria & Albert Museum (p. 113)	Friday to 10pm (last of month)
Wellcome Collection (p. 93)	Thursday to 10pm
Whitechapel Gallery (p. 131)	Thursday to 9pm

gesture, the trace of an action," whatever that means—Rothko and Krasner are here); on Level 3, you'll see the paid exhibitions (usually £12 or more); on Level 4, Structure and Clarity (abstract art) and Energy and Process (*arte povera,* a radical movement). Descriptions dwell on pretentious doubletalk and the incestuous art world culture, something you may ameliorate with the "Modern Art Terms" glossary smartphone app ($3), one of many apps the museum puts out to explain what its signs won't, so bring headphones. Onsite, rent a tremendous tour (£4, one version for adults, another for kids, and you can switch between them) of the highlights on a smartphone-like video device that embellishes on the works' meaning and context.

The formidable collection, one of the world's best for breadth, is always shifting, not just because the museum owns more than it can display (even in this hangar), but also because works vanish on short-term loans. Some heavy hitters never leave. My favorite: In Making Traces, seven of the nine mono-tonal series created by Mark Rothko for New York City's Four Seasons restaurant never fail to put visitors in a meditative mood (one of them, *Black on Maroon,* was restored after a 2012 vandalism incident). There are four free daily guided tours, usually at 11am, noon, 2pm, and 3pm; ask at the ground-floor desk to find out where. At the family desk, open on weekends and busy days, kids pick up free drawing kits or tours based on sounds. The shop on the bottom floor is a wonderland. Carve out refreshment time: The sit-down Tate Modern Restaurant on Level 6 can be inhospitable due to crowds (make a reservation: ✆ **020/7401-5103**)—but when I'm here, I beeline for the 30 first-come bar stools facing floor-to-ceiling glass over St Paul's and the Thames. Afternoon tea is just £15 (Fri–Sun), and the fish and chips platter with mushy peas has my approval for flavor if not price (£18). You can get the same dish for £5 less in the Tate Café on the second floor, but without that stirring view. At lunch there, kids 11 and under eat free if a grown-up buys a main course.

Bankside, SE1. www.tate.org.uk/modern. ✆ **020/7887-8888.** Free admission. Sun–Thurs 10am–6pm; Fri–Sat 10am–10pm. Tube: Southwark.

View from the Shard ★ OBSERVATION DECK   In 2013, the Shard, the tallest building in Europe (but not even in the top 50 worldwide), added an extremely expensive observation deck with timed tickets—sunset sells out ahead of time. Jude Law called it "about the most unfortunate name for a building in the world," and the jagged 306m/1,016 ft.-tall tower doesn't exactly fit in with its neighbors. Even its prices are bigger: green-screen souvenir photos, which staff desperately hustles you to purchase, start at £22, and a glass of champagne will be £10 to £12. After airport-style security and two ear-popping fast elevator rides, you emerge 244m/800 ft. up to some weird angel-like choir music and vertiginous floor-to-ceiling windows far, far over the city—so far that after the initial impression, the casual visitor isn't likely to discern most of what they're seeing. A few levels up (hoist yourself upstairs for the last three floors), there's a second patio level shielded at body-level from the elements. You can stay as long as you want, but there's no seating and no washrooms up there, so take care of business on Earth. There is one novel addition: Point a digital "TellScope" in the distance, and its screen reveals the same view at different times of day. The unblinking truth? The London Eye is more memorable.

Joiner St., SE1. www.theviewfromtheshard.com. *(C)* **0844/499-7111.** Admission £30 adults, £24 children 4–15, £5 discount booked 24 hr. ahead. Apr–Oct daily 10am–10pm; Nov–Mar and Sun–Wed 10am–7pm; Thurs–Sat 10am–10pm. Tube: London Bridge.

Other Area Attractions

Brunel Museum ★ MUSEUM/HISTORIC SITE Although the engineering contributions of Marc Brunel and his son Isambard Kingdom Brunel are largely taken for granted, here they're given their due. With the help of a shield system they invented, these pioneers executed the first tunnel to be built under a navigable river, but London's soft earth didn't make it easy. It took from 1825 to 1843, and this redbrick building marked by a chimney was where steam engines pumped the seeping water out as diggers toiled. The tunnel, lined with arches and Doric capitals, was a commercial flop that deteriorated into a subterranean red-light district. But it later found new purpose as a part of the Overground Line and new respect through this museum, which often creates special events to bring guests into the tunnel.

Railway Ave., SE16. www.brunel-museum.org.uk. *(C)* **020/7231-3840.** Admission £3 adults, £2 seniors, students, and children. Daily 10am–5pm. Tube: Rotherhithe.

The Design Museum ★ MUSEUM Just east of the Tower Bridge on the southern bank of the Thames, you'll find strictly contemporary top-drawer talent—the cool kids of current style. That makes it more of a gallery than a museum. The steep fee also means it's best for devotees of high design, not for average sightseers. Shows are explorations of random topics (race cars, architect Louis Kahn, the annual "Designs of the Year"), and if they're sometimes ostentatious, at least they're thought-provoking. In late 2016, the museum will move out to Kensington.

Shad Thames, SE1. www.designmuseum.org. *(C)* **020/7403-6933.** Admission £13 adults, £10 students, £7 children 6–15. Daily 10am–5:45pm; last admission 5:15pm. Tube: London Bridge or Tower Hill.

The Golden Hinde ★ MUSEUM Tucked into one of the few remaining slips that enabled ships to unload in Southwark (another is Hay's Galleria, downstream by the HMS *Belfast,* now converted to a boutique shopping area), is a 1:1 replica of Sir Francis Drake's square-rigged Tudor galleon, which circumnavigated the world from 1577 to 1580. This 1973 version, which is so tiny you will forever feel pity for those old explorers, made its own circumnavigation in 1980. Self-guided and hour-long guided tours are available daily, but check the schedule for regular Pirate Fun Days, Battle Experience events, and Tudor Fun Days for kids as well as sleepovers (£43, Mar–Oct) during which the little ones can dress in period clothes, hear tales from costumed actors, and help with shipboard tasks on an imaginary voyage.

Pickfords Wharf, Clink St., SE1. www.goldenhinde.com. © **020/7403-0123.** Tours £6 adults; £5 seniors, students, and children. Daily 10am–5:30pm. Tube: London Bridge.

HMS *Belfast* ★ MUSEUM   You'll feel as if the powerful 1938 warship, upon being retired from service in 1965, were simply motored to the dock wearing its grey patchwork camouflage livery and instantly opened as an attraction. Nearly everything, down to the checked flooring and decaying cables, is exactly as it was (although those mannequins with the bad toupees might have been added), making the boat a fascinating snapshot of mid-century maritime technology. Authenticity also makes it a devil to navigate, especially if you have any bags with you—sorry, no cloakrooms, sailor. Getting around its various decks, engine rooms, and hatches requires dexterity and a well-calibrated inner compass. You can roam as you wish, visiting every cubby of the ship from kitchen to bridge, all the while being thankful that it wasn't you who was chasing German cruisers (the *Belfast* sank the *Scharnhorst*) and backing up the D-Day invasion in this tough tin can. The price is too high for those with a lukewarm interest, but the new Upper Deck bar, atop the visitor center (a wine bar over a warship—appropriate?), has stellar views of the Tower of London and Tower Bridge—and an afternoon champagne tea that's just £15. Thanks, World War II!

Morgan's Lane, Tooley St., SE1. www.iwm.org.uk. © **020/7940-6300.** Admission £15 adults, £13 seniors and students, £7 children 5–15; posted prices are higher and include a "voluntary donation." Mar–Oct daily 10am–6pm; Nov–Feb daily 10am–5pm; last admission 1 hr. before closing. Tube: London Bridge.

THE CITY

Museum of London ★★★ MUSEUM   This repository's miraculous cache of rarities from everyday life wouldn't be out of place in the greatest national museums of any land, and it's sure to satisfy true history buffs. Displays contain so many forehead-smackingly rare or fascinating items that by the time you're two-thirds through it, you'll start to lose track. Exhibits start with local archaeological finds (including elephant vertebrae and a lion skull) before continuing to 3,500-year-old spearheads and swords found in the muck of the Thames. Voices from the past come alive again in chronological order: There's a 1st-century oak ladder that was discovered preserved in a well, Norman chain mail, loaded gambling dice made of bone in the 1400s, a leather bucket used in vain to fight the Great Fire of 1666, a walk-in wooden prison cell from 1750, Selfridge's original bronze Art Deco elevators, and far, far more. The biggest drawback is that you need to budget a few hours, otherwise you'll end up in a mad rush through the entire lower floor covering the Great Fire to now—and it'd be such a shame to miss diver Tom Daley's teeny Stella McCartney swim trunks. You also don't want to miss the Victorian Walk, a kid-friendly re-creation of city streets, shops and all from the 1800s (grab a card at its entrance to know what you're seeing). Also seek out the Lord Mayor's state coach, carved in 1757, which garages here all year awaiting its annual airing at the Lord Mayor's Show in November, and Great Britain's petal from the Olympic flame cauldron, on display alongside a re-creation of a portion of it (the original petals were given to each country they represented).

The museum, built into the Barbican complex beside a Roman wall fragment, is easy to combine with a visit to St Paul's, and it sells one of the best selections of books on city history. It also runs an excellent second museum in East London about Docklands (p. 134). Download its absorbing (and free) Streetmuseum app, which shows you archival images and historic facts that relate to wherever you're standing in London. So rich is this city in history that behind the scenes, the Museum owns the world's largest archaeological archive, which is open for tours a few times a year.

150 London Wall, EC2. www.museumoflondon.org.uk. © **020/7001-9844.** Free admission. Daily 10am–6pm. Tube: Barbican or St Paul's.

St Paul's Cathedral ★★★ HISTORIC SITE   The old St Paul's, with its magnificent spire, stood on this site for 600 years before it was claimed by 1666's Great Fire. It was so beloved that when Sir Christopher Wren was commissioned to rebuild London's greatest house of worship, he tried to outdo the original, devoting 40 years to the project and going one further by crowning it with a mighty dome—highly unusual for the time. My, how people talked.

St Paul's cost £750,000 to build, an astronomical sum in 1697 when the first section opened for worship, and now, it costs £3 million a year to run. Wren overspent so badly that decoration was curtailed; the mosaics weren't added until Queen Victoria thought the place needed spiffing up. Stained glass is still missing, which allows the sweep and arch of Wren's design to shine cleanly through. Many foreigners were introduced to the sanctuary during the wedding

A Poignant Pocket Park

Little-known **Postman's Park** is beloved by those lucky enough to have stumbled across it. Hemmed in between buildings, its central feature is the moving **Watts Memorial,** a collection of plaques dedicated to ordinary people who died in acts of "heroic self sacrifice." Have a seat on a bench and ponder John Clinton, 10, "who was drowned near London Bridge in trying to save a companion younger than himself" in July 1894. In 1893, William Freer Lucas tantalizingly "risked poison for himself rather than lessen any chance of saving a child's life and died." Alice Ayres saved three children from a burning house in 1885 "at the cost of her own young life." The commemorations ceased in Edwardian times, making these forgotten faces obscure once again. (West side of St Martin's-Le-Grand between St Paul's Cathedral and the Barbican Centre; 8am–dusk; Tube: St Paul's or Barbican.)

City & South Bank Attractions

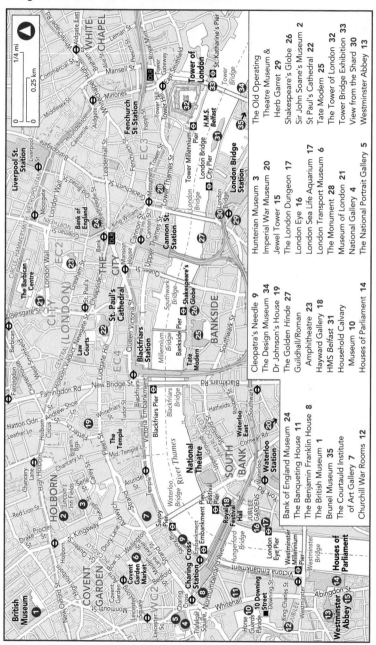

The Old Operating Theatre Museum & Herb Garret **29**
Shakespeare's Globe **26**
Sir John Soane's Museum **2**
St Paul's Cathedral **22**
Tate Modern **25**
The Tower of London **32**
Tower Bridge Exhibition **33**
View from the Shard **30**
Westminster Abbey **13**

Hunterian Museum **3**
Imperial War Museum **20**
Jewel Tower **15**
The London Dungeon **17**
London Eye **16**
London Sea Life Aquarium **17**
London Transport Museum **6**
The Monument **28**
Museum of London **21**
National Gallery **4**
The National Portrait Gallery **5**

Cleopatra's Needle **9**
The Design Museum **34**
Dr Johnson's House **19**
The Golden Hinde **27**
Guildhall/Roman Amphitheatre **23**
Hayward Gallery **18**
HMS Belfast **31**
Household Calvary Museum **10**
Houses of Parliament **14**

Bank of England Museum **24**
The Banqueting House **11**
The Benjamin Franklin House **8**
The British Museum **1**
Brunel Museum **35**
The Courtauld Institute of Art Gallery **7**
Churchill War Rooms **12**

of Prince Charles and Lady Diana Spencer in 1981, but the cathedral also saw a sermon by Martin Luther King in 1964 and Churchill's funeral the next year.

The **High Altar** has a canopy supported by single tree trunks that were hollowed out and carved, and its 15th-century crucifix and candlesticks require two men to lift. (They're nailed down, anyway. As one docent, a half-century veteran of Cathedral tours, lamented, "You'd be surprised what people try to steal.") Behind it is the **American Memorial Chapel** to the 28,000 American soldiers who died while based in England in Word War II. In a glass case, one leaf of a 500-page book containing their names is turned each day. The **organ,** with 7,000 pipes, was regularly played by Mendelssohn and Handel, and the lectern is original. The **Great West Doors,** largely unused, are 27m high (90 ft.) and on their original hinges; they're so well-hung that even a weakling can swing them open. In 2005, the Cathedral completed a £10.8-million cleaning program; a stone panel beside the doors was left filthy to show just how bad things were.

Eight central pillars here support the entire weight of the wood-framed Dome; Wren filled them with loose rubble. In 1925, engineers broke them open to find the debris had settled to the bottom, and they filled them again with liquid concrete. If you're fit, you can mount the 259 steps (each an awkward 13cm/5 in. tall, with benches on many landings) to the **Whispering Gallery,** 30m/98 ft. above the floor. Famously, its acoustics are so fine you can turn your head and mutter something that can be understood on the opposite side. That's in theory; so many tourists are usually blabbing to each other that you won't hear a thing, although it is a transcendent place to listen to choir rehearsal on a mid-afternoon. Climb higher (you've gone 378 steps now) to the **Stone Gallery,** an outdoor terrace just beneath the Dome, and catch your breath, if you choose, for the final 152-step push to the **Golden Gallery,**

The Forgotten Colosseum

Guildhall, a magnificent stone structure originally completed in 1440 but heavily rebuilt time and again, was once where Londoners went to pay taxes but today is used as the City's most regal events space. Partly due to World War II's wrath, the collection at its **Guildhall Art Gallery** is perhaps second-rate (for this city), although its works depicting London can be interesting. But the real reason to come is in the cellar: the foundation remains of the eastern entrance of **London's Roman Amphitheatre,** 2,000 years old, that was the largest in Britannia but was only discovered when the gallery was being built in 1987. It could hold some 7,000 spectators at a time when the entire population of London was only about 25,000, and slots carved into one of the rooms suggest there was once a trap door that could release wild animals to fight in the arena. Sometimes it's hard to believe the Romans trod the same streets as you, but here in the darkness deep underground, the bones of their abandoned plaything provide an eerie reminder. (Gresham St., EC2; www.guildhall.cityof london.gov.uk; ✆ **020/7332-3803;** Free admission except for exhibitions; Mon–Sat 10am–5pm, Sun noon–4pm; Tube: Moorgate or St Paul's.)

which requires you to scale the inner skin of the Dome, past ancient oriel windows and along tight metal stairs. It's safe, but it's not for those with vertigo or claustrophobia. The spectacular 360-degree city view from the top (85m/279 ft. up), at the base of the Ball and Lantern (you can't go up farther), is so beautiful that it defies full appreciation. For more than 250 years, this was the tallest structure in London, and therefore the top of the world.

If you miss the **Crypt,** you'll have missed a lot. In addition to memorials to the famous dead (such as Florence Nightingale and plenty of obscure war heroes), you'll find the tombs of two of Britain's greatest military demigods: **Admiral Horatio Nelson** (whose body was preserved for the trip from the battlefield by soaking in brandy and wine; the 72,000-ton weight of the Dome is borne by the walls of this small chamber), and **Arthur Duke of Wellington** (flanked by flags captured on the field of battle; they will hang there until they disintegrate). To the right of the OBE Chapel, in **Artists Corner,** there's a monument to poet **John Donne** that still bears the scorch marks it suffered in Old St Paul's during the Great Fire (they're on its urn, and it was the only thing that survived the conflagration), and you'll find the graves of the artists **J. M. W. Turner** and **Henry Moore,** plus **Christopher Wren** himself, who rests beneath his masterpiece. "I build for eternity," he once said, and so far, so good: In 2010, the cathedral celebrated 300 years since its completion. If you're hungry, scope out the cafe, since it's one of the cheaper options in this neighborhood.

Tours by volunteers, called "supers," leave at 10 and 11am, and 1 and 2pm. Listen closely, because they are the elder statesmen; many have been here for decades. Lest you forgot it's actually a cathedral, you can also worship here outside of sightseeing hours—for free.

St Paul's Churchyard, EC4. www.stpauls.co.uk. © **020/7246-8357.** Admission £17 adults, £15 seniors and students (including 90-min. guided tour, up to £2 cheaper online), £8 children 7–16, free for children 5 and under. Mon–Sat 8:30am–4:30pm; Sun open for worship only. Whispering Gallery and Dome 9:30am–4pm. Tube: St Paul's.

Tower Bridge Exhibition ★★ LANDMARK   In the late 1800s, there was no bolder display of a country's technological prowess than a spectacular bridge. Consider the Brooklyn Bridge or the Firth of Forth Bridge. This celebrates one such triumph. The museum is like two attractions in one. The first satisfies sightseers who have dreamed of going up in the famous neo-Gothic towers and crossing the high-level observation walkways. For them, it's a close encounter with a world icon. The second aspect delves into the steam-driven machinery that so impressed the world in 1894, and that will hook the mechanically inclined. The original bascule-raising equipment, representing the largest use of hydraulic power at the time, remains in fine condition despite being retired in favor of electricity in 1976. The raising of the spans is now controlled by joystick from a cabin across the road from the entrance (check "Bridge Lift Times" on the website to find out when, or download the free "Raise Tower Bridge" app to watch it happen in 360-degree augmented reality), and recently, a glass floor was installed in a portion of the upper walkway so visitors can get giddy to the sight of the river 42m (138 ft.) below their feet. How could such a proud monument survive the Blitz when everything around it got flattened? The Luftwaffe needed it as a visual landmark. It discounts tickets if you also buy entry to the Monument (p. 132).

Tower Bridge, on the side closest to the Tower of London, SE1. www.towerbridge.org. uk. ℂ **020/7403-3761.** Admission £9 adults, £6 seniors and students (discounts available online), £4 children 5–15. Apr–Sept daily 10am–6pm; Oct–Mar daily 9:30am–5:30pm; last admission 30 min. before closing. Tube: Tower Hill or Tower Gateway DLR.

The Tower of London ★★★ MUSEUM/HISTORIC SITE Every morning at 9am, a military guard escorts the keys to the Tower and its huge wooden doors yawn open again for outsiders. It's the most famous castle in the world, a UNESCO World Heritage Site, and a symbol of not just London, but also of a millennium of English history. Less a tower than a fortified mini-town of stone and timber, its history could fill this book. Suffice it to say that its oldest building, the four-cornered White Tower, went up in 1078 and the compound that grew around it has served as a palace, prison, treasury, mint, armory, zoo, and now, a lovingly maintained tourist attraction that no visitor should neglect. It's at the very heart of English history, and exploring its sprawl should take between 3 and 5 hours.

Tickets are sold outside the battlements. Hit the Welcome Centre, just past the Ticket Office, and grab a copy of the free "Daily Programme," which runs down the times and places of all the free talks, temporary exhibitions, and mini-performances. Plenty are offered—the Tower at times feels more like a theme park than a living museum with 1,000 years of history behind it. The prime excursion is the **Yeoman Warder's Tour,** led with theatrical aplomb by one of the Beefeaters who live in the Tower (there are about 100 residents, including families, but only one Beefeater, Moira Cameron, is female) and preserve it. Those leave every 30 minutes from just inside the portcullis in the Middle Tower. They're engaging, but juvenile—expect bellowing and histrionics, each reciting an identical script with a gleeful fetish for yarns about beheadings and torture. (In truth, you can count the people executed inside the Tower on your fingers and toes; it was considered an honor to be killed here, since it was private.) For reasons I'm about to explain, I suggest you double back and join the tour later in the day. If you'd like your history delivered without vaudevillian shenanigans, head to the gift shop on the right after Middle Tower and grab an audio tour (£4, but do it early; headsets run out). The official guidebooks (£5) here are pretty good, and they certainly help with orientation.

The key to touring the Tower is to arrive close to opening. At 9am, there's a short ceremony (see p. 149) during which guards unlock the gates for the day. Make a beeline for the two-star attractions since intimidating queues form by lunch: the Crown Jewels, in the Waterloo Block at the north wall (farthest from the Thames) and the White Tower, in the center.

As you enter the **Crown Jewels** exhibition, you'll see archival film of the last time most of the jewels were officially used, at the coronation of Queen

Elizabeth in 1952. After passing into a vault, visitors glide via people-movers past cases of glittering, downlit crowns, scepters, and orbs worn (awkwardly—they're 2.3kg/5 lb. each) by generations of British monarchs. Check out the legendary 105-carat Koh-I-Noor diamond, once the largest in the world, which is fixed to the temple of the **Queen Mother's Crown** (1937), along with 2,000 other diamonds; the Indian government has been begging to get the stone back. The 530-carat Cullinan I, the world's largest cut diamond, tops the Sovereign's **Sceptre with the Cross** (1661). The **Imperial State Crown,** ringed with emeralds, sapphires, and diamonds aplenty, is the one used in the annual State Opening of Parliament. After those come candlesticks that could support the roof of your house, trumpets, swords, and the inevitable traffic jam around the **Grand Punch Bowl** (1829), an elaborate riot of lions, cherubs, and unicorns that shows what it would look like if punch bowls could go insane. Because Oliver Cromwell liquidated every royal artifact he could get his hands on, everything dates to after the Restoration (the 1660s or later). Clearly, the monarchy has more than made up for the loss.

Touring the four levels of the cavernous **White Tower** requires much stair-climbing but takes in a wide span of history, including a fine stone chapel, Norman-era fireplaces and toilets, the gleaming **Line of Kings** collection of the Royal Armoury (even small children can't help but notice the exaggerated codpiece of King Henry VIII's intricately etched suit from 1540), and some models depicting the Tower's evolution (it's been much altered, but the six smallest arched windows on the White Tower's south side are original to the 11th century). After you're finished in here, you'll have an excellent overview of how the whole complex worked.

Once you've got those two areas under your belt, take your time exploring the rest. I suggest a stop in the brick **Beauchamp Tower** (pronounced "*Beech*-um," 1280), where important political prisoners were held and where you can still glimpse graffiti testifying to their suffering. In front of it on Tower Green is the circular glass memorial designating the **Scaffold Site,** where the unlucky few (including sitting queens Anne Boleyn and Lady Jane Grey) are said to have lost their heads. In reality, we don't know exactly where they were killed, but Queen Victoria wanted a commemorative site set, and because of the obvious dangers of displeasing the Queen, this spot was chosen.

The Ravens, Forevermore

Ravens probably first visited the Tower in the 1200s to feast on the dripping corpses of the executed, who were taken from Tower Hill (the public execution ground, near the present-day Tube stop) and hung outside the battlements as a warning. You've probably heard the modern legend that if the ravens ever leave the Tower, England will fall—so seven of the carnivorous birds are kept in cages north of Wakefield Tower, where they are fed raw meat, blood-soaked cookies, and the occasional finger from a tourist dumb enough to stick one between the bars.

The **St Thomas's Tower,** from the 13th century, is closest to the Thames and re-creates King Edward's bedchamber with authentic materials. Beneath it, **Traitor's Gate,** once called Water Gate, originally was used to ferry prisoners in secret from the Thames. Torture was never a part of English law, but it happened here anyway, and the **Bloody Tower** was where some of the worst stuff went down. Don't forget to climb the ramparts for that classic photo of the Tower Bridge. But save the extra quid and skip the Royal Fusiliers Regimental Museum, a dreary hodgepodge of military memorabilia.

Daily at 2:50pm, the guards parade outside the Waterloo Block to the Byward Tower. On Sundays, your admission ticket allows you to attend services at the **Chapel Royal of St. Peter ad Vincula,** the Tower's church, at 9:15 or 11am; otherwise, the only way to get in, and to see the marble slab beneath which Boleyn and Grey's decapitated bodies were entombed, is with a Yeoman Warder's Tour.

Tower Hill, EC3. www.hrp.org.uk. ⓒ **084/4482-7777.** Admission £22 adults, £17 students and seniors, £10 children 5–15; posted prices are higher and include a "voluntary donation." Nov–Feb Tues–Sat 9am–4:30pm and Sun–Mon 10am–4:30pm; Mar–Oct Tues–Sat 9am–5:30pm and Sun–Mon 10am–5:30pm; last admission 30 min. before closing. Tube: Tower Hill or Tower Gateway DLR.

Galleries of Valor

Hayward Gallery ★ MUSEUM   The principal exhibition space of the Southbank Centre, hidden on a back rampart of the vital nonprofit arts center, hosts terrific blockbuster shows, usually £11 to £20, which have included Ansel Adams, Roy Lichtenstein, 1920s Surrealism, and a 60-artist panorama of modern African art. It also takes itself quite seriously, which can be good for a laugh.

South Bank Centre, Belvedere Rd., SE1. www.southbankcentre.org.uk. ⓒ **087/1663-2501.** Admission £11–£20. Mon noon–6pm; Tues–Wed and Sat–Sun 11am–7pm; Thurs–Fri 11am–8pm. Tube: Waterloo.

House of Illustration ★ GALLERY   Among the just-rehabilitated warehouses and hot new hangouts at the back end of Kings Cross station, this newly opened gallery-cum-museum is dedicated to the art of illustration—sometimes the children's book kind (world-famous Roald Dahl illustrator Quentin Blake is on the board), sometimes the magazine kind, but always well-selected and a showground for talent. You'll find two changing exhibitions at a time plus a fantastic little gift shop.

2 Granary Sq., N1. www.houseofillustration.org.uk. ⓒ **020/3696-2020.** Free admission to 1 gallery; usually £7 adults, £5 seniors, £4 students. Tues–Sun 10am–6pm. Tube: King's Cross St Pancras.

Saatchi Gallery ★ MUSEUM   This collection of avant garde contemporary art, ranging from shockingly revealing self-sculpture to exhibitions of bright new names from around the world, used to be unmissable, but now it's too often a shill for luxury brands (Hermés, Rolls-Royce) that mount advertisements that masquerade as exhibitions. Check the current fare before committing. The collection is the only resident in the three-story, 6,500-sq.-m (70,000-sq.-ft.) former Royal Military Asylum building (1801) in Chelsea. It's not a good place for kids, though, since the philosophy is to present room-filling pieces without rope barriers.

Duke of York Sq., SW3. www.saatchi-gallery.co.uk. ℂ **020/7811-3070.** Free admission. Daily 10am–5pm. Tube: Sloane Square.

Stephen Wiltshire Gallery ★★ GALLERY   Stephen Wiltshire's ink-and-paper landscapes are haunting. They are twisting, intricately detailed, and eerily transporting although they use only black squiggles. Often they are several yards long. But there's one other thing about them: Wiltshire is an autistic artistic savant. He can draw accurate cityscapes from memory, correct to the number of windows and proportions of every house, after seeing the real view for just a few seconds. His studio is elsewhere, but you can marvel at his work, or take some home, at his gallery, open since 2006. Its location, the Royal Opera Arcade off Pall Mall, dates to 1818 and it's the world's oldest shopping arcade. It was essentially the first indoor shopping mall.

5 Royal Opera Arcade, Pall Mall, SW1. www.stephenwiltshire.co.uk. ℂ **020/7321-2622.** Free admission. Mon–Fri 10am–5:30pm; Sat 11am–4pm. Tube: Charing Cross or Piccadilly Circus.

Whitechapel Gallery ★★ GALLERY   When it opened in 1901, con-temporary art was viewed as a degenerate indulgence. Since then, the White-chapel has reliably led the development of new artistic movements. There's no permanent exhibition, freeing it to import whatever will grip audiences, so every new visit is a fresh experience. In 1939, it brought to Britain Picasso's newly painted *Guernica* as part of an exhibition protesting the then-current Spanish Civil War. Later it introduced Jackson Pollock's abstracts (now they're staples in the Tate museums), and now it gives berth to titillating sculptors such as Sarah Lucas and Rachel Whiteread. It's also something of a community center, and there's always a talk or screening going on.

77-82 Whitechapel Rd., E1. www.whitechapelgallery.org. ℂ **020/7522-7888.** Free admission. Tues–Sun 11am–6pm (Thurs 9pm). Tube: Aldgate East.

Other Area Attractions

Bank of England Museum ★ MUSEUM   The intermittently compelling tale of the B of E is recounted in appealingly patronizing but generous detail, accompanied by plenty of antiques from the vaults. That's fine if you understand finance, but most people lose the plot pretty quickly. Along the way are some fun oddities, including a million-pound note, printed in the early–19th century for internal accounting, and reimbursement claims from families of *Titanic* victims. There's lots of expensive swag, such as a primitive safe from 1700, heaps of silver treasures, and a gold bar so pure (1 part in 10,000 impure) that it was given to Queen Elizabeth as a coronation gift. Guess she didn't need it. It's also fun to watch Her Majesty age on the money over the years. The most popular exhibit is probably a 28-lb. standard gold bar encased in a clear plastic box, that you're challenged to lift. The rest of the Bank isn't open, but you can peek inside with the free Bank of England Virtual Tour app.

Threadneedle St., EC2. www.bankofengland.co.uk/museum. *© **020/7601-5545.** Free admission. Mon–Fri 10am–5pm. Tube: Bank.

Dr Johnson's House ★ MUSEUM/HISTORIC SITE   A rare surviving middle-class home from the 18th century (built in 1700), this slouching and brick-faced abode happens to be that of the famous lexicographer Samuel. He lived here from 1748 to 1759. If you're hoping to learn a lot about him, you'll have to spring for a book in the gift shop. Little substance is provided in the house itself, which fortunately merits some mild interest on its own terms (the corkscrew latch on the front door, which prevented lock-picking from above, is an example). The rooftop garret in which Johnson and his six helpers toiled to publish the first comprehensive English dictionary was burned out in the Blitz, ironically, by a barrel of burning ink which flew out of a bombed warehouse; you can still see some scorch marks on the ceiling timbers. Ink defined the house and nearly destroyed it, but it also saved it, because the printers who used it in the intervening years boarded up the walls, preserving them. While you're here, pop round the corner to the wonderful Ye Olde Cheshire Cheese pub (p. 85). Dr. Johnson sure liked to.

17 Gough Sq., EC4. www.drjohnsonshouse.org. *© **020/7353-3745.** Admission £5 adults, £4 seniors and students, £2 children 5–17. May–Sept Mon–Sat 11am–5:30pm; Oct–Apr Mon–Sat 11am–5pm. Tube: Blackfriars.

The Monument ★ LANDMARK   Back in 1677, it was the tallest thing (61m/200 ft.) in town and it made people gasp. Today, it's hemmed in by personality-free glass buildings. The Monument was erected to commemorate the destruction of the city by the Great Fire in 1666. Its 61m (202 ft.) height is also the distance from its base to the site of Thomas Farynor's bakery in Pudding Lane to the east, where the conflagration began. There's only one thing to do in this fluted column of Portland stone: Climb it. The spiral staircase of 15cm (6-in.) steps, which has no landings, gradually narrows as it ascends to the outdoor observation platform—a popular suicide spot until 1842, when a cage was installed. They'll tell you it's 311 steps to the top, but they're lying. It's 313 if you count the two steps before the box office. Check out the metal band snaking down the north side; it's a lightning rod, and it crosses along an inscription, in Latin, that blamed Catholics for starting the fire (the insult was chiseled off in 1831). It discounts tickets in combo deals with the Tower Bridge Exhibition (see above). Go on a pleasant day unless you'd like a good wind whipping, and be prepared to leave large bags downstairs.

Monument St. at Fish St. Hill, WC4. www.themonument.info. *© **020/3627-2552.** Admission £4 adults, £3 seniors and students, £2 children 15 and under (cash only). April–Sept daily 9:30am–6pm; Oct–Mar daily 9:30am–5:30pm; last admission 30 min. before closing. Tube: Monument or Bank.

EAST LONDON & DOCKLANDS

The part of London east of the City encompasses many square miles and dozens of separate neighborhoods, but most visitors will only hear it referred to broadly as "East London." It starts around Shoreditch and Whitechapel and as you go east, begins to incorporate rehabbed former industrial wastelands. Docklands, the area bordering the river, is rich in upscale condos and corporate offices. Greenwich is a gorgeous village-like neighborhood on the southern bank of the Thames. And in Stratford, the biggest population center of East London, everything seems newly made, including the Queen Elizabeth Olympic Park.

Dennis Severs' House ★★★ MUSEUM   This 1724 town house was dragged down by a declining neighborhood until the 1970s, when eccentric Californian Dennis Severs purchased it for a pittance, dressed it with antiques, and delighted the intelligentsia with this amusingly pretentious imagination odyssey—he called it "Still Life Drama." Other museums are unrealistically neat and cordoned off, but his house looks lived-in so the past feels as real as it truly was. As Severs, who died in 1999, put it, "In this house it is not what you *see,* but what you have only just *missed* and are being asked to imagine." You could go during the day, but it's the best Monday or Wednesday after dark for "Silent Night." As you approach, the shutters are drawn and a gas lamp burns. You're admitted by a manservant who speaks little. He motions you to explore the premises, silently and at your own pace. Suddenly, you're in the parlor of a prosperous merchant in the 1700s, and the owners seem to be home but in the next room. Candles burn, a fire pops in the hearth, the smell of food wafts in the air, and a black cat dozes in the corner. Out on the street, you hear footsteps and hooves. Room by dusky room, you silently explore corners overflowing with the implements of everyday life of past ages. It's as if the residents were just there, leaving toys on the stairs, beds rumpled, mulled wine freshly spilled, and tea growing cold. By the time you explore the attic, you'll have accompanied the house and its occupants through its decay into a collapsing slum. "Silent Night" is one of London's most invigorating diversions.

18 Folgate St., E1. www.dennissevershouse.co.uk. © 020/7247-4013. Admission £10 Mon daytime or Sun visits, £15 Silent Night visits. Day visits: Sun noon–4pm; selected Mon noon–2pm; last admission 45 min. before closing. Silent Night: Mon and Wed 5–9pm. Reservations required only for evenings. Tube: Liverpool Street.

Geffrye Museum ★★ MUSEUM   The complex, a U-shaped line of dignified brick houses built in 1714 for ironworkers, feels removed from the rush of the East End. Inside is a walk through the history of the home: re-creations of typical middle-class London abodes from the 1600s to the late–20th century, artfully arranged to appear lived-in, and complete with explanations of each item on display, including illuminating information about which pieces were necessary and which were merely trendy. To some, they're rooms full of furniture. To others, the Geffrye is a chance to understand how people of the past lived. You know which person you are. One building here is a restored almshouse for the poor; book timed tours to see how charity cases lived back in the day (check the website for the schedule; £3 adults, free for children 15 and under). On weekends, curators plan discussions, lectures, and kid-oriented crafts workshops, which gives the place much more energy than you'd expect from a design-based attraction. Especially on fine days from April to October, the grounds are an exceptional place to relax. The walled herb garden encourages touch, to release scents, and its period plots are historically accurate, cultivated with plants used in several eras, including Elizabethan and Victorian times.

136 Kingsland Rd., Shoreditch, E2. www.geffrye-museum.org.uk. ✆ **020/7739-9893.** Free admission, including audio tour. Tues–Sun 10am–5pm. Tube: Hoxton.

Museum of Childhood ★★ MUSEUM   The awesome V&A Museum chronicles kid-dom through the ages in this location, pulling from a considerable collection of toys, clothing, dollhouses, books, teddy bears, and games. Objects are placed at kids' eye level with simplified descriptions. Some young ones don't grasp the concept—toddlers burst into tears when they see a crib behind glass that they can't climb into—but if they're too young for exhibits, bring them to one of the four to five daily kids' activities, such as stories or drawing. Child-rearing history is also addressed; look for the "Princess Bottle" of 1871, which had a reservoir shape that allowed for quick milk dispensing but also incubated bacteria, a fact that wasn't realized until countless babies died. The MoC's double-galleried glass-and-steel hall, which has a cafe, is itself an artifact; it began its life in South Kensington as the home of the nascent V&A collection but was re-erected here in the 1860s—the fish-scale mosaic floor was made by female prisoners, many of whom were separated from their own kids.

Cambridge Heath Rd., E2. www.museumofchildhood.org.uk. ✆ **020/8983-5200.** Free admission. Daily 10am–5:45pm. Tube: Bethnal Green.

Museum of London Docklands ★★★ MUSEUM   Most of the city's museums would have you believe that London was always a genteel bastion of refined gentlemen. The real story lies in working men who shortened their own lives to put teacups into more privileged, manicured hands and in the labor that circulated profits from slavery into banks and onto City gallery walls. Housed in a brick rum-and-coffee warehouse from 1804, the three-floor museum, strong on plain-speaking explanations, traces the history of working on the Thames, starting with Anglo-Saxon times and ending now. You can inspect an intricate model of the medieval London Bridge, which like the Florentine Ponte Vecchio was stacked with homes and businesses but clogged the river's flow so drastically that it was a threat to life. You'll also roam "Sailortown," a creepy warren of quayside alleys, all shanties and low doorways, meant to evoke the area's early-19th-century underworld. Finally, the spotlight shifts to the harrowing Blitz, when the East End, taking the brunt of the Reich, was obliterated by fire from the sky and forced to reinvent itself as

Docklands Attractions

a corporate citadel. The whole circuit takes 2 to 3 hours. There's also an inter-active, river-themed play area for kids, Mudlarks.

No. 1 Warehouse, West India Quay, E14. www.museumoflondon.org.uk/docklands. © **020/7001-9844.** Free admission. Daily 10am–6pm. Tube: West India Quay DLR or Canary Wharf.

Whitechapel Bell Foundry ★ MUSEUM/HISTORIC SITE   America's Liberty Bell. Montreal Cathedral's Great Bell. Big Ben himself. Name an important chimer from Western history, and chances are Whitechapel Bell Foundry cast it. Sure, the Liberty Bell cracked, by which time it was too late to exchange it, but the foundry's craftsmanship is not in question—Guinness verified it as Britain's oldest manufacturing company, established in 1570, with lineage traceable to 1420. Back then, fulsome industries such as metal-working were found in the East End, where the prevailing winds would carry the grime out of town. This foundry, still operating in a brick-front building from the late 1600s, conducts tours of its cramped, messy workshops on some Saturdays—always when workers are off duty, because flying sparks and molten metal sting a little. A visit isn't plastic in any way; tours (full weeks or months ahead) dodge piles of metal dust, sand, shavings, and aged work-benches to collect around heavyweight bells cooling in their molds. Every aspect of the craft, from casting to buffing, is given its due. You'll even learn that the foundry uses a siren to tell workers when it's time for a break. Why? "Well," says the guide, "when you work in a bell factory . . . ." There's also a small museum and shop (teeny bells, musical scores for handbells), open weekdays, which don't require tickets.

32-34 Whitechapel Rd., E1. www.whitechapelbellfoundry.co.uk. ℂ **020/7247-2599.** Admission £14; children 13 and under not permitted. Shop open Mon–Fri 9am–4:15pm; tours once or twice monthly, Sat 10am, 1:15, and 4pm. Tube: Aldgate East.

GREENWICH

As soon as you step off the ferry 30 minutes east of Central London, you're in a UNESCO World Heritage Site. If you don't have time to go into the countryside, Greenwich will give you that small-town English feel. Start a visit at the city's official mini-museum, Discover Greenwich (10am–5pm), across from the Cutty Sark.

Cutty Sark ★★ HISTORIC SITE   The only clipper ship left in the world was launched in 1869 and by the end of its 52-year career had traveled the equivalent of to the moon and back carrying cargos including tea, wool, and furniture. By the sunset of its sailing life, it was a decrepit old thing, renamed *Ferreira,* having survived hurricanes in America and the loss of its mast in Cape Town, but its worst indignities came more recently. A 2007 fire twisted its iron frame and devastated its hull planking but fortunately, sails, masts, prow, figurehead, and deckhouses had been safely stored for a restoration. As you tour its hold, climbing stairs and weaving across decks, the white-painted framework is original, grey is new. Restoration provided an opportunity for the present lavish presentation: Today, it's as gorgeous as when Britain dominated the seas, and instead of floating in the Thames, it floats 3.6m (11 ft.) over a dry dock skirted by a glass canopy. At the end of their full ship tour, after much accidental head-banging on low thresholds, visitors can peep beneath the streamlined brassed keel. It's a slight cheat, because the hull originally was coated with Muntz metal, bitumen, and felt, but hey, it looks incredible. It'll never be speedy again, but it's never looked hotter. If you're also entering the Royal Observatory (p. 139), buy a combo ticket and save a few pounds.

King William Walk, SE10. www.rmg.co.uk/cuttysark. ℂ **020/8312-6608.** Admission £12 adults, £10 seniors and students, £6 children 5–15; posted prices are higher and include a "voluntary donation." Daily 10am–5pm; last admission 4pm. Tube: Cutty Sark DLR, Greenwich river ferry, or Greenwich National Rail.

Maritime Greenwich ★★★ HISTORIC SITE/LANDMARK   Situated on a picturesque slope of the south bank of the Thames, Greenwich once was home to Greenwich Palace, where both Henry VIII and Elizabeth I were born. The last part of the palace to be constructed, **The Queen's House** (1616, Inigo

THE MAGIC OF mudlarking

Twice a day, the Thames tide swells, rising as much as 23 feet. And when that great churn of water departs the city again at low tide, it leaves behind newly exposed detritus that has been lost in time, be it 16th-century clay pipes, fragments of Tudor beer steins, or pieces of Roman pottery. There is no program in place by the City to protect the incredible finds that are washing up every day. One of London's biggest secrets is you're free to pluck the remnants of centuries past before it's washed away again.

It's called mudlarking, and because it has its dangers, the wisest course is to go with a guide. I recommend joining one of the monthly Sunday morning mudlarking events run by London Walks (www.walks.com, p. 155). They're cheap (under £10), don't require reservations, and they're led by a trained archaeologist who can help you identify the bits you find, be it pebble or prize. Best of all, they'll make sure you don't wander somewhere illegal or get trapped somewhere dangerous by the quick-rising tide. You should also bring sensible, grippy shoes, clothes that can get dirty,

and consider rubber gloves. The river may not smell like it, but London's Victorian-era sewers sometimes release human effluvia into the flow and you could potentially catch something if mud gets into your body—and Georgian glass slices flesh as neatly as modern glass.

Rule Number One of mudlarking is: Eyes only. You're not allowed to dig, scrape, turn over rocks, or use a metal detector, at least not without a permit (obtained from the Port of London Authority). But "getting your eye in," as locals say, still allows you to discover incredible objects. If you find anything of archaeological significance, such as gold, silver, collections of coins, or truly remarkable whole potteries, you're supposed to let the experts at the Museum of London (www.museumoflondon.org.uk, p. 123) know, even if it's only through photographs. Mudlarking is something you can't do in Europe's other major population centers, where river flow was channeled into paved canals. But London is different. Here, history discovers *you* as you walk past. You only have to get close enough to identify it.

Jones, p. 138), still stands, but most of the grounds were rebuilt in the late Georgian period as the equally palatial Royal Hospital, a convalescence haven for disabled and veteran sailors now known as the **Old Royal Naval College** (p. 138). High on the hill, in Greenwich Park, is the **Royal Observatory** (p. 139), and between them stands the **National Maritime Museum** (see below). So many of these treasures are owned by the state that many entrance fees are waived; you can play the whole day without paying more than a few pounds. Stop by the Discover Greenwich visitor center, alongside the *Cutty Sark,* for background information.

Old Royal Naval College, SE10. www.ornc.org. © **020/8269-4747.** Free admission. Grounds: daily 8am–6pm. Buildings: daily 10am–5pm. Tube: Cutty Sark DLR or Greenwich National Rail.

The National Maritime Museum ★★ MUSEUM   Don't be put off by the topic. The world's largest maritime museum is extraordinarily kid-friendly, brimming with buzzy set-piece toys such as steering simulators and a giant play area that looks like a world map. So it's not as, ahem, dry as most would expect. Because so much of Britain's history from the 17th to 20th centuries was transacted via the high seas, this place isn't just about boats and knots. The facility has an endless supply of Smithsonian-worthy artifacts that would do any museum proud. Highlights include a musical stuffed pig clutched in a lifeboat by a *Titanic* passenger; and, most ghoulishly, the blood-stained breeches and bullet-punctured topcoat that Admiral Lord Nelson wore on the day he took his fatal shot (in a new gallery devoted to the man). Get the creeps from relics from Sir John Franklin's ill-fated 1848 Arctic expedition, including lead-lined food tins that likely caused the explorers to go mad and probably eat each other. Also excellent is the Atlantic Worlds display, which plumbs the British role in the slave trade, something few London museums touch upon. The museum is also not too flashy to present the viewpoint that through the East India Company, England looted India—in fact, the English word *looted* has Hindi origins. It's not all so gloomy, though; there are big set pieces such as figureheads, models, antique instruments, and entire wooden vessels. Weekends are full of free kids' events (storytelling, treasure hunts) that bring suburban London families pouring into the gates, and the fun Greenwich Market is running nearby then, too. Maps cost £1.

Romney Rd., Greenwich, SE10. www.nmm.ac.uk. ✆ **020/8858-4422.** Free admission. Daily 10am–5pm. Tube: Cutty Sark DLR, Greenwich river ferry, or Greenwich National Rail.

Old Royal Naval College ★ HISTORIC SITE/LANDMARK   This 1696 neoclassical complex, primarily the work of Wren, is mostly used by a university but offers two main sights: the Painted Hall and the Chapel. The **Painted Hall,** fresh off a major conservation, has incredible paintings by Sir James Thornhill that took nearly 2 decades to complete. It was the setting for the funeral of Admiral Nelson, but it may never have looked more glorious than today, because a 2013 restoration removed years of candle grime and even crusty food splatters from rowdy pensioners' banquets. **The Chapel,** in the Greek Revival style, is the work of James Stuart. Tours by accredited guides run daily at 11:30am and 2pm. If the ORNC's stately symmetry rings a bell, that's because it was used as a stand-in for Paris in the movie musical *Les Misérables.* It's also where you'll find **Meantime Brewing Company** (www.meantimebrewing.london), one of the city's hottest microbrewers and a supplier of restaurants across the city. It has plenty of garden space where you can kick back with very stiff pints.

Greenwich, SE10. www.ornc.org. ✆ **020/8269-4747.** Free admission. Grounds daily 8am–6pm; buildings daily 10am–5pm; Royal Chapel Sun at 11am for worship. Tours: reservations ✆ **020/8269-4799,** 90 min., £5 adults, free for children 15 and under. Tube: Cutty Sark DLR, Greenwich river ferry, or Greenwich National Rail.

The Queen's House ★ MUSEUM/HISTORIC SITE   Viewed from the river and framed by the newer Old Royal Naval College, the Queen's House enjoys as elegant a setting as a building could wish for. Inigo Jones took 22 years to come up with a then-revolutionary, Palladian-style summer retreat for Charles I's wife, Henrietta Maria, but it was completed only in 1638, just before the Civil Wars cut both Charles and his building schemes off at the head. Henrietta scurried off to France. The house has a few ho-hum galleries and displays (lots of paintings of ships and battles), but its nautilus-shaped Tulip staircase, plus other rooms, are considered to be haunted by an unknown specter, so have a camera ready.

Romney Rd., SE10. www.rmg.co.uk. © **020/8312-6565.** Free admission. Daily 10am–5pm. Tube: Cutty Sark DLR, Greenwich river ferry, or Greenwich National Rail.

The Royal Observatory ★ HISTORIC SITE/MUSEUM Commanding a terrific view from the hill in Greenwich Park, with the towers of Canary Wharf spread out in its lap, the Observatory is yet another creation of Christopher Wren (from 1675), and the place from which time zones emanate. Historically the Empire's most important house for celestial observation, it houses significant relics of star-peeping, but the paid areas aren't worth the money. Most of the good stuff—marked on the map in red—is free, including a small Astronomy Centre and an exhibition on time. The only things admission buys you is an unremarkable ceiling-projection planetarium and the sparsely furnished, borderline-interesting Flamsteed House by Wren, which includes a collection of clocks used in an 18th-century competition to crack the mystery of measuring longitude, the solution of which ushered the English Empire to worldwide dominance. You'd have to really be interested in that contest to make the ticket pay off, and there's only a dry audio tour for illumination. Most people plunk down admission not because they care about those but to gain access to the Meridian Courtyard. The Prime Meridian, located at precisely 0° longitude (the equator is 0° latitude), crosses through the grounds and hordes of coach tourists pay to wait an hour for a silly Instagram moment of straddling the line with a foot in two hemispheres at once—but the secret is they don't have to. The line continues down the wall on the walkway north of the courtyard, where the Meridian is free and there's never a wait. In the old days, the red Time Ball fell precisely at 1pm daily so that the city could synchronize its clocks; it still rises at 12:55pm and drops 5 minutes later. You could set your watch by it, but technically, you already do. If you're also interested in the *Cutty Sark* (see above), a combo ticket will save you a few pounds.

Greenwich Park, Greenwich, SE10. www.rmg.co.uk. © **020/8312-6565.** Free admission for most of grounds. Flamsteed House and Meridian Courtyard: £6 adults, £5 seniors and students, £2 children 15 and under. Planetarium: £7 adults, £6 seniors and students, £5 children 5–15. Combination ticket: £12 adults, £10 seniors and students, £6 children 15 and under. Daily 10am–6pm; last admission 5:30pm. Tube: Cutty Sark DLR, Greenwich river ferry, or Greenwich National Rail.

Up at the O2 ★★ TOUR Climbers, about 10 at a time, hook into a safety rigging system and follow a guide over a tensile fabric catwalk laid a

The Millennium Dome was built on a toxic peninsula wasteland on the Thames in the '90s. Conceived as a showplace for what turned out to be a poorly attended turn-of-the-century exposition, it had some elements that were clever in theory: The world's largest domed structure, it was (and is) supported by a dozen 100m-tall yellow towers, one for each hour on the clock in honor of nearby Greenwich Mean Time. But that preening and meaningless symbolism cost a shocking £789 million, and then it stood empty for half a decade while locals cursed the eyesore and argued about how to use it. In 2007, it was finally reborn as the city's finest performance arena, with 20,000 seats, scads of women's restrooms, and seemingly limitless corporate branding potential. There are still plenty of Londoners who would love to stomp on it, and with the debut of Up at the O2, now they can.

few feet over the Dome's (see box) roof, from south to north, to an observation platform at the zenith of the structure. There they pause for 15 minutes of photos of East London (the City is mostly hidden behind Canary Wharf's towers). Beneath them, humming like a ship at sea, is a Dome conquered. The excursion isn't for the height-averse—at your highest, you're 52m (171 ft.) above the ground, and it's not for big eaters or children, either (the weight cutoff is 130kg/286 lb, and you have to be at least 10 years old), but it's also not scary since you're tethered, the shoes they lend you grip well, and if the weather's bad, you get matching jumpsuits like Ooompa-Loompas. The climb, which is more like a stroll up a steep hill, takes 45 minutes, and the rest of a 90-minute experience consists of getting harnessed and psyched up.

Peninsula Sq., SE10. www.theo2.co.uk. ℗ **020/8463-2680.** Climbs from £28 adults and children. 10am to 6–10pm, depending on season. Tube: North Greenwich or North Greenwich ferry.

OUTER LONDON

Dulwich Picture Gallery ★★ MUSEUM A 15-minute train ride from Victoria and an 8-minute walk lands you in a pretty village-like enclave of South London, and something about the leafy stroll acclimates one to contemplation and appreciation. In just a few rooms, the Gallery keeps one of the world's most vital collections of Old Master paintings of the 1600s and 1700s. Magnanimous donors made it England's first public gallery (opened 1817), designed with a surplus of light by Sir John Soane (who left us his own cramped museum; p. 98). A visit is almost indescribably serene, the better to stare into the Cheshire Cat face of one of its star masterpieces, Rembrandt's *A Girl at a Window*—how did he capture her bemusedly frank expression? A handheld video tour unspools fascinating backstories of 10 works you might otherwise pass by, such as the portrait of young Venetia Stanley, which exists because she was discovered dead in bed and her distraught husband summoned Van Dyck to capture her beautiful corpse. Twist ending: Her beloved might have poisoned her. At the airy cafe, grab tea with Devon clotted cream for £6.

Gallery Rd., Dulwich Village, SE21. www.dulwichpicturegallery.org.uk. ℭ **020/8693-5254.** Admission £5 adults, £4 seniors and students, free for children 17 and under; special exhibitions cost more. Tues–Fri 10am–5pm; Sat–Sun 11am–5pm. National Rail: West Dulwich Station.

The Freud Museum ★ MUSEUM   In a hilly Hampstead neighborhood of spacious brick-faced homes, Sigmund Freud, having just fled the Nazis, spent the last year of his life here. His daughter Anna, herself a noted figure in psychoanalysis, lived on in the same house until her own death in 1982. Sigmund's study and library, which came from the doctors' famed offices at Berggasse 19, Vienna, were left precisely as they were on the day he died—which he did on a couch, of course.

20 Maresfield Gardens, NW3. www.freud.org.uk. ℭ **020/7435-2002.** Admission £7 adults, £5 seniors, £4 students, free for children 11 and under. Wed–Sun noon–5pm. Tube: Hampstead.

Hampton Court Palace ★★★ MUSEUM/HISTORIC SITE   If you have to pick just one palace to visit in London, select this one because there's so much more to do than look at golden furniture. A 35-minute commuter train ride from the center of town, Hampton Court looks like the ideal palace because it defined the ideal: The redbrick mansion was a center for royal life from 1525 to 1737, and its forest of chimneys stands regally in 24 hectares (59 acres) of achingly pretty riverside gardens, painstakingly restored to their 1702 appearance. Visitors come looking for vibrations left by Henry VIII during the 811 days he spent here (yes, that's all; he had more than 60 houses), and the Crown still stocks many of the 70 public rooms, which start out Tudor and end up Queen Anne, with rare art.

Current curators pander to Tudor scandals to make history more interesting to tourists, and days are full of events, which may include re-enactments of gossipy events by costumed actors, Tudor-style cook-offs in the kitchens, Shakespeare plays in the hammer-beamed Great Hall, or ghost tours. Whatever you do, don't neglect the 24-hectare (59-acre) **gardens** and make time to lose yourself in the Northern Gardens' shrubbery **Maze,** installed by William III; kids giggle their way through to the middle of this leafy labyrinth. The well-mannered **South Garden** has the Great Vine, the oldest vine in the world, planted in 1768; its black grapes are sold in the gift shop in early September.

East Molesey, Surrey. www.hrp.org.uk. ℭ **084/4482-7777.** Admission £18 adults, £15 seniors and students, £8 children 5–15; posted prices are higher and include a "voluntary donation." March to late Oct daily 10am–6pm; late Oct to Mar daily 10am–4:30pm; last admission 1 hr. before closing. National Rail: Hampton Court from Waterloo Station.

TAKING THE thames TO HAMPTON COURT OR KEW

From April to September daily, you can take **London River Services** (www.wpsa.co.uk; ℂ **020/7930-2062;** £15 adults, £10 seniors, £8 children 5–15) all the way from Westminster in central London, the way Henry VIII did on his barges, but it can be a commitment of 3 hours and tides sometimes play such havoc with schedules that you may arrive too late to see much. You will have to take the train the other way. Trains go twice an hour from Waterloo, take 35 minutes, and let you off across the river from the Palace: much easier. Kew is simpler: The ferry's return fare is £23 adults, £15 seniors, and £11 children. It goes four times a day and takes 90 minutes.

Royal Botanic Gardens, Kew ★★ PARK/GARDEN   The 121-hectare (300-acre) gardens, with many expansive lawns, earned a spot on the UNESCO list of World Heritage Sites in 2003. As you'd expect, the glasshouses are world-class—there are 2,000 varieties of plants, many descended from specimens collected in the earliest days of international sea trade. Of the seven conservatories, the domed **Palm House,** built from 1844 to 1848 and jungle-warm, is probably the world's most recognizable greenhouse, while the **Temperate House** is the world's largest glasshouse containing the world's largest indoor plant (the 17.7m/58-ft.-tall Chilean wine-palm, planted in 1843—not a typo). It's undergoing a £34 million restoration until 2018 but they've relocated most of its plants (except the *Encephalartos woodii* cycad, extinct in the wild and too fragile to move). Other attractions include a bamboo garden, a water lily pond, **Treehouse Towers** (a tree-themed play area for children 3–11), and, it must be said, a heartwarmingly charming village outside the gates. The gardeners are champs; in 1986, they coaxed a bloom from a portea that hadn't flowered in 160 years. Kew's contributions to botanical science are ongoing since 1759, but not mired in the past; it also provides a free app that lets you scan labels to learn more and find blooms. Unless you're a fevered horticulturalist, it will ultimately feel like a park you have to pay for—and a lot at that. Also be aware that many of the goodies clamp down in winter (including Kew Palace, included in the price, p. 144), so this is best in the summer.

Kew, Richmond, Surrey. www.kew.org. ℂ **020/8332-5655.** Admission £15 adults, £14 seniors and students, free for children 16 and under; discounts sometimes available online. Daily 9:30am–4:15pm in winter (6pm in fall and 6:30pm in spring and summer). Tube: Kew Gardens.

Warner Bros. Studio Tour London—The Making of Harry Potter ★★★ MUSEUM   London's most popular new family outing is like a DVD extra feature that comes to life, and it's as gripping as the fine museums can be. On the very lot where the eight movies of history's most

One of the most iconic symbols of London life is that of the Pearly King and Queen. You've seen pictures: grinning folks in suits outrageously embroidered with white buttons and baubles. The tradition began in the Victorian markets, when traders trumpeted their status by decorating their seams with smoke pearl buttons. A poor street sweeper named Henry Croft evolved this esoteric nomenclature into fully embellished outfits, weighing up to 14kg (30 lb.) and worn to attract charitable donations. Soon the idea spread to a whole league of approved wearers, each with their own suit representing a different borough of London. The tradition is dying out, and costumes are increasingly more likely to be found hanging in a museum than on the streets. Some of those appearances are announced on the official site of **London Pearly Kings and Queens Society** (www.pearlysociety.co.uk; ℂ **020/8778-8670**), but you can usually find them one Saturday a month at Covent Garden, from 10:30am to 2:30pm.

successful film franchise were shot, it seems that every set, prop, prosthetic, wig, and wand—and I mean every last thing—was lovingly saved for this polished, informative, and exhaustive walk-though feast. You could spend hours grazing the bounty, from the students' Great Hall to Dumbledore's roost to Dolores Umbridge's den to the actual Diagon Alley. There's little filler, so book your entry time for early in the day so you'll have time to wander. Even if you care nothing about the movies, you will be blown away that items that got barely 2 seconds of long-lens screen time could possess such intricate craftsmanship. The finale, an astounding 1:24 scale model of Hogwarts Castle embedded with 2,500 fiber optic lights, is 50 feet across and takes up an arena-size room lit to simulate day and night. Midway through the tour, in an outdoor area containing 4 Privet Dr. and the actual Knight Bus, you'll find the only place outside of Orlando where you can taste Butterbeer (£3). And you won't *believe* the gift shop. Easy 15-minute trains go three times an hour from Euston Station—but not, fans sigh, from Platform 9¾ at King's Cross. (Although there, an enterprising Potter souvenir stall affixed a sign and takes pictures for £9.)

Warner Bros. Studios Leavesden, Aerodrome Way, Leavesden, Hertfordshire. www.wbstudiotour.co.uk. ℂ **08450/840-900**. Admission £33 adults, £26 children 5–15, free for children 4 and under, £101 family of 4, return train ticket £10. Reservations required. Daily. First tours 9–10am, last tours 4–6:30pm, closes 3 hr. after last tour time. National Rail: Watford Junction, then a £2 shuttle bus that meets trains.

Other Area Attractions

Home of Charles Darwin (Down House) ★★ HISTORIC HOUSE
Charles Darwin made one of history's most important voyages, but once back in England, he barely left his home here in the idyllic parish village of Downe. Upstairs you'll find out about the man and his life (did you know the father of evolution married his own first cousin?) and downstairs,

guided by an audio tour narrated by Sir David Attenborough, you'll explore his study, his greenhouse, and his enchanting garden of lawns and breezy fields. No wonder he never left again. There are two charming country pubs to enjoy while you wait for the bus back; your Oyster card will get you here.

Luxted Rd., Downe, Kent. www.english-heritage.org.uk. ℂ **0370/333-1181.** Admission £11 adults, £10 seniors and students, £6 children 5–15. April–Sept daily 10am–6pm; Oct–Nov daily 10am–5pm; Nov to mid-Feb Sat–Sun 10am–4pm; mid-Feb to Mar Sat–Sun 10am–4pm. National Rail: Bromley South, then bus no. 122 and 7-min. walk.

Horniman Museum ★ MUSEUM   A rich Victorian dilettante collected crazy stuff from all over the world, and rather than let it gather dust, he built a museum in South London. This repository of some 350,000 items has since blossomed into something for everyone, particularly children, including a cherished collection of 7,000 musical instruments (Boosey & Hawkes, once the U.K.'s largest instrument maker, donated its archive) and a huge range of stuff regarding anthropology (masks, puppets, folk art) and natural history (stuffed creatures galore). There's even a modest aquarium, a cafe, and some gorgeous gardened grounds on a hill with a panorama of London 6 miles north.

100 London Rd., Forest Hill. www.horniman.ac.uk. ℂ **020/8699-1872.** Free admission. Daily 10:30am–5:30pm. Tube: Forest Hill Overground.

Kenwood ★★ HISTORIC HOUSE   Bask in a country house high without leaving the city. Just restored, Kenwood is a sublime 18th-century job by Robert Adam with a sigh-inducing southern view across Hampstead Heath. Inside, the walls are hung with paintings that would be the envy of the National Gallery, including Vermeer's *The Guitar Player,* a John Singer Sargent, and a Rembrandt self-portrait. The title character of the 2014 film *Belle* was raised by Lord Mansfield in this house, and the film was shot here. There's no better place to enjoy an English summer than on its acres of lawns or alongside its ornamental pond.

Hampstead Lane, NW3. www.english-heritage.org.uk. ℂ **020/8348-1286.** Free admission. House: daily 10am–5pm; grounds: 8am–dusk. Tube: Archway or Golders Green, then bus no. 210.

Kew Palace and Queen Charlotte's Cottage ★ MUSEUM/ HISTORIC SITE   Remember George III? He's the dilettante ruler who, during his reign from 1760 to 1820, lost the American colonies and went crazy from suspected porphyria: see the movie *The Madness of King George* for the tragic tale. Kew is where he spent his childhood and went insane, and you can tour a piece of his vanished palace, recently restored with scientific exactitude. It's only the size of a standard manor house and lacks interpretation except for some ill-advised histrionic audio enactments that no one pauses to endure. Upstairs in the little Queen Charlotte's Cottage, an imitation of a humble village home, the Picnic Room is painted with vines across its vaulted ceiling. The work is attributed to King George's daughter, Princess Elizabeth. In late April, the Cottage, which is at Kew's southwest end, is surrounded by bluebells in bloom.

Royal Botanic Gardens, Kew, Richmond. www.hrp.org.uk. *©* **020/8332-5655.** Admission to Kew Gardens required: £15 adults, £14 seniors and students, free for children 16 and under; discounts sometimes available online. Kew Palace: Mar–Sept 10am–5:30pm; closed Oct to late Mar. Cottage: Sat–Sun and bank holidays 10am–4pm. Tube: Kew Gardens.

Mandir ★ LANDMARK   The breathtakingly gorgeous, many-pinnacled Mandir in northwest London is the largest Hindu temple outside of India. This fabulous concoction was only completed in 1995. Some 5,500 tons of Italian Carrara marble and Bulgarian limestone were carved in India and shipped here, where they were assembled by volunteers—its dome was built without using steel or lead. The interior is as complicated and as white as a doily and is apt to amaze even people generally unimpressed by such virtuosity. Tourists are welcomed—there's even an "Understanding Hinduism" exhibition. If you're entering, shorts or skirts must not fall higher than the knee (although ankle-length is preferable and sarongs are available to borrow); visitors must also remove their shoes.

105-119 Brentfield Rd., NW10. www.mandir.org. *©* **020/8965-2651.** Free admission. Daily 9am–6pm. Tube: Wembley Park, then bus no. 206, or Stonebridge Park, then bus no. 112.

Thames Barrier Visitor Centre ★ LANDMARK/MUSEUM   People forget that London floods. Parliament has been under water, and in 1953, surges killed 307 people in the U.K. At least, London *used* to flood. The Thames Barrier is the city's primary defense against it and comprises 10 20m (66-ft.) steel-and-concrete gates. These can be raised to block the 520m (1706-ft.) span of the river in just 10 minutes. Most of the time you can't see the gates, which rest on the riverbed, but the piers that raise and lower them are always visible, strung across the river like a row of mini Sydney Opera Houses. At the visitor center you plumb the Barrier's construction and, if you're lucky, see a test raise.

Unity Way, Woolwich, SE18. *©* **020/8305-4188.** Admission £4 adults, £3 seniors and students, £2 children 5–15, free for children 4 and under. Thurs–Sun and bank holiday Mon 10:30am–5pm. Rail: Woolwich Dockyard or Charlton.

Wimbledon Lawn Tennis Museum ★ MUSEUM   Most of us can't get to the tournament. For us, there's still something to see the rest of the year. It's sort of like a Hall of Fame with an emphasis, of course, on Wimbledon, with artifacts going back to 1555, although the British have never been prouder than they are now that Scotsman Andy Murray brought home the

It's easy watching the Wimbledon Championships on TV for 2 weeks in late June and early July, but seeing it in person is a trickier matter. High hotel prices are just the beginning. Because tickets for the final matches go to VIPs, you're more likely to catch famous players during the early rounds, when the club's 19 grass courts are all in use. Roaming access to all but three of those (surcharges of £39–£160 are levied for Centre, No. 1, and No. 2 courts, and tickets are distributed by lottery the previous summer) can be had for the price of a "ground pass" (£5–£25). Around 6,000 ground passes are distributed each morning starting at 7:30am, so arrive many hours before that to Wimbledon Park, Church Road side (no large luggage allowed), and if you snag one, you'll probably be inside by noon, before matches begin; you'll still need to get into the courts. Ticketmaster (and no one else; ticketmaster.co.uk) may release several hundred tickets for Centre Court and Court 3 the day before play. Another clever way to get in is to bum tickets off people as they get tired and leave for the day; just don't offer money—the organizers hate that because they sell unused tickets, too, for charity. Those are resold after 3pm to those already on the grounds (£5–£10). On weekdays and rainy days, your chances of getting unfilled seats for the best courts are better, since people are working or huddling indoors. And after 5pm, ground-pass rates dip to, at most, £18, which isn't such a bad deal since matches continue until 9pm. It's all ridiculously complicated—the English love complicated admission schemes—so check ahead on Wimbledon.com to ensure rules are the same.

trophy after 77 years. There is no other museum in the world where a ghostly video apparition of John McEnroe appears in a locker room to vent about opponents. He comes in peace. No need to duck.

Church Rd., SW19. www.wimbledon.com/museum. © **020/8946-6131.** Admission £13 adults, £11 seniors and students, £8 children 5–16. Daily 10am–5pm. Tube: Southfields or Tooting Broadway, then bus no. 493; or National Rail to Wimbledon Station, then bus no. 493.

OVERRATED ATTRACTIONS

In every city, you invariably find attractions that are heavily publicized but, once seen, are revealed to be time poorly spent. In every city, you will also find a subset of visitors who have no idea why they came. London provides a variety of overpriced pursuits catering to people with an unaccountable aversion to its true treasures—there's even an elaborate attraction by the London Eye devoted to the movie *Shrek*, which needless to say you can safely skip. Still, parents of bored children might discover these inauthentic sights are just the tonic to jolt them back into a compliant mood.

ArcelorMittal Orbit OBSERVATION TOWER   The 114.5m (376-ft.)-tall vertical scribble, a publicity exercise by a steel concern, has observation decks at 76m (249 ft.) and 80m (262 ft.), but it barely matters when there's not much to look at. It originally overlooked the Olympics but the torch and the games are gone, so it peers into a stadium many miles from town. Wear a jacket because it gets windy in the exposed areas, and take your vitamins because a lift takes you up, but you have to use 455 steps down. And no, it doesn't orbit.

Queen Elizabeth Olympic Park. arcelormittalorbit.com. *©* **0333/800-8099.** Admission £15 adults, £12 seniors and students, £7 children 3–6. Daily 10am–6pm; last admission 5pm.Tube: Stratford.

Emirates Air Line OBSERVATION GONDOLA   Opened in time for the Olympics as a Thames crossing between the ExCeL convention center and the O2 dome, it's simply an enclosed, 10-person gondola that shuttles between two places most tourists never go, and it's too far from the City to be of much panoramic use. Oyster cards work on it. The ride takes 5 to 10 minutes.

www.emiratesairline.co.uk. *©* **0843/222-1234.** Admission: journeys £5 adult, £2 children (without Oyster card); or £3 adults, £2 children 5–15 (with Oyster card). Mon–Fri 7am–9pm; Sat 8am–9pm; Sun 9am–9pm. Tube: North Greenwich or Royal Victoria DLR.

The Household Cavalry Museum MUSEUM   Along Whitehall, where guards try mightily to ignore buffoonish tourists who try to get them to crack a smile, this tiny museum pays soporific tribute to the martial ceremonies of the Queen's Life Guard. You might see troopers groom horses through a glass partition or regard cases of uniforms and regalia with glazed eyes, but—nothing against these dedicated men—you won't get much back on your investment. On the hour, mounted dutymen change, and at 11am, the Life Guard changes, but you can see those outside for free.

Horse Guards, Whitehall, SW1. www.householdcavalrymuseum.co.uk. *©* **020/7930-3070.** Admission £7 adults, £5 seniors and children 5–16. Apr–Oct 10am–6pm; Nov–March 10am–5pm. Tube: Embankment.

The London Dungeon HAUNTED HOUSE   Avoid it like the plague. It's a sophomoric gross-out with locations in nine cities that sops up overflow from the London Eye. Costumed actors bray at you as you're led through darkness from set to set, each representing a period of English history as a 13-year-old boy might define them. Plague-ridden rubber corpses "sneeze" on passersby, a whore exposes one of Jack the Ripper's mutilated victims, and Sweeney Todd commands you to sit in his chair. The climax is a pair of indoor carnival rides. If you dread being picked on by bad stand-up comics, you're going to hate this place. Booking ahead may not save you having to queue. If you can't resist, at least bundle it with a ticket on the London Eye for a discount.

County Hall, Westminster Bridge Rd., SE1. www.thedungeons.com. *©* **0871/243-2240.** Admission £26 adults, £23 students, £21 children 5–15, £7–8 cheaper booked online. Times change but roughly daily 10am–5pm. Tube: Westminster or Waterloo.

London Sea Life Aquarium AQUARIUM   Sure, it's fun to see sharks under your feet and penguins on a faux floe. But sorry Charlie, the truth is there is nothing here you can't see at other fish zoos, there are more than three dozen other locations by Sea Life, the McDonald's of fish tanks, and this one feels as cramped as a 16th-century galleon.

County Hall, Westminster Bridge Rd., SE1. www.sealifelondon.co.uk. ✆ **0871/663-1678.** Admission £24 adults, £17 children 3–15, free for children 2 and under, 10% discount online. Mon–Thurs 10am–6pm; Fri–Sun 10am–7pm; last admission 1 hr. before closing. Tube: Waterloo or Westminster,

The London Zoo ZOO It's not about the pedigree. No, it has an esteemed history going back to 1828 as a menagerie for members of the Zoological Society of London. It's just that it's ultimately only a zoo, and a smallish one at that, with few large animals. A pair of Sumatran tigers arrived in 2013, but they're not enough to justify the high ticket price, especially for a first-time London visitor who could be learning about the city instead.

Outer Circle Rd., Regent's Park, NW1. www.zsl.org. ✆ **020/7722-333.** Admission £24 adults, £17 children 3–15; 10% discount online. Daily 10am–6pm. Tube: Camden Town, then bus no. 274.

Madame Tussauds TOURIST MUSEUM Have you ever heard of Shah Rukh Khan? Cheryl Cole? Jonny Wilkinson? If your answer is no, you're not going to get much joy out of this ferociously priced, miserably crowded wax trap. The execution of its doppelgangers, which you can usually touch (Harry is behind ropes, girls), is generally superb. That's not the issue. But the focus of this world-famous waxworks is on British celebrities. A 5-minute, Disney-esque ride, "The Spirit of London," invokes every conceivable London stereotype, from the Artful Dodger to plague victims. As you glide through, you'll suddenly wonder if you're the real dummy here.

Marylebone Rd., W1. www.madame-tussauds.com/london. ✆ **0871/894-3000.** Admission based on time of year and time of day, peaks at £33 adults, £29 children 4–15; up to 25% discount online or via its app. Daily 9:30am–5:30pm, slightly longer Sat–Sun and holidays. Tours continue at least 45 min. past posted closing time. Tube: Baker Street.

The Queen's Gallery MUSEUM The Queen inherited the mother of all art collections—7,000 paintings, 30,000 watercolors, and half a million prints, to say nothing of sculpture, furniture, and jewelry—but she shows only a tiny fraction. The few works (budget 1 hr.) are undoubtedly exceptional (one of the world's few Vermeers, a Rubens' self-portrait given to Charles I, glittering ephemera by Fabergé), but they're not the cream of what she owns. There's more exciting stuff to be had for free at the National Gallery. The Gallery and the Royal Mews can be seen on a joint ticket (£16 adults, £15 seniors and students, £9 children 5–16).

Buckingham Palace Rd., SW1. www.royalcollection.org.uk. ✆ **020/7766-7301.** Admission £10 adults, £9 seniors and students. £5 children 5–16. Sept–July daily 10am–5:30pm; Aug–Sept daily 9:30am–5:30pm; last admission 4:30pm. Tube: Victoria.

Ripley's Believe It or Not! TOURIST MUSEUM Like foot fungus, the worthless rip has spread wherever tourists stagger. Now it's in London. Its halls of oddities (sample: a portrait of Diana made from lint) are useless and

ritual ABUSE

I'm only telling you this because I love you: **Changing the Guard** (Buckingham Palace; www.royal.gov.uk; free admission; May–July daily 11:30am and every other day in other months, cancelled in heavy rain; Tube: St James's Park, Victoria, or Green Park), sometimes called Guard Mounting, is an underwhelming use of 40 minutes of your time. Arrive at Buckingham Palace at least 45 minutes ahead if you don't want to face the backs of other tourists—Buckingham Palace sells a $1 smartphone app that will help decode the ritual. A marching band advances from Birdcage Walk (often, playing themes from *Star Wars*, *West Side Story*, or ABBA—so much for traditional English customs), then members of the Queen's Life Guard—two if the Queen's away, three or four if she's in—do a change around their sentry boxes. And that's it, give or take additional prancing.

Guards patrol all day, without crowds, at both Buckingham Palace and at Horse Guards Arch on Whitehall (which does its own, uncrowded change daily at 11am, 10am Sun). Or park yourself at **Wellington Barracks,** just east of the Palace along Birdcage Walk, by 11am, and catch the Inspection of the Guard that happens before the same guards march over to the Palace for the main event. Then use the day's golden hours for something less touristy.

Ceremony of the Keys (Tower of London; www.hrp.org.uk; ✆ **020/3166-6278;** free admission; nightly 9:53pm; Tube: Tower Hill or Tower Gateway DLR), held every night as the Yeomen lock up the Tower of London, has been a routine for more than 700 years—not even German bombs cancelled it. But it's an awful lot of work for not much payoff: You must enter the Tower at 9:30pm (several hours after closing time, so you can't combine it with a day's visit) and won't leave until around 10:05pm, even though the whole show takes less than 7 minutes—plus, photos aren't allowed. As for the event, the Chief Yeoman Warder approaches the heavy wooden gate with keys and a lantern, is asked "Halt, who comes there?," passes muster, and locks up the gates to a bugle call. The end. If you want to see that, apply for tickets online, with a nightly maximum of six places April to Oct. It sells out 8 months in advance.

not worthwhile even for the kitsch value. This is the definition of a tourist trap. And it costs more than Westminster Abbey! Fortunately, "or Not" is an option.

1 Piccadilly Circus, W1. www.ripleyslondon.com. ✆ **020/3238-0022.** Admission £27 adults, £25 seniors and students, £20 children 5–15; £4 discount online. Daily 10am–midnight. Tube: Piccadilly Circus.

The Royal Mews MUSEUM   Most visitors pop in to what amounts to the Queen's garage in about 15 minutes. You'll see stables fit for a you-know-who (they barely smell at all) and Her Majesty's Rolls-Royces (many of which, at Prince Charles' behest, run on green fuels). You'll also overdose on learning about regulations for when this set of harnesses may be used and when that leather must be polished. The Queen's Gallery and the Mews can be seen on a joint ticket (£16 adults, £15 seniors and students, £9 children 5–16).

Buckingham Palace Rd., SW1. www.royalcollection.org.uk. ✆ **020/7766-7302.** Admission £9 adults, £8 seniors and students, £5 children 5–17. Apr–Oct 10am–5pm; Nov–March 10am–4pm; last admission 45 min. before closing. Tube: Victoria.

The Sherlock Holmes Museum TOURIST MUSEUM   Set up a house as if it were really the home of a fictional character, prop up some shabby mannequins, and then charge tourists to see it. That's the scheme and it has worked for years, so well there's often a line.

221b Baker St., NW1. www.sherlock-holmes.co.uk. ✆ **020/7224-3688.** Admission £10 adults, £8 children 15 and under. Daily 9:30am–6pm. Tube: Baker Street.

OUTDOOR LONDON

Buildings come and go, but London's open spaces have remained unchanged for centuries. They're the city's oldest places.

Epping Forest ★★★ PARK/GARDEN   Mostly because its soil is unsuitable for farming, for a millennium it remained a semi-virgin woodland, so it's the best place to get a feel for what Britain felt like before humans denuded its land. It's the largest open space in London, 6,000 acres, 12 miles long by 2½ miles wide, and containing a universe of diversion—650 plant species, 80 ponds where waterfowl splash, and even some 1,500 species of fungi. Getting lost in the woods is feasible, but not likely, since it stretches in a single direction. Henry VII built a timber-framed hunting lodge in 1542 that was inherited by his daughter Elizabeth and, astoundingly, still stands: **Queen Elizabeth's Hunting Lodge** (reach that via the Chingford rail station).

Rangers Rd., Chingford, E4. www.cityoflondon.gov.uk. ✆ **020/8529-6681.** Free admission. Daily 6am–dusk. Lodge: daily 10am–5pm. Tube: Snaresbrook or Wood Street. National rail: Chingford.

The Green Park ★★ PARK/GARDEN   The area south of Mayfair between Hyde Park and St James's Park was once a burial ground for lepers, but now is a simple expanse of meadows and light copses of trees. It doesn't have much to offer except pastoral views, and most visitors find themselves crossing it instead of dawdling in it, although its springtime flower beds (which bloom brightest Mar–Apr) are marvelous. Don't sit in one of those picturesque striped deck chairs unless you've got a few quid to pay as rent.

Piccadilly, SW1. ✆ **030/0061-2350.** Free admission. Daily 24 hr. Tube: Green Park.

Greenwich Park ★★ PARK/GARDEN   Decently sized (74 hectares/183 acres), it was once a deer preserve maintained for royal amusement; a herd of them still have 5 hectares (13 acres) at their disposal. It's been a Royal Park since the 15th century, although the boundary wasn't formally defined until James I erected a brick wall around it in the early 1600s, much of which still survives. On top of its clean-swept main hill are marvelous views of the Canary Wharf district, and the world-famous **Royal Observatory** (p. 139), commissioned in 1675 by Charles II, serves as the intersection point for the Prime Meridian as well as the center of Greenwich Mean Time. Most people combine a visit with the many other museums of Greenwich.

Greenwich Park, SE10. www.royalparks.gov.uk. ✆ **030/0061-2380.** Free admission. Daily 6am–dusk. National Rail: Greenwich or Maze Hill, or Cutty Sark. DLR or Greenwich ferry.

Hampstead Heath ★★★ PARK/GARDEN Some 7 million visitors a year come to the 320-hectare (791-acre) Heath, in northwest London, to walk on the grass, get enveloped by thick woods, and take in the view from the magnificent Pergola, a beguiling, overgrown Edwardian garden, and a true London secret. The Heath is a perennial locale for aimless strolls and (it must be confessed, George Michael) furtive trysts. The Heath has several sublime places to rest, including the just-restored **Kenwood House** (p. 144), a sumptuous neoclassical home from 1640 adorned with miles of gold leaf and important paintings by Reynolds, Turner, and Vermeer (*The Guitar Player*); and the inviting and woody **Spaniards Inn** (Spaniards Rd. at Spaniards End, NW3; www.thespaniardshampstead.co.uk; ℂ **020/8731-8406;** Tube: Hampstead). The Heath's hilltop is another favored lookout point. The Heath isn't considered a park by locals, but a green space. The difference is irrelevant. It's transporting.

www.cityoflondon.gov.uk/hampsteadheath. ℂ **020/7606-3030.** 7:30am–dusk. Tube: Hampstead or Hampstead Heath Overground.

Hyde Park & Kensington Gardens ★★★ PARK/GARDEN Bordered by Mayfair, Bayswater, and Kensington, together the two conjoined are the largest park in the middle of the city. Hyde Park is home to the famous **Speakers' Corner** (Tube: Marble Arch, p. 116), a meandering lake called the Serpentine, and the Diana, Princess of Wales Memorial Fountain (Tube: South Kensington, p. 109). The most famous promenade is Rotten Row, probably a corruption of "Route de Roi," or King's Way, which was laid out by William III as his private road to town; it runs along the southern edge of the park from Hyde Park Corner. Kensington Gardens, which flows seamlessly from Hyde Park, only opened to plebes like us in 1851, and it hasn't yet shed its country-manor quality. You'll also find the **Serpentine Gallery** (west of W. Carriage Dr. and north of Alexandra Gate; www.serpentinegallery.org; ℂ **020/7402-6075;** free admission; Tues–Sun 10am–6pm; Tube: South Kensington), a popular venue for its modern art exhibitions and an art bookshop. Each summer, a leading architect creates a fanciful pavilion there. Volunteers sometimes run guided tours of the park's quirks; check the bulletin boards at each park entrance to see if one is upcoming. Borrow a Boris Bike and cruise around this giant green playground, and don't forget to look for Sir George Frampton's marvelous bronze statue of Peter Pan (1912) near the west shore of the Long Water.

Hyde Park, W2. www.royalparks.org.uk. ℂ **030/0061-2100.** Free admission. Hyde Park daily 5am–midnight; Kensington Gardens daily 6am–dusk. Tube: Hyde Park Corner, Marble Arch, or Lancaster Gate.

Queen Elizabeth Olympic Park ★ PARK/GARDEN A bracing dearth of trees, paired with a layout that herds crowds, make the park feel a lot like a theme park in which all of the attractions got up and left. Most of the amenities are things that only excite locals who remember when it was formerly a wasteland. The Pringle-shaped Aquatics Centre and Velopark are striking, but this park is only of interest if you want to see the stadium you

THE hidden park

Sure, everybody knows about London's famous green spaces, but there's one recreation area, which stretches from London's northwest to its east through gentrified lanes and industrial wasteland alike, that few tourists are told about. It's the **Regent's Canal,** which threads from Paddington through Camden, Islington, and East London before joining with the Thames (26m/86 ft. lower) just before Canary Wharf. It was completed in 1820 to link with canals all the way to Birmingham and feed the city's massive seagoing trade. In those days, barges were animal-drawn and the districts along the waterway were rat-infested and perilous, but today, it's one of the frontiers for development; many of the horse tracks are leafy promenades and shadowy warehouses have become affluent loft condos. A new development north of King's Cross station is revealing even more glories. Along the shore, you'll pass docks where houseboat barges tie up; their owners can be found topside, making conversation with passersby. The most popular segment is probably the crescent just north of Regent's Park. The **London Canal Museum** (12-13 New Wharf Rd., N1; www.canalmuseum.org.uk; ℂ **020/7713-0836;** admission £4; Tues–Sun 10am–4:30pm; Tube: Kings Cross St Pancras;), in a former icehouse, is devoted to the waterway and operates tours of its towpath and boat tours of the Islington Tunnel, which stretches for 1.2km (¾ mile) under the streets. **London Waterbus** (www.londonwaterbus.com; ℂ **020/7482-2550**) and **Jason's Trip** (www.jasons.co.uk; no phone) ferry riders through the 270-foot Maida Hill Tunnel and the glorious villas that line the canal between Little Venice (Tube: Warwick Avenue) and Camden's markets (Tube: Camden Town) in longboats (£8 adults, £7 seniors and children 3–15) in either direction, year-round. There are no tourist boats that currently ferry riders east of the locks at Camden.

saw on TV; even the torch is gone, and the ArcelorMittal Orbit tower (p. 146) is ultimately mostly pointless.

Stratford, E20. www.QueenElizabethOlympicPark.co.uk. ℂ **020/3288-1800.** Free admission. Daily 6am–dusk. Tube: Stratford.

Regent's Park ★★★ PARK/GARDEN   It's the people's park (195 hectares/487 acres), best for sunning, strolling long expanses—it can take a half-hour to cross it—and darting into the bohemian neighborhoods that fringe it. Once a hunting ground, it was very nearly turned into a development for the buddies of Prince Regent (later King George IV), but only a few of the private terrace homes were built; Winfield House, on 5 hectares (12 acres) near the western border of the park, has the largest garden in London, after the Queen. The American ambassador lives there—surprised? The most breathtaking entrance is from the south through John Nash's elegant Park Crescent development, by the Regent's Park and Great Portland Street Tube stations. North of the park, just over the Regent's Canal and Prince Albert Road, **Primrose Hill Park** (Tube: Chalk Farm or Camden Town) affords a panorama of the city from 62m (203-ft.) high.

Regent's Park, NW1. www.royalparks.gov.uk. ℂ **030/0061-2300.** Free admission. Daily 5am–dusk. Tube: Baker Street, Great Portland Street, or Regent's Park.

St James's Park ★★ PARK/GARDEN The easternmost segment of the contiguous quartet of parks that runs east from Kensington Gardens is bounded by Whitehall to the east and Piccadilly to the north. James I laid it out in 1603 and Buckingham Palace redeveloped it a century later. Its little pond, St James's Park Lake, hosts ducks and other waterfowl. The Russian ambassador made a gift of pelicans to the park in 1667, and the Brits would rather pour the milk after the tea than give up tradition, so six (three of them a 2013 gift from the city of Prague) still call it home; they're fed their 13kg (28 lb.) of whiting daily at 2:30pm at the Duck Island Cottage. The park has a fine view of Buckingham Palace's front facade, where royal couples smooch on balconies (but live in a section of the building you can't see). The real draw is people-watching, since a cross-section of all London passes through here. Not a place for picnics or ball throwing, there's little in the way of amenities or activities, unless you count voyeurism, and why wouldn't you?

The Mall, SW1. www.royalparks.org.uk. ℂ **020/7930-1793.** Free admission. 5am–midnight. Tube: St James's Park.

Victoria Park ★★ PARK/GARDEN The largest and finest open space in East London, this was, when it opened in 1845, the capital's first public park. Bordered by canals and divided in two by Grove Road, it covers an area of just under 87 hectares (220 acres) and contains two lakes, formal gardens, sports facilities, and a bandstand. Other notable features include a Grade II-listed 1862 drinking fountain and two arches from the pre-1831 London Bridge—now turned into benches. In summer, big music events such as Lovebox come here. The park also forms the central section of the **Jubilee Greenway Walk,** a route marked out in 2009 with glass paving slabs in honor of the Queen's Diamond Jubilee, and stretching for exactly 60km (37 miles)—1 kilometer for each year of her reign—from Buckingham Palace to the Olympic Park. She doesn't use it.

Grove Rd., E3. www.towerhamlets.gov.uk/victoriapark. ℂ **020/7364-2494.** Free admission. Daily 6am–dusk. Tube: Mile End/Overground, Hackney Wick, or Homerton.

Walking Tours

There are so many guides to choose from—the best ones are led by government-accredited "Blue Badge" professionals, so always look for the Blue Badge—that you could fill a week with walking tours alone. Plenty of qualified operators cater to custom business (many only cater to groups), but these will let you join individually. Also check the online compendium of day tours, Viator (www.viator.com), plus the "Around Town" section of *Time Out* magazine, where museums and organizations announce one-off tours.

City of London Guided Walks ★★ The government gives written and performance-based exams to the experts who lead its excellent weekly tours. The experience is less theatrical and denser with facts than what London Walks generally provides, and group sizes tend to be smaller, too. There are

17 from which to choose, including ones on Dickens, the City's top 10 sights, and Roman London. Tours are 1½ to 2 hours.

City Information Centre, St Paul's Churchyard, EC4. www.cityoflondonguides.com. Tours £7 adults, £6 seniors and students, free for children 11 and under. Tube: St Paul's.

City of Westminster Guides ★★ Westminster, the area of London west of the City that includes Whitehall, also contracts officially tested guides to lead tours there. Advance booking isn't required, but tours sometimes only go in summer. Tours are 1½ to 2 hours; locations vary.

www.westminsterguides.org.uk. Tours £7 adults, £5 seniors and students, free for children 11 and under.

Context Travel ★ Leave the greasepaint in the hotel room. These tours are for those with intellectual leanings. Context bills them not as hammy storytelling sessions but as "walking seminars," some several hours long and for premium rates, hosted by professors, historians, and other scholars. For example, one of its 2014 additions was about London's role in the colonial slave trade, a topic most museums ignore. Some tours are only available to groups, but inquire about availability. Locations vary.

www.contexttravel.com. ✆ **800/691-6036** (U.S.).

Dotmaker Tours ★★ Dotmaker's weekend walks delve into offbeat topics such as chimneys, tunnels, the story of sounds like St Paul's bells, where the city dumps its rubbish, and where London's past geniuses have found their inspiration. Tours are 2 hours; locations vary.

www.dotmakertours.org.uk. Tours £18 adults, £15 seniors and students.

Eating London Tours ★★★ I recommend this 3½-hour, stuff-yourself-silly walking romp though some of the greatest victuals in the East End. You'll get to try eight tastings of flavors that are truly East End and not faked for tourists, from fish and chips to Brick Lane curry to Beigel Bake salt beef to a pint in an old-fashioned pub—all while getting a solid lay of the land by an entertaining guide. It also does a more expensive 5pm tour of Soho. Locations vary.

www.eatinglondontours.couk. ✆ **020/3289-6327** or 215/688-5571 (U.S.). Tours £65–£75 adults, £50–£60 children 13–18, £40–£50 children 12 and under. East End: Mon–Sat 10am and 10:45am. Soho: Mon–Fri 5pm.

Greenwich Guided Walks ★ Like London, Greenwich operates its own official tours with carefully vetted guides. There are usually two basic 90-minute tours daily from the Greenwich Tourist Information Centre (Discover Greenwich) taking in the main sights plus the Royal Observatory and the Meridian Line.

www.greenwichtours.co.uk. ✆ **020/8858-6169.** Tours £8 adults, £7 seniors and students, free for children 13 and under. Tube: DLR: Cutty Sark.

London Beatles Walks ★ Richard Porter, an extensive writer on the Fab Four, has led tours for 2 decades; the most regular are the Magical

Mystery Tour (landmarks in the development of the band; Sun, Wed, and Thurs) and In My Life (landmarks in their lives; Tues and Sat). You don't have to book ahead. Tours are 2 hours; locations vary.

www.beatlesinlondon.com. ℘ **020/7624-3978.** Tours £10 adults, £8 seniors and students.

London Walks ★★★   Undoubtedly one of the city's best tourist services, its tour list is inspiring. On weekdays, there are often more than a dozen choices, and on weekends, nearly 25, which means that if you ever find yourself with a few hours to kill, you can always find instant occupation. Every tour (most are £9) departs from a Tube stop, and none require reservations, which makes arrangements easy. The marquee tour is probably "Jack the Ripper Haunts," which heads out to the streets of Whitechapel around sunset and, in the pursuit of ghoulish entertainment, employs considerably more grotesquerie than uncontested facts. Many of the group's other walks are more informative, including "The Blitz," "Old Mayfair," Harry Potter filming sites, and my favorite, "Thames Beachcombing" (see box, p. 137). Other topics can supply authoritative tours on lesser-visited themes such as Hampstead village, the "Little Venice" near Regent's Canal, places few other touring companies touch. The group also provides guidance (and discounts) for Westminster Abbey, as well as "Great Escapes!" of Bath, Stonehenge, Cambridge, Canterbury, and other day-trip favorites (entry fees and train transit are included in the price (£34–£72); they may go weekly or seasonally. If there's any fault with London Walks, it's that some groups swell to untenable sizes, and many of the guides, although proven knowledgeable when pressed, rely too commonly on canned performance shtick (in fact, many are actors, but then again, histrionics are preferable to a narcotic delivery). The best way to remedy both problems is to pick a tour with narrower appeal; you'll have a better chance to ask questions. Tours are 2 hours; prices and locations vary.

www.walks.com. ℘ **020/7624-3978.** Tours £9 adults, £7 seniors and students.

Muggle Tours ★★   Although it's based on a mass-appeal trend, it's worthy. This well-assembled tour dispenses reams of Harry Potter trivia, from the books to the movies and locations from the movies. Groups of 20 start at London Bridge, near Borough Market (p. 72), and wind up in Leicester Square, and because so much London history is folded in, there's enough for non-Potterheads. Book online. Tours are 2½ hours. Tube: London Bridge.

www.muggletours.co.uk. ℘ **07917/411-374.** Tours £12 adults, £10 children 11 and under.

Unseen Tours ★★★   London is more than kings, art, and canned tall tales. See it from a raw angle, and plumb its modern issues, on a walk guided by homeless and former homeless residents. Walks go on six different routes—around Shoreditch, Brick Lane, Covent Garden, London Bridge, Brixton, and Camden/Primrose Hill. Tours last 2 hours; locations vary.

www.sockmobevents.org.uk. ℘ **0751/426-6775.** Tours £10 adults, £7 seniors and students.

Escorted Tours

There are many reasons to lean against those hop-on, hop-off bus tours. First, they're expensive. Also, after 10 minutes of rolling down the streets in these tourist-processing machines, everything you've seen will blend into a miasma of antiquity. Third, these tours are like playing Russian roulette, because your experience depends on the skill and brains of your guide and/or the quality of the amplification system, over which you have no control.

Narrated bus tours often make you wait 15 to 30 minutes to catch your next leg, which can add up to hours wasted, and although your ticket will be good for 24 hours, don't expect to catch anything from 6pm or so until after 9am the next morning. Day tickets may come with a free walking tour (Changing the Guard, Jack the Ripper) and a hop-on, hop-off pass for the river shuttle boat (although some report that paying customers may crowd out passholders like you). Unfortunately, both of those perks must often be used during the same 24 hours as the bus ticket's validity, demolishing their usefulness.

In sum, London is a walker's city, and you're better off getting an overview on foot or, if you really want a ride, from a window seat on a real double-decker bus, which is £4 for the whole day if you use Oyster pay-as-you-go (see p. 255 for the best routes for sightseeing), or £21 for the whole week. But if you insist on perceived convenience, you can buy tickets at any marked bus stop.

HOP-ON, HOP-OFF

Big Bus Tours Like its competition, it offers three circuitous routes, although two of them (Red and Blue) cover much of the same ground and narration is frequently prerecorded (it's live on Red, recorded on Blue) with out-of-date information. It doesn't matter at which of the 50-odd stops you get on, but drivers often change at Green Park on Piccadilly, so you'll avoid that wait by starting there. You can catch this one at any stop, but most people get on at Marble Arch, Regent Street south of Piccadilly Circus, Charing Cross Road north of Trafalgar Square, or under the South Bank Lion at Westminster Bridge. Prices can be a few pounds higher if you don't book ahead.

48 Buckingham Palace Rd., SW1. www.bigbustours.com. © **020/7808-6753.** Tours £32 adults, £12 children 5–15 (including City Cruise tour and 3 walking tours); £8 discount online; 48-hr. tickets additional £6 adults/£3 children. Daily 8:30am–8pm.

Golden Tours Open Top Bus Tours The discount option. Golden Tours is one of the big machines in town, offering every permutation of bus tour and day-trip excursion you can imagine. None are particularly special, but they get the job done, and they do it with a flesh-and-blood narrator at low-ish prices, which means crowds. Its main product is a system of routes granting 24-hour access to a network of 44 stops (which can be a waste of money since stops are generally only open from 8am–4:30 or 5pm), plus one free walking tour and one free river boat ride. Its Blue Line covers most of the core city including South Kensington, and the Red Line forgoes South

Ken for the Docklands area. Commensurate with the lower prices, buses are in poor repair.

11a Charing Cross Rd., WC2, 156 Cromwell Rd., SW7, and 4 Fountain Sq., 123-151 Buckingham Palace Rd., SW1. www.hoponhopoffplus.com. © **020/7630-2028** and 800/509-2507 (North America). Tours £29 adults, £12 children 5–15, £75 for family of 2 adults and 2 children (including 1 river cruise and 1 walking tour). Add £4 adults, £2 children for 2nd 24-hr. period. Daily 9am–4:30pm.

The Original Tour London Sightseeing Tours, conducted on open-top coaches, are covered for 24 hours with a ticket, so you can go around five times if your feet hurt. You can catch the bus (three interconnecting circuits that supply solid coverage of the main sights) at any of the 80-odd stops on the routes, but most people begin at Piccadilly Circus, Trafalgar Square, Embankment Station, near Victoria Station, or outside Madame Tussauds. Live narrators appear, without much vigor or inspiration, on the Yellow Line, which covers the broadest swath of town, while other lines are likely to have digital spiels, sometimes too quiet. Two of its routes come with audio/booklet packs for kids, but you have to pick them up at its office.

17-19 Cockspur St., SW1. www.theoriginaltour.com. © **020/8877-1722.** Tours £29 adults, £14 children 5–15; £4 adults, £2 children discount online (including river cruise). Nov–Feb Fri–Sun 8:30am–5:20pm and Mon–Thurs 8:30am–4:50pm; Mar–Oct daily 8:30am–5:20pm.

OTHER TOURS

Brit Movie Tours Increasingly, people feel more connection with movies and TV than with the history that actually wrought them, and for them, it hosts an array of excursions ranging from walking tours to full-day coach, including an 8-hour *Downton Abbey* visit (£95 adults, £85 children 15 and under) that sells out months ahead, and tours for James Bond, *Doctor Who,* and Harry Potter locations (£26 adults/£19 children 15 and under).

www.britmovietours.com. © **0844/2471-007.**

City Cruises When you take a standard trip on its generously glass-sided and -topped boats, live narrators point out details of interest. The "Red Rover" ticket allows you to hop on and off all day. Boats go every 30 minutes, generally between 9am and 9pm, at four piers: Westminster, London Eye, the Tower, and Greenwich. Note that two of those stops are across the river from each other, leaving the stretch between the London Eye and the Tower of London (the meatiest section) without a stop. Using it to add Greenwich can save money off buying several one-way tickets on standard ferries, but simple return tickets are cheaper on Thames Clippers. The 40-minute **London Eye River Cruise** (londoneye.com; © **0870/500-0600;** £13 adults, £12 seniors Mon–Fri; £7 children 5–16; daily 11:45am–4:45pm), from London Eye pier, is less of a value because you can't get off to explore.

www.citycruises.com. © **020/774-0400.** Tours £8 single, £12 return. 24-hr. passes: £16 adults, £11 seniors and students, £8 children 5–16, £32 for 2 adults and 3 children; 10% online discount.

London Ducktours   Like their forebears that have plied the Wisconsin Dells for decades, these 75-minute tours are conducted in clumsy, American-made DUKW amphibious vehicles, which roll down streets like buses and then plow into the Thames and motor along briefly as boats. Roofed and mostly splashless, these vehicles were developed as Word War II transports. You can't hop off and you only see Whitehall, Westminster, and Vauxhall. A 2013 fire incident (everyone was fine) was blamed on too much foam applied to keep the vessels extra buoyant. That's been fixed.

55 York Rd., SE1. www.londonducktours.co.uk. ✆ **020/7928-3132.** Tours £24 adults, £20 seniors and students 13–17, £16 children 12 and under. Daily 10am–late afternoon. Reservations recommended. Tube: Waterloo.

London Helicopter Tours   Six-seated choppers take off from Battersea and supply an epic bird's-eye view of the city, following the Thames to Greenwich, back to Hammersmith, and returning to Battersea in 12 to 18 minutes (the "Buzz" route covers less ground). Your pilot is pressed uncomfortably into double duty as a guide, dispensing dubious information such as dating the *Cutty Sark* 300 years before its actual construction. Never mind; the view is the thing, and it's an unrepeatable view. You'll see the Shard from above, the ligature of countless rail lines binding the city together, and flights at 11:30am will spy Changing the Guard in the distance at Buckingham Palace. One downside: There are two seats in the front at the dashboard and four in a row along the back, so those two middle passengers are getting a poorer view for the same money.

London Battersea Heliport, Bridges Court, Battersea, SW11. www.thelondonhelicopter. com. ✆ **020/7887-2626.** Tours £150–£200. Tube: Clapham Junction.

Thames Rib Experience   Touristy to the core, this outfit loads you in semi-inflatable RIB speedboats with twin 245-horsepower engines and flits you downriver to Canary Wharf, around the O2, or Greenwich from Embankment. Make a lasting memory of St Paul's flying past, blurry from cold estuary spray in your eyes. Tours are 50 to 75 minutes. Its competition, offering similar thrills, is **London RIB Voyages** (www.londonribvoyages.com; ✆ **020/928-8933;** £40–£50), which goes from close to the London Eye and from St Katharine's Pier near the Tower of London.

Victoria Embankment, WC2. www.thamesribexperience.com. ✆ **020/3432-6856.** Tours £25–£52 adults, £22–£36 children 15 and under; prices depend on tour length. Tube: Embankment or Charing Cross.

LONDON SHOPPING

B lame Elizabeth I. Sure, the old girl loved her baubles and gold-embroidered bodices, but her biggest contribution to English consumerism was defeating the Spanish Armada. You see, that established England as the dominant player on the high seas, which opened up channels of international trade and soon, the Thames was more jammed with bounty than the parking lot at the mall on Christmas Eve. Ever since then, London has had a hankering for the finer things. Gird your pocketbook!

Stores across the city generally open at 9 or 10am daily and close at 7 or 8pm, although boutiques may close at 6pm and the department stores and Oxford Street shops are often open as late as 9pm. On Sundays, relatively new terrain for British shopping, 11am or noon to 6pm is common (although arcane laws mean some stores won't make a sale until noon); very few places will stay open past then. Expect crowds on weekends, when people pour into town from the countryside.

THE GREAT SHOPPING STREETS

Appropriately for a city obsessed with class, London's prime shopping streets aren't usually defined so much by what they sell as by how much you'll spend to bring home their booty.

THE ARCADES OF PICCADILLY & OLD BOND STREET

Tube: Green Park: There are several iron-framed, skylighted "arcades" (closed Sun), built by 19th-century blue bloods for shopping in any weather along these streets. The best include the longest one, Burlington Arcade, a block long parallel to Old Bond Street at Piccadilly (silverware, cashmere, handbags, Ladurée *macarons*); the Royal Arcade, south of Burlington Gardens (antiques, shoes, watches); and Piccadilly Arcade, across from Burlington Arcade (men's tailoring; it leads to Jermyn St. [below], a heart of haberdashery).

CARNABY STREET

Tube: Oxford Circus or Piccadilly Circus: This used to be for the mod crowd, but today its legendary hyper-alternative looks are mostly found on Memory Lane. Instead, expect mainstream sporty choices such as North Face and Vans. Better for browsing is Kingly Court, a former timber warehouse converted into a mini-mall for 30-odd upcoming designers. (carnaby.co.uk)

CECIL COURT

Tube: Leicester Square: Distinguished by original glazed-tile Victorian storefronts, matching green-and-white shop signs, and a refreshing lack of cars, this block (it and St Martin's Court just north are said to have inspired Harry Potter's Diagon Alley) was the cradle of British cinema, but today is a holdout of the antiquarian book trade that once dominated Charing Cross Road. Favorites are Marchpane, at 16, a trove of vintage children's literature; Pleasures of Past Times' David Drummond, at 11, an "ephemerist" collecting theatrical memorabilia; and Travis & Emery, at 17, specializing in music and books about music. (www.cecilcourt.co.uk)

SEVEN DIALS

Tube: Covent Garden: Every lane around Covent Garden is an obvious shopping drag, full of the usual brands but increasingly some one-off names. Check out Neal Street for shoes, Long Acre for big clothing stores, and Floral Street for designers. (www.coventgardenlondonuk.com)

JERMYN STREET

Tube: Piccadilly Circus or Green Park: The quintessential street for the natty man is home to several multi-named haberdashers that have been in business for more than a century (Harvie & Hudson, Hilditch & Key, Hawes & Curtis, and Turnbull & Asser—dresser of Chaplin, Churchill, Prince Charles, and James Bond) as well as specialists such as Tyrwhitt for shirts, Daks, and T. M. Lewin. It connects to Piccadilly by Princes Arcade, strong on shoes.

KENSINGTON HIGH STREET

Tube: High Street Kensington: London's coolest department store street in the '60s, the big ones have since decamped for the malls, and it's now a hodgepodge of upmarket brand names, young trendy stuff on the east end, plus some boutiques on Kensington Church Street.

KING'S ROAD

Tube: Sloane Square or South Kensington: The Chelsea avenue where affluent "Sloaneys" spend is where you go to dream—increasingly, about what King's Road used to be. Most of the truly unique stores have recently been elbowed aside by the same old names, but amid the familiar (Ted Baker, Rag & Bone, Anthropologie), you'll find a few independent boutiques, high-end mommy wear, and some designer furnishings. That doesn't mean the French cafes on Sloane Square aren't prime real estate for watching those happy rich kids pass by.

NEW BOND STREET

Tube: Bond Street or Green Park: The ultimate high-end purchasing pantheon runs from Oxford Street to Piccadilly, partly as Old Bond Street. Every account-draining trinket maker has a presence, including Sotheby's, Van Cleef & Arpels, Graff, Alexander McQueen, Harry Winston, Tiffany & Co., Chopard, and Boucheron. Asprey's, at 165-169, sells adornments few can afford, but its Victorian facade is a visual treat for all incomes. Nearby, South Molton Street continues the luxury, but at half-step down in expense, with Brown's Ted Baker, Karen Millen, and other fashion houses.

OXFORD STREET

Tube: Marble Arch, Bond Street, or Oxford Circus: The king of London shopping streets supports the biggest names, including Topshop, H&M, the ever-mobbed Primark, and a few lollapalooza department stores like Selfridges, John Lewis, and Marks & Spencer. Boy, are weekends crowded! (www.oxfordstreet.co.uk)

REDCHURCH STREET

Tube: Shoreditch High Street: This down-at-heel Shoreditch alley, once rammed with cabinetmakers, is at the forefront for stylists. The 150-year-old menswear brand Sunspel opened its first retail shop, Labour & Wait vends desirable kitchen toys, Maison Troi Garçons does slick interiors, and Terence Conran's super-chic hotel/restaurant/cafe complex Boundary seals the deal for scenesters. Around the corner, **Boxpark,** a hipster mall comprised of five dozen rehabbed shipping containers, hosts pop-up boutiques and not-really-slumming corporate brands alike.

SLOANE STREET

Tube: Knightsbridge: Offshore millionaires come here to feast at the top of the consumerist food chain: Bulgari, Valentino, Miu Miu, Prada, Armani, and everything else haute and showy. And no farther than you can throw a chocolate truffle, Harvey Nichols and Harrods. (www.sloane-street.co.uk)

TOTTENHAM COURT ROAD

Tube: Tottenham Court Road or Goodge Street: Locals sniff, but the street's lower half, between Oxford and Store streets, is their only drag for cut-rate electronics (including voltage converters). North to Torrington Place, pickings shift to brilliantly designed housewares and furnishings at Habitat (later in this chapter) and London's grande dame of smart styling, Heal's (later in this chapter).

UPPER STREET

Tube: Angel: Islington's chief avenue is emerging as a low-key location for boutiques, vintage outfits, and kitchen-sink junk shops, all pleasantly spelled by unpretentious pubs and cafes. While you're south of the Green, explore the sidewalks of Camden Passage, known for antiques and bric-a-brac.

THE SHOPPING PALACES

Fortnum & Mason ★★★ Tesco it isn't. So venerable is this vendor, which began life in 1707 as the candle maker to Queen Anne, that in 1922 archaeologist Howard Carter used empty F&M boxes to tote home the treasures of King Tut's tomb. The veddy British, modestly sized department store, which has a focus on gourmet foods, is renowned for its glamorous hampers, which were first distributed in the days before World War I, when soldiers' families were responsible for feeding their men on the field. Such picnic sets now come with bone china and can cost £300, but you can also pack your own. For the full experience, which will leave your family with no inheritance, head to the first floor to peruse its famous wicker hampers, which you can then fill with goodies from the ground-floor Food Hall and have shipped. Select from a cornucopia of such tongue-teasing triumphs as jarred black truffles and fresh Blue Stilton cheese in ceramic pots. In addition to a huge selection of tea packaged in distinctive canisters (*so* much tea), F&M makes its own "parlour ice" (ice creams), "royal game pie" (loafs of seasonal game meats layered with cheese), and something called Rubies in the Rubble (chutney made from fruits obtained in London's markets). Content yourself, as most do, with a wander through the carpeted upper-floor departments, which are lit by chandelier, serenaded by classical music, and illuminated by a lotuslike atrium skylight. The fragrance department smells like a rose garden. High tea can be taken in the top-floor St James's tearooms, among the city's most sumptuous (reservations: ✆ **0845/602-5694**), while lunching ladies can be found in the banquettes of the Fountain Restaurant. When the clock strikes the hour over the store's Piccadilly entrance, two modern mechanical representations of Mr. Fortnum and Mr. Mason emerge, bow to each other approvingly, and return to business inside.

181 Piccadilly, W1. www.fortnumandmason.london. ✆ **020/7734-8040.** Tube: Green Park or Piccadilly Circus.

Harrods ★ Now owned by the Qatari royal family's financiers, a miraculous holdover from the golden age of shopping has been retooled into a bombastic mall appealing largely to free-spending out-of-towners. Few London-born people bother with it, yet it thrives, proof of just how awash with foreign fortunes the city truly is. Its thronged Food Hall rooms are a glut of exorbitantly priced meats and cheeses, its ornate seven-floor facade emblazoned like a Christmas tree after dark, its jewelry hall attended by robotic staff plying the husbands of spoiled wives with champagne until they give in. But much floor space, where too-loud rock music blares nonstop, is either devoted to brands you'd find for a third of the price at your local mall or to One-Percenter nonsense such as £150,000 sculptures. The artificial environment, from the overpriced razzmatazz to the clerks wearing straw hats, would be more authentic at Disneyland than in London of old, and in fact, in the souvenir "emporium" on the second floor (£17 for sandwich-size gusset bags; £15 mugs; teddy bears aplenty), I sense the air has been pumped with the same scent you smell at Disney wherever the company wants to coax customers into purchasing (a trick called "olfactory coding"). Of the many escalator banks, the most interesting is the uproarious Egyptian-themed one at the store's center. At its base is a tacky brass fountain memorial to Dodi Al-Fayed and Princess Diana, who died together in Paris in 1997—his father owned Harrods at the time and campaigned to prove Prince Philip ordered the murder of Diana lest she marry a Muslim. A lipstick-smudged wine glass from the couple's final tryst is preserved along with a ring with which al-Fayed claims his son intended to propose to Diana. Tacky! If you crave a real British department store, visit Fortnum & Mason or Selfridges; if you want to be flabbergasted by the pompous excesses of the jet set, Harrods is the overly shellacked circus for you, but don't be fooled into thinking it's something traditional.

87-135 Brompton Rd., SW1. www.harrods.com. ℭ **020/7730-1234.** Tube: Knightsbridge.

Harvey Nichols ★ *Absolutely Fabulous'* shallow anti-heroines Patsy and Edina spoke of it with the same breathless reverence most people reserve for deities. You'll need the income of a god to afford a single thread of Harvey Nick's women's and men's fashions, and although the British-owned store isn't as popular as it used to be—it's been here since the 1880s—a stroll through this eight-floor spendthrift's heaven is entertaining. In addition to the lunching ladies on display in the fifth-floor restaurant—think of it as a zoo for old money.

109-125 Knightsbridge, SW1. www.harveynichols.com. ℭ **020/7235-5000.** Tube: Knightsbridge.

John Lewis ★★ Every Englishman knows that if you want a sound deal, you go here, where there's a price guarantee; it employs an army of people to scout for the lowest prices in the area, which it matches. That may sound like the gimmick of a low-rent wannabe, but John Lewis, established in 1864, is in fact a respected cooperative owned by its employees, and their interest in its success shows in their attentive service and seemingly limitless product line. It also has some exceptional buyers; you'll find things here no other store carries (the bedding department is renowned). Art fans shouldn't miss the building's eastern face, upon which is mounted an abstract cast-aluminum sculpture, *The Winged Figure* (1960), by one of the most important artists of the 20th century, Dame Barbara Hepworth. She's also in the Tate Britain (p. 104).

Oxford St. at Holles St. www.johnlewis.com/oxfordstreet. ℭ **0844/693-1765.** Tube: Oxford Circus.

Liberty ★★ Founded in 1875, it made its name (and earned some mockery) as an importer of Asian art and as a major proponent of Art Nouveau style. Now its focus is distinctly British. The timber-and-plaster wing looks Tudor, but is actually a 1924 revival constructed from the salvaged timbers of two ships, HMS *Impregnable* and HMS *Hindustan;* the length of the latter ship equals the building's length along Great Marlborough Street. The store's stationery and scarf selections are celebrated, as are its fabrics (many of which are designed in-house), and the beauty hall is one of the best. The soft wooden spaces are creaky and seductive, while the staff service is so obsequious it evokes a bygone era.

210-220 Regent St., W1. www.liberty.co.uk. ℰ **020/7734-1234.** Tube: Oxford Circus.

Marks & Spencer ★★★   The beloved M&S is the country's favorite mid-level department store for good-looking clothing staples. Its own-brand wears, once shoddy and ill-fitting, have been re-envisioned as affordable riffs on well-tailored fashions, and it sells the go-to suit for many a young man starting out in life. M&S is particularly beloved for its underwear, and its bathrobes are preternaturally soft, but its crowning achievement is its giant **food halls** ★★★ (usually tucked underneath the store but sometimes a stand-alone shop called **Simply Food**), which sell an astonishing array of prepared meals, soups and sandwiches, and well-selected yet inexpensive wines. M&S is a national treasure, with nothing like it in other countries, and it's about time the English remembered that.

Flagship: 458 Oxford St., W1. www.marksandspencer.co.uk. ℰ **020/7935-7954.** Tube: Marble Arch.

Selfridges ★★★   Selfridges fills the real-life role in London life that many tourists think Harrods does, and aside from Harrods' olive drab sacks, no shopping bag speaks louder about your shopping preferences than a canary yellow screamer from Selfridges. It's unquestionably the better of the two stores, since it's not merely a sprawling sensory treat, but it also sells items you'd actually buy. Since its 1909 opening by Harry Gordon Selfridge, an immoderate American marketing genius from Marshall Field's in Chicago (it was designed by Daniel Burnham of Chicago and Manhattan's Flatiron Building fame), Selfridges pioneered department store practices, including placing the perfumes near the front door, filling its 27 ground-floor windows with consumerist fantasias, and coining the phrase "the customer is always right"—all Selfridges inventions. Some one million products are for sale, and the beauty department is Europe's largest. The thicket of food counters on the ground floor gets busy at lunchtime, and the rest of the store is just as popular at other times; some 17 million visits are recorded each year. Selfridges has traded in history, too; the first public demonstration of television was held on the first floor in 1925, and 3 years later, the store sold the world's first set. During much of the Blitz, Churchill's transatlantic conversations with FDR were encoded via a scrambler stashed in the cellar. The store's popularity is enjoying a goose thanks to the series *Mr. Selfridge,* starring Jeremy Piven barking his way through the title role, which gives the store the soapy treatment.

400 Oxford St., W1. www.selfridges.com. ℰ **0800/123-400** (U.K.) or 113/369-8040 (overseas). Tube: Bond Street or Marble Arch.

RECOMMENDED STORES

For a city world-famous for shopping, where people from around the world arrive with one fat wallet and leave with 10 stuffed suitcases, there's no way to give proper celebratory due to everything that is wonderful and for sale. Some stores, though, are so original and site-specific that they can sweeten the experience of being in London even if you don't buy a thing.

Art & Antiques

After Noah ★   More like an upscale junk shop with restoration chops, it makes its name on vintage toys, crockery, bathroom fittings, cheerful celluloid jewelry, and wooden desks and bedsteads, sadly too large to get home. Its refurbished mid-20th-century telephones are particularly sought after. 121 Upper St., N1. www.afternoah.com. ℂ **020/7359-4281.** Tube: Angel.

Blue Mantle ★   For dream renovations back home, the largest antique fireplace showroom in the world salvages the good stuff with warm English touches when developers knock down classic buildings—which is happening more than we like. 306-312 Old Kent Rd., SE1. www.bluemantle.co.uk. ℂ **020/7703-7437.** Tube: Borough.

Camden Passage ★★   Plenty of tourists swing through the booths, so bargains aren't always very easy to come by. Still, shimmering examples of china, silverware, cocktail shakers, military medals, coins, and countless other hand-me-downs overflow the cases. Despite the name, it's in Islington. Off Upper St., N1. www.camdenpassageislington.co.uk. Market Wed, Sat, Sun. Tube: Angel.

Grays ★★   Not the place to go if you're looking for the lowest deal (it's in Mayfair), but it's definitely a source for variety. There are some 200 vendors, many experts registered in the official antiques societies, split among two buildings, and they sell everything from Victorian jewelry to toys to strange bric-a-brac and collectible silverware. Weekdays are best. Head into the basement of the Mews building to see the River Tyburn, which was buried by 18th-century redevelopment but now feeds into Grays' goldfish trough. 58 Davies St., W1. www.graysantiques.com. ℂ **020/7629-7034.** Closed Sun. Tube: Bond Street.

LASSCo ★★   From stained glass to paneling and faucets to wood flooring, you'll get an incredible selection of fittings and furniture rescued from museums, churches, pubs, and homes at LASSCo (The London Architectural Salvage and Supply Company). 41 Maltby St., SE1. www.lassco.co.uk. ℂ **020/7501-7775.** Tube: Bermondsey. Also at Brunswick House: 30 Wandsworth Rd., SW8; ℂ **020/7394-2100.** Tube: Vauxhall.

Books

The territorial nature of publishing means that many books that are for sale in London won't be in print back home. Take time to trawl the used-book stores along **Charing Cross Road** and off that, the adorable collectible bookstores lining **Cecil Court** (p. 160), which runs to St Martin's Lane. For scripts, acting guides, and performers' biographies, **French's Theatre Bookshop** (52 Fitzroy St., W1; www.samuelfrench-london.co.uk; ℂ **020/7255-4300;** Tube: Warren Street), north of lovely Fitzroy Square, is the city's most reliable publisher and supplier. But you mustn't ignore the **National Theatre Bookshop** (Royal National Theatre, Southbank, SE1; shop.nationaltheatre.org.uk; ✆ **020/7452-3456;** Tube: Waterloo).

Daunt Books ★★   Lined with oak galleries and lit by a long, central skylight, it prides itself on its travel collection, which is located down a groaning wooden staircase. Everything is arranged by the country it's about—Third Reich histories under Germany, Tolstoy under Russia. It's no slouch in the general interest categories, either. Clerks seem to know what will interest the vaguest browser, and the cashier's desk is always piled with choice curiosities. 83 Marylebone High St., W1. www.dauntbooks.co.uk. ✆ **020/7224-2295.** Tube: Baker Street.

Foyles ★★   In business since 1903, this institution has thus far navigated the onslaught of high rents and low readership. After the 1999 death of its off-putting and tyrannical owner, the store was once again passed to the next generation of the Foyle family, and it finally caught up with modernity just in time to avoid closure. In 2014, it left its cobbled-together home of more than 80 years for a custom-designed book palace a few meters south. Its huge inventory of 200,000 titles straddles both popular and specialty topics. There are small outlets at St Pancras, Waterloo, and the Southbank Centre, but this beloved HQ is more like a theme park for readers full of talks, special events, and signings. If you sign into its free Wi-Fi, you can get walking directions to the shelf containing the title you want. 107 Charing Cross Rd., WC2. www.foyles. co.uk. ✆ **020/7437-5660.** Tube: Tottenham Court Road.

Hatchards ★★   Although the Duke of Wellington and the Queen herself are counted among its customers, Hatchards, the oldest bookseller in the city (1797), is also noted for its famous shoplifters: An 18-year-old Noël Coward was apprehended as he stuffed a suitcase full of books. (Characteristically, he talked his way out of trouble.) It has been trading since 1801 at its current location, which means it was selling books before Hardy, Dickens, or the Brontës were writing them. You'll find it not far west of Waterstones (see below). 187 Piccadilly, W1. www.hatchards.co.uk. ✆ **020/7439-9921.** Tube: Piccadilly Circus.

Housmans Booksellers ★   London supports a vibrant protest community—don't forget this is where Karl Marx fashioned his views that changed the world. Since 1945, the city's preeminent store for radical books has been Housmans. It also boasts the United Kingdom's largest collection of magazines and newspapers, with some 200 titles on offer at any time, plus stationery and a cafe (free trade all the way). You're not going to find most of the stuff here published back home. Wednesdays at 7pm, an author speaks. 5 Caledonian Rd., N1. www.housmans.com. ✆ **020/7837-4473.** Tube: King's Cross St Pancras.

Stanfords ★★★   Marvelous since 1901, it has traded in globe-trotting goodness, from guides to narratives to fiction with a worldview. Should you accidentally leave your map in your hotel room, beeline to the basement; the

The Royal Warrant

When you're snooping around the stuffy shops of St James's or Mayfair, keep an eye out for a royal crest near the store's sign. That insignia is a seal of approval—its presence means that the business counts a member of the royal family as a customer and has done so for at least 5 years. To earn Prince Charles' plumed crest, stores have to do even more, and prove they abide by a sustainable environmental policy. The Queen is represented by a lion and a unicorn, but William doesn't have any warrants registered yet. Once a business wins a warrant—about 800 have done it, from chandeliers to elevator repair— it's extraordinarily rare to see it withdrawn, but to its humiliation, Harrods lost its seal in 2000. Which hotel does the Queen prefer? The Goring (p. 69), which earned its warrant in 2013. More great retailers: Anderson & Sheppard (Prince Charles' clothing), Corney & Barrow (wine), Jeroboams (cheese), and Dewar's (the Queen's quaff). But don't ask what specific items businesses are delivering to the Palace; shopkeepers aren't permitted to tattle. To learn which companies supply the Windsors— say, where the Queen buys her corgis' dog food—search the current warrant holders at www.royalwarrant.org.

floor there is covered with an oversized reproduction of the London A-Z map as well as reams of maps for purchase, especially for walking trails across Britain. 12-14 Long Acre. www.stanfords.co.uk. © **020/7836-1321.** Tube: Covent Garden.

Waterstones ★★★ Its location was opened in 1936 as Simpson's clothiers, the Art Deco model for Grace Brothers in the saucy Britcom *Are You Being Served?,* and now this branch of the giant chain is Europe's largest bookshop. Even if Waterstones is a Big Gorilla of bookselling, it handles the stewardship of that dubious title with dignity; there are six sweeping floors, an enormous London section, plenty of easy chairs for freeloaders, scads of discount offers, and a dedicated events space for visiting authors. The top floor's panoramic cafe, 5th View, hops after work and into the evening. 203 Piccadilly. www.waterstones.com. © **0843/290-8549.** Tube: Piccadilly Circus.

Clothing & Accessories

The clothes you find in the U.K. will not be the same as in major stores elsewhere. Site **Dressipi.com** tracks the current pulse of English High Street women's fashions.

Albam ★★ Unusually, this men's boutique seeks out well-constructed, honest clothing (most made in the U.K.) but doesn't mark it up by insane factors. Although its prices are similar to those of high-casual chain stores, the store (which was its first) has a following among guys because its clothing lasts longer. 23 Beak St., W1. www.albamclothing.com. © **020/7247-6254.** Tube: Piccadilly Circus or Oxford Circus.

Beyond Retro ★★ A one-stop for classic items (jeans, jackets, boots, and other casuals), it's a haunt of the poor and stylish, who can put together an off-margin look without overdrawing. There's a branch in Soho (58-59 Great Marlborough St., W1; ✆ **020/7434-1406;** Tube: Oxford Circus), but this is the location with the cat Tiny, who lives in the store and has become a local mascot. 110-112 Cheshire St., E2. www.beyondretro.com. ✆ **020/7613-3636.** Tube: Shoreditch High Street or Whitechapel.

Browns ★★   Some 100 designers, all of them for higher-end purchasers, fill the five connected shops at the top of Mayfair. For 40 years, it's been a marketplace for upscale women, but increasingly, it's pitching to a younger and more casual set. 24-27 South Molton St., W1. www.brownsfashion.com. ✆ **020/7514-0016.** Tube: Bond Street.

Burberry Factory Outlet ★   Although its East London location is charmless and somewhat laborious to reach, it's worth it for overstock prices that dip 30% to 70% lower than what's on sale in its high-end stores—still expensive, but a lot less than the usual damage. 29-31 Chatham Place, E9. ✆ **020/8328-4287.** Tube/National Rail: Hackney Central.

Cordings ★★   Britain's top manufacturer of Wellington boots, which were invented for the first Duke of Wellington, can be found at this well-heeled and very English emporium of field clothing, waistcoats, tweeds, and knitwear. 24-27 Piccadilly, W1. www.cordings.co.uk. ✆ **020/7734-0830.** Closed Sun. Tube: Piccadilly Circus.

Dover Street Market ★   A high-minded multidesigner concept, heavy on pretentious industrial architecture, is supported by couture (all of Comme des Garçons' lines) fused with multimedia art installations, all in a six-story department store–like space with a bakery on the top floor. 17-18 Dover St., W1. www.doverstreetmarket.com. ✆ **020/7518-0680.** Tube: Green Park.

Diverse ★   One of the first boutiques to move into Islington's Upper Street, it keeps stock changing even as it spotlights white-hot labels, many of which go on to greatness. Clothes tend toward arty, which is to say interesting but not irresistible. 294 Upper St., N1. www.diverseclothing.com. ✆ **020/7359-8877.** Tube: Angel.

Eleven Paris ★★   After 16 stores in France and 8 in Paris, in 2013 the French rocker brand hit London, bringing with it the smart-aleck T-shirts and natty casual wear with a sophisticated urban edge. Next target: the U.S.A. 46 Carnaby St., W1. www.elevenparis.com/en. ✆ **020/7434-1171.** Tube: Oxford Circus.

The Goodhood Store ★★   Consummately East End, the clothing and "life store" products sold in this popular, half-serious two-story emporium are all about what it means to feel cool. Don a faux-vintage T-shirt printed with inscrutable gibberish, carry home "The Masses are Asses" mug for your latte, and stock up on the latest on-trend grooming products. Independent, self-knowing—but it only *looks* secondhand. 151 Curtain Rd., EC2. www.goodhood store.com. ✆ **020/7729-3600.** Tube: Old Street.

Herbert Johnson ★★   This hatter, in business since 1889, made Indiana Jones' famous fedora, called The Poet Hat, for Steven Spielberg in 1980.

That's so awesome, not much more needs to be said, except it can make a cool hat for you, too. BRIGG, 7 Piccadilly Arcade, SW1. www.herbert-johnson.co.uk. 𝒞 **020/7409-7277.** Closed Sun. Tube: Green Park or Piccadilly Circus.

Jack Wills ★★ "Fabulously British," it brags, but this line comes off a bit like American Eagle Goes to Eton. It goes for a sporty prep school look with rugby shirts, tweeds, cute striped trunks, and brightly hued jumpers. It has expanded internationally, but here's the three-story flagship. 136 Long Acre, WC2. www.jackwills.com. 𝒞 **020/7240-8946.** Tube: Marble Arch.

James Smith & Sons ★★★ This shop out of time, hung from the outside with old-style Victorian lettering, is rattling the rafters inside with handmade umbrellas and walking sticks. That's all it makes, as it has done since 1830, so you can imagine the wonders: handles of hazelnut wood, buffalo horn, and antler, from £25 to over £300. Clerks can also fashion a box so you can check your purchase onto the plane. Hazlewood House, 53 New Oxford St., WC1. www.james-smith.co.uk. 𝒞 **020/7836-4731.** Tube: Holborn or Tottenham Court Road.

Jimmy Choo ★ The legendary Malaysian cobbler started his luxe line in 1996 with a fashion editor from the British edition of *Vogue.* Today, he designs a couture line that is sold by appointment only at 18 Connaught St. (𝒞 **020/7262-6888**), a location so exclusive it's not posted on the corporate website. If you're not a celebrity or MP's wife, you'll have to content yourself with the flagship store. 27 New Bond St., W1. www.jimmychoo.com. 𝒞 **020/7493-5858.** Tube: Bond Street.

The Laden Showroom ★★ Barry Laden takes chances on eager, young designers when no one else will. Since 1999, this lifelong Whitechapel resident has given counsel and space—a shelf here, a cubicle there—to newbie designers, about 40 at a time. Once you go in, it's tough to leave without something. Most items, but not all, are for women. 103 Brick Lane, E1. www.laden.co.uk. 𝒞 **020/7247-2431.** Tube: Whitechapel.

Levisons ★ In a single room with that vintage smell and an ever-puffing steamer, find era men's jackets and suits you could only locate in England— tweeds, hip school uniforms, tailored peacoats. The stock changes weekly. In fact, all of Cheshire Street is lined with boutiques for unusual and vintage duds. 1 Cheshire St., E2. www.levisons.co.uk. 𝒞 **020/3609-2224.** Tube: Marble Arch.

Mango ★ Take the cream of high fashion and make it accessible for the typical English young woman—that's the formula at this slightly upmarket label, which does well when you want your look to be colorful, casual, and maybe even beachy. 225-235 Oxford St., W1. monsoon.co.uk. 𝒞 **020/7534-3505.** Tube: Oxford Circus.

Monsoon ★ One of the favored High Street brands for women, its outfits are for independent dressers who favor bright hues and aren't afraid of a few embellishments. It also does good eveningwear. 498-500 Oxford St., W1. monsoon.co.uk. 𝒞 **020/7491-3005.** Tube: Marble Arch.

New Look ★★   Another reliable and very successful High Street chain, it does a huge amount of cute casual wear fashionably and cheaply. Its specialty is women's clothes, but it does a few men's, and it captures trends without going overboard. 500-502 Oxford St., W1. www.newlook.co.uk. ℂ **020/7290-7860.** Tube: Marble Arch.

Nick Tentis ★   This London-born men's designer (favored by Eddie Redmayne and Martin Freeman) revitalizes the neighorhood's fusty looks with ready-to-wear suits in youthful, Mod-culture cuts and modern, sometimes daring, fabrics. 37 Savile Row, W1. www.nicktentis.com. ℂ **020/7287-1966.** Tube: Marble Arch.

Office ★★★   The H&M of footwear rips off designer styles cheaply but effectively, and you'll find it everywhere in town, but one of the most convenient locations is in the Seven Dials area of Covent Garden. Its major competition **Schuh,** found around town, mostly stocks other brands (although it has its own sub-line). 57 Neal St., WC2. www.office.co.uk. ℂ **020/7379-1896.** Tube: Covent Garden.

Opening Ceremony ★★   The first European outpost of the American marketplace that promotes the most promising local artists, the shop sells a variety of British designers, new and established, cult favorites and its own house label, in a mix that appeals to a fashion-obsessed crowd. 35 King St., WC2. www.openingceremony.us. ℂ **020/7836-4978.** Closed Sun. Tube: Putney Bridge.

Primark ★★★   The most intense, most crowded, most oppressive store on Oxford Street roils with young families stuffing baskets with cheap-as-chips fashionable outfits, shoes, luggage, and outrageously lowballed accessories. Unfortunately, we're also talking about a clientele that discards garments wherever they want, staff that deals with the rubble using big push brooms, no washrooms, and products that won't last a year. But the bargains! Oh, the bargains—most stuff is less than £10, and £1 deals are common. You just can't help leaving with sacksful. "The devil wears Primark," mutter the snobs. 213 Oxford St., W1. www.primark.co.uk. ℂ **020/7495-0420.** Tube: Marble Arch. Also at 14-18 Oxford St., W1. ℂ **020/7580-5510.** Tube: Tottenham Court Road.

River Island ★★   Another of the popular, affordable women's High Street fashion brands, it's headquartered in West London and designs most of its wares in-house. Dresses are affordable, shoes are cool, leather jackets well-cut, and there's a kid's line. In 2013, Rihanna tried her hand at formulating a collection for the brand. Police had to restrain the crowd. The course of fashion did not change. 470-482 Oxford St., W1. www.riverisland.com. ℂ **0844/826-9835.** Tube: Marble Arch; 207-213 Oxford St., W1. ℂ **0844/847-2666.** Tube: Oxford Circus; 309 Oxford St., W1. ℂ **0844/395-1011.** Tube: Oxford Circus.

Rokit ★★   Because it's been cool for longer than many of its competitors have been in business, it has a strong following. Probably the largest collection in the city, Rokit sells retro and vintage threads, shoes, and accessories

WHAT CAN I bring home?

Although you should always claim edibles when you pass through Customs, very few things will be confiscated. Most stuff, including baked goods, honeys, vinegars, condiments, roasted coffee, teas, candy bars, crisps, pickles, and homemade dishes are good to go. Always check your country's requirements, but these things are certain to make the inspector dog's nose twitch:

o Meat and anything containing meat, be it dried, canned, or bouillon.

o Fresh fruit and vegetables.

o Runny cheeses, but not firm ones, which make up most cheeses (rule of thumb: if you have to keep it chilled, leave it behind).

o Rice. As if you would import rice.

o Plants, soil, wood, and seeds (non-edible). Ask the nursery whether you need paperwork, because many varieties are permitted. And be warned that officers in Australia respond to wood like it's kryptonite.

o Cadbury chocolate. Stores can't import it to the U.S. now, so grab all you can!

that are funky and hipster-prone, from 1950s industrial uniforms to tracksuits. 42 Shelton St., WC2. www.rokit.co.uk. © **020/7836-6547.** Tube: Covent Garden. Also in Whitechapel (101 and 107 Brick Lane, E1. © **020/7375-3864.** Tube: Shoreditch High Street) and Camden (225 Camden High St., NW1 © **020/7267-3046.** Tube: Camden Town).

Topshop ★★★   At this 8,361-sq.-m (90,000-sq.-ft.) store, some 1,000 employees are on hand, many charged expressly with helping shoppers put together a smashing new outfit. The range of accessories is dizzying—you can even get tattooed or pierced if you're so inclined. It's not just women, either, because the incorporated **Topman** is crammed with deal seekers, too, and its colorful socks are legion and fun. Designs are at the vanguard of youth fashion, yet the prices are defiantly low, which makes this forward-thinking store a primary stop. 214 Oxford St., W1. www.topshop.com. © **020/7636-7700.** Tube: Oxford Street.

Uniqlo ★★★   Savvy and of unexpectedly low prices, the Japan-based, rapidly multiplying megastore is another staple on any sensible Oxford Street shopping spree. The first renter to pay £1,000 per foot in rent for its £40,000-square-foot store on Oxford Street, it does jeans and tops extremely well, but it's also known for cool socks and sweaters, though its hallmark is poppy colors and sporty casuals. 311 Oxford St., W1. www.uniqlo.co.uk. © **020/7290-7701.** Tube: Oxford Street.

World's End ★   For a few years in the 1970s, Vivienne Westwood's shop was the coolest place on the planet. The clock at this guerilla boutique still runs backwards, but London's punk heyday is long over, and Westwood went from rebel to royalty. Never mind the bargains—her Anglomania label is a living museum, but it's not cheap. Still, the fanciful couture inventions, flowing with fabric, are outlandish enough to enchant. 430 Kings Rd., SW10. www.viviennewestwood.com. ℓ **020/7352-6551.** Closed Sun. Tube: Fulham Broadway.

Food

Don't neglect the markets (see below), Borough Market (see p. 72 in chapter 4), or the food halls of the shopping palaces (earlier in this chapter). One warning: Don't buy tea from a touristy shop. Stick to the reputable sellers like Twinings (below) or Fortnum & Mason (p. 162).

A. Gold ★★   English food has been a punch line for so long that even the British were starting to believe the reputation. A. Gold looks longstanding because of its vintage fittings, but is actually a newcomer. It peddles country comfort food that you can't even find at the English supermarkets anymore, such as Cornish salted sardine filets, Romney's Kendal mint cakes, Geo. Watkins Anchovy Sauce, and Yorkshire brack—okay, those names aren't helping, are they? 42 Brushfield St., E1. www.agoldshop.com. ℓ **020/7247-2487.** Closes 4pm. Tube: Liverpool Street.

Hope and Greenwood ★★   A contemporary evocation of an old-fashioned confectionery, with striped wallpaper, a back wall gleaming with glass jars filled with throwback goodies, and wooden tables piled high with addictive soft Terrific Toffees, Salt Caramel Popcorn, boiled sweets, and lavender-and-geranium truffles. 1 Russell St., WC2. www.hopeandgreenwood. co.uk. ℓ **020/7240-3314.** Tube: Covent Garden.

The SAvanna ★   For a taste of South Africa, try *biltong* or *droëwors,* two flavorful jerkies made of local beef. SAvanna will also sell you antipodean candy (Lunch Bar) and sodas—the Stoney ginger beer curls your toes. There are locations in Victoria, Paddington, Liverpool Street, and London Bridge stations, testament to the number of expats from former Empire nations who live here. Multiple locations. www.thesavanna.co.uk. ℓ **020/8971-9177.** Tube: London Bridge.

Twinings ★★   Does this tea boutique rely on tourist traffic? Definitely. But it's still steeped in tradition, having taken over from a coffee shop in this location in 1706. Here you can sample, taste, mix-and-match, and savor the leaf in all its varieties—or just peruse its little tea museum. 216 Strand, WC2. www. twinings.co.uk. ℓ **020/7353-3511.** Tube: Temple.

Health & Beauty

Boots ★   Do I dare suggest you patronize the ubiquitous High Street brand that has devoured all other drugstores? Yes, I certainly do. Something like 80% of fragrance sales in the U.K. are conducted over Boots' counters, and the chain's endless 3-for-2 promotions almost always include something worth taking home, be it Berocca vitamins or other hard-to-get items. Makeup costs a few pounds less than at most other stores. It's authentically British, too—its founder, John Campbell Boot, the second Baron Trent, has his picture in the National Portrait Gallery. Multiple locations. www.boots.co.uk.

Humidorable

Cigars are big business in London, and not just because the city was once the capital of the world tobacco trade. Many wealthy visitors from Arab countries are not permitted to drink alcohol by dint of their religion but they may enjoy a fine stogie, so finer hotels like the Wellesley (p. 40) and No. 10 Manchester Street (p. 40) offer humidors as well as cocktail bars. Dating to 1787, **James J. Fox** claims to be the oldest cigar merchant in the world, and its pedigree is peerless: Oscar Wilde indulged himself here, and Winston Churchill slouched in its weary brown leather armchair while he perused the Coronas. Come to inhale the rich, musky aroma, to select one of its fine bowl pipes, or even to smoke—the city's public smoking ban does not apply here (19 St James's St., SW1. www.jjfox.co.uk. 𝄞 **020/7930-3787.** Tube: Green Park).

Neal's Yard Remedies ★★★ At the forefront of Britain's powerful green movement, it supplies beauty aids, holistic treatments, massage oils, and even make-your-own-cosmetics ingredients, all cruelty-free, clear of toxins, and naturally formulated. Its products—London's answer to the New York beauty boutique Kiehl's—are respected for their quality and ethical standards, and the brand is expanding rapidly across the city. The primary store is squirreled away between Monmouth Street and Shorts Gardens, just northeast of Seven Dials. 15 Neal's Yard, WC2. www.nealsyardremedies.com. 𝄞 **020/7379-7222.** Tube: Covent Garden.

Penhaligon's ★★★ I don't enjoy the image of Prince Charles lighting a Lily of the Valley candle and anointing his body with English Fern eau de toilette, but the fact is that Penhaligon's, established in 1870, is listed as an official supplier of "toilet requisites" to the Prince of Wales, so it may be happening right now. It hand-squeezes and custom designs its own fragrances for both men and women—generally floral-based and gentle—and sidelines in luxury shaving and grooming products. A picturesque location is at 16-17 Burlington Arcade (Tube: Green Park). 41 Wellington St., WC2. www.penhaligons. co.uk. 𝄞 **020/7836-2150.** Tube: Covent Garden.

Housewares

Conran Shop ★★ Gorgeous, contemporary, smartly selected pieces made its name in housewares, and its flagship store is a master class in elegant urban furnishings and desirable home accessories. Its building is just as worthy: the 1911 Art Nouveau headquarters of the Michelin Tire Company, coated with decorative tiles of era racing cars and Bibendum, although the newer location in Marylebone is more convenient (55 Marylebone High St., W1.; 𝄞 **020/7723-2223;** Tube: Baker Street). 81 Fulham Rd., SW3. www.conran shop.co.uk. 𝄞 **020/7589-7401.** Tube: South Kensington.

Habitat ★★★ Consider it not for furniture but for its cheerful linens, kitchen tools, and bath fabrics. In pursuit of the department store's mandate (set by founder Sir Terence Conran) to bring high design to the masses at

Cracking the DVD Code

The dwindling population that still watches discs must contend with "region codes." American and Canadian players will only play Region 1 discs, and Australia and South America are zoned Region 4, but the DVDs you buy in the U.K. will be coded Region 2. This is annoying, to put it politely for a family-friendly guidebook, because many DVDs for sale in Britain—TV shows, documentaries, and so forth—simply aren't available anywhere else. The only legal solutions for now: Buy DVDs marked "All Regions," (sometimes noted as Region 0) or, at home, pick up a "multizone" DVD player that accepts discs from any region. Those are sold in neighborhoods where recent immigrants have settled.

affordable prices, A-list artists (Tracey Emin, Manolo Blahnik) have been recruited to contribute temporary items, and products are always peppy and practical. Although this store is Habitat's showpiece, a nice-size outpost is at 208 King's Rd. in Chelsea (Tube: Sloane Square or South Kensington). 196-199 Tottenham Court Rd., W1. www.habitat.co.uk. ✆ **084/4499-1122.** Tube: Goodge Street.

Heal's ★★ A stalwart since 1810, but not stuffy like one, Heal's (like Liberty, p. 163), was instrumental in forwarding the Arts and Crafts movement in England, and its furniture and housewares, which are usually defined by chic shapes, have proven so influential that in 1978 it donated its archive to the Victoria & Albert museum. The kitchen department is popular. 196 Tottenham Court Rd., W1. www.heals.co.uk. ✆ **020/7636-1666.** Tube: Goodge Street.

Labour and Wait ★★ The most expensive dustpan you'll ever own will be the envy of dirt everywhere. Gorgeously designed kitchenware, bathroom items, gardening tools, and stationery—from vintage enamel to new sculptural metalwork—will put some chic into your chores. Even its location, an emerald-tiled former pub, is functionally fabulous, and its neighbors along Redchurch Street, selling clothes and interior items, are just as stylish. 85 Redchurch St., E2. www.labourandwait.co.uk. ✆ **020/7589-7401.** Closed Mon. Tube: Shoreditch High Street.

Pitfield London ★★ Funky and smart homewares and kitchenwares that are, as the kids say, "cafefully edited." This means they're often one-offs or artist-made (bamboo cups and plates, for example) or hard-to-find (vintage Bakelite radios). Find it here and no one will have anything like it back home. 31-35 Pitfield St., N1. www.pitfieldlondon.com. ✆ **020/7490-6852.** Tube: Old Street.

Stationery

Paperchase ★★★ Paperchase does for stationery what Habitat does for chairs and tables: imbues them with infectious style, bold colors, and wit. Its journal selection is incomparable. Starting in summer, stock up on holiday cards, not only since they're much cheaper in the U.K. than abroad, but also because some proceeds go to charity. There are many so-so branches in this chain, but this three-floor flagship is a big paper cut above. There's even a cafe. 213-215 Tottenham Court Rd., W1. www.paperchase.co.uk. ✆ **020/7467-6200.** Tube: Goodge Street.

Ryman Stationery ★ If you're into office supplies (admit it—it's time to come out of the supply closet), the ubiquitous chain, which makes an appearance on almost every busy shopping street, is a good place to stock up on hard-to-find English-size A4 paper, clamp binders (not common in the U.S.), and convenient "box files" (also absent from other countries' stationers), available in a spectrum of sprightly colors. Multiple locations. www.ryman.co.uk.

Smythson of Bond Street ★★★ In addition to a line of leather journals, organizers, and handbags, it does stationery impeccably. The Queen, a one-woman thank-you note industry, buys her paper here. The cotton-fiber content is probably higher than in your bedsheets. 40 New Bond St., W1. www. smythson.com. ✆ **020/7629-8558.** Closed Sun. Tube: Bond Street.

Toys

Hamleys ★★★ Remote-control helicopters in your hair, magicians at your elbow, rugrats at your knees. This high-octane toy store is run by a gaggle of cheerful young floor staff, themselves kids at heart, who giddily demonstrate the latest toys. The experience will send you into sensory overload. The seven floors are stuffed with amusements—the fifth floor is nothing but sweets. Depending when you go, there may be free pirate face painting, a caricaturist, or even a beach party. It's one of the world's few department stores devoted just to children, and the only must-see toy store in London—even if you don't have kids with you. 188-196 Regent St., W1. www.hamleys.com. ✆ **0871/704-1977.** Tube: Oxford Circus.

LONDON'S GREATEST MARKETS

Unfortunately, with the inexorable spread of megastores, outdoor markets that have been feeding Central Londoners since the Dark Ages are finding themselves extinguished. The following markets soldier on. Not every market sells something you can take home, unless you count memories: For example, the **Columbia Road Flower Market** (Sun at 8am; Tube: Old Street), is an Eden for English blooms, which get cheaper around 2pm, near closing time. **Borough Market,** which is fully described on p. 72, is all about prepared foods or things you can't get past Customs. Even if you aren't keen to buy anything, stroll down one of these market lanes. Whether for gourmets, tourists, or locals, it's like a front-row seat to the ongoing opera of everyday life, and a taste of London as it once was.

BERWICK STREET MARKET ★

Berwick St. around Broadwick St. www.berwickstreetlondon.co.uk. Daily 9am–6pm except Sun. Tube: Piccadilly Circus.

Good for: The last daily street market in the West End, dating to the crowded days of the 1840s, is now being produced by developers. Gone with the

Cockney calls, in with overpriced baked goods and hipster coffee—delicious, but false.

Also check out: The gourmand-pleasing specialty shops lining the route.

BRICK LANE MARKETS ★★★

Brick Lane at Buxton St. www.bricklanemarket.com. ☏ **020/7770-6028.** Tube: Shoreditch High Street.

Good for: The Vintage Market (Fri–Sun, clothes), Backyard Market (Sat–Sun, crafts), Boiler House (Sat–Sun, food), and Tea Rooms (Sat–Sun, antiques). On Sundays, UpMarket does trendy fashions and food.

Also check out: The Beigel Bake (p. 78) for London's version of a bagel.

BRIXTON MARKET ★

Electric Ave. at Pope's Rd. brixtonmarket.net. Mon–Sat. Tube: Brixton.

Good for: Exotic produce, spices, halal meats, soul to reggae and hip-hop.

Also check out: Brixton Village, stalls selling African and Caribbean clothes, foods, and housewares; Ritzy's Art Fayre, a designer market, every Saturday.

CAMDEN ★★

Camden High St. at Buck St. www.camdenlock.net. Daily (weekends best). Tube: Camden Town.

Good for: Tourists favor this rambling warren of 700 stalls for vintage wear, sunglasses, leather, goth gear, and fast foods, partly in a canal-side setting. Between the Lock Market, the Market Hall, the Horse Stables, and Camden Lock Village across the street, options seem never-ending, but the crowds are utterly exhausting.

Also check out: Stables Market, on the other side of the railway off Chalk Farm Road, sells vintage clothes, antiques, and pop culture knick-knacks; Electric Market (on Camden High St.) is an indoor fair of vinyl, programs, and film posters (Saturdays) and retro and punk clothes (Sundays).

CHAPEL MARKET ★★

Islington. Tues–Sun. Tube: Angel.

Good for: Cheese, dumplings, meat pies, toiletries—it's a real catch-all working-class market that actually feeds workaday Londoners.

Also check out: The antithesis of a market, the gleaming N1 Islington mall, dominates the eastern end of the street; it's New London versus Old London.

GREENWICH MARKETS ★★

11A Greenwich Market. www.greenwichmarketlondon.com. Tues–Sun (weekends best). Tube: Cutty Sark DLR or Greenwich National Rail.

Good for: 40 stalls of antiques (Tues, Thurs, Fri), plus crafts, honeys, breads, and cakes under a historic market roof.

Also check out: The cafes lining the covered Craft Market.

LEATHER LANE MARKET ★

Leather Lane between Clerkenwell Rd. and Greville St. Mon–Fri 10:30am–2:30pm. Tube: Farringdon.

Market Hours
Unless otherwise noted, markets are mostly outdoors and generally kick off at around 8 or 9am in the morning and start packing up at around 3pm.

Good for: Local flavor. Hot and ready-to-eat food, be it Jewish (latkes, salt beef), Mexican (burritos), or universal (salads); sweat suits and skirts, jeans.

Also check out: Ye Olde Mitre pub (p. 85), a street away.

MALTBY STREET MARKET ★★★

Maltby St., SE1. www.maltby.st. (C) **020/7394-8061.** Sat 9am–4pm, Sun 11am–4pm. Tube: London Bridge or Bermondsey.

Good for: Refugee vendors from overrun Borough Market decamped to here, south of the Tower Bridge, and they share railway vaults with an antiques salvage company. Shuffle along gathering gorgeous flavors such as pork with sweet chili jam, mugs of horseradished Bloody Marys, and "African volcano" hot sauce.

Also check out: Historic pie and mash vendor M. Manze (p. 73) is nearby.

PORTOBELLO ROAD MARKET ★

www.portobelloroad.co.uk. (C) **020/7727-7684.** Fri–Sat. Tube: Notting Hill Gate or Westbourne Park.

Good for: Antiques, hot foods, jewelry, vintage clothes, tourist tat by the ton. Overcrowded and overrated, but thanks to the movies, it's not going anywhere.

Also check out: The packed pubs along the route; the galleries and antiques shops in the storefronts, where prices can be better than at the stalls.

QUEEN'S MARKET ★

Green St. at Queen's Rd. www.newham.gov.uk. (C) **020/8475-8971.** Tues and Thurs–Sat. Tube: Upton Park.

Good for: 80 stalls and 60 local stores for ingredients from Asia, Africa, Russia, the Caribbean, and elsewhere; international clothes and rugs. Although it's not very posh, it is very Everyday London. Sunday is a quieter day.

Also check out: Its defenders' website, www.friendsofqueensmarket.org.uk, which has argued their market is half as expensive as Walmart.

RIVERSIDE WALK MARKET ★★

Southbank under the Waterloo Bridge. Daily noon–7pm in good weather. Tube: Waterloo.

Good for: Tables of used books, maps, lithographs, and wood engravings.

Also check out: Lower Marsh Market on Lower Marsh between Westminster Bridge and Baylis roads (south of Waterloo station), a classic produce market.

SPITALFIELDS MARKET ★★

Commercial St. between Brushfield St. and Lamb St. www.visitspitalfields.com. Daily. Tube: Liverpool Street.

Good for: Up-and-coming designers and artists, prepared world food, handmade housewares, jewelry, vintage posters. It's the most gentrified market in

HACK THE tax attack

First, the good news: When you see a price in England, that's the full price. Tax is always included. Now, the bad news: That tax is usually charged at a rate of 20%. It's called VAT (Value-Added Tax), and it goes to enviable programs such as national health care, so that any British citizen who needs health care doesn't have to go into debt to get it.

And more good news: Tourists can often get a little of that back. As long as the store you're patronizing participates in the VAT Retail Export Scheme (many don't) and you get the paperwork from them while you're there (stores have varying minimum-purchase requirements), you can apply for a refund, minus a dismaying chunk for administrative fees. The only purchases it doesn't work for are vehicles, unmounted gemstones, and anything requiring an export license (except antiques). The system mostly benefits those who spend hundreds or thousands of pounds, not tourists with casual purchases.

To get money back:

○ Be a non–European Community visitor to the U.K.

○ Obtain stamped tax refund documents from each retailer. At big stores, you may have to wait in line with I.D. and receipts for as long as a half-hour and the store may take a cut of several pounds as a processing fee.

○ On the day you leave Britain, present that document to the VAT refund desk at the airport. The line may be extreme. You must also have the goods on hand, which means a) you must put them in your carry-on, or b) you pack the goods in your baggage but first check in at your airline to pick up your travel documents, then bring your yet-to-be checked baggage for inspection, and then resubmit your baggage at the airline counter once that is finished. This process can take up to 2 hours, and even then you may only get £7 back for every £100 spent, so decide if it's really worth the hassle.

Britain maintains information via www.hmrc.gov.uk. or ☎ 029/2050-1261.

---

town, and especially on Saturdays, there are one-of-a-kind clothing items, not all of them affordable. Sit-down restaurants surround the covered market. The market's success was a linchpin in East London's revitalization.

Also check out: Visit the Style Market for fashions on Saturday afternoons.

WALTHAMSTOW MARKET ★
Walthamstow Market St. Tues–Sat. Tube: Walthamstow.

Good for: 450 non-touristy stalls selling everything from knockoff clothes to food to Chinese-made batteries—it's the longest market street in Europe.
Also check out: You may not have the energy to see much else in this multicultural neighborhood, since the market is a kilometer long.

LONDON NIGHTLIFE

Let no one tell you that London tucks itself into bed early. Perhaps that was true in your grandfather's day. Now, the U.K. rocks 'til dawn. The Tube may shut down after midnight on weeknights, but as of last year, the main lines go all night on weekends, so for the intrepid, the entertainment can rollick until morning. With hundreds of theaters, nightclubs, cinemas, and music halls, London has more to offer on a single night than many cities can muster in an entire year, and its output influences the whole world.

That said, London's nights aren't perfect. The city's prevailing liquor laws force places to sometimes unceremoniously dump their clientele on the streets in mid-toast. Whereas in Spain, Greece, and New York, the night rarely begins before 1am, that's usually when the DJ packs up even at many of London's top clubs. If you require just one more cocktail to close the deal, a very few clubs will serve until 3am; ask your new friends at the bar which place is the cool one right now (in Soho, it's the **Shadow Lounge** at 5 Brewer St.). The Night Bus system (p. 255) assuages some financial pain, but it's a buzzkill to end a festive night of drinking with your legs crossed on a slow-moving bus.

GETTING THE SCOOP   Complete listings information for entertainment is published Saturdays in the London papers, but you don't have to wait until you arrive. Excellent online sources for things to do include **Londonist.com**, **LondonCalling.com**, **TimeOut.com**, **Townfish.com**, and the Twitter accounts Everything London (**@LDN**), **@LeCool_London** (nightlife); and **@SkintLondon** as well as the app **Frugl** (for finding cheap or free activities). The free app **DICE** collects upcoming music gags and sells mobile tickets to them. These are good, too:

- **Visit London:** The "What's On" section of its website is assiduously updated and, even better, it's free. (www.visitlondon.com)
- *Metro:* Free in racks at Tube stations, most copies are gone by mid-morning, but commuters leave copies behind on the trains; it's considered green to recycle a pre-read newspaper. (www. metro.co.uk)

○ The *Evening Standard:* Free at Tube stop entrances in midafternoon—some days, there's an accompanying lifestyle magazine in a nearby stack. *ES* is also available online for free. (www.standard.london)

THEATER

If you leave London without seeing at least one stage show, then you'll have missed one of this city's most glittering attractions. This is where Shakespeare defined great writing and Gilbert and Sullivan shaped modern musical theater. London's influence isn't just in antiquity; the great work continues to this day, and if you doubt it, look at the lists of Oscar, Emmy, and Tony winners from the past decade. With that kind of heritage, London theaters are intrinsically more daring than American ones, where an overemphasis on profits and critics mar creativity.

Whenever you hear the phrase "West End" in relation to shows, think of the term as describing the 60-odd top-tier theaters in the middle of town. These are the shows that most tourists flock to see, but that doesn't mean they're always the best—the West End is increasingly clogged with mediocre dramas propped up by Hollywood names and by so-called "jukebox" musicals that are the intellectual equivalent of bubble gum.

A great many West End shows begin their lives at companies found elsewhere in town. For challenging work mounted by producers intent on taking artistic risks, look to them. Many of them have designed and built facilities expressly for pumping out fresh projects, and each of them has a devoted following of fans and donors that most tourists, because of the circles they travel in, don't hear about. What's more, you're just as likely to catch stars—all at prices that are half what you'd shell out for a West End megamusical that was created by committee.

Standard curtain times range from 7:30 to 8pm for evening shows, and matinees start anywhere between 2 and 4pm. Every theater is different, so check your ticket. Nearly all shows are closed, or "dark," on Sundays.

It's easy to make a night of it. Every theater has its own bar, and many sell ice cream and snacks at intermission ("interval"). Companies with their own buildings might even run their own mid- to high-end restaurants.

Theater Tickets for Less

If you are desperate to see a specific show, book tickets before you leave home to ensure you won't be left out. Check with **The Society of London Theatre** (www.officiallondontheatre.co.uk), the trade association for theater owners and producers (established in 1908), for a rundown of what's playing and soon to play, as well as discount offers. Keep in mind that many links, including Visit London's, will deliver you to ticket sellers who'll hit you for a premium of as much as 20% for your booking. Only use that method if you'd be heartbroken to miss a particular show.

Given a lead-time of a few weeks, the established **LastMinute.com** sells tickets for half price, as does **LoveTheatre.com** (click "Special Offers").

saving ON THE STAGE

Apart from using TKTS, how can you save on a show?

- **Matinees are often cheaper than evening shows.** Unfortunately, they also cut into your daylight touring time.

- **Ask about standing room tickets and "day seats."** Many theaters sell standing room for a tenner (£10–£20. "Day seats" are a daily allotment of cheap seats, but you'll have to queue in the morning. *The Book of Mormon* begins a fun lottery for £20 seats 2½ hours before curtain.

- **Buy at the box office** to avoid paying booking fees.

- **In one of the older theaters, you can often settle for a restricted-view seat.** You may have to crane your neck to see around the edge of a balcony or a pillar, but you'll be in the room. They cost about a third of top-price seats. **Theatremonkey.com** posts theater-specific ratings.

- **If you're a student, some box offices (but not TKTS) may offer you discounts of 20% to 40%.** Carry a recognized ID card.

BroadwayBox.com's **www.theatre.co.uk** posts the known discount codes for the West End shows.

Once you get to London, grab a copy of *The Official London Theatre Guide,* dispensed for free in nearly every West End theater's lobby and at countless brochure racks; it tells you what's playing, where, for how much and how long, and the location of each theater. Unless you buy discounted seats directly from the box office of the theater, there's only one intelligent place to get same-day tickets: **TKTS** (south side of Leicester Square; tkts. co.uk; Mon–Sat 10am–7pm, Sun 11am–4:30pm; Tube: Leicester Square), operated by the Society of London Theatre. It sells same-day seats for as much as half off—the best stuff is sold in the first hour of opening. While the white-hot shows won't be represented here, about 80% of West End shows are—TKTS posts a list of its available shows on its website so you can know ahead of time. When musicals are half off, they're around £30 to £40, and plays cost £20 to £30, although the prices fluctuate per production with up to a £3 per ticket service charge. Come armed with a magazine or a newspaper that lists what the shows are about because TKTS offers no descriptions. Also put the free app **TodayTix** on your phone—it also discounts shows in the hours and days before curtain.

The West End is dotted with closet-size stalls hawking tickets to major shows and concerts. Don't deal with them. They are for audiences who simply *must* get tickets to their chosen show regardless of the fees as high as 25% over cost. Before you give your money to any of these outfits, check with the self-policing **Society of Ticket Agents and Retailers** (www.star.org.uk; ✆ **01904/234-737**) to find out who is reputable. Scalpers, called **touts** here, often issue counterfeit tickets or abscond with your cash before forking over anything at all. Some sightseeing discount cards also brag about discounts, but their deals are mostly for the longest-running, touristy shows and they don't save you nearly as much as TKTS would—only around £20 off the top price.

London's Landmark Theaters

The Barbican Centre ★★ In the 1950s, earnest but misguided city fathers turned their attentions toward redeveloping a bombed-out crater. The end result was a haltingly forbidding, mixed-use residential/business concrete complex that took more than 20 years to finish. They optimistically planned for lively crowds by adding Europe's largest arts and conference center, too, with a concert hall, two theaters, three cinemas, and two galleries, and now they're the best thing about the place—and one of the best things about London arts in general. You can't always find something going on in all of its venues, and even when things are rocking full-tilt, the bunkered Barbican is so windswept it makes *Blade Runner* look like Candy Land, but what does play here is rarely dull. It's nearly impossible to classify the Barbican's fare, since it receives a wide range of the world's great orchestras, singers, and composers, plus a handful of banner festivals each year, particularly in the realm of contemporary music and experimental theater. Its cinemas often screen features fresh from major film festival triumphs, and the long-running Bite festival brings in work from new names and white-hot international producers. Silk St., EC2. www.barbican.org.uk. ℰ **020/7638-8891.** Tube: Barbican.

The Bush Theatre ★★★ The Bush, which for more than 40 years has created a formidable output from new writers, started as a pub theater and in 2011, thanks to a lifesaving campaign that rallied support from the likes of Judi Dench and Daniel Radcliffe, got its own facility in a disused Victorian library. Besides attracting exciting writers, it brings in stars (like Kate Beckinsale and Alan Rickman) who want to connect with audiences. 7 Uxbridge Rd., W12. www.bushtheatre.co.uk. ℰ **020/8743-5050.** Tube: Shepherds Bush.

Donmar Warehouse ★★★ You can't often snag a last-minute ticket to the 250-seat house without standing in line for returns. Its productions, mostly limited runs of vividly reconceived revivals, are edgy and buzzy. Past coups for this comfortably converted brewery warehouse include the *Cabaret* revival that introduced Alan Cumming to the world and appearances by world-class performers such as Ian McKellen and Nicole Kidman. The front row of full-price, same-day tickets are dished out each Monday at 10am sharp for performances 2 weeks later, with a maximum of two tickets per person. 41 Earlham St., WC2. www.donmarwarehouse.com. ℰ **0844/871-7624.** Tube: Covent Garden.

Menier Chocolate Factory ★★ In an intimate setting among exposed beams and cast iron columns, converted you-know-what from the 1870s, is where some of the city's hottest musical revivals have been mounted. Its *Sunday in the Park with George* and *A Little Night Music* transferred to the West End and later to Broadway. This company, which also does plays, is one of the few to do Sunday shows; it's dark Mondays. 51-53 Southwark St., SE1. www.menierchocolatefactory.com. ℰ **020/7378-1713.** Tube: London Bridge.

Old Vic ★ The fruits of Kevin Spacey's late stewardship largely revitalized the venerable company, and upon his departure in 2015, he was feted by the city's arts community. Hitmaking director Matthew Warchus (*Matilda*) is now in charge, and celebrities like Vanessa Redgrave, Kim Cattrall, and Kristin Scott Thomas are drawn to star in its mountings of intellectual, meat-and-potatoes drama—stuff actors love to sink their teeth into. The 200-year-old building is pulling bigger crowds than ever before, and The Pit Bar, downstairs, is a stylish pre- and post-show hangout. The hot ticket for 2016 is the musical version of *Groundhog Day* by Tim Minchin. The Cut at Waterloo Rd., SE1. www.oldvictheatre.com. ⓒ **0844/871-7628.** Tube: Waterloo or Southwark.

Royal Court Theatre ★★ The preeminent writer's theater, it has fought censorship and unveiled international brilliance for so long that it's now a preeminent actor's theater as well. On the east side of jaunty Sloane Square, it devotes a hefty portion of its schedule to important premieres by the likes of Bruce Norris and Caryl Churchill and performances from fierce actors such as Ben Whishaw and Fiona Shaw. Among the plays launched here include *Look Back in Anger, The Rocky Horror Picture Show* (in its upstairs studio theater), George Bernard Shaw's *Major Barbara* and *Heartbreak House,* and Mike Bartlett's *Cock.* Sloane Square, SW1. www.royalcourttheatre.com. ⓒ **020/7565-5000.** Tube: Sloane Square.

Royal National Theatre ★★★ The government-subsidized powerhouse people simply call The National is the country's, and possibly the world's, most noted showpiece for top-flight drama and classical acting. Laurence Olivier was its first director, and the tradition of world-class performances has been unerring: Judi Dench, Ralph Fiennes, Anthony Hopkins, Maggie Smith, and Benedict Cumberbatch have been regulars. The National always mounts a diverse repertoire of British works on its three permanent (and one temporary) theaters spanning Shakespeare to classic musicals (the *Oklahoma!* that made Hugh Jackman a star) to no-seat experiments in which you follow the actors (Punchdrunk's *The Drowned Man*) to emotional spectacles (*War Horse* began here) to world premieres of well-made plays by the world's best playwrights. A recent renovation made the brutalist riverside complex a pleasure to hang out in, having added several places to eat, caffeinate, or tipple, and the fascinating and free Sherling High-Level Walkway allows anyone off the street to watch the activity backstage; there's even a periscope so kids can peer over railings into the scene shops. To find that, head down the eastern side road toward the Dorfman, go inside, and take the lift to the second level. As the people's theater, the National's pricing is populist. Some 100,000 tickets a year are discounted to £15 for the Travelex season (ⓒ **020/7452-3000**). Catch one of the 75-minute tours (£9–£13) showing off the inner workings or costume department, or shop in the lobby bookstore, a performing arts nirvana. South Bank, SE1. www.nationaltheatre.org.uk. ⓒ **020/7452-3000.** Tube: Waterloo.

Sadler's Wells ★ Sadler's Wells has been a part of the fabric of London life for so long (since 1683) that its current two-house home, dating to 1998, is actually the sixth. You can turn to this Islington establishment to catch some of the world's greatest companies in movement- or rhythm-based performances that transcend language. Its specialties are ballet (Matthew Bourne is a frequent guest artist), contemporary dance, and daring opera (Rufus Wainwright's *Prima Donna* premiered here). It also programs the Peacock Theatre on Portugal Street near the Holborn Tube. Rosebery Ave., EC1. www.sadlerswells.com. ☎ **020/7863-8198.** Tube: Angel.

Shakespeare's Globe ★★ One would think that a reconstruction of an Elizabethan theater on the Thames (see p. 119 for architectural details) would support mostly kitschy productions for tour groups. That it is, in fact, a serious concern that attracts the finest classically trained performers, is thanks partly to its founding artistic director, the brilliant actor Mark Rylance, who set a tone for quality that is maintained today. The season at the open-air Globe is spring through fall, but in 2014, a 340-seat Jacobean indoor theater, the Sam Wanamaker (named in honor of the American actor who fought to reconstruct the Globe) opened, so now there's something happening year-round. In the candle-lit Wanamaker, actors are so near that you could reach out and touch them. 21 New Globe Walk, Bankside, SE1. www.shakespearesglobe.com. ☎ **020/7401-9919.** Tube: Southwark or Mansion House.

Southbank Centre ★★★ Like the Barbican, it's a bleak canvas-colored slab architects don't know quite how to fix. It was conceived as a postwar pick-me-up, but age was not kind; despite a peerless Thames location, it's got a reputation as a forbidding architectural scowl that looks more like a pile of sidewalk curbs than an artistic capitol. It's perkier on the inside. Some 1,000 programs a year go down here at its three concert venues as well as in its huge central hall, which has a cafe and is open to everybody. Dance, classical and contemporary music, the London Jazz Festival, and films fill the bill, which is prolific if self-important. Don't miss the Undercroft, the hideous concrete negative space under the building along the Thames. When the Centre went up, this area was thought to be useless, so skateboarders and street artists claimed the architectural mistake. Recently, landlords tried to evict them for shops, but too late—the skaters proved too beloved. Belvedere Rd., SE1. www.southbankcentre.co.uk. ☎ **020/7960-4200.** Tube: Waterloo.

London's Great Smaller Theaters

Almeida Theatre ★★ The inviting Almeida, which has its own contemporary pub, sticks to its guns, mounting intelligent plays (some new, some unfairly forgotten, many new) without much regard for pushback—2014 saw *American Psycho,* the musical—and people liked it. The resulting experience is often thought-provoking. Lucy Kirkwood's *Chimerica,* about the Tiananmen Square tank photograph, was a 2013 smash. Almeida St. off Upper St., N1. www.almeida.co.uk. ☎ **020/7359-4404.** Tube: Angel.

THE QUIRKS OF LONDON theatergoing

London theater can be a strange experience for outsiders:

- Programs are not free; they cost from £3 (for plays) to £5 (for musicals). Big productions will also sell a glossy souvenir brochure for £7 to £10.

- Some seats are equipped with plastic opera glasses, which can be rented for the show with a 50p or £1 coin.

- What North American theaters call "orchestra" seats, London houses call the "stalls." And instead of a "mezzanine," they have a "Dress Circle," and above that, "Upper Circle" or "Royal Circle." If there happens to be a third, topmost level, that is the "balcony," or sometimes, the "gallery." And because many theaters were constructed in a class-obsessed era, there will likely be a separate street entrance for each area.

- The break between acts is called an "interval," not "intermission."

- The big snack? Ice cream, sold by ushers (or "attendants").

- Older theaters are required to deploy the "fire curtain," which seals the stage from the auditorium in the event of flames, once during every performance. It's usually done discreetly during the interval.

- Leave big bags at the hotel, because these old seats can be knee-knockers. And ladies, cover your knees, because in the Circles, they will likely be at head-level of the person sitting in front of you.

Hackney Empire ★ One of London's greatest and most ornate old houses (1901) was where, once upon a time, you could catch Charlie Chaplin as a vaudeville act. The ever-changing slate still presents the best of variety, but with an urban, multicultural twist: kids' shows, opera, comedy acts like British smarm-meister Jimmy Carr, hip-hop drama, and concerts. 291 Mare St., E8. www.hackneyempire.co.uk. ℭ **020/8985-2424.** Tube: Hackney Central Overground.

Lyric Hammersmith ★ Riding high after the 2014 opening of a £16.5 million expansion, its core may look like a fusty Victorian jewel-box theater, but you'll find spectacular stuff—a mix of multimedia-based shows, avant-garde experiments, and an annual Christmas show to write home about. Its kids' shows are its bread and butter. Lyric Square, King St., S6. www.lyric.co.uk. ℭ **020/8741-6850.** Tube: Hammersmith.

Roundhouse ★★ Located in a rehabbed 1846 locomotive shed, it picks up on the maverick spirit of neighboring Camden with a frisky lineup of innovative creations such as musical dramas and spectaculars, many of them given a crowd-pleasing, dance-inflected, shock-to-the-system twist. In the 1960s, it was one of London's most important stages, particularly for counterculture concerts. In more recent seasons, you're just as likely to see one-off comedy events or concerts. Chalk Farm Rd., NW1. www.roundhouse.org.uk. ℭ **084/4482-8008.** Tube: Chalk Farm.

Soho Theatre ★   The Soho functions like a one-building arts festival; it casts a wide net in looking for the latest voices in theater, comedy, and cabaret. On weekend days, come for kids' shows. Its Theatre Bar is a fine hangout even sans tickets. 21 Dean St., W1. www.sohotheatre.com. ✆ **020/7478-0100.** Tube: Tottenham Court Road.

The Unicorn Theatre ★   A children's theater that caters to kids without suffering from a debilitating case of preciousness, it runs at least two productions, one for each of its theater spaces. Some are script-based and some sensory-based for younger kids and kids with autism. Many are designed to expose kids to other cultures, places, and classic stories. If only every city had a kids' facility as lush. 147 Tooley St., SE1. www.unicorntheatre.com. ✆ **020/7645-0560.** Tube: London Bridge.

Young Vic ★   Spry and in top form, it programs a mixed bag of jarring plays, conversational touchstones, edgy musicals (*The Scottsboro Boys*), and affordable opera, then stands back and hopes for *frisson*. It often achieves it, and if it fails, it doesn't dally long, since it has three theaters (seating 500, 160, and 80) to fill. There's nearly always something high-quality to plumb here. 66 The Cut, SE1. www.youngvic.org. ✆ **020/7922-2922.** Tube: Waterloo or Southwark.

Pub Theaters

In the early 1970s, a new form of alternative theater swept London: the pub theater. Often just a tatty back room where you can bring your beer from the scruffy front bar, your typical theater pub is where some of the city's most affordable, idiosyncratic, let's-try-this-and-see-if-it-works theater is found—which is why so many megastar actors were launched to fame from them. Some of the most respected fringe venues in town are pub theaters, and they have just as much artistic power as many better-heeled West End palaces. Five fantastic ones are:

The Etcetera Theatre ★★   Odd, challenging fare (sometimes several different shows a night) in its very small black box. 265 Camden High St., NW1. www.etceteratheatre.com. ✆ **020/7482-4857.** Tube: Camden Town.

Hen & Chickens ★   Frequent comedy bookings as well as strong writing presented by a resident company, Unrestricted View. 109 St Paul's Rd., N1. www.henandchickens.com. ✆ **020/7354-8246.** Tube: Highbury & Islington.

The King's Head ★★★   Alums include Kenneth Branagh, Clive Owen, Joanna Lumley, Ben Kingsley, Juliet Stevenson, Hugh Grant, and John Hurt in their younger, braver, poorer days. 115 Upper St., N1. www.kingsheadtheatre.com. ✆ **020/7478-0160.** Tube: Angel.

Landor Theatre ★   Basically just a large room seating about 60, this space specializes in palatable musicals, cabaret, and comedy. 70 Landor Rd., SW9. www.landortheatre.co.uk. ✆ **020/7737-7276.** Tube: Clapham North.

Old Red Lion ★   The very pubby ORL hires its 60-seat space to a variety of aspiring producers and hosts the occasional comedy night. 418 St John St., EC1. www.oldredliontheatre.co.uk. ✆ **020/7837-7816.** Tube: Angel.

OPERA

Opera can be a budget-breaker. Frugal travelers should try the street singers who perform daily at the **Covent Garden Piazza** (Tube: Covent Garden). That's not a joke: Performers are auditioned before being awarded buskers' licenses, so the caliber is high. Also check to see if there's a touring opera putting down stakes at Sadler's Wells (p. 184). Of course, nothing compares to these institutions:

English National Opera ★★   With the Royal Opera entrenched as the country's premium company, the ENO at the London Coliseum (1904) is the progressive one that angles for younger audiences. Gadaffi has been fodder for one opera, and in 2013, Philip Glass' bio-opera *The Perfect American*, was a *Citizen Kane* version of Walt Disney's life. The slate (this season, of 11 major productions, including Glass' *Akhnaten*) consists of both progressive choices and classics. Best of all, it sets aside 500 seats at every performance for £20 or less. St Martin's Lane, WC2. www.eno.org. ✆ **020/7845-9300.** Tube: Leicester Square.

Royal Opera House ★★   Opera fans don't need to be reminded of the role the ROH plays on the world scene, but outsiders might be surprised at how inviting and attractive its terrace and cafe are. The main house, which is shared by the equally prestigious Royal Opera and Royal Ballet, is supplemented with two smaller spaces for chamber opera and studio dance. Happily, 40% of the tickets cost £40 or less—if you move quickly—and surtitles appear on little screens or monitors. There are three daytime tours available, too: backstage; or workshops; or its 2,256-seat, horseshoe-shaped auditorium (✆ **020/7304-4002;** £9–£12; 75 min.; children 7 and under not permitted; sells out 2–3 months ahead, calendar online). Bow St., Covent Garden, WC2. www.roh.org.uk. ✆ **020/7304-4000.** Tube: Covent Garden.

DANCE PERFORMANCE

London's dance scene has yet to achieve the vibrancy of New York's or Germany's, but that's not to say there's nothing to see; it's just that some of the best terpsichorean productions are put on by visiting companies, not by Londoners. The first thing to do is check the schedules at the Barbican (p. 182), Roundhouse (p. 185), Sadler's Wells (p. 184), and Southbank Centre (p. 184), which present a cornucopia of performance genres. The country's largest company, **Royal Ballet ★★** shares space with the Royal Opera (Bow St., Covent Garden, WC2; www.roh.org.uk; ✆ **020/7304-4000;** Tube: Covent Garden). The adventurous **English National Ballet ★** tours Britain much of the time but finds itself in London often (www.ballet.org.uk; ✆ **020/7581-1245**).

   The Place ★★★ (17 Duke's Rd., WC1; www.theplace.org.uk; ✆ **020/7121-1100;** Tube: Euston) is known for contemporary dance—specifically, as the home of the Richard Alston Dance Company—and the host venue of some

100 companies a year from around the world. **Trinity Laban** (Creekside, Greenwich, SW8; www.trinitylaban.ac.uk; ✆ **020/8691-8600;** Tube: Cutty Sark DLR), the lucky tenant of a gleaming translucent building by the same team that designed the Tate Modern puts on a mixed bill of works from around the world and by up-and-comers from its conservatory. To find out about one-off performances, check *Time Out*'s "Dance" section. Also check out the listings for the Barbican (p. 182) and the Southbank Centre (p. 184).

CLASSICAL MUSIC

Cadogan Hall ★   With 900 seats, the onetime Christian Scientist church is now the home of the Royal Philharmonic Orchestra and, in summer, the BBC Proms, which books it during the summer for its chamber music as a supplement to its concerts at Royal Albert Hall. 5 Sloane Terrace, SW1. www.cadoganhall.com. ✆ **020/7730-4500.** Tube: Sloane Square.

King's Place ★★   The relatively new development behind King's Cross has become the city's most versatile, exciting venue, with spaces for multiple galleries, chamber groups, and orchestras. It has some bright ideas to keep programming fresh; regular festivals for global music and opera; and 50 great chamber concerts determined by a vote. Also look into its weekly nights: Thursday is comedy, Friday is folk music, Saturday is jazz, and Monday nights, catch interviews with world notables. 90 York Way, N1. www.kingsplace.co.uk. ✆ **020/7520-1490.** Tube: King's Cross St Pancras.

Royal Albert Hall ★★★   Imposing, ornate, and adored by music lovers worldwide, it's one of the few performance arenas on earth where, once they have performed there, artists can truly claim to have made it. During the summer, the storied BBC Promenade Concerts (the Proms) fill this historic, 5,200-seat circular hall with classical music, but the rest of the year, the space books a hodgepodge of tours, arena-style musicals, Cirque du Soleil, concerts (the house organ is 21m/69 ft. tall and has 10,000 pipes)—even tennis matches. See p. 112 to tour it. Kensington Gore, SW7. www.royalalberthall.com. ✆ **0845/401-5034.** Tube: South Kensington.

St Martin-in-the-Fields ★★★   Right in the thick of Trafalgar Square, this handsome church's evening candlelight concerts and lunchtime performances are London traditions. It's non-fussy with clean acoustics. Trafalgar Square, WC2. www.stmartin-in-the-fields.org. ✆ **020/7766-1100.** Tube: Charing Cross or Leicester Square.

Wigmore Hall ★★   Opened in 1901 as a recital hall for the Bechstein piano showroom that was next door, it was seized (along with the company) as enemy property in World War I. A nasty start, but today the hall, notable for a bombastic Arts and Crafts cupola over the stage, is known for ideal acoustics and a roster of some 450 concerts, mostly classical, each year. Some nights, there's free music in the bar. 36 Wigmore St., W1. www.wigmore-hall.org.uk. ✆ **020/7935-2141.** Tube: Bond Street.

PRINCE CHARLES CINEMA: THE WORLD'S silliest MOVIE THEATER?

The family-friendly "Singalonga" *The Sound of Music*, a silly participatory screening of the 1965 classic, was born here in 1999 and swept the world. Participants—some of whom arrive dressed as Nazis and nuns, without regard to gender—receive a "magic moment" bag with edelweiss, curtain swatches, and a party popper to deploy at the moment of Maria and the Captain's kiss. And it hasn't stopped with "Do-Re-Mi." On Friday nights, other Netflix favorites are given the call-and-response treatment, *Grease, Frozen, Moulin Rouge*, and *Dirty Dancing* among them. On other nights, it's a "bitch along" to *Mean Girls*. Or a *Labyrinth* Masquerade Ball. Or an all-night sleepover to John Hughes movies. Or an *Animal House* Frat Party—just don't tell your hotel you're wearing its sheets (7 Leicester Place; www.princecharlescinema.com; ℂ **020/7494-3654;** Tube: Leicester Square).

THE MUSIC SCENE

Just as many of London's live music venues don't draw a heavy line between the genres they present, no rigid division exists between gig venues and dance venues; in fact, many spaces switch from live music to dance in a single evening. That's one of the things that makes the city's nightlife so vibrant, but it's also why it's important to check programming in advance. Students can often get discounts on entry—as if you needed any more proof that education is valued in England.

Live Music, Including Jazz, Pop, Folk & Rock

Dozens of theaters and arenas in town book concerts by recognizable names, but it would be fruitless to list them since they're almost all rented by promoters and don't always have something going on. The better advice is to stay on top of who's playing by checking *Time Out* (www.timeout.com) or *New Musical Express* (*NME;* www.nme.com) magazines. Since big shows sell out months in advance, the best recourse is to book ahead via **See Tickets** (www.seetickets.com; ℂ **087/1220-0260**); **Stargreen** (www.stargreen.com; ℂ **020/7734-8932**), which has a small office at 20/21a Argyll St., outside the Oxford Circus Tube station; **Ticketweb** (www.ticketweb.co.uk; ℂ **0333/321-9990**) or its partner **Ticketmaster** (www.ticketmaster.co.uk; ℂ **0333/321-9999**), all of which levy fees but let you buy from abroad. Also visit **SouthbankLondon.com** to see what's playing in all the Southbank venues.

The 100 Club ★   Many decades have passed since it was a prime hangout for U.S. servicemen homesick for the jazzy sounds of Glenn Miller and his colleagues. In 1976, after passing through an R&B and jazz period that had Louis Armstrong puckering up for audiences, it sponsored the world's first punk festival, and bands like the Sex Pistols—unsigned at the time—took the stage. This red-walled club still can't decide which era to honor, so it careens between punk, swing, R&B, and jazz. 100 Oxford St., W1. www.the100club.co.uk. ☏ **020/7636-0933.** Cover £10–£21, 25% discounts often available in advance. Music starts around 8:30pm. Tube: Tottenham Court Road.

12 Bar Club ★★★   In 2015, development forced the longstanding club from its postage stamp–size Soho space despite pleas from 25,000 fans including The Who's Pete Townshend. Now it's in Islington, but you'll still find a range of music, indie pop to funk; see several acts a night; and pay just a few pounds for all of them until 3am. 203 Holloway Road, N7. www.12barclub. com. ☏ **020/7240-2622.** Mon–Sat 7pm–3am (may close earlier); Sun 7pm–12:30am. Cover usually £6–£10. Tube: Holloway Road.

Barfly ★   Launch pad for a thousand indie bands, some that actually ended up soaring (Coldplay, Blur, and the like), Barfly is a dark, intimate bar/performance space in Camden with a good mix of students, musicians, and old-time locals. Beware the sometimes overzealous moshers. When the bands wrap up, a house DJ spins for a few more hours while the audience chills. 49 Chalk Farm Rd., NW1. www.barflyclub.com. ☏ **0844/847-2424.** Cover under £10. Tube: Chalk Farm.

The Betsey Trotwood ★★   An adorable, wood-floored Victorian pub on three levels that hosts funk, comedy, and a few singer-songwriters a month—such as Jason Mraz early in his career. 56 Farringdon Rd., EC1. www. thebetsey.com. ☏ **020/7253-4285.** Tube: Farringdon.

Borderline ★   A Soho institution since 1992, this modest (capacity 275) basement space, which was recently renovated to install much-needed AC, books country, folk, Britpop, and blues. Cheap beer, young crowd. Fridays are Bedrock (£4), an indie night featuring DJs "who still accept requests and actually attempt to entertain, rather . . . who should stay in their bedrooms." Orange Yard, Manette St., W1. www.mamacolive.com/theborderline. ☏ **020/7734-5547.** Cover: live music around £15. Tube: Tottenham Court Road.

Dingwalls ★   An ever-popular house of rock, folk, and acoustic guitar since 1973, this former industrial space by Camden Lock grants audiences the dignity of seating and tables for enjoying the music, which has included Mumford and Sons, Jello Biafra, and Foo Fighters. Middle Yard, NW1. www. dingwalls.com. ☏ **020/7428-5929.** Cover ranges from "pay what you roll" on a die to £22. Tube: Camden Town.

Dublin Castle ★   Any bar that proclaims itself the birthplace of the '70s ditty band Madness would not on the surface seem to be a place you'd want to enter without prior insobriety. But it has street cred. It was the first bar in London to win a late liquor license from the government, so it became an important nightspot. Really no more than a threadbare, greenish pub with a teeny backroom stage, it hosts bands struggling to make it—and a few (Blur, for one, and Madness for two) that actually have. On weekends, late-night DJs spin. 94 Parkway, NW1. www.thedublincastle.com. ☏ **020/7485-1773.** Cover £6–£7. Tube: Camden Town.

Electric Ballroom ★★ One of those dicey, utilitarian halls that never loses the lingering smell of old beer, it has hosted the likes of Sid Vicious, The Clash, and Garbage. Steel yourself for a weeklong roster of punk, goth, industrial, glam, hardcore, metal, and other genres whose aficionados are unlikely to do more architectural damage to the premises than what's already been done by the ravages of time and benign neglect. 184 Camden High St., NW1. www.electricballroom.co.uk. ✆ **020/7485-9006.** Cover: live music £15–£20, club nights £7–£14. Tube: Camden Town.

Green Note ★★ Much of London nightlife is mired in dance music and the illusion of luxury, while this welcoming vegetarian cafe/bar books acoustic live gigs, from folk to jazz, roots to singer-songwriters. Softened by pillows and upholstered seating, it's a laid-back scene, and food prices are sensible (no meat, all organic), but you can swing in just for the shows. 106 Parkway, NW1. www.greennote.co.uk. ✆ **020/7485-9899.** Opens 7pm. Cover £2–£15. Tube: Camden Town.

Jazz Café ★★★ The prime venue for "names" keeps the music going to 2am, usually in the form of acts (jazz, soul, bluesy vocalists) with followings. Converted from a bank, there are both cabaret tables and an upstairs gallery with food; show up early for a good position. Saturdays are '80s/'90s parties. 5 Parkway, NW1. www.thejazzcafelondon.com. ✆ **0844/847-2514.** Cover: live music around £10, club nights around £5. Tube: Camden Town.

Koko ★ Favored by visiting indie bands, in its first life as the Camden Palace this 1,500-place, multileveled space saw performances by Charlie Chaplin. In the '70s and '80s, it became an epicenter for pop—The Eurythmics, Boy George, and Wham! played their earliest gigs here, and it's where Madonna made her U.K. debut. The name Koko brings respect. 1A Camden Rd., NW1. www.koko.uk.com. ✆ **087/0432-5527.** Cover under £10, student discounts before midnight. Tube: Mornington Crescent.

Pizza Express Live ★★ Unlikely as it is for a chain restaurant, it hosts lunchtime and night concerts in its on-site jazz club by respected acts such as Jamie Cullum, Norah Jones, and Roy Haynes. Even Amy Winehouse played here. 10 Dean St., W1. www.pizzaexpresslive.com. ✆ **084/5602-7017.** Cover free–£30. Tube: Tottenham Court Road.

Ronnie Scott's Jazz Club ★ Since the 1960s, it has been the standard bearer in London for stylish, American-style jazz, and it honors a long tradition of pairing visiting U.S. greats with local acts. But the old dive got ritzy. After a £2.1-million renovation, the 255-seater began charging prices in the £45 range. But it's true that the club draws names, including Patti Austin, Van Morrison, Tom Waits, Cleo Laine, Chaka Khan, and Kyle Eastwood. 47 Frith St., W1. www.ronniescotts.co.uk. ✆ **020/7439-0747.** Tube: Leicester Square.

Scala ★★ When it was a cinema, Stanley Kubrick shut it down for screening *A Clockwork Orange* without permission. Good thing he did, or this 1920 theater might not have been reborn as a pleasing place to catch an acoustic or lyrical band. Its three levels give nearly everyone a good view of the stage, fostering a sense of intimacy appropriate to its capacity of around 1,000 people. A warren of rooms confuses the drunk ones and conceals the shy ones. Weekdays, it hosts gigs by indie bands, and weekends, it turns to club nights. 275 Pentonville Rd., N1. scala.co.uk. ☏ **020/7833-2022.** Cover £8–£15. Tube: King's Cross St Pancras.

The Water Rats ★★ If you're not a headbanger, its singer-songwriters may appeal more than Camden's squalling pubs. Once it was a pub known as the Pindar of Wakefield, and Bob Dylan made his U.K. debut in its back room in 1962, Oasis braved London audiences for the first time here in 1994, and Katy Perry played its cramped stage before arenas. It's little wonder why the record-label scouts brave the grime to listen to the new acts, be they alt-country, rock, or hip-hop. 328 Grays Inn Rd., WC1. www.water-rats.com. ☏ **020/7209-8747.** Cover from £6. Tube: King's Cross St Pancras.

Major Venues

If you want to get into the big-name shows, you have to book ahead, before you arrive. The most important venues post their schedules and link to ticket sellers on their websites. The grittier, midsize venues include **Bush Hall** (www.bushhallmusic.co.uk); the **O₂ Academy Brixton** (www.O2academy brixton.co.uk); the **O₂ Academy Islington** (www.O2academyislington.co.uk); the recently renovated, Art Deco **Eventim Apollo** in Hammersmith (www. eventimapollo.com); the **O₂ Shepherds Bush Empire** (www.O2shepherds bushempire.co.uk); plus the **Electric Ballroom** and **Koko** (see above). The most massive venues—where your favorite artist will look like a tiny, bouncing smudge on the far side of 10,000 sweaty fans—are the **Copper Box Arena** at the just-renewed **Queen Elizabeth Olympic Park** (www.queen elizabetholympicpark.co.uk), where the park's open but the main stadium remains closed until 2016, when it becomes the home of West Ham United FC; and **SSE Arena Wembley** (www.ssearena.co.uk). Sometimes you'll also see big gigs on the sports pitches at **Arsenal's Emirates Stadium** (www. arsenal.com/emiratesstadium) or **Twickenham Stadium** (www.england rugby.com/twickenham), well outside of town.

The O₂ The £789-million boondoggle on the Thames in East London is a dome 10 times the volume of St Paul's. It's where the gargantuan acts from Dolly to Gaga to Kylie to Monty Python appear, packing in their own religious followings, in a 20,000-place arena (ladies, there are 550 toilets for you, too) fringed by a mall for food and clubs. Michael Jackson was in rehearsal for a concert series for the O₂ when he died, and during the 2012 Olympics, it housed gymnastics and basketball. For those not keen to squint at their favorite artist reduced to a tiny smudge on a distant arena stage, there's O₂ dome's "intimate" performance space, **IndigO₂,** although with 2,350 places in an acoustically superior, contemporary room, it's still plenty big, has four bars, and attracts major talent (Prince, Leonard Cohen). Even if you aren't carrying a ticket for a show, it's worth exploring the massive open spaces inside. The bubbly-blue mega-chandelier hanging above the main entrance is too big for your camera's viewfinder, but if you need something more jolting, you can take a safe, 2-hour climb above it on its **Up at the O₂** roof-walking attraction (p. 139). One of the keys to O₂'s explosive success has been the fact the Jubilee line's sleek North Greenwich station runs beneath it. Thames Clippers (p. 256) docks here, too. Peninsula Square, London, SE10. www.theo2.co.uk. *℘* **020/8463-2000.** Tube and ferry: North Greenwich.

Clubs

The city's dance scene, being embedded in the style scene, is various and shifting, and by the time you read this, the variety will have shifted again. The best source for tips on parties you stand a chance of getting into is Time Out (www.timeout.com/london/clubs). Although the clubs around Shoreditch, Old Street, and King's Cross were until recently the markers of cool, both gentrification and development have squeezed the scene northeast to Dalston, which makes getting home in the middle of the night expensive—freelance cabbies charge double. Covers nudge toward £20.

The king of clubs remains **Fabric** (77a Charterhouse St., EC1; www.fabriclondon.com; *℘* **020/7336-8898;** Tube: Farringdon or Barbican), a former butchery that for more than a decade has had lines around the block. Its all-weekend parties (from Sat 10pm 'til the cock crows on Mon) are engineered to drill teeth-chattering bass frequencies into the souls of those who dare to submit, Friday is dubstep and drum-and-bass night, Saturday is deep house. The City is not lost to the nerds yet; the pedigreed managers of **XOYO** (32-37 Cowper St., EC2; www.xoyo.co.uk; *℘* **020/7729-5959;** Tube: Old Street) turned a former printworks into a stripped-down sound tank, and succeeded. It sometimes throws approachable parties at the South Place Hotel (p. 45) before shifting all night to its home base. The **Ministry of Sound** (103 Gaunt St., SE1; www.ministryofsound.com; *℘* **020/7740-8600;** Tube: Elephant & Castle) is known around the planet for its top-notch sound system, upper-crust DJs, and extreme cover charge in the low £20s. Otherwise, wander Dalston for the leading edge and basement clubs. The **Dalston Superstore** (117 Kingland High St., E8; www.dalstonsuperstore.com; *℘* **020/7254-2273;** Tube: Dalston Kingsland Overground) is a pansexual party mix of DJs, disco, and ravey go-go boys. **The Nest** (36-44 Stoke Newington Rd., N16; www.ilovethenest.com; *℘* **020/7354-9993;** Tube: Dalston Junction rail) is intimate, affordable, and at times sweaty, but has the quality lineup and sound system of a mini Fabric.

COMEDY CLUBS

London's comedy scene is dominated by Edinburgh's. Each August in the Scottish capital, seemingly all of Britain attends the city's famous festival season, where sharp minds vie for awards, audiences, and perversely, that shiniest of brass rings, a major London booking. The rest of the year, it seems that half the stages in town are either helping artists groom material for Edinburgh (June and July schedules are packed with new shows) or cashing in on its past successes. The fevered competition has created a comedy scene that has less in common with the stand-and-discuss neuroses of New York clubs and more to do with the brittle high concepts of, say, Russell Brand or Ricky Gervais. You may miss a few local references, but you're sure to appreciate the wit. All comedy venues serve food and drink, and tickets are almost always under £10 unless it's a big name or a very central location. Main shows are usually at 7:30 or 8pm. The Saturday night stand-up showcase is the main event at **Amused Moose** (Moonlighting Nightclub, 17 Greek St., W1; www. amusedmoose.com; ℂ **020/7287-3727**; Tube: Tottenham Court Road), although big-name comics like Eddie Izzard or Stephen Merchant sometimes appear here without a peep of advance word to test out new material. The cluttered **Canal Café Theatre** (The Bridge House, Delamere Terrace, W2; www.canalcafetheatre.com; ℂ **020/7289-6054**; Tube: Warwick Avenue) puts on a dozen shows a week, but its biggest draw is "NewsRevue" (www.news revue.com) a weekly send-up of current events running since 1979 that holds the Guinness record for the longest-running live comedy show (Thurs–Sun). The 400-seat **Comedy Store** (1a Oxendon St., SW1; www.thecomedystore. co.uk; ℂ **0844/871-7699**; Tube: Leicester Square or Piccadilly Circus) was created in 1979 in imitation of clubs popular in New York and launched Izzard and Jennifer Saunders, but today it does improv (Wed and Sun) and stand-up (Thurs–Sat). **Jongleurs** (61-65 Great Queen St., WC2; www.jongleurs.com; ℂ **08700/111-960**; Tube: Holborn), which has branches all over the country, is the kind of mixed bag where you'll find boozed-up bachelorette parties (here, "hen parties") and possibly crummy food, while **Pleasance Theatre Islington** (Carpenters Mews, North Rd.; N7; www.pleasance.co.uk; ℂ **020/7609-1800**; Tube: Caledonian Road), in a former wood warehouse 20 minutes from the center of town, has stronger ties than most to Edinburgh; it operates the Scottish festival's chief comedy venue and it starts previewing entrants in the spring.

CINEMA

Major movie premieres attended by major movie stars are routinely held at one of Leicester Square's giant cinemas, including the **Odeon** (24-26 Leicester Sq., WC2; www.odeon.co.uk; ℂ **087/1224-4007**; Tube: Leicester Square), from 1937, the largest cinema in the country, with seating for about 1,700. But tickets for Leicester Square theaters can cost an outlandish £18. For better prices—in even more historic houses—look elsewhere. Because so many handsome old cinemas have survived, movie-going can still feel like an event. In most theaters, you even select your seats when you buy your ticket.

BFI Southbank ★★★ The programming of the British Film Institute (BFI) is mind-bogglingly broad and savvy, from classics to mainstream to historic—more than 1,000 titles a year. For example, on a day in a recent July, its three screens unspooled a retrospective of Indian director Satyajit Ray, Alfred Hitchcock's *Dial M for Murder* in 3D, a mid-century series from the largely forgotten Boulting Brothers, and outdoor screenings of Gothic monster schlock. As the country's preeminent archive and exhibitor, it also programs plenty of talks, special previews, and the occasional free screening. The on-premises **Mediatheque** is an arcade for quiet, on-demand viewing of tons of titles you'd never see abroad because of rights issues, and its shop stocks an incomparable list of rare DVDs, including many treasures the BFI has personally restored and re-released—Charlie Chaplin's Keystone and Mutual films being recent triumphs. There are also two popular bars, one in the lobby and one on the water. Belvedere Rd., South Bank, SE1. whatson.bfi.org.uk. ✆ **020/7255-1444.** Tube: Waterloo.

Coronet ★ One of the oldest movie houses in London was built as a small variety house in 1898. A 5-year plan to restore it is currently underway. This is where Hugh Grant's character wistfully attended a movie starring his estranged girlfriend (Julia Roberts) in *Notting Hill*. 103 Notting Hill Gate, W11. www.the-print-room.org. ✆ **020/7727-6705.** Tube: Notting Hill Gate.

The Electric Cinema ★★★ One of the world's great screens: Leather seats are softer and deeper than anything you have at home, and each one is equipped with a footstool, table, and a wine basket—it's a luxurious, romantic way to pass a few hours. The bar in the back of the house sells everything you need, from crudites to booze, and downstairs is a barrel-roofed French-American diner. Meanwhile, the films, which change daily, hop between first-run and well-received art house movies—nothing too obscure. Shockingly, this place stood derelict from 1993 to 2001, and only a fierce campaign saved it. Now it's run by the exclusive Soho House, which opened a private club here. 191 Portobello Rd., W11. www.electriccinema.co.uk. ✆ **020/7908-9696.** Tube: Ladbroke Grove or Notting Hill Gate.

Phoenix Cinema ★ Thought to be the oldest purpose-built cinema in the U.K., it was constructed as the Premier Electric Theatre in 1910; by 1985, despite its handsome Edwardian barrel-vault ceiling, it was nose-to-nose with the wrecker's ball before fans (including director Mike Leigh) rallied. It screens an immense range of films from across eras and borders, plus frequent transmissions of live theater. It also has a liquor license. 52 High Rd., East Finchley, N2. www.phoenixcinema.co.uk. ✆ **020/8444-6789.** Tube: East Finchley.

GAY & LESBIAN

London's gay and lesbian scene is collapsing in the face of development. The last 2 years saw the unthinkable closure of Camden's half-century-old drag landmark The Black Cap, and several important Soho bars including Madame Jojo's have been forced out or have been sold. Nevertheless, the city still has one of the most varied scenes in the world. The city boasts more than 100 pubs, clubs, and club nights, and a dozen saunas—beat that, San Francisco or New York! The music seems to crank a few notches louder when the jolly and outrageous **Pride London** (prideinlondon.org) season rolls along, in late June or early July.

Daily gay-oriented pursuits have traditionally been centered around Soho, where the bars and clubs take on a festive, anyone-is-welcome flair, and after work, guys spill into the streets. But as a mark of a truly integrated city, now nearly every neighborhood has its own pubs and gay nights. Where you spend an evening depends on your proclivities and willingness to commute. At most places, there aren't usually cover charges unless an event or show is on, when they're about £5 at bars and £11 for clubs. Lesbians who want to go out at night must usually plan a little because most girls' events take the form of weekly scheduled nights in bars that might cater to other niches during the rest of the week. The Sapphically inclined should turn to **Gingerbeer** (www.gingerbeer.co.uk) for listings.

The weekly **Boyz** (www.boyz.co.uk) and **QX Magazine** (www.qxmagazine.com) publish schedules that favor club events. *Time Out* also has a weekly "Gay and Lesbian" section that dwells more on clubbing than on well-rounded pursuits.

These standout venues in every flavor are welcoming to tourists and will provide a good overview of the culture.

Barcode Vauxhall ★★   Thanks to its cobalt-and-steel design, it seems on the surface like a snooty setting, but in reality it attracts a varied crowd of friendly over-25s on their pre-club rounds, and it gets far cruisier than its style might suggest. When the other bars close, it heats up and stays hot past dawn. Arch 69, Albert Embankment, SE1. www.barcode-london.com. ✆ **020/7582-4180.** Thurs 10pm–4am; Fri 8pm–8am; Sat 10pm–noon. Tube: Vauxhall.

Central Station ★   For those who like it sexually charged, no other large space in the city can compete. Three floors plus a roof terrace and a drag cabaret mean there can be events of various spiciness going on at once, so it's essential to check its schedule beforehand. Fetish nights aren't the only thing going down in cellar cruise spaces. 37 Wharfdale Rd., N1. www.centralstation.co.uk. ✆ **020/7278-3294.** Tube: King's Cross St Pancras.

Comptons ★★   This old two-level pub wears the tatty garb of a bygone saloon but it's one of Soho's most beloved hangouts for men who are out of their bubble gum years. **Admiral Duncan,** across the street, and the **Duke of Wellington** ("Duke of Welly's"), where Old Compton Street t-bones into Wardour Street a few steps west, cater to the same professional age group. 51-53 Old Compton St., W1. www.centralstation.co.uk. ✆ **020/3238-0163.** Tube: Piccadilly Circus.

G-A-Y ★★   Once renowned for their literary prowess and symbolic subterfuge in hinting at their sexuality, London's homosexuals have allowed their wit to become somewhat less nimble: They named one of their top clubs G-A-Y. Just G-A-Y. It's about partying, cruising, and dancing. The main event is the Saturday night club. No other dance club in Europe, gay or straight, comes close to attracting such a pantheon of legendary live performances: Kylie, the Spice Girls, Cyndi Lauper, Bjork, and of course, Madge, all performed here at the height of their fame, and some have been known to drop by unannounced to collect laurels from 2,000 chipper young things. Every night, G-A-Y also runs a light pre-show hangout, G-A-Y Bar, where a young, twink crowd steeps in cheery Europop and watches videos on the plasma screens. And you can imagine the vibe at its G-A-Y Late venue, which goes until 3am. Club: Heaven, Under the Arches, Villiers St., WC2. Tube: Charing Cross or Embankment. Bar: 30 Old Compton St., W1. www.g-a-y.co.uk. ✆ **020/7494-2756.** Tube: Leicester Square. Late: 5 Goslett Yard, W1. ✆ **020/7734-9858.** Tube: Tottenham Court Road.

The Hoist ★ A well-known leather dive with a dress code that changes per the night, it's not for the female or the fainthearted. Or, on some nights, for the clothed. Railway Arches 47b and 47c, South Lambeth Rd., SW8. www.thehoist. co.uk. ✆ **020/7735-9972.** Tube: Vauxhall.

Ku Bar ★★ A manageably sized, young-skewing, three-level lounge is the place you go when you don't want a scene but you wouldn't mind being served by the shirtless part-time porn stars who work here. It has a later license: until 3am Monday to Saturday. 30 Lisle and 25 Frith sts., WC2. www.ku-bar. co.uk. ✆ **020/7437-4303.** Tube: Leicester Square.

Royal Vauxhall Tavern ★★★ In 2013, a biography revealed that Diana, Princess of Wales, once secretly attended this gay drag landmark dressed as a man. That gives you an idea of its heft in British culture, as well as the fact that anything goes. There are three shows a night, all transgressive. Recently sold, it is considered at risk of imminent development. 372 Kennington Lane, SE11. www.rvt.org.uk. ✆ **020/7820-1222.** Tube: Vauxhall.

She Soho ★ She's one of London's only 7-days-a-week lesbian bars, and given that there aren't too many part-time girl bars, either, it attracts a wide spectrum of types—even tag-along men. 23a Old Compton St., W1. www. she-soho.com. ✆ **020/7437-4303.** Tube: Piccadilly Circus.

XXL London ★★★ London's biggest dance night for "bears" (for the uninitiated, those are men who would never dream of shaving their chests like the young "twinks" do), it's colossal beyond belief. Its arched-ceilinged dance floor—actually you're in vaults beneath a railway—gets super sweaty, which is only why thousands of assembled men strip off their shirts and grind on. 1 Invicta Plaza, South Bank, Blackfriars Rd. at Southwark St., SE1. www.xxl-london.com. ✆ **020/7403-4001.** Wed and Sat. Cover £15. Tube: Southwark.

The Yard ★★ On weekends, all the cute jock types are here, cramming the courtyard-like space, or watching the action from the Loft lounge area upstairs. Weekdays, it's more subdued and a place for the after-work crowd, but it's always straight-friendly. This is another gay bar that is at risk of redevelopment soon. 57 Rupert St., W1. www.yardbar.co.uk. ✆ **020/7437-2652.** Tube: Piccadilly Circus.

WALKING TOURS OF LONDON

Paying for a sightseeing tour seems smart in principle. You glimpse monuments, briefly, and you hear one or two eye-glazing facts about them as they whiz past. But no coach tour, no hokey sightseeing boat, goes at your speed. None convinces you the things you're seeing are quite real, allowing you to mull what's before you, or lets you breathe in the atmosphere. Get up close to London. Don't pass it. Touch it—so that it can touch you.

WALKING TOUR 1: WESTMINSTER, WHITEHALL & TRAFALGAR SQUARE

START:	**Westminster Tube station**
FINISH:	**Trafalgar Square**
TIME:	**Allow 60 minutes, not including time spent in attractions**
BEST TIME:	**Be at the starting line just before noon to hear Big Ben deliver its longest chime of the day**
WORST TIME:	**After working hours, when energy drains out of the area**

When most people hear the word "London," this is the area they picture: the Houses of Parliament, the wash of the Thames, the gong of Big Ben, and the Georgian facade of No. 10 Downing Street. Kings and queens, prime ministers and executioners, despots and assassins—this is where they converged to shape a millennium of events, at the command center for England and the British Empire. History buffs, lace up.

1 ## Westminster Tube Station
   The best train to take here is the Jubilee line, which was added at great expense in 1999. The station's concrete-grey, 36m-deep (118-ft.) cavern, ascended by escalators from the Jubilee's platforms, is one of the city's finest new spaces, providing a modern-day analog to the majestic space of Westminster Abbey nearby. Portcullis House, where many MPs (Members of Parliament) keep offices, is overhead.

Walking Tour 1: Westminster, Whitehall & Trafalgar Square

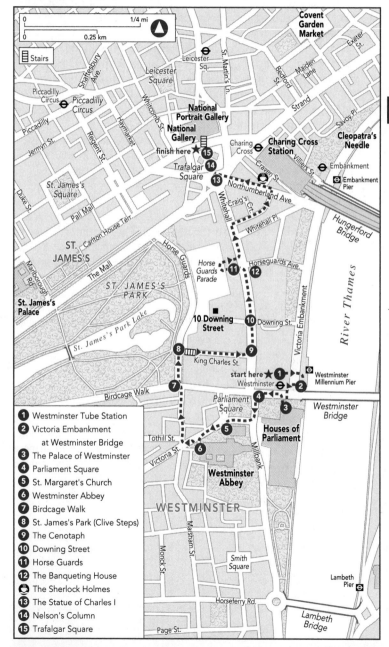

1 Westminster Tube Station
2 Victoria Embankment
   at Westminster Bridge
3 The Palace of Westminster
4 Parliament Square
5 St. Margaret's Church
6 Westminster Abbey
7 Birdcage Walk
8 St. James's Park (Clive Steps)
9 The Cenotaph
10 Downing Street
11 Horse Guards
12 The Banqueting House
The Sherlock Holmes
13 The Statue of Charles I
14 Nelson's Column
15 Trafalgar Square

2 Victoria Embankment at Westminster Bridge

Once you're outside, you'll see the River Thames. If you stood here in 1858, in the midst of what came to be known as The Great Stink, you'd have choked on the fumes rising from the fetid effluvia floating in the river below. Until then, the city had no sewers to speak of—only pipes that dumped into the water. The solution was the Victoria Embankment, a daring engineering project, completed in 1870, that saved engineers from having to dig up the whole city. They simply built a new riverbank, laid sewers along it, paired that with new Underground railway tracks, and topped the unattractive additions with a garden and a road. Destructive, but effective—how Victorian.

Today, the embankments' benches are raised to allow a good view of the water and it's dotted with triumphant statuary like Boudicca in her bladed chariot, which you can also see from here. This tribal queen rose up against the Romans; she failed politically but as you see, succeeded aesthetically.

The London Eye, spinning before you, had a tricky birth in 1999; it was constructed lying flat over the river, resting on pontoons, and then it was laboriously hoisted upright and into place. The mock-baroque building behind it is County Hall—it looks old, but it only dates to the early-20th century, and was once the seat of the London city government.

At the bridge's opposite landing, you can see the South Bank Lion. Weighing 14 tons, 3.6m (12 ft.) tall, and eager-eyed and floppy-pawed as a puppy, he was carved in 1837 by the Coade Stone Factory, which once stood where County Hall stands today. Made of a durable, synthetic ceramic stone formulated by a mother-daughter team, the lion stood proudly for over a century, painted red, atop the Red Lion Brewery that was located past the London Eye. Blitz bomb damage destroyed his roost, but at the request of King George VI, he was saved and placed just feet from his birthplace.

Go back into Westminster station, head down the corridor, and turn left before the set of four stairs. Leave the station via Exit 3, marked Houses of Parliament.

3 The Palace of Westminster

You're now standing under the iconic Elizabeth Tower of the Houses of Parliament, once called St Stephen's Tower but renamed in 2012 in honor of QE2's Diamond Jubilee. This is as close as you can get to it, so have a good look at the assorted crowns, kings, and crests carved into the facade. These buildings may look like they're from the Gothic period, but in fact they date to 1859, when they rose from the ashes of the old Parliament House, destroyed by a nightmarish fire in 1834. Big Ben, the name of the largest of four bells inside (2.7m/9 ft. in diameter, 13 tons), was named for the portly commissioner of works who oversaw its installation. There's actually a bigger bell in town: Great Paul at St Paul's is 2 tons heavier. Each side of the Clock Tower's four faces is 6.9m (23 ft.) long. Since 1923, the very earliest days of wireless, the BBC has broadcast the 16-note prelude (called "Westminster Quarters" and replicated in doorbells around the world) of Big Ben before its news summaries. Thanks to a crack that developed in the 1860s, the bell is now slightly off from its original note: E above middle C, but you'd need perfect pitch to tell.

This plot of land has been used by royals since 1050, when Edward the Confessor built a palace here, away from the hubbub of the walled city. Kings ceased living on this block as of Henry VIII, when nearby Whitehall became his main London pad, followed by St James's and currently, Buckingham—but Parliament's land is nationally owned, so technically it meets in Westminster Palace.

Head away from the river to:

4 Parliament Square

The heavy metal bars on the spiked fence that distances you from this building are not there out of mere paranoia; as far back as the thwarted Gunpowder Plot of 1605, the Houses of Parliament have been a target for would-be revolutionaries. Prime Minister Spencer Perceval was fatally shot on the steps of the House of Commons by a former convict on May 11, 1812, and in the Blitz, the buildings were smashed on more than a dozen occasions, including one (May 10, 1941) that caused the near-total destruction of the House of Commons.

The section of the Houses that juts into the yards, behind the statue of Oliver Cromwell, is Westminster Hall, from 1097, one of the only survivors from the 1834 fire. Charles I, Sir Thomas More, and Guy Fawkes were all condemned to death in the Hall.

Turn left and walk in front of the Houses of Parliament. Use the first crosswalk to your right, heading toward the church. At the far side of the church, enter the gate to see:

5 St Margaret's Church

The little side church by Westminster Abbey (p. 105), the one with the four sundials on its tower, is the Church of Saint Margaret, dating to the early 1500s and much changed over the years. Sir Walter Raleigh, who was executed outside the Palace of Westminster, is buried inside, and both the poet Milton and Winston Churchill married their wives here.

You can see the statues of Parliament Square better from here. Probably the most famous one is that of American president Abraham Lincoln, at the western end; it's a copy of one in Chicago by Augustus Saint-Gaudens. The statue of Winston Churchill received a temporary Mohawk made of grassy turf during the anticapitalist protests of 2000. This square has always attracted well-intentioned screw-ups: In 1868, the world's first traffic light was erected here. Gas powered, it blew up.

Follow the footpath to the front of:

6 Westminster Abbey

The lawn beside the abbey—yes, the one you just walked across—is in fact a disused graveyard. In a city this old, you simply can't avoid treading on final resting places. There is an unknown number of plague pits scattered through the city, into which thousands of victims were hastily dumped to avoid the spread of disease, and several city parks likely had the germ of their beginnings, so to speak, as potter's fields—group graves for paupers.

Although most of the abbey is in the Early English style, the stern western towers above you now were the 18th-century work of Nicholas Hawksmoor, a protégé of Christopher Wren. Hawksmoor's designs are famous for emphasizing the forbidding, angry side of God. Some critics accuse him of using architecture to frighten people into piety. Most of the time the people who use this main entrance in an official capacity do so in a crown, a gown, or a coffin. If you peer down Broad Sanctuary, which becomes Victoria Street, you can see the Italianate tower of Westminster Cathedral, the primary cathedral of England. Good news, Catholics: The English don't execute you anymore!

Cross the street to your right (Broad Sanctuary), and cross again. You should be a block west of Parliament Square on Storey's Gate now. Walk straight until you find yourself at the corner of St James's Park. You're at:

7 Birdcage Walk

You've just walked past a variety of European Union offices; the proximity to the Houses of Parliament has appealed to paper-pushers for centuries. The military has a presence here, too. The road that heads to the left is Birdcage Walk, which leads to the front of Buckingham Palace. Halfway down, you'll find the Wellington Barracks, the headquarters of the Guards Division, where a battalion of one of the Queen's five regiments of foot guards (Grenadier, Coldstream, Scots, Irish, and Welsh) bunks down. There's also a small, curio-packed Guards Museum (© **020/7414-3271;** daily 10am–4pm; £5), where you learn that their tall "busby" helmets are made of Canadian brown bearskin. Who knew?

Storey's Gate, which you just walked, was named for the keeper of Charles II's aviary. Birdcage Walk, the street you have now encountered, was named after a royal aviary that was in St James's Park; until 1928, only the Hereditary Royal Falconer was permitted to drive on Birdcage Walk. The park continues its tradition of hosting bird menageries; the pond is a haven for ducks and geese, and a small flock of pelicans has been in residence since the 1600s.

Cross the street and walk 1 block, passing the Treasury Building on your right, until you reach Clive Steps at King Charles Street on the right. Peek into:

8 St James's Park

See if you can spot the lake in the park. The body of water was originally a formal canal belonging to St James's Palace, the official royal residence from the burning of Whitehall in 1698 to the time Victoria moved into Buckingham Palace in 1837. The old canal was prim and straight in the French style and outfitted with gondolas, a gift of the Doge of Venice. In winter, Samuel Pepys wrote in the 1600s, it would freeze over, and people would frolic upon it using skates made of bone. It was later sculpted into something calculated to appear more random and thus more English. St James's Palace, which is not open to the public (except for Clarence House, in summer, p. 108), is located on the north (far) side of the park. You might be able to make out a rustic-looking shack just inside the park. That's Duck Island Cottage, built in 1840 as a dwelling for the bird keeper. Not shabby for a servant's quarters.

You'd think that if London were under attack from flying bombers that you'd be much safer if you were a little farther from the Houses of Parliament. Yet in the basement of the sturdy 1907 Treasury Building, Britain's leaders orchestrated their country's "finest hour." Unbeknownst to the world, it was the hideout of Winston Churchill and his cabinet. Famously, but hardly wisely, that daredevil Churchill went onto the roof of the building so he could watch one of Goering's air raids slam the city. The cellar, preserved down to its typing pool and pushpins, is now the Churchill War Rooms and a superlative museum paying homage to the bulldoggy prime minister (p. 102).

Who is Robert Clive, the cutlass-wielding subject of this statue on the steps? He was the general who helped the East India Company conquer India and Bengal, partly through a series of underhanded bribes, thus delivering the region into the control of the British Empire for nearly 2 centuries. Don't be too hard on him; the opium-addicted fellow committed suicide by stabbing himself with a penknife.

Walk down King Charles Street and through the arches at the end. You are now on Parliament Street. Look into the center of it. The somber stone column in the traffic island is:

9 The Cenotaph

The Cenotaph (from the Greek words for "empty" and "tomb") is a simple but elegiac memorial to those killed in the two World Wars. A 1919 plaster parade prop that was made permanent in stone by Edwin Lutyens the next year, it was executed with inconceivable restraint when you consider that nearly a million British subjects died in the Great War alone. Its inscription to the "Glorious Dead," coined by Rudyard Kipling, is repeated on other memorials in Commonwealth nations; the Cenotaphs in Auckland, New Zealand, and in London, Canada, are replicas. Uniformed servicemen and -women will always salute it as they pass, and on the Sunday closest to November 11, Britain's Remembrance Day, the sovereign lays the first wreath while other members of the Royal Family observe from the balcony of the Foreign Office. You may see flowers around it, or possibly silk poppies (red flowers with black centers), the national symbol of remembrance.

Walk left up Parliament Street, which becomes Whitehall. In about 30m (98 ft.) on the left, you reach a black fence with glass lanterns. Look inside the gates. This is:

10 Downing Street

On the right, by the tree and tough to make out, is No. 10, the official home of the prime minister. It's famous for its lion's head knocker—although to be frank, if you have to knock, you aren't welcome. Once, you could walk around in there, but Margaret Thatcher made many enemies, so you'll have to make do with peering down the lane. Such security was a long time coming. In 1842, a lunatic shot and killed the secretary to the prime minister, mistaking him for the big man; and in 1912, suffragette Emmeline Pankhurst and friends pelted the house with stones, breaking four windows, in one of many acts of civil disobedience in the fight for voting rights for women. If sentries prevent you from approaching, then the prime minister might be on the move. Prepare for the black gates to burst open, spew forth an armada of cars, and watch the prime minister's Jaguar blast onto Whitehall as if he'd just robbed a bank.

The lane was laid out by George Downing, the second man to graduate from Harvard University in America and by all accounts a shady individual, a turncoat, and a slumlord. He's one of history's great scoundrels; his underhanded dealings resulted in Dutch-held Manhattan being swiped by the British and the slave trade multiplying in the Colonies. Strange that the most important street in British politics should bear his name.

Downing built No. 10 (then, no. 5) as part of a row of terraced houses in the late 1600s, fully intending for it to fall apart after a few years (instead of actually laying bricks, he just painted on lines with mortar). Yet George II had his eye on the house, and he kicked out a man named Mr. Chicken—further information about him, tantalizingly, is lost to the mists of time—to give it as a gift to the first prime minister, Robert Walpole, in 1730. Walpole insisted that the house be used by future First Lords of the Treasury, his official capacity. He also connected it to a grand home behind it on Horse Guards, now nicknamed The House at the Back—this deceptive Georgian facade actually conceals 160 rooms. No. 10 is also connected with nos. 11 and 12, and it's even linked to Buckingham Palace and Q-Whitehall, a sprawling war bunker, by long underground tunnels. Many prime ministers elected to live in their own homes, using No. 10 for meetings, but not William Pitt, who moved in upon becoming prime minister at the virtually pubescent age of 24 in 1783. He lived here for more than 20 years, longer than any other prime minister, until his death at 46. Whitehall became a slum in the mid-1800s, and the house fell out of fashion, but then it served as the nerve center for the two World Wars and became indispensable to the British spirit. You can see the original front door, now replaced by a stronger one, on display at the Churchill Museum at the Cabinet War Rooms (p. 102), two stops back.

A little up Whitehall from Downing Street, look for the bronze monument to "The Women of World War II," which depicts no women, but rather their uniforms and hats, which hang on pegs as if they'd been put away after a job well done. The implication of this 6.6m-tall (22-ft.) tableau is, of course, that the women went back to the kitchen after briefly filling a more robust societal role. This sly bit of statuary-as-commentary was unveiled by the Queen in 2005. Some 80% of the cost of the memorial was raised by a Baroness who won money on ITV's *Who Wants to Be a Millionaire?*

Continue up Whitehall, past the monumental government buildings. In about 60m (200 ft.), you will reach another black gate broken by two stone guardhouses. Head inside the yard to view:

11 Horse Guards

Built in the Palladian style between 1750 and 1758 on a former jousting field of Whitehall Palace, the Horse Guards is the official (but little-used) entrance to the grounds of St James's Palace and Buckingham Palace. Two mounted cavalry troops are posted in the guardhouses every day from 10am to 4pm, and they're changed hourly. At 11am daily and 10am Sunday, the guard on duty is relieved by a dozen men who march in from The Mall behind, accompanied (when the Queen is in town) by a trumpeter, a standard bearer, and an officer. Don't try to crack up guards with your shenanigans. You'll look boorish and rude—and they still won't react.

If you think the clock tower arch looks small, you're right. Its designer made it that way so that its proportions would match the rest of the building. Walk through the clock tower arch to reach the graveled Horse Guards Parade, the city's largest non-park gathering space, which you may recognize as the setting for volleyball during the Olympic Games.

Return from the yard to Whitehall. Across the street you'll see:

12 The Banqueting House

Built by Inigo Jones, this is not a home but it is the last remaining portion of the great Whitehall Palace. Inside is a bombastic ceiling by Rubens depicting the king as a god. That vainglorious posture, and the king's grabs for more power, led to the gory event that happened on this spot on January 30, 1649. If you were standing here then, you would have been in the crowd that watched King Charles I mount the scaffold (wearing two shirts so that he wouldn't shiver—he was no true god, after all), place his head on the block, and be decapitated, handing the reins of the country to a military dictatorship led by Oliver Cromwell. When the executioner held the head aloft, one witness said there was a queasy silence, followed by "such a groan by the thousands then present, as I never heard before and I desire I may never hear again." Charles I was buried privately at Windsor, not at Westminster Abbey, to avoid more unpleasant scenes. If you want to see what poor Charles looked like, hang on for the next stop. The regicide was somewhat for naught; by 1660, the country grew weary of its leadership and Charles I's son, the hedonistic spendthrift Charles II, was back on daddy's throne. In revenge, the second Charles chose the Banqueting House as the site for his restoration party, and then had the nerve to show up late. England was royal again—and how.

Continue up Whitehall. Take the next right, Great Scotland Yard (the corner of Scotland Place was the "visitor's entrance" of the Ministry of Magic in the Harry Potter movies) and then cross Northumberland Avenue, veer slightly left, and head into Craven Passage.

The Sherlock Holmes ☕

Time for a pint and maybe some traditional English pub grub, so head to The Sherlock Holmes (10-11 Northumberland St.). In 1957, a collection of Arthur Conan Doyle memorabilia was assembled as a tourist attraction for the huge Festival of Britain that gave London the Southbank Centre, and it became the centerpiece of this pub. It's nowhere near 221B Baker St., but it has a roof garden and a terrace.

Return to Northumberland Avenue and turn right. When you reach Trafalgar Square, cross the street so you're in the oval traffic island.

13 Statue of Charles I

That this bronze statue stands here is a miracle. It's of Charles I, pre-headectomy, and is a precious Carolinian original from 1633. When the king was beheaded, the Royal Family was deposed (permanently, so people thought). The owner of this statue was commanded to destroy it, but he was clever enough to bury it instead. After the Restoration, it was dug up and placed here, in about 1675. That was even before Trafalgar Square existed (the zone was, as an equestrian statue suggests, used as stables). Charles wasn't a tall man, and boosting him with a horse went some way toward making the luckless fellow seem imposing. Someone stole his sword in 1867, and he went into hiding again during the Blitz, but otherwise, this is one of the oldest things in this part of London that remains in its original place. Its pedestal, unloved and weathered, could use a restoration, too.

This is a good spot, free of traffic and obstructions, to survey your surroundings and take some photos. Look back down Whitehall, from where you just came, and you'll see Big Ben's tower. To the right, the vista through Admiralty Arch concludes in the distance with the grand Victoria Memorial at Buckingham Palace. Important buildings for two Commonwealth nations stand astride Trafalgar Square: Canada House to the left (west) and South Africa House to the right (east; its country's name is inscribed in Afrikaans as Suid-Afrika).

Cross again so that you're on the south side of:

14 Nelson's Column & Trafalgar Square

Not long after Charles's statue lost its original sword, lightning struck Lord Nelson, who is exposed at the top of his column, and damaged his left arm. The city finally got around to eliminating the bronze bands that held him together in 2006, using the same Craigleith sandstone with which he was constructed in 1843. Since the quarry had closed in the 1940s, craftsmen had to find stone left over from the restoration of a school in Edinburgh. During the work, surveying revealed that the monument is actually 4.8m (16 ft.) shorter than guidebooks have been claiming—it's 51m (167 ft.), not 56m (184 ft.), from the street to the crown of his hat. The man himself is 32m (105 ft.) tall. Why is Nelson so revered? The Admiral sacrificed his life in 1805 to defeat Napoleon Bonaparte's naval aspirations, which secured Britain's dominance over the oceans—and thus pumped untold wealth into London. The column's base is lined with four bronze reliefs that were said to be cast using metal from French cannon captured at the battle that each one depicts. All are guarded by four reclining lions (1867), the mascots of the square.

In the southeast corner, you'll see a stone booth big enough for a single person; that's the city's smallest police station, built in 1926. Once a closet for a phone that was used to summon backup, now it's used mostly to store chemicals for the fountains.

Lutyens, who did the Cenotaph, also designed the two fountains (from 1845 originals), which were ostensibly for beautification but conveniently prevented citizens from protesting in numbers. Trafalgar Square has long been the setting for demonstrations that turned from complaint to unrest, such as infamous riots over poll taxes and unemployment. The English gather here for happy things, too, as they did for the announcement of V-E Day (May 8, 1945), and as they still do for free summer performances.

You may have heard about Trafalgar's Square's famous pigeons. So where are they? Banished for overactive excretion. Until the early 1990s, the square swarmed with them—the fluttering flock was estimated to peak at 35,000—and vendors made a living from selling bird feed to tourists. Eventually, the GLC, London's government, grew tired of shoveling streaky poo off the statues and decided to return the square to its original function as a great public space. They began feeding the pigeons themselves first thing in the morning, and then hired a team of six hawks, tended by a leather-gloved keeper, to patrol the square. The flock, which now numbers as low as 400, quickly learned to chow down and then clear out for the day; anyone who feeds the birds is subject to a £500 fine.

Head to the other side of the fountains to:

15 North Trafalgar Square

At night when landmarks are picked out by lights, the views down Whitehall are sublime. Most of the statues dotting the square are of forgotten military and noble men; James II is finely crafted, but he looks ridiculous in those Roman robes. The northwestern plinth of Trafalgar Square was designed for an equestrian statue of its own, but money ran out and it stood empty from 1841. More than 150 years later, the naked spot was named The Fourth Plinth and filled by works commissioned by a subversive panel of top artists. Sculptures show for 12 to 18 months, and they get the city talking. Marc Quinn's *Alison Lapper Pregnant* depicted a snow-white, nude woman born with limb deformities and heavy with child, and *Hahn/Cock* was Katharina Fritsch's two-story, ultramarine rooster, a sly send-up of the pompous military iconography elsewhere in the square. In 2015, it's Han Haacke's *Gift Horse,* a skeleton of a horse with a leg wrapped in a live stock exchange ticker, and then it's David Shrigley's elongated thumbs-up *Really Good* (2016).

Along the north terrace, by the Café on the Square, look for the Imperial Standards of Length, which were set into the wall in 1876 and moved in 2003 when the central stairs were installed. They are the literal yardsticks against which all other British yardsticks are measured, showing inches, feet, and yards, plus mostly obsolete measures such as links, chains, perches, and poles.

And now, reward yourself with a visit to the loo, left of the stairs, and a spot of tea in the cafe. Or, if you crave some more substantial victuals, head over to the street east of the square to St Martin-in-the-Fields church, finished in 1724. Its combination of spire and classical portico was controversial at the time, but today, it pleases people of all persuasions with its excellent Café in the Crypt (p. 64).

WALKING TOUR 2: **ST PAUL'S & SOUTHWARK**

START:	**St Paul's Tube station**
FINISH:	**The George Inn, near London Bridge Tube station**
TIME:	**2 hours, not including restaurant breaks or attractions**
BEST TIMES:	**Weekend days in good weather, when the area is abuzz; Borough Market is most vital from Thursday to Saturday**
WORST TIMES:	**After dark, when cobbled streets are too dark to see well**

It was the best of advertisements, it was the worst of advertisements. Charles Dickens' novels, largely social protests wearing the cloak of entertainment, made readers feel like they had traveled to London when they never left their own armchairs. Trouble is, the city that Dickens has primed visitors to expect—the foggy, coal-smudged metropolis teeming with pickpockets and virtuous orphans—is nowhere to be found. Partly thanks to Dickens' work, London reformed itself. On this tour, you'll explore what's left of its darker side—from the libertine London of Shakespeare's day to the desperate one Dickens sought to solve with his pen. Along the way, you'll enjoy gourmet food and a beer on the Thames, which conceals a body count of its own.

Walking Tour 2: St Paul's & Southwark

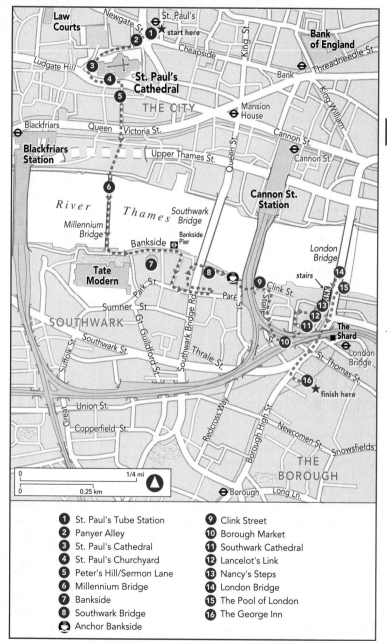

1 St. Paul's Tube Station
2 Panyer Alley
3 St. Paul's Cathedral
4 St. Paul's Churchyard
5 Peter's Hill/Sermon Lane
6 Millennium Bridge
7 Bankside
8 Southwark Bridge
🍵 Anchor Bankside

9 Clink Street
10 Borough Market
11 Southwark Cathedral
12 Lancelot's Link
13 Nancy's Steps
14 London Bridge
15 The Pool of London
16 The George Inn

1 St Paul's Tube Station

If you just took the Central Line here, you rode what was once called the Central Railway. In the first 75 years of the Underground, train lines were independently owned, and separate tickets were required each time a passenger changed trains. Fares were cumbersome, calculated according to the distance traveled and the class of carriage chosen. When the Central Railway held its grand opening in 1900, in the presence of American wit Mark Twain (who lived in London at the time), it soared above its competitors by dint of several innovations, the most important of which was that anyone could ride as far as they wanted on a flat fare. The so-called "Twopenny Tube," which had one class of carriage like today's Tube trains, was a sensation. Gilbert and Sullivan, swept along, amended a line in their operetta *Patience* from a reference to the three-penny bus to "the very delectable, highly respectable Twopenny Tube." The Central Railway helped democratize public transit and accelerated expansion into the suburbs—even if authorities eventually went back to the old format of charging passengers by distance. The St Paul's station opened on July 30, 1900, as Post Office station—the city's main Post Office was then across the street (hence the name of Postman's Park, p. 124, just north).

Exit the St Paul's Underground station and turn left, toward:

2 Panyer Alley

Panyer Alley, where you're standing, was named for the basketmakers, or panyers, who once traded here. Look for a plaque on the wall depicting a child sitting on a basket. This plaque, the so-called Panyer Stone, is dated "August the 27, 1688," and reads, "When you have sought / the citty round / yet still this is / the highest ground." The artists behind this stone surely knew that Ludgate is not the highest point in The City; that's Cornhill, which is about 30cm (12 in.) higher. But the sign has been here so long that it would quite literally be a crime to take it down.

Head left, toward St Paul's, and make a right through the pedestrian alley, Paternoster Row, to Paternoster Square. Go through the ornate arch at the left:

3 St Paul's Cathedral

The area you've just walked through, Paternoster Row, ranks among the most sacred in London. There have been major houses of worship on the plot of St Paul's as far back as 604, and for centuries, these narrow surrounding streets have teemed with ecclesiastical scribes and clergy, as well as with untold hordes of desperate supplicants desperate for a handout from the merciful church. By the 1800s, Paternoster Row was known as the center of literary London, first for its publishers—who replaced the scribes—and later for its book market. Yet what you'll see today is modern. Even its 23m-tall (75-ft.) column was created only a few years ago to appear older than it is. Why would planners permit the wholesale demolition of such a rich heritage? They didn't. This was

Ground Zero of the Blitz in 1940. The Germans, recognizing that the destruction of St Paul's would demoralize the nation, focused their power on it, and the spillover devastated everything around it. Every firefighter was called to the cathedral, saving it at the expense of just about everything else.

The stone archway that you passed through, however, is a true antique, although it didn't originally stand here. It's Temple Gate, one of eight ancient gateways to The City of London, which stood where Strand becomes Fleet Street from 1672. Charles Dickens described it in *Bleak House* as "a leaden-headed old obstruction." It was dismantled in 1878 and was destined for a dump somewhere when a visionary stepped in and brought the stones home. After spending more than a century in the hinterland of his family's Hertfordshire estate, the gate, possibly designed by Christopher Wren, was restored and re-erected here in November 2004. The seven other gates, including Aldgate and Moorgate, were all lost.

A statue of Queen Anne, who ruled England when St Paul's was completed, looks down Ludgate Hill. In attendance are ladies symbolizing England, France, Ireland, and North America, which she considered her subjects. The statue is an 1886 copy of the 1712 original, which (like Temple Gate once did) now resides, in scabby condition, in the countryside.

Herbert Mason's iconic photograph of St Paul's dome, snapped during the mighty conflagration that engulfed London after air raids on December 29 and 30, 1940, was taken from Ludgate Hill. Next time you see that picture, note that it's lit by firelight.

Skirt the cathedral along the busy street called:

4 St Paul's Churchyard

At the crossing, go over the street. Now's a good time to duck into The City of London Information Centre (Mon–Sat 9:30am–5:30pm, Sun 10am–4pm), located inside the origami-style, wing-roofed building, and stock up on free tourist brochures and timetables. It also runs daily guided walks in the afternoon.

If you don't need information, turn left. If you do use the office, when you come out again, turn right. After the patch of grass, turn right again. You can see down Peter's Hill to a white pedestrian bridge over the river. Stroll down:

5 Peter's Hill/Sermon Lane

On the right is the Firefighters National Memorial, which depicts a young man gesturing wildly toward St Paul's as two others grapple desperately with a hose. It's impossible to exaggerate the devastation caused by the Blitz, both in property and in lives. The superheated firestorms created damage greater in area than those of the Great Fire of 1666. More than 20,000 people were killed, and 1.4 million left homeless. The names of some 1,000 victims, all volunteer firefighters defeated by the wild blaze and collapsing buildings, are inscribed on the octagonal base. Winston Churchill dubbed this monument "The Heroes with Grimy Faces." For their families, the survival of St Paul's Cathedral amidst utter devastation remains a testament to their sacrifice. Keep going toward the river.

Go onto the:

6 Millennium Bridge

You're now on the steel Millennium Bridge, the central city's first new crossing over the Thames since the Tower Bridge in 1894. Its design, which features side-located suspension cables that sag about six times shallower than a conventional suspension bridge's supports do, was a little too advanced for its own good. When the bridge opened in 2000, it was discovered that the shifting weight of pedestrians caused it to sway, and people had to grasp the rails for support. (At the start of *Harry Potter and the Half-Blood Prince,* Death Eaters attack the bridge and make it wobble—that was an inside joke for Londoners.) Engineers closed the 325m (1066-ft.) span, poured in another £5.2 million to solve the issue, and reopened it in 2002. Now locals love it because it has transformed accessibility to the river's southern bank, and they're planning more foot crossings. It's still not perfect—it's plagued by joggers with little regard for idle strollers—but crossing the river here, in view of many of the city's landmarks, young and old, makes for some stirring photos.

Straight ahead is the monumental Tate Modern (p. 120), signaled by its factory-like "campanile" smokestack, which from 1952 to 1981 belched exhaust from the Bankside Power Station. Energy has been a fundamental part of the district's character for generations. The power station replaced an earlier one that dusted everything near it with a coating of soot, and that plant, too, supplanted a foul gasworks. Before that, the district was the domain of a legion of coal merchants who shuttled their filthy wares around town in shallow boats. These "lightermen" worked from docks that lined the entire southern shore, where land was cheaper than it was in The City on the northern side. The building you see before you is a direct descendant of the way of life that prevailed on the bank in the 1700s.

How deep is the Thames? The river fluctuates greatly with tides (so it's dangerous for swimming—in fact, that's illegal between Putney and the Thames Barrier), but depending on when you measure around here, it's generally 8.9m (29 ft.) deep at highest tide and 1.8m (6 ft.) at low tide. The Thames' moodiness is the main reason Southwark, the side of the river where the Tate Modern sits, was written off for so many centuries. Until medieval times, the low-lying southern bank was boggy and mostly uninhabitable, so was instead thought of as part of Surrey, the county south of London. Londoners made use of the waterlogged land by turning it into gardens for secret trysts and fish farms (the Pike Garden, or Pye Garden, stood pretty much in front of you around the Tate's eastern flank), but it wasn't until the latter part of the 1700s that people figured out how to drain the water and settle the area fully. Southwark was where you went for a rowdy time—that is, until the Puritans quashed the fun in 1642.

Before you completely cross the river, look down at the debris near the river wall. Turn back for a stupendous view of St Paul's dome symmetrically rising from the center of the bridge.

Once you're on the opposite bank, with the river in front of you, turn right. Stand midway between the cluster of houses and the building with the thatched roof. You're on:

7 Bankside

This river promenade also continues west, past the Tate Modern, to the London Eye and the Houses of Parliament. When Hugh Grant told Andie MacDowell he loved her by way of David Cassidy in *Four Weddings and a Funeral,* he did it farther along this walkway by the National Film Theatre. There's no better place to stroll, people-watch, and appreciate the sweep of the city.

As late as the 1960s, the path you're on, which at this place is called Bankside, was a vehicular street bearing two-way traffic, as it had been since the 1600s. Each building on the street owned rights to the docks or water-stairs on the river opposite it, so tenants were usually people who needed access to the water, such as ferrymen or sailors. The four-story, white house at the left of the blind Cardinal Cap Alley, no. 49, was built around 1710 on the foundations of a pub, the Cardinal's Cap, which itself went up in 1547 to entertain the people who came to Southwark to carouse. No. 49 was home to successive generations of coal merchants, but not, as its plaque purports, to Sir Christopher Wren as he built St Paul's. Wren did live nearby, but in a building that was torn down when the power station needed land—this plaque, which hung on that vanished home, was appropriated by a D.I.Y. revisionist in the mid–20th century. No. 49 has received its own biography, *The House by the Thames* by Gillian Tindall.

To the left is Shakespeare's Globe Theatre, which made a premature exit in its own era, only to be rebuilt in ours. The circular Globe's stage is even at the same compass point as the 1599 original's (p. 119).

Southwark may be famous for Shakespeare, but interestingly, the city's theatrical life was only centered here from about 1587 to 1642, when it was illegal to operate a theater in The City proper. Once the laws relaxed, the entertainment venues moved back into town, where they've been ever since.

Southwark was the Tudor version of a multiplex, and the biggest blockbuster was bear-baiting—the spectacle of vicious dogs let loose upon tethered bears. Even Henry VIII and Elizabeth I were huge fans; he had a bear pit installed at Whitehall Palace, and she barred Parliament from banning the pursuit on Sundays. One short block past the Globe is a lane called Bear Gardens. Three-quarters of the way down, you'll find a small courtyard. That's the former location of the Davies Amphitheatre, one of the most popular bear pits. Samuel Pepys wrote in his diary in 1666 of attending one such slaughter where he "saw some good sport of the bull's tossing the dogs—one into the very boxes. But it is a very rude and nasty pleasure."

Under a modern office building in the next street, Rose Alley, lie the foundations of another theater known to have premiered plays by Shakespeare, the Rose (p. 119). It lasted from 1587 to about 1606. The Swan stood nearby, too, although we may never find the footprint. The Rose's footprint gave us vital clues about what Elizabethan theaters looked like—architects also studied sketches made of it by a Dutch tourist in 1596. (Are you sketching your trip?)

Historians think they know where the original Globe stood. If you'd like to see it, head down Bear Gardens one block to Park Street, turn left and go under the bridge, and just after it, past the buildings on the right, you'll find a semicircular arc of stones. Not very suggestive, is it? In 1949, it was even drearier. It lay behind the locked gate of the decrepit Anchor Brewery, and when American actor Sam Wanamaker (father of Zoë, who played Madam Hooch in the Harry Potter movies) dropped by to pay pilgrimage, the indignity of the meager plaque (still there) so enraged him that he resolved to rebuild the Globe as a living home for England's great theatrical tradition—which is what came to pass, albeit 4 years after his 1993 death.

Retrace your steps to the riverside. On the water at Bear Gardens, look for a stone seat embedded in the wall of Riverside House. It's said to be the last remaining Wherryman's Seat, dozens of which once lined the Thames. Boatmen, the taxi drivers of their day, would lounge in these perches—this one is 15th century—until someone came along and hired them for a trip across the water. Ferrymen would also court business by shouting destinations to theatergoers after their plays: "Eastward ho!" or "Westward ho!"

Continue along the river, keeping it to your left. You'll go through a pedestrian tunnel under:

8 Southwark Bridge

On the walls of the tunnel, you'll see illustrations of skaters and revelers at the bygone "Frost Fairs" that, starting in 1564, were regularly held on the icy Thames. No matter how many winters you spend in London, you'll never see the Thames freeze over. But back then, they had the London Bridge, a few hundred yards downstream. Its 19 arches were so narrow, and its supports so thick, that the river's flow became sluggish, allowing water (and the outhouse filth that churned within it) to freeze. By contrast, during outgoing tides the rush was so fierce that boats capsized and passengers (few of whom knew how to swim, given the filth) drowned. When the bridge was dismantled in 1814, the Frost Fairs melted into history.

Walk past the two modern buildings and take a look underneath South-wark Bridge where it meets the shore. You can still discern the remains of some water-stairs, dating to before the construction of the first bridge here in 1819. In 1912, this bridge's central 72m (236-ft.) span was the largest ever attempted in cast iron. The drab hunk of a building to your right is the headquarters of the *Financial Times*.

The Anchor 🍺

Few pubs are more idyllic than the **Anchor** (p. 80), where Bankside meets the railway viaduct. The riverside patio is open in good weather; otherwise, the interior is charming. This pub was once controlled, as nearly all pubs once were, by a brewery; it was Barclay Perkins, located just behind it from 1790 until about 1980. Even before that, it was a fixture; in 1666, Samuel Pepys watched the Great Fire rage from here before coming to his senses and hurrying across the river to rescue his possessions from his home in Seething Lane, near the Tower of London. In the 1950s, the Anchor was considered a slum and nearly went.

After the Anchor, the path jogs inland. Take the first left onto:

9 Clink Street

Pass under the railway arch. In a few moments, you've gone from Eliza-bethan Southwark (theaters, bear-baiting) to Georgian Southwark (coal merchants, breweries). Now you're in Victorian Southwark, a claustro-phobic underworld teeming with fetid-smelling industry and river rats. You can almost hear distant reverberations on this narrow wharfside street. You might even call the sensation Dickensian, and you wouldn't be wrong, since when the writer was 12 years old, his father was thrown into a debtor's prison near where you're standing, off the Borough High Street.

Prisons were something of a cottage industry for the area; the Clink Street Prison stood here from 1127, when the Bishop of Winchester built it as a lockup for his Winchester Palace, until 1780, when the anti-Catholic Gordon riots saw the dismal hole destroyed. Although the Clink gave its name as slang to all prisons that came after it, no one knows for sure how it got the name itself—Flemish or Middle English words for latch are likely the origin. Suffice to say it was awful—and so is the museum here that purports to tell its story. Avoid it.

In the 1800s, warehousing goods instead of people became this street's stock-in-trade. All around, you'll see hints of the street's past maritime uses, from wooden loft doors to cranes used to hoist crates into upper floors. Today, these spaces house media companies and architects. Dur-ing the week, you'll see them in their fashionable clothes, staggering across the cobbles in their Italian shoes on their way to mid-afternoon cocktails.

The latter Bishops of Winchester were not nice guys. Henry II (1133–89) gave them control of this neighborhood, and because it was outside of the jurisdiction of the city, they could pretty much get away with whatever they wanted to. Principally, they cultivated countless brothels and skimmed the profits for themselves—which is how Southwark got its rap as a den of vice. Anyone who annoyed them (heretics, troublemakers) wound up in the Clink, where no one was likely to find them again. Continue down Clink Street. By the building with the rounded grid of windows, you'll see all that's left of the Bishops' palace. This unique geometric rose window, dating to the 1300s when it lit the great hall, was forgotten behind a wall until a warehouse fire exposed it again. Double back to Stoney Street.

Turn down Stoney Street and walk under the railway. On your left, you'll see:

10 Borough Market
Stop at the frilly grey portico.

The mood of the neighborhood has changed drastically again. To your left, behind the portico, is Borough Market, a fantasy for the tongue (described in gastronomic detail on p. 72) and the oldest fruit and vegetable market in the city. A market has been held around here since A.D. 43, when Roman soldiers noted passing a market on their way to sack The City. More reliable records date it to 1014, when it served the denizens on the old London Bridge, the city's only river crossing. The cream-grey portico is not original to this place; it's the cast-iron Flower Hall of Covent Garden, rescued when the Royal Opera House was renovated in 2003. If it seems to blend seamlessly, it's because it was made around the same time as the rest of the Borough Market structure (1859–60).

The Market is best known for gourmet supplies. Park Street, which runs into Stoney Street, looks as quaint as a movie-set version of old England; in fact, it was used in *Harry Potter and the Prisoner of Azkaban,* and no. 7A was the entrance of The Leaky Cauldron. The Market itself has appeared in films including *Howard's End* and *Bridget Jones's Diary.* The city's first railway, a 6.4km (4-mile) run to Greenwich, plowed its route .8km (½ mile) east of here in 1836. Even after tunneling technology improved, railway tycoons thought nothing of barricading thriving neighborhoods with massive brick viaducts, cutting them off from each other and creating slums. On your tour, you have crossed under a number of railway viaducts built that way, and shortly, you'll see how narrowly one of England's most historic churches averted its own destruction.

Cross the next street and enter the brick arch marked Green Market. Head straight into the grounds of:

11 Southwark Cathedral
(If for some reason the Green Market arch is closed, turn left down Bedale Street—it's not marked—until you see a church appear on your right.)

Before you stands the oldest Gothic church in the city, and the oldest building in Southwark. You'll see its tower appear in every old drawing of the city. In Roman times, it was the site of a villa. Its Christian chapter was begun by the daughter of a ferryman in the 7th century; it was rebuilt in the 850s and again 300 years later. There was once a monastery and a chapel in this yard, where office workers now lunch on gourmet items from Borough Market, but those came and went, too. Southwark teemed with the poor, with factory workers, and with grubby river men. One such blue-collar child was John Harvard, one of nine kids of a man who owned a tavern and butcher shop just northeast of here. John was baptized in this church in the early 1600s but when he grew up, he fled this slum for the Massachusetts Bay Colony, where Harvard University was later named for him. In time this place was limping along as a humble parish church called St Saviour's and it dissolved into dilapidation. The rerouting of London Bridge Road sheared away several small chapels, and in 1863, the rumbling railway forced its way alongside the yard. But by 1905, its fortunes reversed when it was elevated to a cathedral, and now it's so well cared for that it's hard to discern its true age and sordid past.

The cathedral's entrance is to the left. Go straight across the sanctuary, through the glass doors, up a short flight of stairs, and to the end of the glass-roofed corridor, which traces the line of an alley that was called:

12 Lancelot's Link

Nelson Mandela opened this building in 2001. Have a look at the display, which preserves surprising discoveries made in this small area during a 1999 renovation. Look down into the well on the far right, and you'll see the original paving stones from the Roman road that cut through this space in the 1st century. You crossed over this same road several times already today; you were standing above it when you entered Borough Market. Other relics, piled on top of each other, include a stone coffin, probably from the 1200s, with a carved slot for the head, and a kiln from the 1600s, soot marks intact—bits of the Delftware made here have been found as far away as Williamsburg, Virginia.

The cathedral has some beautiful painted monuments, including one of England's oldest wooden effigies (1280). Shakespeare's brother Edmond was buried here in 1607, as was Philip Henslowe, who built the Rose, in an unmarked grave. Other worthwhile sights include Edwardian stained-glass tributes to the Bard's plays, the Harvard Chapel with masonry from the Norman period, and some of the original ceiling bosses, carved in 1469 and saved when things got bad. How bad? During Elizabeth I's reign, the retro-choir (the part behind the altar) was walled off and rented to a baker. Later on, vestrymen discovered the baker was also raising swine in there.

Back down the corridor, exit. Go through the yard into the lane (it's Montague Close; the Thames is in front of you). Turn right, and before the overpass, look left for:

13 Nancy's Steps

These are popularly held to be the location, in the Dickens novel *Oliver Twist,* where Noah Claypool eavesdrops on a conversation that leads to Nancy's murder by Bill Sykes. In the book, those steps faced the Thames, but these steps are indeed a rare surviving remnant of the same New London Bridge, built here in 1821 as a replacement for the 600-year-old, overcrowded London Bridge. The steps that Dickens wrote about were sold in 1968 to an American oilman who had most of the bridge shipped, stone by stone, to Lake Havasu, Arizona, where it remains today. These steps were left behind and attached to this feature-less 1973 replacement.

Just so you know, the existing London Bridge was not the source of the nursery rhyme "London Bridge Is Falling Down"—that either referred to the burning of a wooden version in 1013, during a skirmish between Danes and Norwegians; or to Henry III's "fair lady" Queen Eleanor, who skimmed the tolls of the medieval bridge for her own purse, leaving its maintenance in a parlous state.

Climb the stairs to the road above. You're now on:

14 London Bridge

At the top of the stairs, you'll see a pedestal topped by a dragon, the symbol of the city, holding London's crest. You'll see these dragons at several of the city's medieval borders. About 30m (98 ft.) east of here, under modern buildings, is where you would have entered the Stone Gateway, the entry to the disaster-prone medieval London Bridge. For more than 3 centuries, tar-dipped heads of executed criminals were impaled on pikes and stuck atop the Gateway as a vivid warning to would-be ne'er-do-wells.

Turn to the right to use the crosswalk. Go to the opposite side of the street and walk onto London Bridge, over the river. Don't cross the river—just enjoy the view of the:

15 Pool of London

This section of the Thames between London Bridge and the Tower Bridge is known as the Pool of London. It may be quiet now, but for nearly 2,000 years, it was the heart of international trade. So many goods passed through here that warehouses along the southern bank became known as "London's Larder." Ships finally became so large that they had to unload downstream, closer to the sea. The section of river in front of you, parallel to this bridge, is where the medieval London Bridge stood.

Across the river from the Tower, you'll just make out an egg-shaped glass building. That's City Hall (2002), designed by Norman Foster (who also did the Millennium Bridge) to be ergonomic, with a huge spiral staircase curling around its atrium and "smart" windows that open on hot days. Just like a politician, it has no edge and you can't tell if it's coming or going. Former London mayor Ken Livingstone, a man not known for tact or restraint, called it "a glass testicle." Anyone can have a ball in its public spaces from 8:30am to 5:30pm on weekdays (www.london.gov.uk).

Turn around and follow London Bridge inland, keeping on the left side of the road. This street becomes Borough High Street. You will pass under a railway arch. Just after you pass Southwark Street forking off to the right, look for "The George" sign. It marks:

16 The George Inn

Because the London Bridge was the only crossing to the city from the south for so many centuries, this area became the equivalent of a train depot, and it was dotted with inns, stables, coach yards, and pubs. Everyone going to or coming from southern England or Europe stopped here, often spending the night before pushing into the shoulder-to-shoulder crowds of London Bridge. If you've ever read *The Canterbury Tales,* you'll recall that in 1386, the pilgrims began their journey to the shrine of Thomas à Becket from the Tabard Inn. Until 1873, that was located a short walk farther down Borough High Street, on the left. The George, described on p. 81, is the last survivor from this bustling coaching era. Although the wooden building, which once encircled the entire yard, dates to 1677, the inn was here for at least another 130 years before that, if not longer. We know it was typical of the time because John Stow, in *A Survey of London* (1598), termed it "a common hostelry for travelers." A drink here makes a fitting end to your journey through time. Look up and you'll see the jagged glass spire of The Shard (p. 121), Europe's tallest building, peering down as you sit where people have lifted beer for nearly half a millennium.

WALKING TOUR 3: SHOPPING, SOHO & GIMME SHELTER

START:	**Oxford Circus Tube station**
FINISH:	**Goodge Street Tube station**
TIME:	**2 hours, not including shopping or restaurant breaks**
BEST TIMES:	**Weekdays, when Berwick Street's market is on and Oxford Street is slightly less crowded**
WORST TIMES:	**Evening rush hour, when Oxford Circus Tube stop is positively rammed, and after dark, when stores and markets close**

All churched out? London is more than stories about dead queens and bloody uprisings. It's always been cosmopolitan, too, and the flash point for trends that ripple out to the rest of the world. Songs first sung at the clubs of Soho soon caused toes to tap on the other side of the planet, and fashion trends born on Carnaby Street remain internationally iconic 40 years later. Bring along your credit cards as we roam some of the city's best shopping streets and touch upon a few leftovers from London's recent past, including forgotten air-raid shelters and the settings for some good, old-fashioned sexual scandals. This is the London you found out about from the radio and the runways, not from your social studies teacher.

---

1 Oxford Circus

Leave the Tube station using Exit 2. Position yourself out of the fray.

You are in the thick of the mile-long Regent Street, which to the right is punctuated by the witches-hat steeple of All Souls Church and to the left curves toward Piccadilly Circus. When the Prince Regent, later George IV, was planning his new pet project, Regent's Park, he decided he also wanted a road to connect his house to it. He chose this particular location because, in his mind, it would provide a suitable demarcation line between the gentry of Mayfair, to the west, and the rabble of the traders who lived in Soho, to the east. George tapped John Nash to do the job, completed in 1825. Originally, the sidewalks were covered by stone colonnades, but when those attracted prostitutes, they were removed, and most of the original buildings were later rebuilt—the only Nash original is now All Souls. Even if most of the facades you see now mask more modern buildings, few streets in London impart such a sweeping, uplifting feeling, though few are also as congested with the hoi polloi George would have spurned.

The other avenue intersecting before you is Oxford Street, following the same line as a Roman road. George's class-centered definition of the landscape has more or less held: The exclusive shops of Oxford Street still lie west of Regent Street, and the downmarket stores tend to be east of it. Having a presence on Oxford Street is considered crucial for brands with mass appeal.

Head right, east on Oxford Street. You will pass Argyll Street on the right. When you pass Ramillies Street, prepare to stop in front of:

2 Marks & Spencer

London has a love-hate relationship with Oxford Street. People come here to shop by the thousands, but they often despair of the crush of the experience. Charles Dickens, Jr., described the street thusly in 1888: "It ought to be the finest thoroughfare in the world. As a matter of fact it is not by any means, and though it is, like all the other thoroughfares, improving, it still contains many houses which even in a third-rate street would be considered mean." We're only going to walk down a sample of Oxford Street. It's usually so crowded, it's all you can probably handle if you're keeping one eye on this book.

Marks & Spencer (p. 164), or M&S, dates to 1894 and is the favored British department store for staples. Perhaps proof of its appeal is that the chain can afford to run two giant frontages on Oxford Street; its flagship store is remarkably near here, between Bond Street and Marble Arch Tube stations. Its Food Halls (at this store, in the cellar) are well known

Walking Tour 3: Shopping, Soho & Gimme Shelter

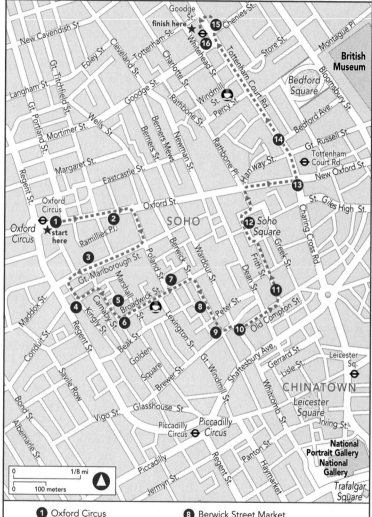

1. Oxford Circus
2. Marks & Spencer
3. Great Marlborough Street Magistrate's Court
4. Foubert's Court
5. Carnaby Street
6. Kingly Court
- The John Snow
7. Berwick Street
8. Berwick Street Market
9. Brewer Street
10. Old Compton Street
11. Frith Street
12. Soho Square
13. St. Giles Circus
14. Tottenham Court Road
15. The Goodge Street Deep Level Shelter
16. Goodge Street Tube station

as an ideal place to pick up prepared foods, sandwiches, and inexpensive but well-selected wines.

Turn right at Poland Street, walk 1 block, and turn right again onto Great Marlborough Street. Soon on your right, at nos. 19-21, you'll see a stout white building. That's the:

3 Great Marlborough Street Magistrate's Court

Charles Dickens worked here as a reporter just before hitting it big as a novelist, and a variety of other big names appeared before the judges here, including the Marquess of Queensbury (defending himself from Oscar Wilde's libel charge). When this neighborhood turned bohemian in the Swinging '60s, it began trying a string of drug charges against the likes of Mick Jagger, Johnny Rotten, Keith Richards, Francis Bacon, and, curiously (and coming full circle), the guy who wrote the musical *Oliver!*, Lionel Bart. It's now a luxury hotel, but I suggest you go inside briefly, because much of the old judicial fittings were left intact. You can have a cocktail in one of the old jail cells—now converted into private booths—or even peek into Silk, a restaurant slotted into the authoritative Number One court, which still has its witness stand, bench, wood paneling, and vaulted glass ceiling.

Beyond the Courthouse Hotel on the left, you'll see a Tudor-style building of black beams and white plaster. This is Liberty (p. 163), famous for its haute fabrics. It's also famous for its building—it was made in 1924 using wood recycled from junked ships.

Great Marlborough Street runs into Regent Street. Turn left there and walk the short distance to:

4 Foubert's Court

Times have been better on Regent Street. Walmart-style box stores in the suburbs have put the screws on the destination shops of the city, and this avenue saw long-termers lose their sizzle. Dickins & Jones, a department store at the corner you just turned, closed its doors in early 2006 after nearly 170 years, and the same old shopping mall brands are moving in.

Two doors farther from Foubert's Court, though, at nos. 188-196, is a well-loved holdover from the street's glory days. It's Hamleys (p. 175), one of the largest toy stores in the world. Some 5 million customers pour through its doors every year, but since the sales force is famous for putting on a nonstop show on every floor, it's understandable if many of those customers come to gawp and not to buy. If you go into Hamleys, when and if you come out again, turn right and go back to Foubert's Court.

Walk down the very short Foubert's Court for 1 block; you'll see "Carnaby" on a metal arch. Go under it and head 1 block. Go right, and now you'll see a larger arch on:

5 Carnaby Street

Yes, those obnoxious arches proclaim your location with a self-promotion that proves this street is no longer the super-cool, forward-trending street of the kids in the know. It's more of a mall with an edge. The days of Swinging London, when men could cruise from store to store trying on hip-hugging black trousers and frilly shirts, are behind it. *Time* magazine spilled the secret of Carnaby Street in 1966, and by the 1970s, it was pedestrianized as a shopping street, making hipness a matter of retrospect.

Just after you cross Ganton Street, where Broadwick Street hits Carnaby Street, duck into the passageway on the right:

6 Kingly Court

Clever entrepreneurs capitalized on Carnaby Street's rep with this development, a retail experiment in a former timber warehouse. The stores here are mostly boutiques pushing young designers.

Slip out the back door of Kingly Court, opposite its front door, and hang a left on Kingly Street. No. 9 is the Bag 'O Nails pub, where future Wings-mates Paul McCartney and Linda Eastman first clapped eyes on each other—and also where John Profumo met Christine Keeler, kicking off the notorious Profumo Affair. It's also where Fleetwood Mac's John McVie proposed to Christine.

Return to Kingy Court. Retrace your steps out of it, cross Carnaby Street, and head down Broadwick Street. You'll stop around:

John Snow Pub 🍺

So grateful were Dr. Snow's neighbors that they renamed their pub for him, albeit a century later. It stands at no. 39, at Lexington Street, on the site of his practice. Raise a pint in his honor here, as we read the words of Dr. Snow himself: "I feel it my duty to endeavor to convince you of the physical evils sustained to your health by using intoxicating liquors even in the greatest moderation." (Oops.)

7 Berwick Street

About 160 years ago, this block was a foul slum. French, Greek, and Italian immigrants fled hard times and revolutions by cramming into these tight streets, and by the 1850s, cholera was storming through the overstuffed city. An 1854 outbreak killed 500 people in barely 10 days. Common wisdom at the time held that the disease was spread through the air—a reasonable conclusion, given how terrible the sewage-smeared city smelled—but a local anesthetist, John Snow, suspected polluted water was the cause. He got permission to inspect the public pump at Broad Street, now Broadwick Street (in the block before Berwick Street) and he found that it was being contaminated with sewage leaking from no. 40 nearby, proving his theory. The saga was recently retold in the book *The Ghost Map* by Steven Johnson, and in 2015 the site of no. 40 was dug up to build a giant new development.

When you reach Berwick Street, look left. Think of this location as the modern-day Abbey Road. It's where, in 1995, Oasis photographed the cover of *(What's the Story) Morning Glory?*, one of the seminal CDs of the age. The photographer shot from farther down the street, aiming south, toward where you're standing. (Noel Gallagher, with characteristic tact, said he thought the album cover was "s**t.")

And here's another slice of rock history: One miniblock farther down Broadwick Street at no. 7, the corner shop covered in striking rust-colored tiles (now Sounds of the Universe record store, a local landmark for world music), was the Bricklayers Arms pub. Brian Jones auditioned the Rolling Stones here in 1962, and they held formative rehearsals upstairs. Across the road at no. 6 is Agent Provocateur, a noted lingerie shop, a hint of how unsavory the area once was. The word "Soho" is probably derived from a hunting cry used when this area was parkland—it's nice to see that some folks around here are still on the hunt.

Turn south on Berwick Street. Walk down it to:

8 Berwick Street Market

This is the vestige of the last great market in the center of the city, and it has been in operation since the 1840s, although vestry records indicate some illicit trading was going on as far back as 1778. London's first publicly available grapefruit was sold here in 1890. Now that the Cockney produce sellers have been mostly elbowed aside for gourmet nibbles, the market again caters to those with exotic, expensive tastes. How much has this hood transformed? Portions of London Fashion Week are now held at the Brewer Street Car Park, around the corner.

Pass over Peter Street and under Maurice House, going under the crossover and winding up on:

9 Brewer Street

From the late 1700s to the 1950s, it was impossible for a single gentleman to pass unpropositioned through Soho. A 1959 act chased the open salesmanship indoors, to be replaced by drinking joints where men could buy lap time with a lady, and by the 1970s, even those were forced to seek a lower profile. By law, today's displays are not permitted to titillate, complying with the British reputation (inaccurate in my book) for sexual modesty.

It was in this fleshy carnival that Laura Henderson bought a theater at Great Windmill and Archer streets and got around indecency laws by ensuring that the performers in her naughty entertainment, the Revudeville, never moved a muscle. Famously, the Windmill never closed, not even during the Blitz. You might have seen it in the film *Mrs Henderson Presents*. By the 1950s, Soho was a den of gang warfare and prostitution, full of craftsmen of every sort—costumers, ostrich feather trimmers, gun makers—until the Conservative government rezoned the neighborhoods to admit offices and the old ways were priced out.

Go left to Wardour Street, make a right and then a quick left. You'll be at the head of:

10 Old Compton Street

First, note the church of St Anne's, a few yards down Wardour Street, on the left. It was built in 1685, possibly by Wren (which ones weren't?), 2.5m (8 ft.) higher than the street because it went on top of a graveyard with 60,000 bodies that until 1853, when burials stopped, made the neighborhood reek. Everything save the tower was creamed by the Nazis.

Walk down Old Compton Street, Soho's de facto main street, which is busy round the clock and a center of gay life. No. 54 is the Admiral Duncan. Dylan Thomas once drank there (then again, where didn't he?). It was here, in 1999, that Nazi sympathizer David Copeland planted a bomb stuffed with 500 nails. It killed three people and injured many more. Copeland, an obvious madman, also bombed the South Asian population of Brick Lane and blacks in Brixton, but his only fatalities were here.

On the corner of Dean Street, look right. Down the block on the left, at no. 49, is the French House, more commonly called the French Pub. During World War II, it was the drinking haunt of Charles de Gaulle, and it was where the exiled leader formed the Free French government and army. The street beyond the French House is Shaftesbury Avenue, the famous theatrical thoroughfare; many of the side streets between Old Compton and Shaftesbury contain the stage doors for the major playhouses, where famous actors report to work. Now look left, north up Dean Street. In the attic of no. 28, Karl Marx dwelled in abject poverty with his wife and several kids, but no running water or toilet. Three of his kids died while he was in residence in Soho in the early 1850s. No wonder he thought communism would be better.

Turn left at:

11 Frith Street

Bar Italia, the stylish cafe at no. 22, is a nightlife landmark of its own (p. 63). Upstairs is where, in 1925, John Logie Baird privately tested a homemade invention he called "noctovision," using his grocer's delivery boy as a test subject. The next year, he unveiled an improved model for the science nerds of the Royal Institution upstairs in this building. (Unsatisfied, he made another attempt in 1928 that involved hooking up a fresh human eyeball he'd rushed by taxicab from Charing Cross Ophthalmic Hospital. It created a mess.) Baird's system, which used a spinning disc, was eventually discarded, but it debuted ahead of American Philo T. Farnsworth's more famous electronic version. Within a decade, the BBC was broadcasting "television"—its new name—regularly. In the 1940s, Baird invented the first color picture tube.

Walk up three doors. For 10 months starting in September 1764, the 8-year-old Mozart lived with his father and sister at a house at no. 20 (the building was replaced in 1858). While he was in London, the prodigy amused King George III, wrote his first two symphonies, and befriended fellow composer J.C. Bach, who mentored him. By the 1800s, Soho's Wardour Street was the violin-making center of Europe. Music history of another kind happened at no. 47, which in 1969 hosted the first public performance of The Who's *Tommy,* then Jimi Hendrix's last one, in 1970.

Use the gate to head into:

12 Soho Square

Laid out in 1681, Soho Square was, early on, fashionable and mansion-lined. Later it became the center of the ambassadorial and scientific cliques. Sir Joseph Banks, who made his name collecting exotic specimens as a tagalong on Captain Cook's voyages, moved here in 1777. These days, Soho is a center for the music and film industries.

In the center of the square, which is technically a private garden even though it's been open to the public for half a century, is a cottage you'd swear was Tudor in origin. In fact, it's an 1895 pastiche made to hide an electrical transformer. Beneath the lawns lie empty air-raid shelters.

Exit the opposite side of the square and go straight down Soho Street. You'll soon hit Oxford Street again. Turn right and head for the next major intersection, officially called:

13 St Giles Circus

Look across the next major street, and you'll see the 35-story Centre Point development. Built in 1964 with heavy government concessions, it was kept empty for years by its unscrupulous owner, partly to hold out for astronomical rents and partly because doing so would get him off the tax hook, even as the city struggled through a homeless crisis. The charity Centrepoint, which started in the basement of St Anne's church in Soho and grew into a force in housing issues, derisively took its name from the waste. Still, it's indisputably one of the landmarks of the skyline.

The area around the Tube station, which contains some tile mosaics by the great artist Eduardo Paolozzi, is under major redevelopment as part of the mammoth Crossrail project, a train line that will connect Canary Wharf in Docklands with West London. The project is slated to open in 2018.

Turn left and head up:

14 Tottenham Court Road

Fans of Andrew Lloyd Webber (anyone?), or at least of T.S. Eliot, will recall that this is the "grimy road" roamed by Grizabella, who sings "Memory." On the first corner, the Dominion Theatre was where, in 1957, Bill Haley and the Comets were the first American rock act to play Britain. Just 5 minutes ahead, on your left, you will see Goodge Street, with pubs frequented by students who attend the several universities in this area.

Duck into Chenies Street, on your right. At the curving side alley of North Circle, look for the striped, rounded buildings. That's:

15 The Goodge Street Deep Level Shelter

In 1939, planners decided to build an express train line beneath the existing Northern line platforms of Goodge Street. War intervened. In 1942, the unfinished tunnel was allocated to the Americans, and it was under the ground here where General (later President) Dwight D. Eisenhower orchestrated D-Day and announced it to the world, in 1944. There were eight deep-level shelters, and five were open to bomb-shocked civilians; this is one of the most central and best kept. It retains its ground-level entry blocks, one pillbox and one octagonal, connected by a brick building—thousands of Londoners pass them daily but don't know their original purpose. Since the Cold War, the onetime shelters, now innocuously painted grey with blue stripes, have been used for storage.

Double back onto Tottenham Court Road. Across the street will be:

16 Goodge Street Tube Station

Before you end your tour at the Tube station opposite, turn right. The Goodge Street Deep Level Shelter could originally be accessed from a second point on the west of Tottenham Court Road opposite Torrington Place; some brick-and-concrete structures and vents linger. Back on Tottenham Court Road, notice how no. 79, the building containing the Caffè Nero, stands alone—its neighborhood was blasted away by the final V2 rocket attacks in 1945. Nine people died here—but 2,700 perished this way citywide—and the site remains undeveloped. Goodge Street Underground station, opened in 1907 and still sporting much of its original tile work, uses elevators, not escalators. You can always take the 136 steps—that is, if you have the juice after your walking tour.

DAY TRIPS FROM LONDON

You've flown all the way to England. It would be a shame to miss seeing some of the sights that make it special—the rolling countryside, the stately mansions cradled by ancient trees, the ageless villages built alongside slow-flowing rivers. You can't get these things in London, but you can sample them in nearby places that have played an integral role in the development and culture of London life. An excursion enriches you with two experiences for the price of one: You'll taste everyday English life while you immerse yourself in world-famous landmarks.

Britain has comprehensive transport, but it's not quick as mercury. Because of traffic and a dearth of superhighways, you can expect a 48km (30-mile) trip to take an hour, so a spot that's 129 to 161km (80–100 miles) each way, such as Stonehenge or Bath, will require you to rise at dawn if you want to buy yourself much touring time at all. Going by bus is often less expensive than by rail, but the inefficient journey will involve narrow roads.

The tourist offices listed will be able, for a fee (£4–£5, plus 10% of the room rate), to hook you up with a bed for the night, should you decide that you'd rather not trek back to London right away. You can find lots more information at **Visit England** (www.visit england.com) and **Visit Britain** (www.visitbritain.com).

For in-depth coverage of everything outside of London, get a copy of *Frommer's England & Scotland*. For casual day-trippers, though, here's what you need to know to dash out of the city and see the best of these destinations.

WINDSOR & ETON

Buckingham Palace is a mere *pied-à-terre*. The Queen actually prefers this great castle, which dominates the skyline of town like a cloud of stone. Windsor Castle (32km/20 miles west of London) has been the home of the Royal Family for some 900 years, far longer than anything in London. Queen Victoria is buried in the backyard (although they don't phrase it quite that way). Despite the inevitable crowds, this is unmissable.

Essentials

GETTING THERE   The price difference between transport options is negligible. Riding the rails is quicker, so it's got the edge. **Trains** (www.national rail.co.uk; ✆ **08457/48-49-50;** 38–56 min.; £10–£12) go directly from Waterloo station to Windsor & Eton Riverside or from Paddington to Windsor & Eton Central with a change at Slough. Both Windsor stations are a 3-minute walk from the Castle. Trains requiring no changes leave twice an hour, and trains requiring a change leave a little more frequently. Or take a coach by **Green Line** (www.greenline.co.uk; ✆ **0871/200-2233;** 1 hr. 45 min.; £10 single, £15 return, 40% less after noon) nos. 700, 701, or 702 from Hyde Park Corner or Victoria Coach Station south of Victoria Station.

VISITOR INFORMATION   **Royal Windsor** (Old Booking Hall, Windsor Royal Station, Thames St.; www.windsor.gov.uk; ✆ **01753/743-900;** windsor. tic@rbwm.gov.uk). From there, you can be referred to Blue Badge guides for **town walks.**

TOURS   The most appealing way to see the area is by **boat,** which departs from Windsor Promenade, Barry Avenue, for a 40-minute round-trip with fine views of the castle. Tours are operated by **French Brothers,** Clewer Boathouse, Clewer Court Rd., Windsor (www.frenchbrothers.co.uk; ✆ **01753/851-900;** 40-min. trip: £7 adults, £6 seniors, £5 children 3–13, cheaper online; 2-hr. trip: £11 adults, £10 seniors, £7 children 3–13).

Exploring Windsor

Legoland Windsor (www.legoland.co.uk; ✆ **0871/222-2001;** Mar–Oct; £48 adults, £44 seniors and children 3–15, cheaper online), 2 miles from town, has top-notch rides catering to small children and some impressive Lego constructions. The Green line from London goes there, or shuttles go from the Theatre Royal. The tourist office sells discounted tickets for late-afternoon entry.

Windsor Castle ★   You may have had your fill of palaces in London proper, but you haven't seen the best. A fortress and a royal home for more than 900 years, it was expanded by each successive monarch who dwelled in it—more battlements for the warlike ones, more finery for the aesthetes. The resulting sprawl, which dominates the town from nearly every angle, is the Queen's favorite residence—she spends lots of time here—and its history is richer than that of Buckingham Palace.

The castle's **State Apartments** are sumptuous enough to be daunting, and a tour through them, available unless there's a state visit, includes entrance to some mind-bogglingly historic rooms. Around a million people file through every year, so sharpen your elbows, and there are no cafes, so eat first. **St George's Chapel** (closed Sun), a delicately vaulted Gothic spectacle opened by Henry VIII, is his final resting place and that of nine more monarchs, including Elizabeth II's father (George VI). Elizabeth II's mother (the Queen Mum) and sister (Princess Margaret) are with him in a side chapel and it's safe to assume that this is where she will wind up one day, too. The palace also has a cache of priceless furniture (some of it solid silver), paintings, ephemera (look for the bullet that killed Lord Nelson, sealed in a locket) and weaponry, all of which, frustratingly, the audio guide, signage, and £5 souvenir book do little to describe, so the only recourse is to pepper staff with questions. In 1992, one-fifth of the castle area was engulfed by an accidental fire; the Queen recounted her despair over that, plus the breakup of two of her children's marriages, in her now-famous "annus horribilus" Christmas speech to the nation, and much effort and funding went into putting everything back to the way it was before. In fact, the Queen originally opened Buckingham Palace to visitors to fund the restoration. **St George's Hall,** one of the repaired areas, is the Queen's chosen room for banquets. Kids love **Queen Mary's Doll's House,** a preposterously extravagant toy built for the allegedly grown-up Queen Mary in the 1920s with working electricity, elevators, plumbing, specially written library books, and other details so extravagant they're borderline offensive. From October to March, the tour also includes the **Semi-State Rooms,** George IV's private area, considered by many to be among the best-preserved Georgian interiors in England. In August and September, you can climb the **Round Tower** for views, and sometimes in January and midsummer, the castle's ancient **Great Kitchen** is open. There's also a **Changing the Guard** ceremony at 11am (Mon–Sat, but alternate days Aug–Mar; check the website).

The Castle is the superstar here, but supporting roles are played by the succinctly named **Great Park** adjoining it, and the 4.8km (3-mile) pin-straight **Long Walk** that culminates with an equestrian statue of George III. **Frogmore,** open a pitiful few days in August, is the house where Victoria and Albert share their mausoleum. Just south of the castle is the **Guildhall,** where Prince Charles and Camilla Parker-Bowles had a quiet civil marriage in April 2005; it's no St Paul's, where in 1981 Charles wed his first wife, what's-her-name, but it is also the work of Christopher Wren (note its delicate arches). The building was apparently designed without the center columns, which made councilors nervous; Wren threw up some columns but left them an inch shy of the ceiling, just to prove that his architecture was sound.

Castle Hill. www.royalcollection.org.uk. ℭ **020/7766-7304.** Admission £19 adults, £18 students and seniors, £11 children 5–16, free for children 4 and under, £50 family of 5 (2 adults and 3 children 16 and under). Mar–Oct daily 9:45am–5:15pm, last admission 4pm; Nov–Feb daily 9:45am–4:15pm, last admission 3pm. Closed for periods in Apr, June, and Dec, when the royal family is in residence. National rail: Windsor Central or Windsor & Eton Riverside.

Eton College ★ A 15-minute walk over a footbridge on the Thames (narrow at this western remove), you're in a world of snooty stationers and haberdashers. Eton is probably the most exclusive boys' school on Earth. Princes Harry and William are alums, known as Old Etonians, as are kings and princes from around the world. There's a museum in its wine cellars—and the fact this school has a wine cellar tells you what kind of rich these kids are. Be nice to

Train fares listed in this section are provided as a guideline; National Rail pricing schemes are complicated and unpredictable. The good news is that for all of the destinations served by trains, if you return to London on the same day that you leave it, you can pay just a little more than the price of the usual one-way (single) ticket. Rail clerks call this a "day return." More tips:

○ Tickets tend to be most costly on Fridays, when Londoners head out of town.

○ You can find incredible deals (up to 70% off) if you happen to be among the first customers to get tickets for a given departure. Book starting 12 weeks out.

○ Prices are highest for "open" tickets with no restrictions, so opt for the restricted fare since you probably won't need to change your plans.

them. They're tomorrow's dictators. Check ahead to verify opening times because recent renovations have wreaked havoc on public access.

Keats Lane, Eton, Windsor. www.etoncollege.com. ☏ **01753/671-177**. Admission £8 adults, £7 children 8–13. 1-hr. tours Mar–Oct daily 2 and 3:15pm, with some blackout days during school term; check website's schedule.

BATH

Easily roamed on foot, Bath, about 161km (100 miles) west of London, is revered as a splendid example of Georgian architecture—to tourists, Bath is resolutely stuck in that past. The pleasing sandstone hue of its buildings set against the slate-grey British sky, the assiduously planned symmetry of its streets, the illusion that Jane Austen (who lived here in 1800–05) is taking tea within one of its 18th-century Palladian town houses—Bath's magic comes from its consistent and regal design. No wonder the upper crust of the 1700s found it so fashionable, and no wonder their descendants have not dared to alter it. And no wonder UNESCO inscribed it as a World Heritage Site—a rarity for an entire city.

Essentials

GETTING THERE   The fastest **trains** (www.nationalrail.co.uk; ☏ **08457/ 48-49-50**; 90 min., twice an hour; £18 with advance purchase) leave from Paddington and let off in Bath Spa, an ugly section of town about 5 minutes' walk from the good stuff. Because buses take twice as long, I don't recommend National Express (www.nationalexpress.com; ☏ **08705/80-80-80**; 3 hr.; £12 single).

VISITOR INFORMATION   Visit Bath/Bath Tourist Information Centre (Abbey Chambers, Abbey Churchyard; www.visitbath.co.uk; ☏ **090/6711-2000** [50p/min.], from overseas ☏ **011-44-844-847-5257**; tourism@bathtourism.co.uk).

TOURS The Mayor's office provides professionally guided, free 2-hour **Walking Tours of Bath** (www.bathguides.org.uk; Sun–Fri 10:30am and 2pm, Sat 10:30am; May–Sept also Tues and Fri 7pm). Meet by the Abbey Church-yard entrance to the Pump Room. Download the free **Official Bath App** for orientation.

Exploring Bath

Begin your tour of Georgian Bath at **Queen Square** for some of the famous streets laid out by John Wood the Elder (1704–54). Walk up to the **Circus,** three Palladian crescents arranged in a circle, with 524 different carved emblems above the doors. His son designed the **Royal Crescent,** an elegant half-moon row of town houses. Robert Adam put up **Pulteney Bridge,** a shop-lined crossing of the River Avon, in 1773, just as a similar bridge in the same medieval style, London Bridge, was crumbling.

Roman Baths ★ The Romans were the first to recognize the tourism potential of the natural hot springs, which bubble at a rate of 250,000 gallons a day. These steamy facilities were discovered in the late 1800s, and the res-toration and accompanying museum are excellent. The Victorians mounted a proud colonnade around the excavation, and water has long been drawn in the adjoining Pump Room; you can drink a glass of the sulfuric stuff if you like, or settle down for a pricey lunch in neoclassical style. It's been the done thing in Bath since your great-great-great-grandma was in bloomers.

Bath Abbey Church Yard, Stall St. www.romanbaths.co.uk. ✆ **01225/477785.** Admis-sion £14 adults (£15 July–Aug), £12 seniors and students, £9 children 6–16. July–Aug daily 9am–10pm; Sept–Oct and Mar–Jun daily 9am–6pm; Nov–Dec daily 9:30am–5:30pm, Jan–Feb daily 9am–4:30pm; last admission 1 hr. before closing.

No. 1 Royal Crescent ★ First-time visitors are blown away by the sweep and elegance of the Royal Crescent, a dazzling 30-house development that took some 8 years to complete, from 1767 to 1775. Its first house, which recently absorbed the old servants' quarters in a massive restoration that reli-giously presents daily life in those days, is worth a swing-by if you want the full Regency effect.

1 Royal Crescent. www.no1royalcrescent.org.uk. ✆ **01225/428126.** Admission £9 adults, £7 students and seniors, £4 children 6–16, family ticket £22. Tues–Sun 10:30am–5:30pm; Mon noon–5:30pm; last admission 1 hr. before closing. May be closed late Dec to Jan.

Fashion Museum & Assembly Rooms ★ The grand **Assembly Rooms,** designed by the younger John Wood and completed in 1771, once played host to dances, recitals, and tea parties. Damaged in World War II, the elegant rooms have been restored and look much as they did when Jane Austen and Thomas Gainsborough attended events here. Housed in the same building, the **Fashion Museum** offers audio tours through the history of fashion from the 16th century to the present day through some 165 dressed

Taking Tea in Bath

Yes, it's super-touristy—just go with it. The Regency stiffness of Bath is bound to give you a craving for that quintessentially English tradition of afternoon tea served with jam, clotted cream, and scones. Try the **Pump Room** at the Roman Baths (p. 232), which serves "Bath buns" (sweet buns sprinkled with sugar), or **Sally Lunn's** at 4 North Parade Passage (www.sallylunns.co.uk; ℂ **01225/461634**), which makes such a big deal of its light Sally Lunn buns you'd swear you'd even heard of them

before, which you haven't. The latter's building itself is one of the oldest in Bath, dating from 1482, and shows little hint of any changes with its crooked floors and low ceilings. For £7 to £12, you can sample a range of cream teas, which include toasted and buttered buns served with strawberry jam and clotted cream. The **Regency Tea Rooms** at the Jane Austen Centre offer "Tea with Mr. Darcy" sets (yes, I know . . .) for £17 to £30 for two, and basic cream tea from £8.

mannequins. Exhibits change every 6 months. There's also a "Corsets and Crinolines" display where enthusiastic visitors can experience the masochism of period garments.

Bennett St. www.fashionmuseum.co.uk. ℂ **01225/477-789.** Assembly Rooms: free admission. Fashion Museum: admission (includes audio tour) £8 adults, £7 students and seniors, £6 children 6–16, £24 family ticket, free for children 5 and under. Nov–Feb daily 10:30am–4pm; Mar–Oct daily 10:30am–5pm.

Jane Austen Centre ★   This small homage to Britain's favorite 19th-century writer isn't in her house, but Miss Austen did live up the hill (at no. 25) for a few months in 1805. Exhibits and a video convey a sense of what life was like when Austen lived in Bath between 1801 and 1806. Ladies can also learn the esoteric skill of using a fan to attract an admirer. Wholesome, corny fun. Allow at least 45 minutes. The tearoom is worth a visit (see "Taking Tea in Bath," above).

40 Gay St. www.janeausten.co.uk. ℂ **01225/443-000.** Admission £9 adults, £8 seniors, £7 students, £6 children 6–16, £23 family ticket. Apr–Oct daily 9:45am–5:30pm; Nov–Mar daily 11am–4:30pm.

OXFORD

Whereas the face of London, 92km (57 miles) east, has been forcibly reshaped by the pressures of war, disaster, and commerce, Oxford was made stronger by them. When plague killed townspeople, the colleges snapped up their houses, and when the Reformation cleaned out the churches, the colleges took their land, too. Academies used the extra space to carve out some of the most beautiful college buildings in the world. Here, the reverence for education borders on the ecclesiastical. Yet Oxford is no cloister; it's a decidedly modern city—thriving, sophisticated, and busy.

Essentials

GETTING THERE   The least expensive, easiest method is by coach, since companies compete for students with regular buses rolling round the clock. The so-called **Oxford Tube** bus (www.oxfordtube.com; ⓒ **01865/772250;** 100 min. with no traffic; £15 same-day or £18 next-day return) leaves every 10 to 20 minutes at all hours. It picks passengers up near the Tube stations at Marble Arch, Victoria, Notting Hill Gate, and Shepherd's Bush. Give rush hours wide berth. **Trains** (www.nationalrail.co.uk; ⓒ **08457/48-49-50;** 1 hr.; £15–£25 single with advance purchase) go from Paddington station to Oxford, sometimes via Reading.

VISITOR INFORMATION   In addition to selling (yes, selling—not giving) maps and guides, **The Oxford Information Centre** (15-16 Broad St.; www.visitoxford.org; ⓒ **01865/686430;** info@experienceoxfordshire.org) offers daily walking tours using accredited guides. You can download free maps of the city from Visit Britain (www.visitbritain.com).

TOURS   The Information Centre offers excellent **theme tours** such as "Pottering in Harry's Footsteps," "C.S. Lewis and J.R.R. Tolkien," and "Stained Glass"; book ahead. **Oxford River Cruises** (www.oxfordrivercruises.com; ⓒ **0845/226-9396**) runs several boat tours along the River Thames; the tranquil 50-minute Oxford Experience (cheaper online: £12 adults, £6 children 15 and under) is popular.

Exploring Oxford

Wandering Oxford's cobbled streets and ducking into its colleges to soak up their abject loveliness makes for a happy afternoon, particularly for fans of architecture. Many of the most iconic building clusters in this city of 140,000 (30,000 of whom are students) are collected together in the center of town, and they were built to house the university's nerve center. Oxford, like Cambridge, is comprised of individual colleges that feed off a central university system. Each of the 39 colleges has its own campus, tradition, character, and disciplines, although many close their grassy inner sanctums to visitors. During the school term (mid-Jan to mid-March, late April to mid-June, Oct to early Dec), some university buildings required for study (libraries, residence halls) are closed, or only open on Saturdays. At all times of year, watch out for zooming bicyclists; an unwritten law appears to grant them ownership of the city.

   To get the most out of Oxford, poke around, looking both inside cloisters and above rooftops. The doors between the inner and outer quadrangles of **Balliol College** (Broad St. and St Giles; www.balliol.ox.ac.uk; ⓒ **01865/27-77-77;** £2 adults, £1 seniors and students; daily 10am–5pm) still bear scorch marks from where Bloody Mary burned two Protestants alive for refusing to recant. Viewpoints are popular attractions here: The 22m (72-ft.) rectangular **Carfax Tower** (Carfax; ⓒ **01865/790522;** £2 adults, £1 children 15 and under; Apr–Sept daily 10am–5:30pm, Oct–Mar daily 10am–4:30pm), the last remaining chunk of the 13th-century St Martin's Church, has only 99 steps so it's not too taxing, which may be why it's a well-known suicide spot. It's located by the crossroads of the city center. Other popular panoramas are from the octagonal cupola above Sir Christopher Wren's **Sheldonian Theatre** (Broad St.; www.sheldon.ox.ac.uk; ℘ **01865/277-299**; £4, £8 with guided tour; Feb–Nov Mon–Sat 10am–4:30pm, plus July–Aug Sun 10am–4pm; closed 3pm Dec–Jan). Perhaps the top view is from the **University Church of St Mary the Virgin** (www.university-church.ox.ac.uk; ℘ **01865/279113;** free admission; daily 9am–5pm, closes 6pm July–Aug).

Bodleian Library ★ The main research library in town that made its name in research, "the Bod" opened in 1602 and has been burrowing under the streets of Oxford, trying to find new places to store its multiplying collection (11 million tomes and counting), ever since. The round **Radcliffe Camera** ("Rad Cam"; open via guided tours at the Bodleian) was built in the 1740s to house scientific books. It stands on the north side of Radcliffe Square.

Catte St. www.bodleian.ox.ac.uk. ℘ **01865/287-400.** Admission £1, Divinity School only; £7 (standard tour) or £5 for mini-tour (30 min.); £13 (extended tour); check current tour times online. Mon–Fri 9am–5pm; Sat 9am–4:30pm; Sun 11am–5pm. Closed for week around Christmas and New Year's.

Magdelen College ★ Pronounced "*Maud*-lin," it is one of the largest and most peaceful colleges here; its tower is the city's highest point, and its chapel is carved with breathtaking detail. Its site has a virtual tour to prep you on your explorations. U.S. Supreme Court justice Stephen Breyer attended.

High St. www.magd.ox.ac.uk. ℘ **01865/276-000.** Admission £5 adults; £4 seniors, students, and children. July–Sept daily noon–7pm; Oct–Jun daily 1–6pm or dusk (whichever is earlier). Closed for a week around Christmas and New Year's.

Christ Church ★ The largest, most beautiful, and most popular college to visit looms large in children's literature; it was copied for Hogwarts School in the Harry Potter films, and it was where Lewis Carroll (aka mathematician Charles Dodgson) befriended the little girl for whom he wrote *Alice in Wonderland.* The college chapel, which dates from the 12th century, also serves as Oxford Cathedral for the local diocese; and bowler-hatted "custodians" still patrol the pristine lawns. Its Meadow, still grazed by cattle, is a delightful place to watch punters on the rivers Isis and Cherwell. Just being here makes you feel smarter.

St Aldate's. www.chch.ox.ac.uk. ℘ **01865/276-150.** Tours £13 adults, £11 students, seniors, and children 5–17, free for children 4 and under. Mon–Sat 9am–5pm; Sun 2–5pm. Last admission 4:30pm. Closed for week around Christmas and New Year's.

The Ashmolean Museum ★ Offering more than just a pretty facade, it was founded way back in 1683, literally before anyone knew what the word "museum" actually meant. It houses an important hodgepodge of antiquities and art on par with (but on a smaller scale than) the British Museum, including a lantern carried by Guy Fawkes during the foiled Gunpowder Plot; the Anglo-Saxon Alfred Jewel of gold, enamel, and rock crystal; a Stradivarius

| | Punting the River Cherwell |

Punting on the River Cherwell is an essential if slightly eccentric Oxford pastime. From mid-March to October at the **Cherwell Boathouse,** Bardwell Rd. (www.cherwellboathouse.co.uk; © **01865/515-978**), you can rent a punt (a flat-bottomed boat for up to five people maneuvered by a long pole and a small oar) for £15 (Mon–Fri) to £18 (Sat–Sun) per hour. **Magdalen Bridge Boathouse,** the Old Horse Ford, High St. (www.oxfordpunting. co.uk; © **01865/202-643**), charges £20 per hour, daily 10am until dusk. Both outfits will give you some basic training.

violin; and assorted Old Masters paintings. Oh, and you know, minor stuff by Raphael and Michelangelo.

Beaumont St. at St Giles. www.ashmolean.org. © **01865/278-000.** Free admission. Tues–Sun 10am–5pm. Closed Dec 24–26.

The Pitt Rivers Museum ★   In an imposing 1886 cast-iron cathedral-like building not unlike a railway station, oft-freakish blend of folk art and anthropology—think shrunken heads and bundles of poisoned arrows brought back by British explorers over hundreds of years. It is, to use an academic term, totally gnarly.

Parks Rd. www.prm.ox.ac.uk. © **01865/270-927.** Free admission. Tues–Sun 10am–4:30pm; Mon noon–4:30pm.

Blenheim Palace ★   Within 30 minutes, the half-hourly S3 bus from the train station or Gloucester Green whisks visitors to Hensington Road, Woodstock, and the gates of the birthplace of Winston Churchill, now a UNESCO World Heritage Site. The British rarely remind you that their oh-so-English savior was, in fact, half American; his mom Jennie, who was from Brooklyn, married an English lord, and Winston was born here in 1874, several hundred years into the palace's history. A few decades later, the home was saved from financial ruin when the Duke of Marlborough married another American, a Vanderbilt; their descendants still live here for part of the year. Tours of the grounds, landscaped by Capability Brown, and the state rooms, which are in excellent nick, take about 3 hours.

Hensington Rd., Woodstock, Oxfordshire. www.blenheimpalace.com. © **01993/810-530.** Admission: palace and grounds £23 adults, £18 seniors and students, £12 children 5–16. Daily 10:30am–5:30pm.

CAMBRIDGE

Oxford is a city in its own right, but Cambridge, in the marshes 79km (49 miles) northeast of London, would barely have a pulse without its university. That makes Cambridge manageable. It feels in some ways like a typical English town, with a daily market for crafts and food on its central square, Market Hill. Its best rewards come when you wander through

BLETCHLEY PARK: ENIGMA no more

For decades, it was top secret. Few people realized what had happened during World War II in its rotting temporary wooden huts, which were nearly bulldozed for a housing development. But in time, we learned what codebreaker Alan Turing and his brilliant team accomplished at **Bletchley Park** (www.bletchleypark.org.uk; ✆ **01908/640-404**; admission £17 adults, £15 seniors, £10 students 12–16, free for children 11 and under; Nov–Feb daily 9:30am–4pm, Mar–Oct daily 9:30am–5pm, last admission 1 hr. before closing), hidden from the world on a former estate 88km (55 miles) northwest of London, where they cracked the Enigma machine code, breaking the German blockade that threatened to starve an entire country. In 2014, the year their story, *The Imitation Game,* was released, the fully restored Bletchley Park campus was opened as a fascinating day out, like a spy novel set in a park, suffused in the urgency, intrigue, and excitement of those terrifying years when computers were born and Nazis were a few chess moves away from storming England. You can tour more than a dozen buildings around its soothing central pond, exploring the methods, experiments, and lucky breaks that enabled round-the-clock workers, including many gifted women, to translate a jumble of meaningless letters into life-saving intercepted secrets. The cramped, rudimentary Huts 3, 6, and 8, dressed to look like they probably did then (no one is sure—photographs were forbidden), were the heart of the operation, but you can also tour the ground floor of the mansion that served as its command post and outbuildings that housed the computers, which were later dismantled down to the rivets to prevent anyone from duplicating them. Head to the basement of Block B, where modern fans have rebuilt one. The number of Enigma-related artifacts and the level of codebreaking detail can be headspinning, so children may tire quickly, but interested adults could spend 3 or 4 absorbed hours wrapping their heads around it, a pursuit made easier by the three cafes spread around its grassy acres.

Next door, you'll find the **National Museum of Computing** (www.tnmoc. org; ✆ **01908/374708**; admission £8 adults, £5 seniors, students, and children), where volunteers are rebuilding historic systems that were lost to time, including Bletchley's own Colossus. That exhibit is open daily, but the rest of that museum, including the world's largest collection of historic computers, is only open Thursday, Saturday, and Sunday from noon to 4pm. The level of computing detail there isn't for everyone. Trains to Bletchley leave Euston a few times an hour (50 min.; £16 single) and the gates are 182m (200 yd.) from the station; sit on the left of the carriage for good views of the Grand Union Canal as you go. If you fancy a country drive, Avis, Enterprise, and Budget are clustered near the Bletchley train station.

randomly chosen iron gates or along a river path—that's when the inviting little town really opens up.

Essentials

GETTING THERE Nonstop **coaches** from National Express (www. nationalexpress.com; ✆ **08705/80-80-80**; 2½ hr.; £7–£8 single) leave hourly from Victoria Coach station; don't get off at Trumpington, but wait for the city center stop. There are **trains** from Liverpool Street or King's Cross, but be warned that Cambridge's station is several miles from the city center, so you will need to bike or call a taxi; coaches are the smarter way to travel. If you insist, though, note that some trains take about 45 minutes and some take twice that, so ask about journey times (www.nationalrail.co.uk; ℗ **08457/48-49-50;** 45–90 min.; £10–£23).

VISITOR INFORMATION **Cambridge Visitor Information Centre** (Peas Hill; www.visitcambridge.org; ℗ **0871/226-8006** in U.K. or ℗ 011-44-1223/464-732 overseas; info@visitcambridge.org) sells maps and guides but won't dispense them for free. Cambridge also sells hour-long walking tours on downloadable MP3s (www.tourist-tracks.com; £5 for two). You can download free maps of the city from Visit Britain (www.visitbritain.com).

TOURS The **Cambridge Tourist Information Centre** (see "Visitor Information," above) has several types of walking tours of the city, from £6 to £16 for adults, and up to £8 for children 11 and under. Book tours at www.visit cambridge.org/official-tours (℗ **01223/457-574**).

Exploring Cambridge

Like Oxford, Cambridge's calling card is the elaborate and ancient architecture of its colleges. Unlike in Oxford, it's easy to venture into the cloistered grounds of many of Cambridge's colleges (the oldest was founded in 1286 after a squabble in Oxford necessitated the establishment of a second educational capital), though doing so usually requires a few quid. Mill Lane leads to the River Cam, where you can rent a punting boat for £6 or sit at The Mill pub overlooking the water. (If you want to seem savvy to Cambridge traditions, punt from the back of the boat. In Oxford, they punt from the front.) The meadows along the Cam are known as **The Backs,** and they make for idyllic walks.

The head of Oliver Cromwell, which was impaled outside Westminster Hall in London as a warning against regicide (albeit 3 years after the man died of natural causes), was finally buried within an antechapel (not open to visitors) at Sidney Sussex College in 1960. It's in an unmarked grave to keep pranksters from pinching the much-abused thing. That's Cambridge in a nutshell: It has many secrets, but since it's still a working university town, marvels won't be handed to you. You have to wander, wonder, and ask questions. Colleges aren't open, and street life is at a minimum, outside of term (mid-Jan to mid-Mar, late Apr to mid-June, Oct to early Dec).

King's College Chapel ★ For some reason, the marauding Puritans neglected to smash the 16th-century stained-glass windows of its chapel—they probably thought they were just as divine as you will. The chapel's fanned and vaulted ceiling, a work of craftsmanship that stuns even those who care little for such things, was completed at the behest of Henry VII. Its famous choristers sing at services during term time.

King's Parade. www.kings.cam.ac.uk. ℗ **01223/331-212.** Admission £8 adults, £6 students and seniors, free for children 11 and under. Mon–Fri 9:45am–3:30pm; Sat 9:30am–3:15pm; Sun 1:15–2:30pm; check website ahead for changes.

Pembroke College ★   The third-oldest college in town is one of the best, distinguished by the oldest gatehouse in Cambridge and by a chapel with an ornate plaster ceiling, which was the first completed work by Christopher Wren (after finishing, the man seemed never to rest again). Unlike many of the colleges, Pembroke never charges visitors to poke around its common areas.

Trumpington St. www.pem.cam.ac.uk. ℂ **01223/33-81-00.** Free admission. Daily 2–5pm, except mid-May to mid-June when closed for exams.

Trinity College ★   Trinity is the largest and most endowed of Cambridge's 31 colleges. Sir Isaac Newton first calculated the speed of sound here, at Neville's Court, and Lord Byron used to bathe naked in the Great Court's fountain with his pet bear. The University forbade students from having dogs, but there was no rule against bears. In *Chariots of Fire,* sprinters tried to get around the .8-hectare (2-acre) yard in the time it took for its clock to strike 12. Your attempts will not be appreciated.

Trinity St. www.trin.cam.ac.uk. ℂ **01223/338-400.** Free admission. The Wren Library: Mon–Fri noon–2pm; Sat 10:30am–12:30pm. Various other areas are open at different times and may incur a £2 charge; inquire at the porter's lodge.

Queen's College ★   Founded by the wife of Henry VI and the wife of Edward IV, the college dates from 1448 and is regarded as the most beautiful of Cambridge's colleges. Entry and exit are by the old porter's lodge in Queens' Lane. Tourists are often told that the wooden **Mathematical Bridge** (1749) spanning the Cam behind it (see it from Silver St.) was constructed using no nails, and when curious students disassembled it to figure out how, they couldn't put it back together without using screws. The college is curiously defensive about the accusation, saying that anyone who believes this story "cannot have a serious grasp on reality."

Silver St. www.quns.cam.ac.uk. ℂ **01223/335-511.** Admission £3 adults (including guide booklet), free for children 9 and under. Jun–Sept and Nov–May daily 10am–4:30pm; Oct Mon–Fri 2–4:30pm and Sat–Sun 10am–4:30pm. Closed late May to late June.

Fitzwilliam Museum ★   Cambridge's most storied attraction is a first-rate neoclassical building full of applied arts and Old Masters that a city 10 times Cambridge's size (pop. 108,000) would covet. If a colonial Englishman could carry it home on a ship, it's here: precious antiquities from Rome, Greece, Egypt, Asia, and paintings by every famous name under the European sun.

Trumpington St., near Peterhouse. www.fitzmuseum.cam.ac.uk. ℂ **01223/332-900.** Free admission; donations appreciated. Tues–Sat 10am–5pm; Sun noon–5pm. Closed Mon, Good Friday, Dec 24–26 and 31, and Jan 1. Sat guided tours at 2:30pm (£6).

STONEHENGE & SALISBURY

Stonehenge is a circle of rocks. If it's raining, it's a damned circle of rocks. But people still ask to go, and if that's their dream, then they should do it. Just understand that it may not blow you away.

Essentials

GETTING THERE This one's a pain. Trains don't go directly to Stonehenge; the nearest station is in Salisbury, nearly 16km (10 miles) south. So the easiest way to get here is to drive. The rocks are located 3.2km (2 miles) west of Amesbury in Wiltshire on the junction of A303 and A344/360. Or take a half-hourly **train** (www.nationalrail.co.uk; ℂ **08457/48-49-50;** 90 min.; £38 single with advance purchase) from Waterloo station to Salisbury station. There used to be a cheap public bus to the rocks from there, but it says a lot about the values of the local tourism authorities that they replaced that route entirely with the expensive but convenient Stonehenge Tour Bus by **Wilts & Dorset Buses** (www.thestonehengetour.info; ℂ **0845/0727-093;** 30 min.; round-trip £14 adults, £9 children 7–18, buy from driver), which leaves seven times a day between 10am and 4pm from Salisbury station. A few extra buses are tossed in during the summer; check its website for updated schedules. Many tour companies offer round-trip all-day coach tours from London that take 10 or 11 hours. One of them is **Premium Tours** (see above) for £67 adults, £64 seniors, and £57 children 3 to 16.

VISITOR INFORMATION Salisbury and Stonehenge (Fish Row, Salisbury; www.visitwiltshire.co.uk; ℂ **01722/342-860;** visitorinfo@salisbury citycouncil.gov.uk). VisitWiltshire produces a free app that rounds up the area's offerings.

TOURS You can easily see Salisbury on foot, either on your own or by taking a guided daytime or evening walk run by **Salisbury City Guides** (www. salisburycityguides.co.uk; ℂ **07873/212941**). Tickets are £5 for adults, £3 for students, and free for kids.

Exploring Stonehenge & Salisbury

Stonehenge ★ Construction on this bucket-list sight began about 5,000 years ago, and the first recorded day trips to the megalith were in 1562. Arranged in such a way that it aligns with the rising of the sun during the midsummer solstice, this Neolithic circle of stones is certainly Britain's most important ancient wonder, and it's a UNESCO World Heritage Site (together with Avebury, a far less interesting, but still important, line of rocks 39km/24 miles north). Whether its builders, who remain anonymous, worshiped the sun or merely appreciated astronomy is only the beginning of the mystery. We also can only make educated guesses as to how these prehistoric people, using only rudimentary tools, managed to hoist these slabs from Wales to here, and then into place. Even if you don't salivate over such long-ago feats of ingenuity, the distinctive profile of the stones, surrounded by empty plains, "henge" earthworks, and hundreds of lumpen burial mounds, will surely be iconic.

You're not allowed to walk amongst the rocks the way visitors once were; you have to stick to a footpath that curves near the circle but keeps the formation at a safe distance, good for pretty photographs but bad for curiosity. Most tourists like you and me are being kept at arm's length (exception: Clark Griswold, who managed to topple them like dominoes in *National Lampoon's European Vacation*),

THE TRADE-OFF WITH escorted tours

Arranging your own day trips using public transportation will almost always be the most cost-effective method, but there are cogent reasons for choosing a guided coach tour. It's simply quicker to allow someone else to drive you around, making sure you cram a laundry list of major sites into a short time span, and consuming spoon-fed nuggets of information about each place. What you learn won't have much depth, but at least you'll have been there.

Problem is, you'll have paid a pretty penny for it: Most tours cost at least £70 a day, not including food. You get a richer experience (and one that doesn't have you idling in traffic and trooping into gift shops all day), when you do it yourself. But some people desperately want to soak up as many sights as they can, even if it means they skim the surface. For them, here are the major players in the coach-tour biz, sold aggressively through the concierges at expensive hotels (who love getting the commissions):

o **Evan Evans Tours** (www.evan evanstours.co.uk; in the U.K. ✆ **020/7950-1777,** in the U.S. 866/382-6868)

o **Gray Line's Golden Tours** (www. goldentours.co.uk; in the U.K. ✆ **020/7630-2028,** in the U.S. 800/509-2507)

o **Premium Tours** (www.premium tours.co.uk; in the U.K. ✆ **020/ 7713-1311,** in the U.S. 800/250-5775)

Better yet are the more affordable **London Walks** (www.walks.com; ✆ **020/ 7624-3978**), which run frequent day trips (see p. 155). These use public transportation and don't include admission fees, but you'll have a guide every step of the way to show you how it's all done.

but you can apply in advance for a 1-hour pass to stroll among the rocks, timed just before or after the site closes to the public for the day. These passes are never given for Tuesday or Wednesday mornings, and October through February is usually blocked off, too, and slots must be applied for in writing. The forms are at the English Heritage website. The limited experience (a disappointment for many who trudge 129km/80 miles west of London to have it) is why few people see Stonehenge without passing through Bath on the same day. That itinerary is offered by coach tours; putting it together yourself with trains and buses is not ideal because the connections chew up too much time. Salisbury is doable, though, since trains headed there connect with a bus (see "Getting There," above). Alternatively, climb **Amesbury Hill,** clearly visible 2.4km (1½ miles) up the A303. From here, you'll get a free panoramic view.

At the junction of A303 and A344. www.english-heritage.org.uk/stonehenge. ✆ **08703/ 331181.** Admission £15 adults, £13 students and seniors, £9 children 5–15, £38 family ticket; posted prices are higher and include a voluntary donation. June–Aug daily 9am–8pm; April–May and Sept–Oct 15 daily 9:30am–7pm; mid-Oct–mid-Mar daily 9:30am–5pm; last admission 2 hr. before closing. Train: Salisbury, then Stonehenge Tour Bus.

Salisbury Cathedral ★ Built with uncommon efficiency between 1220 and 1258 and barely touched since, this early English Gothic masterpiece is considered by many to be the most breathtaking church in the world. After you've seen it, and lost yourself in gazing at it and sighing, the rest of your

VISITING HIGHCLERE CASTLE, THE real DOWNTON ABBEY

The 8th Earl and Countess of Carnarvon still dwell under the sandstone turrets of **Highclere Castle** (Highclere Park, Newbury; www.highclerecastle.co.uk; ℭ **01635/253-204;** admission £20 adults, £18 students and seniors, £13 children 4–16), known to TV viewers as the idyllic and stately *Downton Abbey*. Time and spendthrift earls took their toll on this historic home, and as recently as 2009, more than 50 rooms were uninhabitable due to mold and leaks. The current Earl faces repair bills running around £12 million, so he welcomes visitors to spend the day exploring the 1,000 acres of private rolling Berkshire countryside. He also rents out to film production: The upstairs scenes of the ITV/PBS show were shot on the ground floor and first floor using the house's actual furniture, but downstairs was shot on a soundstage in Ealing, west London. At Highclere, the basement is full not of servants but of mummy stuff: The fifth Earl was the guy who bankrolled Howard Carter's 1923 emptying of King Tut's tomb in Luxor, so unseen beneath Lord Grantham's feet lay items taken from the tombs of Egypt. Highclere is only open for 60 to 70 days a year but they're scattered all over the calendar—typically Easter Week, bank holiday weekends, and from mid-August to mid-September. Taking a group tour guarantees a ticket, but those sell out months ahead and herd you along. If you show up independently at either 10am or 2:30pm, you can get a walk-up ticket even though advance tickets are sold out, but that involves taking a 52-minute train from Paddington (from £24) or a National Express bus (1¾ hr.; from £10) to the adorable town of Newbury (stop to admire the longboats on the Kennet and Avon canal) and then a £15 taxi (try www.cabco33333.com or www.newburytaxi.co.uk).

time in Salisbury will be contentedly spent walking medieval streets, which were laid in a loose grid and give the city an airy character. The cathedral complex's octagonal Chapter House possesses one of the four surviving copies of the Magna Carta signed by King John in 1215. Two more are in London at the British Library (p. 86).

The Close. www.salisburycathedral.org.uk. ℭ **01722/555120.** Admission: voluntary donation £8 adults, £7 seniors, £5 students, free for children 7–17, £15 family. Mon–Sat 9am–5pm; Sun noon–4pm. Chapter House closes 4:30pm (Apr–Oct 5:45pm) and all morning Sun.

Old Sarum ★   Believed to have been an Iron Age fortification, Old Sarum was used again by the Saxons and flourished as a walled town into the Middle Ages. The Normans built a cathedral; parts of that were taken down to build the city of "New Sarum," later known as Salisbury, leaving behind dramatically sited remains with unforgettable views of Salisbury and rolling green hills, not to mention the opportunity to commune with grazing sheep.

2 miles north of Salisbury off A345 Castle Rd. www.english-heritage.org.uk/oldsarum. ℭ **01722/335398.** Admission £4 adults, £4 seniors and students, £3 children 5–15; posted prices are higher and include a voluntary donation. Apr–Sept daily 10am–6pm; Mar and Oct daily 10am–5pm; Nov–Mar daily 10am–4pm. Bus: 5, 6, 7, 8, or 9, every 30 min. during the day, from Salisbury bus station.

PLANNING YOUR TRIP TO LONDON

First of all, relax. Getting to London isn't as tricky as it used to be. Some 17.4 million international visitors came here in 2014—making it the most popular destination for travelers from abroad—so they know a thing or two about helping foreigners. Finding airfare isn't much harder than finding a cross-country flight. Being ready for the rest (money, electricity) is simply a matter of having the facts.

GETTING THERE

By Plane

FROM THE AIRPORT

Transatlantic flights almost always land at Heathrow, Europe's busiest international airport (LHR; 17 miles west), or Gatwick, perhaps the most disliked (LGW; 31 miles south). With a few minor exceptions, the other four airports, Stansted (STN; 37 miles northeast), Luton (LTN; 34 miles northwest), London City (LCY; in London's Docklands area), and Southend (SEN; 42 miles easy) serve flights from Europe, and they're where cut-rate flyers and executive jets tend to go. Every airport offers some kind of rail connection to the central city, and that's the smart way to go. Tickets can be bought at windows in the arrivals halls, at machines, or online, where you get a discount. You'll rarely have to wait more than 20 minutes for the next train.

Airport Transportation Options

Heathrow Express (www.heathrowexpress.com; ✆ 08456/00-15-15; £21.50 single, £35 return, kids 5–15 £10.70 single £17.50 return; 15 min.) zooms to Paddington every quarter-hour. First Class is a waste of money; Express Saver, the cheapest option for purchase online or at vending machines, is plenty plush. **Heathrow Connect** (www.heathrowconnect.com; ✆ 084/5678-6975; £10.10 single; 30–45 min.) is designed to give access to local stations, so it takes twice as long (still not long at all). It uses commuter-style carriages and leaves half-hourly. Both trains arrive at Paddington,

AIRPORT	COST/AVG. TIME USING NATIONAL RAIL	HOURS OF RAIL SERVICE
Heathrow (LHR), HeathrowAirport.com	Heathrow Express (www.heathrow express.com): £21.50 single, £35 return, kids 5 to 15 £10.70/£17.50*/15 minutes OR Heathrow Connect: £10.10 single/30–45 minutes	Four times hourly 5:07am to 11:55pm
Gatwick (LGW), GatwickAirport.com	Gatwick Express (www.gatwick express.com): £20 single, £35 return (in person) £18/£31 (online), kids £10/£17.50 and £9/£15.55/30 minutes or Thameslink & Great Northern: £11 single/30 to 50 minutes	Four times hourly 3:30am to 12:30am
Luton (LTN), www.London-Luton.co.uk	Thameslink & Great Northern: £14 single including 5-min. shuttle bus, 45 minutes	Six times hourly 5am to midnight
Stansted (STN), StanstedAirport.com	From £19 single, £32 return/47 minutes	Four times hourly 5:30am to 12:30am
London City (LCY), LondonCityAirport.com	N/A	DLR: 5:30am to midnight
London Southend (SEN), www.southendairport.com	Greater Anglia: £17 single/53 minutes	4am to 11pm

*Online fare. Tickets £5 more if you wait to pay on board.

**As if you'd be daft enough to want a taxi after seeing those prices and times, you're more likely to find one by booking ahead. Check www.london-luton.co.uk, www.stansted airport.com, and www.southendairport.com for list of the latest approved companies. Addison Lee (www.addisonlee.com) is an established minicab company, and Heathrow has a partnership with Green Tomato Cars (www.greentomatocars.com). All services offer discounted prices for children.

where you can hop the Tube system or a taxi (above Platform 12). The cheapest way is by London Underground (£5.70 cash or £5.10 Oyster; 75 min.) using the Piccadilly line. If you need to go in the middle of the night and the Tube isn't running, Night Bus N9 goes to and from Trafalgar Square and Heathrow and takes about 75 minutes.

Gatwick Express (www.gatwickexpress.com; ✆ 084/5850-530; £20 single, £35 return, kids 5–15 £10/£17.50, discounts online; 30 min.) runs from Victoria. On **Thameslink & Great Northern** (www.thameslinkrailway.com; ✆ 0345/026-4700; £11 single; 30–50 min.), you can get to Gatwick via Blackfriars, Farringdon, St Pancras, or London Bridge stations four times an hour—service ends around 11:45pm.

10

RAIL SERVICE TO	COST/TIME USING TUBE OR DLR	COST/AVG. TIME FOR NATIONAL EXPRESS SHUTTLE SERVICE TO CENTRAL LONDON	COST/AVG. TIME TO AIRPORT BY TAXI
Paddington	£5.70 cash or £5.10 Oyster/75 minutes on Piccadilly Line	£6 single, kids 11 to 16 £3, under 11 free, from £5.50 each way (www.nationalexpress.com)/50–70 minutes	£65–£85/70 minutes
Gatwick Express: Victoria; T&GN: St Pancras, Farringdon, Blackfriars, or London Bridge	N/A	£8 each way (www.nationalexpress.com)/90 minutes	£100/70 minutes
St Pancras, Blackfriars, or London Bridge	N/A	From £9 (www.nationalexpress.com)/90 minutes (runs 24 hr.)	£100/80 minutes**
Liverpool Street	N/A	From £12 single (www.nationalexpress.com)/60–100 minutes	£99/80 minutes**
N/A	£4.80 cash, £3.30 Oyster/25 minutes on Docklands Light Railway	N/A	£25–£40/20 to 40 minutes
Liverpool Street	N/A	N/A	£80–£100/60 to 80 minutes

Stansted Express (www.stanstedexpress.com; ℗ **0845/600-7245;** from £19 single, £32 return; 47 min.) runs from Liverpool Street station. **Luton** has rail service from St Pancras station, Blackfriars, London Bridge stations by **Thameslink & Great Northern** (www.thameslinkrailway.com; ℗ **0345/026-4700;** £14 single, including 5-min. shuttle bus; 45 min.; four times hourly). The correct stop is Luton Airport Parkway Station, linked by a 10-minute shuttle (5am–midnight) to the terminals.

City Airport is linked so expediently and affordably by the Docklands Light Railway (£4.80 cash, £3.30 Oyster; 25 min. from Tower Gateway or Bank) that it doesn't support commuter rail or coach service. **London Southend** (www.southendairport.com), too, is so well-connected to a shiny new station by **Greater Anglia** rail from Liverpool Street that buses don't bother to go there, so the train (£17 single; 53 min.) is the sole option.

Door-to-door **car service** (£50–£60) can take 45 min. to 2 hrs., so the train-taxi or train-Tube combo is often faster, although those force you to contend with your luggage. You can book ahead: Check each airport's website for a current list of the latest approved companies. **Addison Lee** (www.addisonlee.com; ☏ 020/7407-9000) is an established minicab company, the website Minicabit.com surveys companies for the best prices, and Heathrow has a partnership with **Green Tomato Cars** (www.greentomato cars.com; (☏ 020/8568-0022). Also try **Airport Cars UK** (☏ **0330/088-2222;** www.airportcars-uk.com) which serves all airports.

Finding the Lowest Airfare

The central question is *when* are they? London is such a popular destination (it's served by more flights from the United States than any other European city) that plenty of airlines vie to carry you across—although the ones that are not American-run are usually of higher quality. If you're not redeeming frequent-flier miles (book very far ahead if you are), there are five rules to finding bargains:

1. **Fly on days when traffic is lightest.** Some airlines post calendars that show you when their best prices are, or test fare trends on a site such as **Hopper.com**.
2. **Depart after dinner.** This saves you from paying another hotel night, since you'll arrive in the morning. You're also likely to find lower fares, because business travelers like day flights.
3. **Go off-season.** London's weather isn't extreme, so there's really not a no-go month. November through March yield the lowest airfares and hotel rates, although the late-December holidays and the last week of November (Thanksgiving in U.S.) can be busy, too. Summer prices (June–Sept) soar over a grand.
4. **Search for fares for or on a weekend.** Many major airlines post lower prices to fly then. You might also save money by booking your seat at 3am. That's because unpaid-for reservations are flushed out of the system at midnight, and prices often sink when the system becomes aware of an increase in supply.
5. **Don't buy last-minute.** Desperation has a price.

Hotwire's **TripStarter** tool (www.hotwire.com/tripstarter/index.jsp) tracks how much the airlines charge, and when. Monitor airline newsletters, sale pages, Twitter accounts, and sites such as **Frommers.com** and **SmarterTravel.com**. Both **Airfarewatchdog.com** and **Yapta.com** spit out emails when airfare drops.

Primary websites that collect quotes from a variety of sources (whether they be airlines or other websites) include **Ebookers.com**, **Expedia.com**, **Kayak.com**, **Lessno.com**, **Mobissimo.com**, **Momondo.com**, and **Orbitz.com**. Always canvas multiple sites, because each has odd gaps in coverage because of how they obtain quotes. Always compare your best price with what the airline is offering, because that price might be lowest of all. Some sites have small booking fees of $5 to $10, and many force you to accept non-refundable tickets for the cheapest prices. If you're hitting a wall, search for transatlantic itineraries that allow for one or two stops, since routes that include stops in Reykjavik or Frankfurt (on Icelandair or Lufthansa, respectively) can produce hidden bargains. No matter which airline you go with, prepare yourself for added taxes and fees, which are usually $500 or higher round-trip from the USA—London's airport fees are truly noxious.

Most times of the year, the least expensive way to reach London is with an **air-hotel package** (p. 43), which combines discounted airfare with discounted nights in a hotel. Most air-hotel deals will allow you to fly back days after your hotel allotment runs out, and at no extra charge. Keep in mind that solo travelers always pay a little more, typically $200.

By Bus

National Express (www.nationalexpress.com; ✆ **08717/818-8179**) buses will also take you from all airports (except Southend) for around £10 each way, although given traffic we don't recommend it. It's also the least expensive way to get from city to city in Britain (but not the fastest—that's usually the train), and because the country is not very big, it rarely takes more than a few hours to reach anyplace. Even Scotland is only 5 hours away. This is a major carrier with scads of departures, but the best-priced is **Megabus** (www.megabus.com; ✆ **090/0160-0900** or +44-141-352-4444), which serves more than 100 cities across Europe, and charges as little as £1.50 for early bookings, although £19 to £45 for Edinburgh is a more typical rate. It accepts bookings 2 months ahead; book online to avoid phone fees. Both coach services depart from the miserable Victoria Coach Station, located behind Victoria railway station.

What's the best place to hear about inexpensive ground tours? Hostels. Drop into one; most of their lobbies are papered with brochures. Don't neglect their bulletin boards, either, since you may catch wind of a shared-ride situation that'll often cost you no more than your share of the gasoline (in Britain, *petrol*).

A few coach companies also travel to Europe, usually crossing the Channel with a ferry. Because of the pressure put on the market by mushrooming no-frills airlines, rates are extremely low. You'll pay as little as £21 one-way to Paris via **Eurolines** (www.eurolines.co.uk; ✆ **08717/81-81-78;** 8–10 hr. each way). Brussels or Amsterdam are £25 with a 7-day advance purchase. The trade-off: It can take all day, sunrise to sunset, to reach Paris by this method.

Young, social adventurers should investigate **Busabout** (www.busabout.com; ✆ **8450/267-514**), a coach system that follows set loops from London to France and Spain, Austria, Belgium, Italy, Switzerland, and Germany and the Czech Republic. Passengers can hop on and hop off as they please. Some other companies arrange full-on organized tours of Europe's greatest hits—but never for less than you could do independently; choose one only because you'd enjoy having company: **Contiki** (www.contiki.com; ✆ **866/266-8454**) is geared toward a party-hearty under-35 crowd, **Tucan Travel Adventure Tours** (www.tucantravel.com; ✆ **855/444-9110**) is for social scrimpers, and **Fanatics** (www.thefanatics.com; ✆ **020/7240-3233**) is for followers of organized sports.

driving **IN LONDON?**

Don't! Roads are clogged. In bad traffic, a trip from Heathrow to the western fringe of London can take 2 hours. And once you're in the city, just about every technology is deployed against you. There's a hefty fee just to drive to the city center. Roads are confusingly one-way. Cameras catch and ticket your honest driving errors. Parking is a fantasy. Many North Americans think of cars as the default transportation mode, but in London, trains are the thing. The only time to *maybe* drive a car is if you're on a cross-country tour—but in cities, it won't be easy for you.

The cheapest coach and van services for each airport are listed in the chart, and they all drop you off at standardized stops such as major train stations. For Gatwick, Stansted, and Luton, in addition to the usual National Express coach options, there's the no-frills **easyBus**

(www.easybus.co.uk). Unless you book far in advance, it may not beat the National Express prices.

If you insist upon wheels, reserving ahead from home yields the best prices. Try to return your car outside the congestion-charge zone to avoid charges and aggravation. You will find similar rates among **Nova Car Hire** (www.nova carhire.com), **Auto Europe** (www.auto europe.com), **Europe By Car** (www.ebc travel.com), **Europcar** (www.europcar. com), and **Holiday Autos** (www.holiday autos.com). Also check the major names like Avis, Hertz, and Budget, in case they can do better. Air-conditioning, something you won't need, adds about £5 to the daily bill. Fuel, or *petrol*, is even more expensive than at home, and although most rentals include unlimited mileage, not all do. Also: Many rental cars are stick-shift models.

By Train

The original railway builders plowed their stations to every town of size, making it easy to see the highlights of the United Kingdom without getting near a car. The British whine about the declining quality of the service, but Americans, Canadians, and Australians will be blown away by the speed (and the cost, if they don't book ahead) of the system. Find tickets to all destinations through **National Rail** (www.nationalrail.co.uk/cheapestfare; © **08457/48-49-50**) or the indispensible **TheTrainLine.com**. Seats are sold 12 weeks ahead, and early-bird bookings can yield some marvelous deals, such as £26 for a 4-hour trip to Scotland (£125 last-minute is common). When hunting for tickets, always search for "off-peak" (non-rush hour) trips going or coming from London in general, not a specific London station, because each London terminal serves various cities. The free app **TicketySplit** also searches the rail companies' byzantine fare schedules for journey configurations that can save you many pounds. Unfortunately, not every train company website accepts international credit cards; TheTrainLine does.

Tickets bought reasonably in advance will still be cheaper than what you'd pay for the same trips on a **BritRail pass** (www.britrail.com; must purchase outside the U.K.), good on long-distance trains but not on local London transport, and few tourists ride rails with the near-daily regularity that would make a timed pass pay for itself. Check prices against the U.S. seller **Rail Europe** (www.raileurope.com; ☎ **800/622-8600**), as quotes vary.

For trips from northwestern Europe, the train is more dignified. Unlike taking a flight, you won't need to set aside extra hours and pounds to get to and from airports; train stations are in the middle of town. We're living in marvelous times: The Channel Tunnel opened 2 decades ago (although they *still* seem to be working out the kinks), so you can reach the heart of Paris in an incredible 2 hours and 15 minutes from London. You can literally ride both the Tube and the Métro before lunch. In fact, you can ride both a black taxi and Space Mountain before lunch, since the Eurostar train alights in the middle of Disneyland Resort. Eurostar links London's St Pancras station with Paris, Brussels, Lille, and Calais, and from there, you can go just about anywhere using other trains.

Book via **Eurostar** (www.eurostar.co.uk; ☎ **03432/186-186** in the U.K. or +44 1233/61-75-75; phone bookings are US$7 more) itself or the U.S.-based **Rail Europe** (www.raileurope.com; ☎ **800/361-7245** in North America), which also sells European rail passes. Check both sites, since prices can differ, but do it early, because rates boom as availability decreases. Pay attention to the special offers on Eurostar's site; deals go as low as £69 round-trip in summer.

By Boat

Ferry travel is obsolete, mostly used by people who need to transfer cars. No ferry to Europe sails directly to London. You'll have to get down to the southern coastal towns of Folkestone and Dover (for France), or Portsmouth (for Spain). Unless you have your own car, it's hard to get to the ports of the France-destined lines. Advance purchase can be from £35 each way with a car and including taxes (150 min.) on **P&O Ferries** (www.poferries.com; ☎ **08716/64-64-64**). The aggregator **DirectFerries.co.uk** sells European routes from a rapidly diminishing roster of companies.

If you despise flying, one ocean liner still makes the storied 7-day trip between New York City and Southampton, which connects by rail to London in an hour. That's the *Queen Mary 2* (www.cunard.com; ☎ **800/728-6273**), intermittently scheduled. Fares start around $900 per person, including all your food.

GETTING AROUND
By Public Transportation

There are three practical methods for taming London's sprawl: by Tube (historic and enchanting, but expensive); by bus (less expensive and less glamorous, but more edifying and often quicker); and by foot (the best method, but not always possible). Taxis are overpriced, Ubers require mobile data usage, and driving a car is lunacy.

The Underground

Londoners call their 402km (249-mile) metro system the Underground, its official name, or just as commonly, "the Tube." Its elegant, distinctive logo—a red "roundel" bisected by a blue bar—debuted in 1913 as one of the world's first corporate symbols, and it remains one of the city's most ubiquitous sights. There's no older subway system on earth—the first section opened in 1863 while America was fighting its Civil War—and it often acts its age, with frequent delays and shutdowns. Check in the ticket hall to see what "engineering works" are scheduled.

The Tube is an attraction unto itself. It's fun to seek out vestiges of the early system (1907 tilework on the Piccadilly Line; the fake house facades built at 23-24 Leinster Gardens to hide exposed tracks; abandoned stations like the one at Strand and Surrey St.). If such "urban archaeology" fascinates you, visit the London Transport Museum in Covent Garden (p. 94), one of the city's family-friendly highlights. The Tube is also much more dignified than most American systems. In fact, seats are upholstered. That's because the British know how to take care of nice things.

There are 13 named lines, plus the Docklands Light Railway (DLR) serving East London and a tram line in South London, which together serve nearly 300 stations. Lines are color-coded: the Piccadilly is a peacock purple, the Bakerloo could be considered Sherlock Holmes brown, and so on.

The Tube shuts down nightly from Sunday to Thursday. Exact times for first and final trains are posted in each station (using the 24-hour clock), but the Tube generally operates from 5:30am (0530) to just after midnight (0000), and Sundays 7am (0700) to 11:30pm (2330). On Friday and Saturday nights, many lines in Central London run every 10 minutes all night long: "Night Tube" trains are the Piccadilly, Victoria, Central, and Jubilee lines, plus the Charing Cross branch of the Northern line. Still, if you plan to take the train after midnight, always check the Night Tube map and schedule beforehand.

What happens if you miss the last train? Don't worry—you're not stranded, although your trip may take longer or cost more. Just turn to the city's network of 24-hour and Night Bus routes (p. 255).

HOW THE TUBE WORKS

Navigating is mostly foolproof. Look for signs pointing to the color and name of the line you want. Pretty soon, more signs separate you according to the direction you want to go in, based on the Tube map. If you know the name/color of the line you want, as well as the direction of your destination, the signs will march you, anthill-like, to the platform you need. Nearly every station is combed with staircases. You'll shuffle through warrens of cylindrical tunnels, many of them faced in custard-yellow tiles and overly full of commuters, and you'll scale alpine escalators lined with ads. Stand to the right so "climbers" can pass you.

On the DLR (the Overground) and commuter trains, the carriage may not automatically open. Push the illuminated button and it will.

frustrations OF THE TUBE

The Tube lists everything about itself in exhaustive detail at **www.tfl.gov.uk**, which contains more maps, planners, and FAQs than a normal person can use. As endearing as the Tube is, it is not perfect. In fact, it can be so dehumanizing that it has had to put up signs begging people not to abuse its staff (sad but true). Be prepared for a few things:

1. **Stairs.** Most stations are as intricate as anthills. Passengers are sadistically corralled up staircases, around platforms, down more staircases, and through still more staircases. Even stations equipped with extremely long escalators (Angel has the longest one in the system—59m/194 ft.) perversely require passengers to climb a final flight to reach the street. So if you bring luggage into the Tube, be able to hoist your stuff for at least 15 stairs at a time. (This is where backpacks make sense.) For a list of which stations are step-free (there are only 66 so far), contact **Transport for London Access & Mobility** (www.tfl.gov.uk; ℂ **020/7941-4600**).

2. **Delays.** When you enter a station, look for a sign with the names and colors of the Tube lines on it. Beside each line, you'll see a status bar reading "Good service," "Severe delays," or the like. Trust this sign—it's updated every 10 minutes and lines close without warning. If you note "Minor delays," don't worry. Do worry about labor strikes—they're unpleasantly common.

3. **Heat.** The network can be stuffy. In summer, health advisories are issued to passengers. AC is being added—slowly.

4. **Hellish rush hours.** Shoulder-to-shoulder, silently shuffling through airless underground cylinders. It's memorable in the wrong way.

5. **Tough weekends.** Unlike modern systems, which generally have two sets of rails in each direction, London's ancient system has one set, so entire lines have to shut down when maintenance is required. Weekends are when this happens. This is a major reason why it's smart to stay in central London, where you don't depend on a single Tube line. Check in the ticket hall to see what "engineering works" are scheduled.

One of the groovier things about the Underground is the electronic displays on platforms that tell you how long it'll be until the next train. A 24-hour information service is also available at ℂ **0343/222-1234.** The best resource is the TfL Journey Planner, online at **www.tfl.gov.uk/journeyplanner**. For specific journey information using a mobile device, you can text your start-point and end-point—as full postcodes (what tourist knows those?), or station or stop names, in the format "A to B"—to ℂ **60835.** TfL will fire off a text with the quickest route and scheduled times. The best resource is the free app **Citymapper,** which tells you which Tube, bus, or train to use, how long it takes, and includes mapped walking directions to the nearest stop.

The most confusing lines for tourists are the Northern line (black on the maps) and the District line (green). Owing mostly to the petty backbiting of the Victorians who built these lines as individual businesses, they split and take several paths. You can handle it. Platform displays and signs on the front of the trains tell you its route before you board, and you won't get too far off course if you mess up. If you ride the DLR (and you should—it provides a lovely rooftop-level glide through the brickwork of the old East End and the monolithic towers of Canary Wharf), those lines split variously, too, but there are lots of chances to rectify mistakes.

Search the **Underground's website** (www.tfl.gov.uk) for the "London's Rail and Tube Services Map." It's a truer picture than the Tube map alone because it shows all the places Oyster will take you by rail. (Buses are on separate maps.) The site also has terrific simplified bus maps that show you routes from any neighborhood. Plug in your hotel's address, access City-mapper via Wi-Fi, and you'll have your options.

FARES

London Underground (**tfl.gov.uk/tickets**) gives 1.1 billion rides a year—and seemingly every passenger pays a different fare. Rates go up every January (these rates were current at press time and will give you a sense of proportion). Britain's train system is so complicated that it's accused of having been engineered to bewilder travelers into paying more than they have to. But it can be boiled down like this:

How much you pay: The center of town—basically everything the Circle line envelops, plus a wee bit of padding—is zone 1. Heading outside of town, in a concentric pattern, come zones 2 through 6. Most tourists stick to zones 1 and 2; very few popular sights are outside those (Wimbledon, Hampton Court, and Kew being the main exceptions). Your fare is calculated by how many zones you go through, and the lower the zone number, the less you pay. If a station appears to straddle zones, you'll pay the cheaper zone's rate. One-way tickets are called "singles" and round-trips are "return."

Astonishingly, **kids 10 and under travel for free** when accompanied by an adult. Adults must buy their own ticket and then ask the staff to wave Junior through the entry gate. Ask an agent about the going discounts for kids.

There are essentially three ticket types for visiting adults.

1. **Via Oyster Pay As You Go (PAYG).** This is the best option, and it's what locals use. Rub this credit card–size pass on yellow dots at the turnstiles and you get the lowest fares. You load it with cash and it debits as you go, no tickets required, on all forms of in-city public transit. No matter how many times you ride the Tube (debited at £2.30 in zone 1—that's a lot better than the £4.80 cash fare!) and bus (debited as £1.50—you can't pay cash on a bus), the maximum taken off your card in a single day will **always be less** than what an equivalent Day Travelcard would cost. Non-stop Oyster use will always peak at £6.40 for anytime travel in zones 1 and 2, versus the flat rate of £12 you'd have paid if you'd bought an equivalent Travelcard. Getting an Oyster usually requires a £5 deposit, but you can get that back before you skip town at any Tube ticket office (there's even one at Heathrow; ID may be requested). It won't get erased if you keep it beside your mobile phone. And if you don't use up all the money you put

on it, you can get a refund as long as there's less than £10 value left on your card. (Travelcards offer no refunds for unused monies.)

2. **Via Travelcard.** Aimed at tourists, it's an unlimited pass for 1 or 7 days on the Tube, rail, and bus. "Day Anytime" Travelcards for zones 1 through 3 with no timing restrictions are £12. If you find you have to pop into a zone that isn't covered by your card, buy an extension from the ticket window before starting your journey; it's usually £1.50 to £2 more. 7-Day Travelcards cost adults £32.10 for travel in zones 1 and 2. For Travelcard prices that include more zones, visit **www.tfl.gov.uk/tickets**. You can load a Travelcard purchase onto an Oyster.

3. **In cash, per ride.** You could, but don't. To travel a mile in zone 1 on the Underground, the cash fare is £4.80 ($7.40). I did the math: It costs 3 and ½ times more to pay cash to go a mile on the Tube than to go a mile in transatlantic First Class. What's more, bus drivers don't even take cash anymore. They *do* take Oyster.

If you're hearing a theme here, it's this: **Buy an Oyster card.** They're sold at vending machines when you enter the Tube and then you can use it on buses, too.

It's most economical to get an Oyster PAYG and then do everything you can to plan days during which you don't take transport at all. A significant aspect of that strategy is choosing a hotel that's within walking distance of lots of the things you want to do. Fortunately, the city's extremely walkable. Trains go shockingly slowly (34kmph/21 mph is the *average* and has been for over 100 years); and in the center of town, stops are remarkably close together and the stairs can wear you out. In fact, if your journey is only two or three stations, you'll often find it less strenuous to simply walk. The Tube does offer **contactless payment**—charges are exactly the same as with Oyster—but there's no telling if your card issuer or bank supports it. Apple Pay and American Express with contactless payment should work. Visit **tfl.gov.uk/contactless-payment-card** and confer with your own issuer to make an educated guess whether you can use contactless payment.

How you ride: If you have a paper ticket for any train (even trains that aren't part of the Tube system), keep it handy because you'll need it to get back out at the end. If you can't find it, you'll have to fork over the maximum rate. If you have an Oyster card, you must remember to touch it to a yellow reader dot both before you board *and* after you get off—even if there are no turnstiles, and that's the part people always forget. Inspectors regularly check passengers' tickets and they won't hesitate to fine you.

How you pay: If you are paying with a swipe credit card, don't pull your card out of the vending machine too quickly or it will register as declined. Vending machines usually accept cash and coins. If your credit card issuer offers a version of your card embedded with a SIM chip, order one ahead of your trip—it makes a lot of transactions a lot easier in London, where chip cards are more common.

Although TfL will mail you tickets ahead of time, that's a waste of money; you can just as easily purchase them without shipping costs at any Tube stop.

National Rail

These are the rail lines that aren't operated by the Underground. These lines, which leave regularly, are covered by Travelcards and Oyster PAYG for roughly the same price as the Tube as long as you stay in the zone system. The major stations have information desks if you're unsure about Oyster's validity on any journey. You must tap Oyster at the start and the completion of each journey or you'll be charged as if you took the train to the end of the line. If you accidentally tap in for a wrong or missed train, alert staff. They can ensure you aren't penalized.

There are many termini, but you don't have to hunt by trial and error. Call the 24-hour operators at **National Rail Enquiries** (www.nationalrail.co.uk; ℭ **08457/48-49-50**) or check **TheTrainLine.com**. Alternatively, each station posts timetables. Schedules are listed by destination; find the place you're going, and the departures will be listed in 24-hour time.

National Rail stations (not Eurostar or the Underground) accept discount cards for certain folks. Each card requires proof of eligibility (passport, ISIC student ID), but since they can be used for trips to distant cities, they pay for themselves quickly if you're doing lots of rail-riding. Get them at rail stations:

- The **Senior Railcard** (www.senior-railcard.co.uk, £30 a year): Discounts of about 33% for those 60 or over.
- The **16–25 Railcard** (www.16-25railcard.co.uk, £30 a year): Discounts of 33% for those 16 to 25, plus full-time students of any age. It requires a passport-size photo, which may be uploaded from a computer. If you're applying in the U.K., bring a passport photo for that purpose.
- The **Family & Friends Railcard** (www.family-railcard.co.uk, £30 a year) is for at least one adult and one child age 5 to 15, with a maximum of three adults and four kids on one ticket; at least one child must travel at all times. It awards adults 33% off and kids 60% off. But know that two kids age 4 and under can travel with an adult for free at all times, even without this card.

By Bus

This is what smart Londoners use. The buses in your city may not come often, but London's are frequent (every 5 min. or so on weekdays), plentiful (some 100 routes in central London and 700 in the wider city), and surprisingly fast (many operate in dedicated lanes). Sitting on the second level of a candy-apple red double-decker, watching the big landmarks roll past, is one of London's priceless pleasures. Best of all, the bus is cheaper than the Tube. The 1-day Oyster PAYG price cap for bus-only travel is £4.40, no matter the zone. Travelcards and Oysters (per-trip £1.50; buy in Tube stations) are the best way to pay. There are no free transfers, and be warned that surprise ticket inspections are common nowadays.

RED-LETTER double-deckers

A few routes are truly world-class, linking legendary sights. With routes like these, you won't need to splurge on those tedious hop-on, hop-off tour buses:

○ The **15 bus,** which crosses the city northwest to southeast, takes in Paddington, Oxford Street, Piccadilly Circus, Trafalgar Square, Fleet Street, St Paul's, and the Tower of London. And it has antique Routemaster vehicles.

○ The **10** passes Royal Albert Hall, Kensington Gardens,

Knightsbridge (a block north of Harrods), Hyde Park Corner, Marble Arch, Oxford Street, Goodge Street (for the British Museum), and King's Cross Station.

○ The **159** links Paddington, Oxford Circus, Trafalgar Square, and Westminster.

○ The **RV1** hits Covent Garden, Waterloo, the Tate Modern, and as a bonus, you get to ride over the Tower Bridge to the Tower of London.

Some shelters have automated ticket machines (cash only, and don't expect change; drivers do not accept money anymore), but all have easy-to-read maps that tell you where to catch the buses going to your destination. Major intersections have multiple stops named with letters, and each stop services different routes; check the map in the bus shelter to find the letter stop you need. Many shelters even have electronic boards that approximate the arrival time of the next bus. Board by the driver and get off via the door at the middle; newer buses have also reinstated the rear-door design with its own conductor, and you can leap off that back entrance whenever you want, but of course that comes with hazards. An automated voice announces stops with plenty of warning. Press a button on a handrail to request a halt at the next one.

Routes that start with N are Night Buses, which tote the clubbers home after the Tube stops around midnight; many connect tediously in Trafalgar Square, so pee before setting off. Bus passes and Travelcards expire at 4:30am the day after you buy them. TfL 24-hour information: ✆ **0343/222-1234.**

By Ferry

One of the happy outcomes of the Olympics was a revitalization of London's river ferry services, which are now one of the most pleasurable ways to get around. The boats, nicknamed River Bus, cover a surprising amount of terrain quickly, with 14 stops, including right outside the London Eye, the Tate Modern, the Tower of London, Greenwich, and the O_2 dome, among others. Getting from Greenwich to Embankment takes all of 45 idyllic minutes. You can go right under the famous Tower Bridge—and because it's intended for commuters, it's at a fraction of the price of a tourist boat.

Fares depend on how far you're going, but for a trip from Westminster to Greenwich, expect a one-way fare of £7.15. You will always save money if you buy a return trip instead of two one-ways (round-trips are £12.60). **Thames Clippers** (www.thamesclippers.com; ✆ 020/7930-2062; generally 6:30am–10:30pm) fast catamarans go every 20 minutes during the day. Passes that allow you to take as many trips as you want on a single day are called River Roamer passes, and they cost £17.35 for adults and £36 for a family of two adults and up to three kids. Showing an Oyster card gets 10% off singles, and those with Travelcards loaded into their Oyster can get a third off single fares. You can buy at the piers or buy ahead via the Thames Clippers Tickets app, downloadable via thamesclippers.com/app.

By Cycle

Scattered throughout town, you'll see racks of identical red bikes in racks. They're yours to borrow, day or night! They are officially called **Santander Cycles** (until 2015 sponsored by Barclays; www.tfl.gov.uk/modes/cycling/santander-cycles), but Londoners call them **Boris Bikes,** after the blowsy mayor who brought them here, and they provide more than 10 million rides a year. Interestingly, it's been reported this is the only part of Transport for London that makes a profit.

It works like this: You choose one and pull it out of the rack by lifting the seat. You ride it to any other docking station in the city with a free space, and you park it by slotting the front wheel in until a green light appears on the dock. When you're ready to ride somewhere else, just get another bike. You buy the right to borrow bikes for £2 for 30 minutes (payments are on your credit card) every time you pull a bike out of the rack. Go past that, and you pay the same rate: £2 per extra 30 minutes. The idea is for you to use the bikes in place of public transport, not to keep it with you all day. You are required to follow the same traffic rules that cars do, which won't be easy, although the city's huge parks are safer, ideal places to cycle. Locations of nearby docks are listed on every pylon. Use the free apps **Santander Cycles, Spotcycle,** or **Citymapper** to find nearby stations with space.

By Taxi

Even Londoners think taxis are crazy expensive. It's not the fault of the cabbies. They're the best in the world. Before they're given their wheels, every London taxi driver (there are some 24,000 of them) must go through a grueling training period so comprehensive that it's dubbed, simply, "The Knowledge." On Sundays, you'll see trainees zipping around on mopeds with clipboards affixed above their dashboards. Cabbies arrive inculcated with directions to every alley, mews, avenue, shortcut, and square in the city, and if they don't know, they'll find the answer so discreetly you won't catch the gaffe. And then there are those adorable vehicles: bulbous as Depression Era jalopies, roomy as a studio apartment, yet able to do complete U-turns within a single lane of traffic.

But for this admittedly peerless carriage, you'll pay a £2.40 minimum. Trips of up to 1.6km (1 mile) cost £5.60 to £8.80 during working hours; 3.2km (2-mile) trips are £8.60 to £14; 6.4km (4-mile) trips are £15 to £22; and trips

CAN I do that?

Some things that are considered sins back home may lead to legal pleasures in London. Which means they're not sinful as long as you're on British soil! To wit:

- The drinking age is 18. But if you're having your first legit night out, take it easy, because beers here have higher alcohol content than in many countries.

- There are no open container laws. That means you can drink beer in public. The one exception is on public transportation, where you need a drink the most.

- You may smoke Cuban cigars. Get them at any tobacconist and puff away. If you're American, though, don't try smuggling them home.

- Absinthe, the brutal quaff nicknamed "The Green Fairy," is available here. Drink up because American Customs frowns on many versions of it.

- The age of consent is 16 no matter the sexual preference.

---

of around 9.6km (6 miles) hit you for a painful £23 to £29. Rates rise when you're most likely to need a taxi: by about 10% from 8pm to 10pm or all day on weekends, and roughly another 20% from 10pm until dawn. Trips that start at Heathrow cost an extra £2.80. Mercifully, there is no charge for extra passengers or for luggage. It has become customary to tip 10%, but most people just round up to the nearest pound. Some taxis accept credit cards plus a 12.5% surcharge, but mostly, they are a cash-only concern.

Taxis are often called "black cabs," although in fact 12 colors are registered, including "thistle blue" and "nightfire red." If you need to call a cab, **One Number** (© 087/1871-8710) pools all the companies, with a surcharge of £2.

Minicabs, which are hire cars that operate separately from the traditional black cab system, are easy to find using apps. Don't accept a ride from an unsolicited one. Among the top free apps that can hail the nearest ride: **Kabbee** (www.kabbee.com; or book via © 020/515-1111) which canvasses some 70 cab fleets for the best price; **Minicabit** (www.minicabit.com); **Cabwise** (www.tfl.gov.uk/cabwise); taxi-calling app **Hailo** (hailoapp.com/locations/london/; minimum charges of £10 outside of weekdays), to which about half the city's black cabs subscribe; independent share ride app **Uber** (www.uber.com); **Gett.com** (cashless app with no minimum fare or surge pricing); **Maaxitaxi.com** (an app that hails shareable black taxis); and London's reigning power minicab operator **Addison Lee** (www.addisonlee.com), which makes £100 million in bookings a year from its free app alone.

Renting a Car

Are you insane? Rare is the local who drives in central London, where there's a mandatory daily "congestion charge" of £11.50 (Don't believe me? See **www.cclondon.com**), and where parking fees look like your rent back home.

When you're online in the U.K., such as when you sign up for free Wi-Fi, you may be asked to input a mobile number and a postcode before you can submit a form. Of course you don't have those—you're visiting! Bulldoze through this shortsightedness by giving a fake number you can invent at http://fakenumber.org/generator/mobile. As for a postcode, use your hotel's. Better yet, use the following code: EH2 2AN. After all, if that postcode is good enough for the Queen, it's good enough for you!

Streets were cramped even when people rode horses, plus they're dogged with one-way rules and police cameras will ticket you for even honest errors, which you'll make since you're visiting. You'll go crazy and broke, so why do it? If you're driving out of the city for a tour of the country, fine, but *do not* rent a car for a London vacation.

WHEN TO GO

CLIMATE It's always time to visit London. Even though it's approximately at the same latitude of Edmonton, Alberta, weather patterns keep the environment from being extreme. It gets cold in the winter, but rarely snowed in. It gets warm in the summer, but rarely blisteringly so (in fact, most buildings don't even have air-conditioning). The winter months are generally more humid than the summer ones, but experience only slightly more rain. Locals use the free, reliable **Met Office Weather app,** by the U.K.'s national weather service, to pinpoint forecasts by GPS.

The principal art season (for theater, concerts, art shows) falls between September and May, leaving the summer months for festivals and park-going. A few royal attractions, such as the state rooms of Buckingham Palace, are only open in the summer when the Queen decamps to Scotland. In summer, when the weather is warmest, the sun sets after 10pm, and half of Europe takes its annual holiday, the airfares are higher, as are hotel rates, and the queues for most of the tourist attractions, such as the London Eye and the Tower of London, might make you wish you'd come in March. For decent prices and lighter crowds, go in spring or fall—April and October seem to have the best confluence of mild weather, pretty plantings, and tolerable crowds. Prices are lowest in mid-winter, but a number of minor sights, such as historic houses, sometimes close from November to March, and the biggest annual events take place during the warmer months.

London's Average Daytime Temperatures & Rainfall

	JAN	FEB	MAR	APR	MAY	JUNE	JULY	AUG	SEPT	OCT	NOV	DEC
TEMP. (°F)	39	39	43	46	52	58	62	62	57	51	44	42
TEMP. (°C)	3	3	6	7	11	14	16	16	13	10	6	5
RAINFALL (in.)	3.1	2	2.4	2.1	2.2	2.2	1.8	2.2	2.7	2.9	3.1	3.1
RAINFALL (mm)	49	39	40	43	47	52	59	57	56	62	59	53

London's Public Holidays

England observes **eight public holidays** (also known as "bank holidays"): New Year's Day (Jan. 1); Good Friday and Easter Monday (usually Apr); May Bank Holiday (first Mon in May); Spring Bank Holiday (usually last Mon in May, but occasionally the first in June); August Bank Holiday (last Mon in August); Christmas Day (Dec. 25); Boxing Day (Dec. 26). If a date falls on a weekend, the holiday rolls over to the following Monday.

London's Calendar of Events

Special events are an integral part of London's calendar, and many regular happenings draw tourists from around the world. Find even more events at London's **city website** (www.london.gov.uk/get-involved/events), at the **official tourism site** (www.visitlondon.com), the blog **Londonist** (www.londonist.com), and *Time Out* **magazine** (www.timeout.com/london).

JANUARY

London New Year's Day Parade. As many as 10,000 dancers, acrobats, musicians, and performers (heavy on the marching bands) promenade from Parliament Square to Piccadilly for 500,000 spectators and TV audiences. www.londonparade.co.uk. January 1. ℭ 020/3275-0190.

Chinese New Year Festival. In conjunction with the Chinese New Year, the streets around Leicester Square come alive with dragon and lion dances, children's parades, performances, screenings, and fireworks displays. www.chinatownlondon.org. ℭ 020/7333-8118.

Get into London Theatre. Theatre gets a jolt of new audiences during this promotional period during which producers get together to sell some 75,000 tickets at big discounts. www.getintolondontheatre.co.uk. Early January to February.

London International Mime Festival. Not just for silent clowns, but also for funky puppets and Blue Man–style tomfoolery, it's held around town in mid-January. www.mimelondon.com. ℭ 020/7637-5661.

FEBRUARY

London Fashion Week. Collections are unveiled for press and buyers at a biannual fashion festival also held in September. It's tough to get a runway show ticket, but there's a raft of slick events and parties across the city. www.londonfashionweek.co.uk. Mid-February and mid-September.

MARCH

St Patrick's Day Festival. When you're this close to Dublin and you consider England's long rivalry with the Emerald Isle, you can expect lots of raging Irish pride—parades, music, cultural village, and food stalls around Trafalgar Square, where the fountains gush green. The city also sponsors concerts and craft fairs promoting Irish culture and heritage. It's not just about drinking—it just looks that way. March 17. www.london.gov.uk. ℭ 020/7983-4000.

BADA Antiques & Fine Art Fair. Sponsored in mid- to late March by the British Antique Dealers' Association, it's considered to be the best in Britain for such collectors. Some 100 exhibitors move into a mighty tent in Duke of York's Square, in Chelsea, for the 7-day sales event. Don't expect a bargain. www.bada-antiques-fair.co.uk. ℭ 020/7589-6108.

Oxford and Cambridge Boat Race. Taking place in late March or early April, the popular annual event (since 1829) held on the Thames in Hammersmith takes less than a half-hour, but the after-party rollicks into the night and the good-natured rivalry is undying. www.theboatrace.org.

APRIL

London Marathon. Although it draws some 35,000 runners, the Marathon is also a kick for spectators, so hotels tend to fill up ahead of it. The starter pistol fires in Greenwich, and the home stretch is along

Birdcage Walk near Buckingham Palace. If you want to run, apply by the previous October. www.virginmoneylondonmarathon.com. Sunday in mid-April.

Udderbelly Festival. Mounted for 3 months in a giant inflatable purple cow's udder by the riverbank (really), this 410-seat offshoot of Edinburgh Fringe Festival's variety venue the Underbelly sold some 750,000 tickets in 2013. Dozens of acts range from comedy to musicals to circus, plus there's food, a beer garden, and other amusements. www.udderbelly.co.uk. ✆ **0844/545-8282.** April to mid-July.

MAY

London Wonderground. An ever-surprising summer-long, 200-performance festival of offbeat, family-friendly circus, comedy, and cabaret acts from around the world—plus fairground rides—has taken over a temporary spiegel tent on Southbank to great acclaim since 2012. www.londonwonderground.co.uk. ✆ **0844/545-8282.** Early May through September.

Regent's Park Open Air Theatre. Forget stuffy auditoriums. There's little shelter from sudden downpours, but in good weather the repertoire of high drama, musicals, and Shakespeare sparkles under a canopy of blue skies, towering trees, and natural beauty. www.openairtheatre.org. ✆ **0844/826-4242.** St. Mid-May to September.

Chelsea Flower Show. The Royal Horticultural Society, which calls itself a "leading gardening charity dedicated to advancing horticulture and promoting good gardening" (don't you just love the English?), mounts this esteemed show for 5 days in late May on the grounds of the Royal Hospital in Chelsea. The plants, all raised by champion green thumbs, are sold to attendees on the final day, but sadly, foreigners aren't usually able to get their plants past Customs. Tickets go on sale in November for this lily-palooza, and they're snapped up quickly. The event is so celebrated that it is covered on nightly prime-time TV. Really. www.rhs.org.uk. ✆ **0845/260-5000.**

JUNE

Beating Retreat. Drum corps, pipes, and plenty of bugle calls: This anachronistic twilight ceremony, held for two evenings in early June at Horse Guards Parade by St James's Park, involves the salute of the Queen (or another member of the royal family) and the appearance of many red-clad marchers. Scholars trace its origins to 1554—so for tradition's sake, it's deeply meaningful. It's the nearest relative to the better-known Trooping the Colour, but without the crowds. Reserve ahead. ✆ **020/7839-5323.**

Hampton Court Palace Festival. High-end niche names (Burt Bacharach, Van Morrison, Russell Watson) perform early in the month in a temporary theater on palace grounds. Tickets are around £50. www.hamptoncourtpalacefestival.com. ✆ **084/4412-2954.**

The Royal Academy Summer Exhibition. Artists have been in a frenzy to win entry to this blind competition for nearly 250 years. Paintings, sculpture, drawings, architecture—if you can dream it, you can enter it, and if you're one of the most talented, your piece is anointed as the best that year. The show is what the Royal Academy is known for, and although it's not envelope-pushing, it's a seminal event in British art culture and shouldn't be missed if you're in town. www.royalacademy.org.uk.

Trooping the Colour. Never mind that the Queen was born in April. This is her birthday party, and as a present, she gets the same thing every year: soldiers with big hats. A sea of redcoats and cavalry swarm over Horse Guards Parade, 41 guns salute, and a flight of Royal Air Force jets slam through the sky overhead. The Queen herself leads the charge, waving politely to her subjects before they lose themselves in a hearty display of marching band prowess. Held in mid-June, it starts at 10am. If you want grandstand seats instead of standing in the free-for-all along the route, where you'll only get a fast glimpse of passing royalty, send a request in January or February only to Brigade Major, Headquarters Household Division, Horse Guards, Whitehall, London, SW1A 2AX, United Kingdom. SASEs are required, so include an International Reply Coupon from your post office so that your return postage is paid. Otherwise, check out the Beating Retreat for a similar, if less elaborate, experience. www.household division.org.uk/trooping-the-colour. ✆ 020/7414-2479.

Taste of London Festival. For 5 days in mid-June, the city's top chefs and the region's finest farmers convene in Regent's Park for a belly-stuffing. London.tastefestivals.com ✆ 087/1230-5581.

Pride London. A signature event on the world's LGBT calendar, in a good year London Pride can pull some 825,000 revelers, many of them heterosexual, with a buoyant roster of concerts and performances by famous names plus a parade (the U.K.'s largest) in the center of the City. The gay pride week, co-sponsored by the Mayor's office, also makes for an excellent excuse for some blowout dance parties. Late June or early July. www.prideinlondon.org.

Wimbledon Championships. Why watch on television yet again? Check p. 146 for how to be one of the 500,000 to witness it in person. Late June to early July. www.wimble don.org. ✆ 020/8971-2473.

Greenwich and Docklands International Festival. An ambitious program of free theatrical and musical pieces, many of them developed by artists expressly for the spaces they're performed in. It's held in late June. www.festival.org. ✆ 020/8305-1818.

City of London Festival. Traditional and high-minded classical music concerts are held toward the end of the month in some of the City's oldest buildings. www.colf.org. ✆ 0845/120-7502.

Meltdown. A compendium of hip prestige arts held at the end of June at the Southbank Centre, curated each year by a notable such as Patti Smith, David Bowie, or Yoko Ono. www.southbankcentre.co.uk/melt down. ✆ 020/7960-4200.

JULY

Calling. Tickets are steep (around £70), but the lineup for this 1-day classic rock festival on Clapham Common is A-list; names have included Eric Clapton, The Police, Bon Jovi, Aerosmith, and Bruce Springsteen. www. callingfestival.co.uk.

BBC Promenade Concerts. The biggest classical music festival of the year, held primarily at the Royal Albert Hall, "the Proms" consists of orchestral concerts for every taste. Seats start at £6. www.bbc.co.uk/proms. ✆ 020/7589-8212.

Lovebox. The weekend-long music marathon held in Victoria Park in northeast London mixes newcomers with giants of sound, including past guests Azealia Banks, Mark Ronson, Little Dragon, and Goldfrapp. The crowd is young and fun, starting with nitrous-huffing kids on Friday and morphing into a de facto gay pride day by Sunday. lovebox festival.com.

New Look Wireless Festival. Held alfresco in Finsbury Park for 4 days in July, it books the best names in the biz. In 2015, those included Drake, Avicii, and Nicki Minaj. www.wirelessfestival.co.uk.

The Lambeth Country Show. A free, old-fashioned farm show overtakes Brixton's Brockwell Park (for a single weekend in July, anyway) with farm animals, jam-making contests, a fun fair, tractor demonstrations, and Punch and Judy puppet shows. Very English stuff. www.lambeth.gov.uk.

AUGUST

London Triathlon. Some 13,000 participants cycle through the City from Westminster, sprint around the ExCeL center in Docklands, and swim in Royal Victoria Dock in this annual early August event. Sir Richard Branson attends. www.thelondontriathlon.co.uk. ✆ 020/8233-5900.

Notting Hill Carnival. In August 1958, roving bands of white racists combed the slums of Notting Hill in search of Caribbean-owned businesses to destroy. Resulting community outrage and newly rediscovered cultural pride led to the formation of a new festival, which today is Europe's largest street parade, a powerhouse smorgasbord of cultures spanning the rest of the Caribbean as well as Eastern Europe, South America, and the Indian subcontinent. It attracts some 2 million people during the August Bank Holiday weekend, which includes the last Monday in August. Sunday is kids' day, with scrubbed-down events and activities, but on

10

PLANNING YOUR TRIP TO LONDON

London's Calendar of Events

Monday, the adults take over, costumes get skimpy, floats weave through small streets, and rowdy hordes celebrate into the wee hours. www.thelondonnottinghillcarnival.com.

Great British Beer Festival. Just like it sounds: More than 900 British ales and ciders are available to try at London Olympia—after all those tastings, you'll be relieved to learn the Tube is within easy reach. It runs 5 days. www.gbbf.org.uk. ℂ **0844/412-4640.**

SEPTEMBER

The Great River Race. Always over too soon, the Race is the aquatic version of the London Marathon, with rowers vying to beat out 300 other vessels—Chinese dragon boats, Canadian canoes, Viking longboats, and even Hawaiian outriggers—on a morning jaunt upriver from the Docklands to Richmond. It's held on a Saturday in mid-September. www.greatriverrace.co.uk. ℂ **020/8398-8141.**

Totally Thames. In conjunction with the Great River Race, nearly half a million souls attend London's largest free open-air arts festival, which includes more than 150 events (Southwark Bridge is closed for a giant feast), a flotilla of working river boats, circus performers, and antique fireboats, tugs, and sailboats. Sunday sees the Night Carnival, a lavish procession of thousands of lantern-bearing musicians and dancers crawling along the water. Everything is topped off with barge-launched fireworks. It takes place over September. totallythames.org. ℂ **020/7928-8998.**

Open House London. More than 800 buildings, all of them deemed important but normally closed to the public, yawn wide for free tours on a single, hotly anticipated weekend in mid-September. Past participants have included the skyscraper headquarters of Lloyd's and Swiss Re (officially "30 St Mary Axe" but usually called "The Gherkin") and even No. 10 Downing Street. The list of open buildings comes out in August, and some require timed tickets, but for most the line forms at dawn. Open House also organizes year-round walking tours. www.openhouselondon.org. ℂ **020/3006-7008.**

London Fashion Weekend. It's got nothing on its kin in New York or Milan, but here, pop-up shops from more than 100 designers are put on sale at deeply discounted prices in the hopes they'll build style buzz. www.londonfashionweekend.co.uk.

OCTOBER

Frieze Art Fair. More than 175 galleries vie for big money from collectors in a colossal 4-day tent show in Regent's Park. It has become influential in the contemporary art world. www.friezeartfair.com. ℂ **0871/230-3452.**

Diwali. One advantage of visiting a multicultural city like London is that it affords you the chance to sample major international holidays in an English-speaking environment. One such treat is Diwali, the Indian "festival of light," when Trafalgar Square is transformed with lights, floating lanterns, massive models of the elephant god Ganesh, music, dance, and DJs. It's free and held in mid- to late October.

BFI London Film Festival. An important stop on the cinema circuit, this event, sponsored by the British Film Institute, is geared toward media exposure, but there are plenty of tickets for the public, too. www.bfi.org.uk/lff. ℂ **020/7928-3232.**

Dance Umbrella. One of the world's best contemporary dance festivals, with plenty of standing-room seats for as little as £5; it peaks in late September. www.danceumbrella.co.uk. ℂ **020/7407-1200.**

NOVEMBER

Guy Fawkes Night. In 1605, silly old Guy Fawkes tried to assassinate James I and the entire Parliament by blowing them to smithereens in the Gunpowder Plot. Joke's on him: To this day, the Brits celebrate his failure by blowing up *him*. His effigy is thrown on bonfires across the country, fireworks displays rage across the autumn night sky, and more than a few tykes light their first sparklers in honor of the would-be assassin's gruesome execution. Although displays are scattered around town, including at Battersea Park and Alexandra Palace, get out of the city for the weekend nearest November 5, also called Bonfire Night, because the countryside is perfumed with the woody aroma of burning leaves on this holiday. Mount Primrose Hill or Hampstead Heath for a view of the fireworks going off around the city.

Lord Mayor's Show. What sounds like the world's dullest public access program is actually a delightfully pompous procession, abut 800 years old, involving some 140 charity floats and 6,000 participants to ostensibly show off the newly elected Lord Mayor to the Queen or her representatives. The centerpiece is the preposterously carved and gilt Lord Mayor's Coach, built in 1757—a carriage so extravagant it makes Cinderella's ride look like a Toyota Corolla. That's a lot of hubbub for a city official whose role is essentially ceremonial; the Mayor of London (currently Boris Johnson) wields the true power. All that highfalutin strutting is followed by a good old-fashioned fireworks show over the Thames between the Blackfriars and Waterloo bridges. It's held on the second Saturday in November. www.lord-mayorsshow.org.

London Jazz Festival. Some 165 mid-November events attract around 60,000 music fans. Many performances are free, and tickets are distributed by the venues. www.londonjazzfestival.org.uk. ✆ **020/7324-1880.**

Remembrance Sunday. Another chance to glimpse Her Royal Highness. She and the prime minister, as well as many royals, attend a ceremony at the Cenotaph, in the middle of Whitehall, to honor the war dead and wounded, of which Britain has borne more than its share. Those red flowers you'll see everywhere—red petals, black centers—are poppies, the symbol of remembrance in Britain. It takes place on the Sunday nearest November 11.

DECEMBER

Carols by Candlelight. Royal Albert Hall's annual evening of sing-along Christmas carols, readings from Dickens, and music by Handel, Bach, Mozart, and Corelli played by the Mozart Festival Orchestra—in period costume. Late December. www.royal alberthall.com. ✆ **020/7589-8212.**

New Year's Eve Fireworks. As Big Ben strikes midnight, London rings in the New Year with fireworks over the Thames and the Eye. It's so crowded that in 2015, the city began limiting attendance to 100,000 and requiring tickets. They cost £10 and a few tickets can be booked via www.london.gov. uk/nye in mid-June, with the rest available in September.

[FastFACTS] LONDON

Accessible Travel

London can be hard going. It can't seem to strike the right balance between preserving old buildings and making sure they're accessible to all. With the laudable exception of the Docklands Light Railway, only a slim selection of Tube stations offer lifts, and those with plenty of escalators still require passengers to climb several flights of stairs. The situation is so scrambled, and positive changes so slow, that you'll need to do a bit of research. Your first stops should be

Visit London (www.visit london.com/access) and **Transport for London** (www.tfl.gov.uk/access guides). The website **UpDownLondon.com** keeps tabs on current step-free access at Tube stations, including temporary maintenance obstacles. Many London hotels, museums, restaurants, Tube stations, and sightseeing attractions have dedicated wheelchair access, all taxis and buses will, and persons with disabilities are often granted admission discounts. Generally speaking, the more

expensive a hotel is, the more likely it is to be wheelchair accessible, but not always. The website for **Nationwide Disabled Access Register** (www. directenquiries.com) tattles about the accessibility features of a wide range of facilities, from attractions to car renters.

Artsline (www.artsline.org. uk) distributes information about accessible entertainment venues, including which ones have infrared hearing devices for rental; it also welcomes calls. Blind or partially sighted travelers will find useful advice from the **Royal National Institute of Blind People** (www.rnib.org.uk; ✆ **0303/123-9999**) and **Royal London Society for Blind People** (www.rlsb.org.uk; ✆ **020/7808-6170**), which has been developing an app, Wayfindr, that helps visually impaired passengers navigate the Tube. **Tourism for All** (www.tourismforall.org.uk; ✆ **084/5124-9971**) passes accessibility information to older travelers as well as to travelers with disabilities. The British agency **Can Be Done** (www.canbedone.co.uk; ✆ **020/8907-2400**) runs tours adapted to travelers with disabilities. **Wheelchair Travel** (www.wheelchair-travel.co.uk; ✆ **01483/23-76-68**) rents out self-drive and chauffeured chair-accessible vehicles (including ones with hand controls), provides day tours, and arranges city sightseeing in special vehicles.

Area Codes The country telephone code for Great Britain is **44.** The area code for London is **020.** The full telephone number is usually 8 digits long. Businesses and homes in central London usually have numbers beginning with a **7;** those from farther out begin with an **8.** For more info, see "Telephones" later in this section.

ATMs/Banks See "Money" later in this section.

Business Hours Offices are generally open weekdays between 9 or 10am and 5 or 6pm. Some remain open a few hours longer on Thursdays and Fridays. Saturday hours for stores are the same, and Sunday hours for stores are generally noon to 5 or 6pm. Banks are usually open from 9:30am to 4 or 5pm, with some larger branches open later on Thursdays or for a few hours on Saturday mornings.

Cellphones See "Mobile Phones," later in this section.

Crime See "Safety," later in this section.

Customs Rules about what you can carry into Britain are standard but ever-shifting, so get the latest restrictions from **HM Revenue & Customs** (www.hmrc.gov.uk; ✆ **011-44/2920-501-261**). Your own government is responsible for telling you what you can bring back home.

Doctors Ask your hotel first. Then try the G.P. (General Practitioner) finder at **www.nhs.uk**. North American members of the **International Association for Medical Assistance to Travelers** (IAMAT; www.iamat.org; ✆ **716/754-4883**, or 416/652-0137 in Canada) can consult that organization for lists of local approved doctors. **Note:** U.S. and Canadian visitors who become ill while they're in London are eligible only for free *emergency* care. For other treatment, including follow-up care, you'll pay £60 to £150 just to see a physician.

Drinking Laws Legal drinking age is 18. Children 15 and younger are allowed in pubs only if accompanied by a parent or guardian. Although there are no open container laws, drinking on London's **public transport network** is forbidden and on-the-spot fines are issued to transgressors.

Electricity The current in Britain is 240 volts AC. Plugs have three squared pins. Foreign appliances operating on lower voltage (those from the U.S., Canada, and Australia use 110–120 volts AC) will require an adapter and possibly a voltage converter, although the range of capability will usually be printed on the plug. Many modern phone chargers and laptops can handle the stronger current with only an adapter. A few hotels provide outlets for a non-heating appliance such as a shaver.

Embassies & Consulates Until 2017, the **U.S. Embassy** is at 24 Grosvenor Sq., London W1 (http://london.usembassy.gov; ✆ **020/7499-9000**; Tube: Bond Street or Marble Arch). Standard hours are Monday to Friday 8:30am to 5:30pm. Most non-emergency inquiries require an appointment.

The **High Commission of Canada,** 1 Trafalgar Sq., London W1 (www.canadainternational.gc.ca/united_kingdom-royaume_uni/index.aspx; ✆ **020/7004-6000;** Tube: Charing Cross), handles passport and consular services for Canadians. Hours are Monday, Wednesday, and Friday 8 to 10:30am.

The **Australian High Commission** is at Australia

House, Strand, London WC2 (www.uk.embassy.gov.au; ✆ **020/7379-4334;** Tube: Temple). Hours are Monday to Friday 9am to noon.

The **New Zealand High Commission** is at New Zealand House, 80 Haymarket, London SW1 (www.nzembassy.com/uk; ✆ **020/7930-8422;** Tube: Charing Cross or Piccadilly Circus). Hours are Monday to Friday 9am to 5pm.

The **Irish Embassy** is at 17 Grosvenor Place, London SW1 (www.embassyofireland.co.uk; ✆ **020/7235-2171;** Tube: Hyde Park Corner). Hours are Monday to Friday 9:30am to 5pm.

Emergencies The one-stop number for Britain is ✆ **999**—that's for fire, police, and ambulances. It's free from any phone, even mobiles. Less urgent? Call 111.

Family Travel Attractions cater to the family market. The kingly treatment starts, at many places, with the so-named **Family Ticket,** which grants a low price for parents and kids entering together. For any length of stay, you can rent baby equipment from **Chelsea Baby Hire** (www.chelseababyhire.com; ✆ **07802/846-742**). Babysitting: **Sitting Pretty Babysitters** (www.sittingprettybabysitters.com; ✆ **07971/083-207**) will come to your hotel and has a minimum commitment of 3 or 4 hours, depending on the time of week; rates are around £9 an hour with a

£5.50 booking fee and a £15.50 membership fee.

If you are a **divorced parent** with joint custody of your children, bring proof that you are entitled to take your kids out of the country.

Some resources for family-specific travel tips include the **Family Travel Network** (www.familytravelnetwork.com), online since 1995. **Travel with Your Kids** (www.travelwithyourkids.com) specializes in tips for international travel, and it also maintains a section just about London's finds. **The Family Travel Files** (www.thefamilytravelfiles.com) rounds up tour operators and packagers geared to families, but its suggestions aren't always the most economical or efficient. *Time Out* (www.timeout.com/london) also includes a section on kids' activities.

When it comes to baby supplies, pacifiers are called "dummies," diapers are "nappies," a crib is a "cot," and Band-Aids are "plasters."

Health Traveling to London doesn't pose specific health risks. Common drugs are generally available over the counter and in large supermarkets, although visitors should know the generic rather than brand names of any medicines they rely on. Pack **prescription medications** in carry-on luggage and in their original containers, with pharmacy labels—otherwise they may not pass airport security. Also bring copies of your prescriptions, just in

case. Don't forget an extra pair of contact lenses or prescription glasses. The general-purpose painkiller known in North America as acetaminophen is called **paracetamol** in the U.K. If you don't feel well and you need the advice of a doctor or a nurse, the national health care system operates a free, 24-hour hotline: **National Health Service Direct** (www.nhs.uk; ✆ **111**). Citizens of many European countries are entitled to free health care while in Britain (see www.dh.gov.uk/travellers), but everyone else is not, and although clinics were once known to treat tourists and then look the other way rather than embark upon the odyssey of paperwork required to bill them, private billing companies are now policing for every pound and to see a doctor you could pay between £50 and £150. Non-EU citizens should carry health or travel insurance.

Hospitals In the U.K., the ER is usually called A&E, or Accident and Emergency. If your need is urgent, dial ✆ **999** (it's free no matter where your phone is registered) rather than risk going to a medical center that doesn't offer A&E. You can search **www.nhs.uk** for the nearest A&E, or go to the 24-hour, walk-in A&E departments at **University College London Hospital,** 235 Euston Rd., London NW1 (www.uclh.nhs.uk; ✆ **020/3456-7890** or **0845/155-5000;** Tube: Warren Street) and **St Thomas's**

Hospital, Westminster Bridge Road, entrance on Lambeth Palace Road, London SE1 (www.guys andstthomas.nhs.uk; ☏ 020/7188-7188; Tube: Westminster or Waterloo). **Central London Community Healthcare** (1 Frith St., W1; www.clch.nhs.uk; ☏ 020/7534-6500; 8am–9pm; Tube: Tottenham Court Road) is a central clinic.

Insurance   **U.K. nationals** receive free medical treatment countrywide, but visitors from overseas only qualify automatically for free **emergency** care. **U.S. visitors** should note that most domestic health plans (including Medicare and Medicaid) do not provide coverage, and the ones that do often require you to pay for services upfront and reimburse you only after you return home. Among many options, you could try **MEDEX** (www.medexassist. com; ☏ 800/732-5309) or **Travel Assistance International** (www.travel assistance.com; ☏ 800/821-2828) for overseas medical insurance cover. **Canadians** should check with their provincial health plan offices or call **Health Canada** (www.hc-sc.gc.ca; ☏ 866/225-0709) to find out the extent of their coverage and what documentation and receipts they must take home in case they are treated overseas. **E.U. nationals** (and nationals of E.E.A. countries and Switzerland) should note that reciprocal health

agreements are in place to ensure they receive free medical care while in the U.K. However, visitors from those countries must carry a valid **European Health Identity Card** (EHIC).

So what else may you want to insure? You may want special coverage for **apartment stays,** especially if you've plunked down a deposit, and any **valuables,** since airlines are only required to pay up to $2,500 for lost luggage domestically, less for foreign travel.

If you do decide on insurance, compare policies at **InsureMyTrip.com** (☏ 800/487-4722). Or contact one of the following reputable companies: **Allianz** (www.allianztravel insurance.com; ☏ 866/884-3556); **CSA Travel Protection** (www.csatravel protection.com; ☏ 877/243-4135 or collect: 240/330-1529); **MEDEX** (www. medexassist.com; ☏ 800/732-5309); **Travel Guard International** (www.travel guard.com; ☏ 800/826-4919); **Travelex** (www. travelex-insurance.com; ☏ 800/228-9792). Note that most insurers require you to purchase plans *before* you leave home.

Internet   Wi-Fi flows freely at pubs, cafes, museums, and nearly all hotels. Usually, you will have to fill in an email address to activate it, but often it's a data collection ploy and you can write dummy information. Sometimes you'll be asked for a U.K. postcode. In that

case, I suggest pretending you live at SW1A 1AA—it's the Queen's. Virgin Media (www.virginmedia.com/wifi) provides Wi-Fi in many Tube stations but not between them. Visitors can buy passes for £2 (1 day), £5 (1 week), or £15 (1 month). See "Mobile Phones" later in this section.

Laundry   Launderettes are not easy to find in central London anymore, and expensive hotels will only do laundry and dry cleaning if you're wiling to shell out, but also look into the app **Laundrapp,** which will pick up and drop off to your hotel for free. Prices start at £2 per article or £15 for 8kg (17.6 lb.)

Left Luggage   Useful for taking those cheap European flights with steep luggage fees, **Left Baggage** (www.left-baggage.com; ☏ 0800/077-4530) has locations at Heathrow, Gatwick and the big railway stations: £10 per item per 24 hours for up to a week, then £5 per item per day thereafter.

Legal Aid   If you find yourself in trouble abroad, contact your consulate or embassy (see "Embassies & Consulates," above). It can advise you of your rights and will usually provide a list of local attorneys (for which you'll have to pay if services are used), but they cannot interfere on your behalf in the English legal process. For questions about American citizens who have been arrested abroad, including ways of getting money to them, telephone the **Citizens Emergency Center** of the Bureau of Consular Affairs in Washington, D.C. (📞 **877/487-2778**).

LGBT Travelers Gay and lesbian people have equality and marriage rights. Public displays of affection are received with indifference in the center of the city, although in the outer suburbs couples should show more restraint. Gay bashings are rare enough to be newsworthy, but it's true that an element of society can, once full of ale, become belligerent. Particularly in parks at night, be aware of your surroundings and give wide berth to gaggles of drunken lads. This advice holds irrespective of your sexuality.

The **Turing Network** (www.turingnetwork.org.uk) lists gay and lesbian social events and festivals and is partnered with the **London Gay & Lesbian Switchboard** (www.llgs.org.uk; 📞 **0300/330-0630**), a counseling hotline. For nightlife planning, the best sources for information (among many less handy glossy lifestyle magazines) are the **Boyz** (www.boyz.co.uk), which publishes a day-by-day schedule on its website. The free **QX International** (www.qxmagazine.com) posts a downloadable version of its printed edition every week. Both publications are distributed for free at many gay bars. Also see p. 195.

Mail An airmail letter or postcard to anywhere outside Europe costs £1 for up to 10g (⅓ oz.) and generally takes 5 to 7 working days to arrive. Within the E.U., letters or postcards under 20g (⅔ oz.) cost £1.

Medical Requirements Unless you're arriving from an area known to be suffering from an epidemic, inoculations or vaccinations are not required for entry into the U.K.

Mobile Phones Anytime you call a mobile phone in Britain, the fee will be higher than calling a land line, although there is no fee to *receive* a call or text.

Apart from renting a phone (not recommended to the casual visitor), many tourists simply enable their international **roaming** feature. That works, but your provider will bleed you. You'll pay as much as $2.50 per minute, even if someone from home calls you, and data is a killer. Package plans tend to be stingy with time and data allowances and you'll exceed them without warning.

The best solution, if you do have an unlocked quad- or tri-band phone that uses the GSM system, is to pop into any mobile phone shop or newsstand and buy a cheap **pay-as-you-talk** phone number from a mobile phone store. You pay about £5 for a SIM card, which you stick in your phone, and then you buy vouchers to load your account with as much

money as you think you'll use up (no refunds). That will give you a British number, which you can e-mail to everyone back home, that charges local rates (10p–40p per min.) and a deal on data that might allow 1GB in a month for about £5— much, much cheaper than roaming. Just call your provider before you leave home to "unlock" your phone (out-of-contract and last-generation phones are better candidates), so that the British SIM card will function in it. That service is usually free. U.K. mobile providers with pay-as-you-talk deals, all comparable, include: **Vodafone** (www.vodafone.com), **O₂** (www.o2.co.uk), **Lebara** (www.lebara.co.uk), **EE/T-Mobile** (www.ee.co.uk), and **Virgin Mobile** (www.virginmobile.com). Annoyingly, purchased SIMs come with automatic child content locks, and gay and lesbian travelers will find some of their social sites blocked. To remove the censorship, go to a mobile phone store run by your SIM provider (Vodafone, EE, and O₂ are easiest to find) to prove you're an adult. Bring your hotel's details since you must supply a U.K. address.

Even if your home mobile company won't permit you to unlock your phone, you can always use its Wi-Fi features for Skype, FaceTime, WhatsApp, and the like.

Money The British pound (£1), a small, chunky, gold-colored coin, is usually accepted in vending machines. It's commonly called a "quid." Like dollars in America, Canada, and Australia, pounds are divided into 100 pennies (p)—the plural, "pence," is used to modify amounts over 1p. Pence come in 1p, 2p, 5p, 10p, 20p, and 50p coins. Patterns on the obverse of the £1 and 50p coins periodically change to commemorate areas or events. You'll see large bull's-eye £2 coins, too. Notes come in £5, £10, £20, and £50. Now and then, you'll receive notes printed by the Bank of Scotland; they're valid, but an increase in forgeries means some shops refuse them. Banks will exchange them.

Be quick when using ATMs. Retrieve your card immediately from ATM slots; many machines suck them in within 10 to 15 seconds, for security. Should that happen, you'll have to petition the bank to have it returned to you.

In recent years, the exchange rate has hovered in the vicinity of £1 = US$1.50, but of course that's always changing, so consult a currency exchange website such as **www.oanda.com/currency/converter** or its Oanda app.

All prices (including at most B&Bs but not at all hotels) are listed including tax, so what you see is what you pay. No guesstimating required.

When bringing up prices, always insert the word "pounds"; for example, £2.50 would be uttered as "two pounds fifty" but not "two fifty."

Every visitor should have several sources for money, but cash is still king, as they say (Queen Elizabeth isn't jealous—her face is on all the money). The simple solution is to pull cash from an ATM upon arrival; the rates are the cheapest there. Before leaving home, warn your bank and your credit card issuers that you intend to travel internationally so that they don't place a stop on your account when international charges start cropping up. You may also need to adjust your PIN, since English banks require 4-digit codes. If you know your PIN as a word, memorize the numerical equivalent. Most banks hit you with fees of a few pounds each time you withdraw cash. Your own bank may toss in a small fee of its own (another 2% or 3%, but ask ahead to see what its policy is), so gauge for yourself how much you feel comfortable withdrawing at a time to offset that fee. If you have an account with an international bank chain, ask whether using their machines during your visit will save on fees. Also ask your bank if it has reciprocal agreements for free withdrawals anywhere. One institution known to charge international usage fees that are below the industry standard is **Everbank** (www.everbank.com; ☏ **888/882-3837**); another is **Charles Schwab** (www.schwab.com;

☏ **866/855-9102**), which reimburses ATM fees.

Now that ATMs are common, traveler's checks are nearly dead. Using them, you run the risk of most places declining them. Creditors have come up with **traveler's check cards,** also called **prepaid cards,** which are essentially debit cards loaded with the amount of money you elect to put on them. They're not coded with your personal information, they work in ATMs, and should you lose one, you can get your cash back in a matter of hours. If you spend all the money on them, you can call a number or visit a website and reload the card using your bank account information, although there may be fees of a few dollars for ATM transactions. **Travelex Cash Passport** (www.cashpassport.com; ☏ **877/465-0085** or 01733/501-370 in the U.K) works anywhere MasterCard does and can be loaded in British pounds, Euros, or American dollars; also try **NetSpend** (www.netspend.com; ☏ **866/387-7363**).

Changing cash is also on the outs. ATM withdrawals give the best deals, so old-fashioned cambios are few and far between, although you'll still find a few at the airport and around Leicester Square. If you must change money, better rates are offered by banks (9:30am–4pm).

Credit cards are accepted nearly everywhere. However, **American Express** is accepted less widely. Bring a Visa or MasterCard; they are the chief cards. Many credit card issuers levy an annoying international transaction fee on top of your purchase; **Capital One Venture** (www.capitalone. com; © **800/955-7070**) is one that does not. Small vendors may charge a transaction fee (3% is the norm) as a way of defraying the cost of dealing with credit card companies. Try not to use credit cards to withdraw cash. You'll pay a currency exchange fee, and worse, you'll be charged interest from the moment your money leaves the slot.

Europeans use "chip and PIN" cards requiring a code number. Some vending machines **will not accept** swipe-only cards and may incorrectly inform you that you were declined, so ask your issuer for a card with a chip in it; it may be able to provide one for free upon request. Travelex (see above) sells debit cards that work in chip-and-PIN readers. For swipe-only cards, clerks will always verify your signature, so make sure your card is signed. For security, restaurants will usually process your payment at your table wirelessly.

North American Starbucks cards can be used for coffee in the U.K.

Newspapers & Magazines

London offers more publications than one would think a city of its size could support. The broadsheets, ordered from left to right, politically speaking, are: *The Guardian, The Independent, The Daily Telegraph,* and *The Times.* On the Tube, *Metro* is free in the morning and *Evening Standard* is free in the afternoon. The salmon-colored *Financial Times* covers business. The tabloids are fluffier and more salacious, and they include *The Sun, The Mirror, Daily Star, The Daily Mail,* and *Daily Express. Time Out* publishes a free listing of events and entertainments. International publications such as *USA Today* are widely available. Other popular magazines include *Heat* (celebrity gossip), *The Big Issue* (written and sold by homeless and formerly homeless people, *Radio Times* (TV listings and celebrity interviews), and *Hello!* and *OK!* (fawning celebrity spreads usually planted by publicity agents).

Packing

For your wallet's sake, pack sparingly! You've heard that before, but it's really true this time. It's not as easy as it used to be to wink your way through the weigh-in. In some cases, the conveyor belts at check-in are programmed to halt if they sense a bag over the limit.

British Airways, for example, grants coach passengers a puny **23kg (51 lb.).** If you exceed that, you will be smacked with a flat fee of £25 per flight. That only buys you another 9kg (20 lb.), because bags over 32kg (71 lb.) will be rejected outright. When it comes to carry-ons ("hand baggage"), it's got to measure no more than 56cm long by 45cm wide by 25cm deep (22 × 18 × 10 in.). Some airlines, such as Virgin Atlantic, can be ruthless about making sure even your *carry-on* baggage weighs no more than 10kg (22 lb.). That's very little. If you're taking multiple airlines, stick to the tightest set of restrictions of the lot. Many airlines (even the no-frills) discount for booking baggage at least 24 hours early, and charge more at the airport.

If you need to buy cheap luggage, Primark (p. 170) sells it for less than £20.

Keep prescription medications in their original, labeled containers for Customs even though they're unlikely to be inspected. If you require **syringes,** always carry a signed medical prescription.

Pare toiletries to essentials. You're not going to the Congo. You will find staples like toothpaste, contact lens solution, and deodorant everywhere. Women should bring a minimum of make-up; the British don't tend to use very much themselves. Brits are also more likely to wear trousers than blue jeans. If you plan to go clubbing, pack some fashionable duds—Londoners love to look natty. Speaking of that, don't wear a lot of T-shirts with writing or logos; it marks you as a tourist.

You'll be most comfortable if you dress in clothing that layers well. Even in winter, London's air can be clammy, and dressing too warmly can become uncomfortable. No matter what the average temperature is (see the box on weather, p. 258), the air can grow cool after the sun sets, so plan for that, too. In the winter, a hat, scarf, and gloves are necessities. A compact umbrella is wise year-round, as is an outer coat that repels water, since you never know when you're going to find yourself in one of those misty rains that make the British Isles so lush and green.

Don't bring illegal drugs (duh) or medical marijuana (duh), and also leave the pepper spray and mace at home; they're banned in the U.K.

Passports To enter the United Kingdom, all U.S. citizens, Canadians, Australians, New Zealanders, and South Africans must have a passport valid through their length of stay. No visa is required. A passport will allow you to stay in the country for up to 6 months. The immigration officer may also want to see proof of your intention to return to your point of origin (usually a round-trip ticket) and of visible means of support while you're in Britain (credit cards work). If you're planning to fly from the United States or Canada to the United Kingdom and then on to a country that requires a visa (India, for example), you should secure that visa before you arrive in Britain.

Pharmacies Every police station keeps a list of pharmacies (chemists) that are open 24 hours. Also try **Zafash,** a rare chemist that is open 24 hours, 233-235 Old Brompton Rd., SW5 (✆ **020/7373-2798;** Tube: Earl's Court); and **Bliss,** open daily 9am to midnight, 5-6 Marble Arch, W1 (✆ **020/7723-6116;** Tube: Marble Arch). For non-emergency health advice, call the NHS at ✆ **111.**

Police London has two official police forces: The City of London police (www.cityoflondon.police.uk) whose remit covers the "Square Mile" and its 8,600 residents; and the Metropolitan Police ("the Met"), which covers the rest of the capital and is split into separate borough commands for operational purposes. Opening hours for all the Met's local police stations are listed at **www.met.police.uk/local.** In a non-emergency, you can contact your local police station from anywhere by dialing ✆ **101.** Losses, thefts, and other criminal matters should be reported at the nearest police station immediately. You will be given a crime number, which your travel insurer will request if you make a claim against any losses. Always dial ✆ **999** or 112 if the matter is serious.

Safety Crossing the street is the most perilous thing you'll do. Always look down to see which way traffic is flowing—the street will be painted "Look right" or "Look left" so you'll know. Also, a steady-lit green man on the crosswalk signal means it's safe, but a flashing green man is not like a yellow traffic light—it's a stop sign. When the green man flashes, do not begin crossing, because it means cars are about to gun it again. Few places in London are unsafe. Neighborhoods that pessimistically might be called sketchy are usually distant from the Tube lines, and they only feel tense after dark, when shops close. London is like anyplace; simply be sensitive to who's around you and you'll do fine.

The biggest nuisance tourists might encounter—besides tipsy locals—is pickpockets. As chronicled in *Oliver Twist,* London, like all cities of size, is home to a skilled subspecies of crooks eager to pilfer your valuables, especially your phone. Oxford Street and the Tube are the prime picking grounds. Simply be smart about where you put your cash and what you leave sitting in the open.

Guns are banned—even on most police officers—so you don't often see the kind of violence taken for granted in the United States. Londoners cite knife crime as a problem, but the victims are almost always young men who themselves carry knives. Some male tourists have gotten fleeced at some of the **"hostess bars"** in Soho. If you do suffer a lapse of judgment and accept the barker's invitation to go into one, understand that you might have cash exacted by lunkheaded yobs with tattooed fingers.

Should you find yourself on the business end of the legal system, you can get advice and referrals to lawyers from **Legal Services Commission** (www.legal services.gov.uk; © **084/ 5345-4345**). Victims of crime can receive volunteer legal guidance and emotional fortification from **Victim Support** (www. victimsupport.org.uk; © **0845/30-30-900**). In the unlikely event of a sexual assault, phone the **Rape Crisis Federation** (www. rapecrisis.org.uk; © **0808/ 802-9999**).

Senior Travel Don't hide your age! Seniors in England are usually classified as those aged 60 and over, and they're privy to all kinds of price breaks, from lower admission prices at museums to a third off rail tickets (but you first have to apply for the **Senior Railcard;** www.senior-railcard. co.uk). You may hear seniors being referred to as OAPs, which stands for Old Age Pensioners. That acronym is falling out of use, perhaps because it's rare to find a solvent pension fund anymore. Don't be offended if you're also referred to as a "geezer," though—in England, it's a compliment that means a fun-loving (if sometimes rowdy) bloke.

If you're over 50, you can join **AARP** (601 E St. NW, Washington, DC, 20049; www.aarp.org; © **888/687- 2277**), and wrangle discounts on hotels, airfare,

and car rentals. Elderhostel's well-respected **Road Scholar** (www.roadscholar. org; © **800/454-5768**) runs many classes and programs in London designed to delve into literature, history, the arts, and music. Packages last from a week to a month and include airfare, lodging, and meals.

Smoking Smoking is prohibited by law in any enclosed workplace, including museums, pubs, public transportation, and restaurants. If in doubt, ask permission.

Student Travel Have ID ready to go, and always mention that you're a student, because it'll save you cash, including on trains to other cities. Attractions gladly offer discounts of around 25% for full-time students, but your high school or university ID may not cut it where clerks haven't heard of your school. Before leaving home, obtain a recognized ID such as the **International Student Identity Card** (ISIC; www.isic.org or www. myISIC.com). Those 25 and under who are not in school can obtain an **International Youth Travel Card**, also through ISIC, which performs many of the same tricks as a student discount card.

Before buying airline tickets, those 25 and under should consult a travel agency that specializes in the youth market and is versed in its available discounts: **STA Travel** (www. statravel.com; © **800/781- 4040**) is big.

Taxes Prices of all goods in the U.K. are quoted inclusive of taxes. Since 2011 the national value-added tax (**VAT**) has stood at 20%. This is included in all hotel and restaurant bills, and in the price of most items you purchase.

If you are permanently resident outside the E.U., VAT on goods can be refunded if you shop at stores that participate in the **Retail Export Scheme**— look for the window sticker or ask the staff. See p. 178 for details. Information about the scheme is also posted online at **www. hmrc.gov.uk/vat/sectors/ consumers/overseas- visitors.htm**.

Telephones Directory assistance: www.bt.com or © **118-500.** Local calls start with 020. The main toll-free prefixes are 0800, 0808, and 0500. Numbers starting with 07 are usually for mobile phones and will be charged at a higher rate. Numbers starting with 09 are premium-rate calls that will usually be very expensive (around £1.50 per min.) and may not even work from abroad.

Many attractions, hotel companies, and services have cynically changed their standard phone numbers to profit-generating ones that charge for every minute you call them. Sometimes, these are not reachable from outside the United Kingdom or Internet calling. If you find you cannot reach a number in this book, try from London, or use the website.

When dialing a number in this book from abroad, precede it with your country's international prefix (in the U.S. and Canada, it's 011), add the U.K.'s country code (44) and drop the first zero in the number. Many British companies are cheap and don't offer toll-free numbers. You often can't reach 0845, 0870, and 0871 numbers (charged at 10p a minute or less) from abroad, and when you can, you're charged more; if you have to call one from abroad, use the Web instead to get information. The 0845 numbers are charged at a local rate; 0870 at a national rate. The 0845 prefix enables companies to make a profit for every call received. As you can imagine, this profiteering leads to putting customers on hold.

To make an **international call** from Britain, dial the international access code (**00**), then the country code, then the area code, and finally the local number. If you call a toll-free number located back home, you'll still pay international rates for it.

The majority of London's rapidly vanishing **payphones** are operated by BT (British Telecom), and they are costly. The minimum charge is 60p (nothing under a 10p coin accepted, and phones don't give change), and then you'll be charged in 10p increments. Some payphones accept credit cards at a premium: £1.20 to start and 20p per minute for local and domestic. Full charge breakdowns by country and call duration are at **British Telecom** (www.payphones.bt.com/publicpayphones). Phones at pubs and hotels legally jigger their phones to charge at a higher rate.

When calling from a mobile phone, dial the full number including area code.

Phonecards are often the most economical method for both international and national calls. They are reusable until the total value has expired. Cards can be purchased from newsstands and post offices, and offer rates of a few pence per minute to most countries.

Hotels routinely add outrageous surcharges onto calls made from your room. It's much cheaper to purchase a phonecard.

Time London is generally 5 hours ahead of New York City and Toronto, 8 hours ahead of Los Angeles, 11 hours behind Auckland, and 9 hours behind Sydney. It is 1 hour behind western continental Europe. Greenwich Mean Time is London time.

Tipping Waiters should receive 10% to 15% of the bill unless service is already included—*always* check the menu or bill to see if service was already added, because traditions are changing. At pubs, tipping isn't customary unless you receive table service. Fine hotels may levy a service charge, but at the finest ones, grease the staff with a pound here and there. Staff at B&Bs and family-run hotels don't expect tips. Bartenders and chambermaids need not be tipped. There's no need to tip **taxicab drivers** but most people round up to the next £1, although a 10% to 15% tip is becoming increasingly standard.

Toilets London doesn't have enough of them. Washrooms can be found at any free museum in this guide, any department store, any pub or busy restaurant (though it's polite to buy something), and at Piccadilly Circus and Bank Tube stations. Train stations also have toilets that may cost 30p to 50p. On weekends, open-air *pissoirs* for men are placed throughout the West End.

VAT See "Taxes," above.

Visas No E.U. nationals require a visa to visit the U.K. Visas are also not required for travelers from Australia, Canada, New Zealand, or the U.S. To be sure that hasn't changed, see **www.ukvisas.gov.uk** long before your travel dates. The usual permitted stay is 90 days or fewer for tourists, although some nationalities are granted stays of up to 6 months. If you plan to work or study, though, or if you're traveling on a passport from another country, you'll need to obtain the correct paperwork.

Visitor Information
Three official information units supported by British taxes are set up to help tourists, but only online:

Visit Britain (www.visit britain.com, @VisitBritain); **Visit England** (www.visit england.com, @VisitEng land); and **Visit London** (www.visitlondon.com, @VisitLondon), which possesses the biggest database and publishes a free app with offline maps called **London Official City Guide** and an app collecting upcoming happenings, **London Official Events Guide**. The only official information bureau with a public office is opposite the south side of St Paul's Cathedral: The **City of London Information Centre** (www.visitthecity. co.uk; ✆ **020/7332-1456**) sells attraction tickets and Oyster cards, runs tours, supplies brochures and counsel for daytrips throughout the country. It publishes walking tours, a free City Visitor Trail audio walking tour app, and children's discovery trail maps. Opening hours are Monday to Saturday 9:30am to 5:30pm, Sunday 10am to 4pm.

Excellent independent sources for things to do include **Londonist.com**, **LondonCalling.com**, **TimeOut.com/London**, **Townfish.com**, and the Twitter accounts Everything London (**@LDN**), **@LeCool_London,** and **@SkintLondon**.

Women Travelers   First and foremost, lone women should avoid riding in **unlicensed London taxicabs,** especially at night. However attractive the price you're quoted, flag down a black cab or call a minicab instead. **Addison Lee** (www. addisonlee.com; ✆ **020/ 7407-9000**) has a huge, efficient fleet, and will text you the registration plate of your cab for added security. It has a free app for hailing rides.

A true club and not an agency, **Women Welcome Women Worldwide** (www. womenwelcomewomen. org.uk; ✆ **01494/46-54- 41**) connects travelers worldwide and costs £35 a year.

Index

See also Accommodations and
Restaurant indexes, below.

General Index

RESTAURANTS INDEX

Before, During, or After your use of an EasyGuide... you'll want to consult

FROMMERS.COM

FROMMERS.COM IS KEPT UP-TO-DATE, WITH:

NEWS
The latest events (and deals) to affect your next vacation

BLOGS
Opinionated comments by our outspoken staff

FORUMS
Post your travel questions, get answers from other readers

SLIDESHOWS
On weekly-changing, practical but inspiring topics of travel

CONTESTS
Enabling you to win free trips

PODCASTS
Of our weekly, nationwide radio show

DESTINATIONS
Hundreds of cities, their hotels, restaurants and sights

TRIP IDEAS
Valuable, offbeat suggestions for your next vacation

*AND MUCH MORE!

Smart travelers consult Frommers.com